Rock Climbing
Eldorado Canyon

Richard Rossiter

CHOCKSTONE®

FALCON®

HELENA, MONTANA

A FALCON GUIDE®

Falcon® is continually expanding its list of recreational guidebooks. All books include detailed descriptions, accurate maps, and all the information necessary for enjoyable trips. You can order extra copies of this book and get information and prices for other Falcon® guidebooks by writing Falcon, P.O. Box 1718, Helena, MT 59624 or calling toll-free 1-800-582-2665. Also, please ask for a free copy of our current catalog. Visit our website at www.Falcon.com or contact us by e-mail at falcon@falcon.com.

All Crimp Tower topos © Tod Anderson.
All black-and-white photos by author unless otherwise noted.
All drawn topos by author unless otherwise noted.

Library of Congress Cataloging-in-Publication Data

Rossiter, Richard, 1945–
    Rock climbing Eldorado Canyon / Richard Rossiter.
        p. cm.
    ISBN 1-58592-031-2
    1. Rock climbing--Colorado--Eldorado Canyon--Guidebooks. 2. Eldorado Canyon (Colo.)--Guidebooks. I. Title.

  GV199.42.C62 E437 2000
  796.52'23'09788–dc21   00-034715

CAUTION

Outdoor recreational activities are by their very nature potentially hazardous. All participants in such activities must assume the responsibility for their own actions and safety. The information contained in this guidebook cannot replace sound judgment and good decision-making skills, which help reduce exposure, nor does the scope of this book allow for disclosure of all the potential hazards and risks involved in such activities.

Learn as much as possible about the outdoor recreational activities in which you participate, prepare for the unexpected, and be cautious. The reward will be a safer and more enjoyable experience.

 Text pages printed on recycled paper.

WARNING:
CLIMBING IS A SPORT WHERE YOU MAY BE SERIOUSLY INJURED OR DIE. READ THIS BEFORE YOU USE THIS BOOK.

This guidebook is a compilation of unverified information gathered from many different climbers. The author cannot assure the accuracy of any of the information in this book, including the topos and route descriptions, the difficulty ratings, and the protection ratings. These may be incorrect or misleading and it is impossible for any one author to climb all the routes to confirm the information about each route. Also, ratings of climbing difficulty and danger are always subjective and depend on the physical characteristics (for example, height), experience, technical ability, confidence and physical fitness of the climber who supplied the rating. Additionally, climbers who achieve first ascents sometimes underrate the difficulty or danger of the climbing route out of fear of being ridiculed if a climb is later down-rated by subsequent ascents. Therefore, be warned that you must exercise your own judgment on where a climbing route goes, its difficulty, and your ability to safely protect yourself from the risks of rock climbing. Examples of some of these risks are: falling due to technical difficulty or due to natural hazards such as holds breaking, falling rock, climbing equipment dropped by other climbers, hazards of weather and lightning, your own equipment failure, and failure or absence of fixed protection.

You should not depend on any information gleaned from this book for your personal safety; your safety depends on your own good judgment, based on experience and a realistic assessment of your climbing ability. If you have any doubt as to your ability to safely climb a route described in this book, do not attempt it.

The following are some ways to make your use of this book safer:

1. Consultation: You should consult with other climbers about the difficulty and danger of a particular climb prior to attempting it. Most local climbers are glad to give advice on routes in their area and we suggest that you contact locals to confirm ratings and safety of particular routes and to obtain first-hand information about a route chosen from this book.

2. Instruction: Most climbing areas have local climbing instructors and guides available. We recommend that you engage an instructor or guide to learn safety techniques and to become familiar with the routes and hazards of the areas described in this book. Even after you are proficient in climbing safely, occasional use of a guide is a safe way to raise your climbing standard and learn advanced techniques.

3. Fixed Protection: Many of the routes in this book use bolts and pitons which are permanently placed in the rock. Because of variances in the manner of placement, weathering, metal fatigue, the quality of the metal used, and many other factors, these fixed protection pieces should always be considered suspect and should always be backed up by equipment that you place yourself. Never depend for your safety on a single piece of fixed protection because you never can tell whether it will hold weight, and in some cases, fixed protection may have been removed or is now absent.

Be aware of the following specific potential hazards which could arise in using this book:

1. Misdescriptions of Routes: If you climb a route and you have a doubt as to where the route may go, you should not go on unless you are sure that you can go that way safely. Route descriptions and topos in this book may be inaccurate or misleading.

2. Incorrect Difficulty Rating: A route may, in fact, be more difficult than the rating indicates. Do not be lulled into a false sense of security by the difficulty rating.

3. Incorrect Protection Rating: If you climb a route and you are unable to arrange adequate protection from the risk of falling through the use of fixed pitons or bolts and by placing your own protection devices, do not assume that there is adequate protection available higher just because the route protection rating indicates the route is not an "X" or an "R" rating. Every route is potentially an "X" (a fall may be deadly), due to the inherent hazards of climbing – including, for example, failure or absence of fixed protection, your own equipment's failure, or improper use of climbing equipment.

THERE ARE NO WARRANTIES, WHETHER EXPRESS OR IMPLIED, THAT THIS GUIDEBOOK IS ACCURATE OR THAT THE INFORMATION CONTAINED IN IT IS RELIABLE. THERE ARE NO WARRANTIES OF FITNESS FOR A PARTICULAR PURPOSE OR THAT THIS GUIDE IS MERCHANTABLE. YOUR USE OF THIS BOOK INDICATES YOUR ASSUMPTION OF THE RISK THAT IT MAY CONTAIN ERRORS AND IS AN ACKNOWLEDGMENT OF YOUR OWN SOLE RESPONSIBILITY FOR YOUR CLIMBING SAFETY.

CONTENTS

Crusher on Mouth of the South, *West Bank.* RICHARD ROSSITER PHOTO

CRUSHER'S TWO CENTS WORTH
BY STEVE "CRUSHER" BARTLETT

I have a memory like a sieve. Names, faces—they often just find their way into some kind of black hole in my head. However, after living and climbing around Boulder for 16 years, even my appalling memory can't help but register and retain fond thoughts of the many great climbs and great people. I want to write a little about some of the people who have made living in Boulder so enjoyable, and something about this new guidebook.

First, here's what I'd most like to see, now this new guide is out: hordes of climbers flinging themselves at new classics such as *Sic Mix*, or *There's a Cowboy Up There*. I also expect to see long lines on forgotten gems like *The Dull Men's Club*, and *I've Been Sick*. Perhaps now I'll be able to get on *Touch and Go* without waiting.

> "OK Rob, let's go climb something you've never done before." Rob was a roommate for a few months. Nice guy, but he was convinced that everything had happened before. The conviction was strong enough that after checking himself into Boulder Psychiatric Unit for a few days, he swore that one of the doctors had finally told him, "Well, we couldn't cure you, but it looks like we did a great job of taking all your money." I handed Rob the guidebook. He stalled, then finally admitted that he'd never done Anthill Direct. "I'm positive!" He generously offered to drive. On the way he had to stop to buy cigarettes. Twice. The car was strewn with about 20 cigarette packets, all with just one cigarette missing. "They're drugged. I try to buy them at different random places, but the Bureau always gets there first, and they make me buy a packet that has been drugged." Ah yes, I thought, this is shaping up to be a really fun day in Eldo....

Richard Rossiter's beautiful topos need little introduction. Richard was one of the first people to "draw" a guidebook. His early versions of the Boulder guides (dating back to 1981) were in pure topo format, no text and no photos. I loved using my old yellow topo guide. I still have it, coffee and beer stained, swollen, fluffy, and re-bound with duct tape: so easy to understand and a pleasure to look at. Plus, seeing as I seem incapable of remembering a description for more than 20 feet up a pitch, I could tuck it under my shirt or in my pocket and carry it up the climb.

Since the publication of *Boulder Climbs North* in 1988, Richard has incorporated text and photos to make the guide easy to use even for those of us for whom looking at pictures is challenging. He also included lots of historical information/slander.

> Derek Hersey was a roommate for several years. He would be out in Eldo (the Office) almost every day, and supping Toothsheaf in Old

Chicago's most nights. He never met a climbing partner he didn't
have a great time with and who didn't have a great time with him.
His soloing exploits are legendary. Reading his old Eldo guidebook is
shocking, so many "solo" notations, written next to hundreds of
climbs. One day we calculated that he'd soloed Outer Space at least
a hundred times. Another day, seeing him lounging lazily on the
couch, he told me he was having a (rare) rest day because the day
before he'd soloed Le Toit, The Naked Edge, Climb of the Century
and back down Center Route—all in an hour and a half.

Hiding behind the dry pages of a guidebook are many colorful personalities. Knowing something of these people, and their exploits, adds to the appreciation of many climbs. For instance, after cruising up the first pitch of *Blind Faith*, I happily place some Friends and haul my sweating carcass out of the crack onto the thin face moves. After beaching myself on the belay ledge I can't help but wonder how I would feel if I'd done the pitch in the style of the first ascent: on-sight free solo. My stomach churns, my knees wobble, and I scrabble to stuff ever more gear into any empty bits of crack within reach.

In the spirit of enchainment in the mountains, Mic Fairchild once
topped-out on Rotwand, Lower Peanuts, Bastille, Supremacy,
Cadillac, Rincon, Shirttail, Wind Tower, Hawk-Eagle, Potato Chip,
Long John Tower, Lumpe Tower, and Towers One and Two (On
Redgarden Wall), car to car, all in 2 hours, 58 minutes and 55
seconds.

The local scene has a colorful history. Many of the climbs done around here have been of groundbreaking difficulty, from Ray Northcutt's 5.11a lead of the *Northcutt Start* to *Bastille Crack*—in 1959!—to some of the wild leads of the early 1980s, like *Super Fly*, *Red Dihedral*, *Ministry of Fear*, and *Perilous Journey*. These have been—and this applies to a surprising number of these testpieces from this era—repeated by fewer people than have been to the moon.

Steve Dieckhoff, inspired by one of the Celebrate Eldorado events,
managed to sucker people (including my wife Fran) into sponsoring
him climbing, at $2 per pitch. "Oh, last year I did about 25 pitches.
I'll try, but I'm not sure I can do that many this year," and then
promptly climbed 60 pitches in one day.

The history got really colorful in the late 1980s. A full treatment would require my investing in a personal bodyguard. Boulder was dragged screaming and kicking into the modern, sport-climbing era. Conflict and dissent among local activists resulted in retro-bolted routes, chopped bolts, and incidents involving climbers verbally assaulting other climbers and non-climbers.

Christian Griffith put up many of the hardest routes in Eldorado. Behind this dry statement is a person who proudly brings haute couture to the Boulder climbing scene. Few of us get our photos in Rock &Ice *magazine. But how about naked, sitting on the side of a bathtub, carefully shaving our legs? Christian has. Full page, too.*

With the new millennium, things have calmed down. Climbing access and permission to place bolts are still awkward issues, but the future is looking brighter. We are getting smarter and learning that yes, there are other people in the world. Some obvious suggestions: Chipping the rock is best left to one of the local quarrying companies. Private landowners and government employees alike usually don't much care for being insulted. We should walk softly and carry a big clip stick. Join The Access Fund. They don't know all the answers, but they are learning and are the best hope we have for negotiating with government agencies.

"Hey Dan, any idea how many first ascents you've done around here?" Dan Hare looked puzzled. "Hmmm. Well, a few years ago, one quiet day at the Boulder Mountaineer, we sat down and started counting. We got only partway up Boulder Canyon and sort of lost interest at around 200..."

Richard Rossiter is one of the great characters of the Boulder climbing scene. He was a Green Beret during the Vietnam War and ranger for seven seasons in Eldorado Canyon. He is author of many climbing guidebooks, incorporating his inspiring topos. Next time you hear the rumble of a Harley Davidson around Boulder, take a look; it might be Richard. He has also put up many first ascents of (invariably) top quality routes around Boulder. For this guidebook, Richard has kindly given me great freedom to edit/butcher the existing text, while he worked on researching new information on the areas south of Mickey Mouse Wall. I have updated information, added new routes, changed a few ratings, renumbered all the climbs, and reformatted all the descriptions.

Working on guidebooks requires great care. I've had visions of climbers rappelling off the ends of their ropes into a big pile of bodies, just because I wrote the wrong descent rope-length somewhere. The thoroughness (or is it obsessiveness?) needed to produce a guide like this requires an absurd amount of time and patience. Richard seems to have a tradition of losing his girlfriend or wife just as a guidebook is nearing completion. I can see why.

Steve Bartlett
Boulder, Colorado
Spring 2000

ACKNOWLEDGMENTS

I would like to thank the following people for granting telephone interviews; participating in on-site photo sessions; providing topos, photos, and first ascent data; and for making the task of writing the sixth edition of *Boulder Climbs, Eldorado Canyon Area* (now called *Rock Climbing Eldorado Canyon*) a lot more fun, meaningful, and authoritative.

In no particular order, I thank: Will Niccolls, Ken Trout, Dave Crawford, Dave Field, Alan Nelson, Mat Esson, Steve LaPorta, Willie Mein, Melissa Griffith, Serena Benson, Mary Reidmiller, Gail Effron, Fran Bagenal, Steve Sangdahl, Brad White, John Baldwin, Steve Levin, Brad Bond, Keith Ainsworth, Mark Wilford, Annie Whitehouse, Bonnie Von Grebe, Jeff Achey, Kent Lugbill, Barry Brolley, Andy Donson, Ken Trout, Duncan Ferguson, Cameron Tague, Bret Ruckman, Marco Cornacchione, Fred Knapp, Dave Fortner, Robert Fenichel, and Todd Shannon.

The following climbers deserve special recognition for meeting in person with me or Crusher to discuss their areas of expertise related to the book. In no particular order, I thank: George Squibb, Colin Lantz, Tripp Collins, Moe Hershoff, Dan Hare, David Light, Chip Ruckgaber, Mic Fairchild, Christian Griffith, Mark Tarrant, Mike Brooks, Steve Muehlhauser, Ed Webster, Bob Horan, Michael Gilbert, Steve Dieckhoff, Jim Erickson, Mark Rolofson, Dan Hare, Roger Briggs, Rob Candelaria, and Eric Doub.

Special thanks go to Tod Anderson for contributing most of the Ralston Buttes chapter along with Eric Doub.

Special thanks to Chris Archer for contributing the section on fixed hardware policy in Eldorado Canyon.

Special thanks to Kath Pyke for contributing the section on wildlife closures.

Foremost, I am boundlessly thankful for the expert and enduring assistance of Crusher (sometimes known as Steve Bartlett), who devoted hundreds of hours to the editing and reorganization of this guide. Along with all the topo shuffling and daunting stints at the computer, Crusher made many trips to Eldorado Canyon to verify anchors and new route information. He also personally interviewed many of the great characters whose contributions to Colorado climbing may be partially glimpsed in the pages of this book. The fact that this new guide is even available during the year 2000 (and not 2012) is largely due to Crusher's persistence and enthusiasm for the task. He is also responsible for the book's entertaining preface.

Last, I would like to thank Falcon Publishing for putting up most of the money to cover Crusher's invaluable help. And my editor John Burbidge . . . who waited.

MAP LEGEND

Interstate Highway	═══════▷	Interstate Highway	(5)
Paved Road (major)	═══▭═══▷	U.S. Highway	(2) (395)
Paved Road (minor)	═══════▷	State/County Roads	(23) (166)
Gravel Road	═══════▷	Forest Service Road	4420
Tunnel	═▷═══◁═	Peak/Elevation	x
Dirt Road	==========▷	Crag/Boulder	⬭
Trail	················	Pitch Number	28
Railroad	+++++++++++	Bolt Anchor	x x
Railroad Tunnel	++▷····◁++		
Gate	•—•	Compass	**N** ↑
River/Creek	～～～		
Lake	▰	Scale	0 1 2 Miles

ABBREVIATIONS

c.	circa, about, approximately	S	serious fall potential
FA	first ascent	SR	standard rack of gear (see "Equipment")
FFA	first free ascent	TCU	three-cam unit
KB	knifeblade piton	TR	toprope
LA	Lost Arrow piton	VS	very serious fall potential
P1, P2	pitch one, pitch two, etc.	★	route of good-to-excellent quality
QD	quickdraw		

TOPO LEGEND

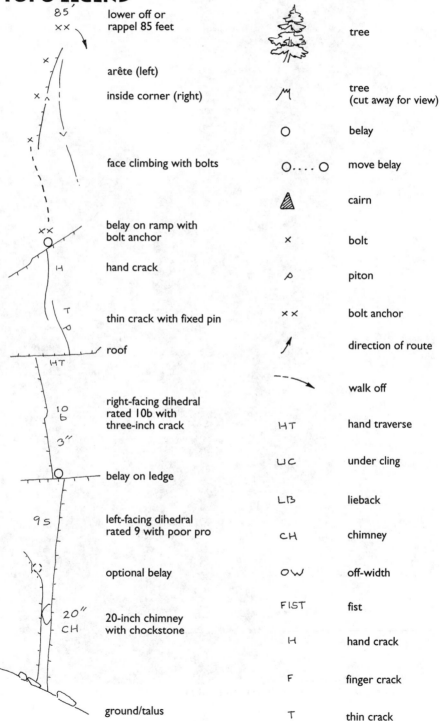

85' ××	lower off or rappel 85 feet
	arête (left)
	inside corner (right)
	face climbing with bolts
×× O	belay on ramp with bolt anchor
H	hand crack
T ρ	thin crack with fixed pin
	roof
HT	
10 b 3"	right-facing dihedral rated 10b with three-inch crack
O	belay on ledge
9 s	left-facing dihedral rated 9 with poor pro
	optional belay
20" CH	20-inch chimney with chockstone
	ground/talus

	tree
M	tree (cut away for view)
O	belay
O·····O	move belay
▲	cairn
×	bolt
ρ	piton
× ×	bolt anchor
↗	direction of route
--→	walk off
HT	hand traverse
UC	under cling
LB	lieback
CH	chimney
OW	off-width
FIST	fist
H	hand crack
F	finger crack
T	thin crack

Jerry Moffat and Skip Guerin on Psycho Roof *(5.12d)*. BOB HORAN PHOTO

INTRODUCTION

BOLTING IN ELDORADO?
HERE'S THE NEW DRILL
BY CHRIS ARCHER

In the late 1980s, the placement of bolts became a topic of controversy in Eldorado. The cause was twofold: the establishment of rap-bolted sport routes and the retro-bolting of established routes. During this period at least two new routes (*Paris Girl* and *Scratch and Sniff*) were chopped by climbers opposed to such tactics. In addition, several climbers began systematically replacing ancient fixed anchors. Unfortunately, in addition to replacing gear with like gear in the same locations, these climbers also added additional bolts to existing routes, replaced pitons with bolts, and altered the locations of bolts. These actions changed the nature of certain classic climbs, such as *Psycho*, *X-M*, *Rosy Crucifixion*, *Le Toit*, and *The Wisdom*, and enraged many local climbers. As a result of this well-meant but misdirected effort, some of the new bolts were chopped and the rock damaged.

Due to these events, in 1991, Eldorado Canyon State Park management concluded that individuals should no longer be permitted to take unilateral actions (like placing and chopping bolts) without the local climbing community's input and support. Bob Toll, the head ranger at Eldorado at the time, approached several local climbers and informed them that the Park would continue to allow climbers to establish new routes requiring bolts, if climbers would establish a process which determined whether the local climbing community supported the proposed routes.

As a result, the Action Committee for Eldorado (ACE) was incorporated in 1992 by The Access Fund. ACE is a tax-exempt, nonprofit organization whose board of directors is comprised of representatives from The Access Fund, American Alpine Club, American Mountain Guides Association, and the Colorado Mountain Club, as well as several at-large members. Because of the Park's willingness to allow climbers to govern themselves and to continue to establish new routes, ACE created Celebrate Eldorado, an annual weekend-long gathering of volunteers who work on Eldorado's trails, replace eroding fixed hardware, and raise thousands of dollars for ACE's work in Eldorado Canyon. To date ACE has raised over $100,000 through Celebrate Eldorado and private donations. The majority of these funds have been spent on Eldorado's trails.

In 1992, ACE created the first fixed hardware review process in the nation. The Fixed Hardware Review Committee (FHRC) is designed to provide the climbing community with the opportunity to comment on and discuss, approve or disapprove of:

1. Proposals to establish new routes requiring fixed gear;

2. Proposals to remove routes with fixed gear;

3. Proposals to change existing climbing routes by adding, removing or relocating fixed gear; and

4. Other proposals or actions that affect climbing in the Canyon.

The goal of the process is the thoughtful development of new routes in Eldorado per community consensus. Each year, ACE appoints local climbers to serve on the FHRC. After publicizing the proposals and surveying the local climbing community through e-mail, at climbing shops and gyms, and at a public meeting, the FHRC informs the Park of the community's opinion. The final decision on all proposals rests with the Park. Since the FHRC's inception, the Park has approved all but one of the proposals recommended by the FHRC.

Given the wide diversity of opinion within the climbing community on fixed hardware, the FHRC process has worked surprisingly well. In the mid- to late-1980s, new routes utilizing fixed hardware were established in Eldorado at the rate of 20 to 45 per year. Since ACE initiated the FHRC process in 1992, a total

Richard Rossiter free-soloing Over the Hill *(5.10b), Rincon Wall.* VALERIE MCKINLEY PHOTO

of 11 new routes has been approved and installed in the canyon. Each route recommended to the Park by the FHRC was approved by the majority of people attending the meeting and voting on the route. These results, however, did not come without a certain amount of strife.

It is probably an understatement to say that the formative years of the FHRC have been a period of intense and passionate debate. Tempers frequently flared at FHRC meetings—the culmination of which was a death threat leveled against the entire committee by a disgruntled applicant! After approving a few routes in the first few years of its existence, in the mid 1990s, the majority of FHRC members were vehemently opposed to any new routes in Eldorado despite public opinion to the contrary. During this period, no new routes were approved, and applications for new routes became scarce to say the least. In the last few years, a moderate FHRC has accurately reported public opinion and recommended several new routes to the Park.

Recently there have been some subtle shifts in the focus of the FHRC process. The very existence of the FHRC means that the ability to establish new routes has become a community centered process. No longer is the creation of a new route requiring bolts an individual decision and a monument to the first ascentionist. In the future, climbers who want to establish new bolted routes in Eldorado will hopefully gain satisfaction from opening routes which many can enjoy, and forego the desire to establish dangerous routes that are seldom climbed.

There is little doubt that there are still worthy new lines to be climbed in Eldorado. The FHRC process seeks to allow the opening of new routes that benefit the climbing community, while at the same time maintaining the traditional routes of Eldorado. The process will hopefully continue to focus on preserving existing routes in the condition of the FFA, while approving new routes with adequate protection which can be led safely by a leader competent at the grade.

If you're interested in establishing a new route, or adding or relocating new fixed gear, get an application from ACE. Applications will be available at ACE's website (currently under development) before the next millennium, and are currently available via e-mail from ACEELDO@AOL.COM, or from ACE at P.O. Box 337, Eldorado Springs, CO 80025. The FHRC publicizes proposals via e-mail and in books distributed to climbing shops and gyms, usually at least three weeks before the FHRC meeting. Check them out between burns. To get onto the ACE e-mail list, send a request to ACE. For new routes, an applicant must have toproped the route and must specifically indicate where he or she proposes to place bolts. If you want to replace worn gear with like gear in the same location, you don't need to apply to the FHRC. Instead, contact the Park directly for permission.

If you'd like to serve on the FHRC, e-mail ACE and ask for an application (which is usually due by mid-December). FHRC members are elected annually by ACE (usually in January) based upon several criteria: an open mind, the

Eldorado Canyon. RICHARD ROSSITER PHOTO

ability to consider each route on its merits, and the ability to vote against one's own personal opinions when the climbing community's opinion differs are among the most important criteria for FHRC members. In addition, years of climbing experience in Eldorado, awareness of Eldorado's history and traditions, willingness to devote a substantial amount of time to working on the committee, and the ability to discuss proposals with other climbers while out climbing are also considered.

The future of Eldorado depends on the involvement and support of all of us who are fortunate enough to climb in this mystical place. If you've been participating in the FHRC process and giving something back to Eldorado by supporting ACE and Celebrate Eldorado, we thank you and hope you'll continue to do so. If you've never been to a FHRC meeting or Celebrate Eldorado, make this year the year you participate. Heck, if you don't like trail work, you can always apply for a new route. See you at the next meeting.

Chris Archer is one of the founding members of ACE and a current director. He is also an Access Fund director and chairs The Access Fund's Legal Committee. When not climbing in Eldorado, he can occasionally be found in his law offices in Boulder.

Note: Mickey Mouse Wall is located within City of Boulder Open Space. Placement of any new fixed hardware in this area is currently prohibited. For information, call (303) 441-3408.

WILDLIFE CLOSURES
BY KATH PYKE OF THE ACCESS FUND

The Access Fund is a national non-profit organization that works to keep climbing areas open and to conserve the climbing environment. The Access Fund supports land and recreation management based on objective analyses, information of critical resources, and how climbers affect these resources. The climbing environment provides crucial habitat for many kinds of plants and animals, some of which are rare or quite sensitive to disturbance from humans.

For this reason The Access Fund supports seasonal climbing restrictions to protect nesting raptors at over 70 climbing locations in the United States. These are targeted to protect endangered or threatened species, such as peregrine and prairie falcons and golden eagles. Typically, restrictions start in early spring and run through early to mid-summer, the critical nesting period when birds are raising their young.

By working in partnership with biologists and land managers, The Access Fund strives to help provide the necessary protection for the nesting birds without excessive climbing restrictions. We encourage lifting restrictions early if nest sites are not established, and the flexibility to change restricted areas if birds vary their nest sites from year to year.

Support from local climbers is vital to the success of the raptor program. Resource managers, with limited budgets for monitoring, welcome raptor sightings or reports of unusual behavior. Equally, The Access Fund needs your feedback. If you need more information or have a concern about a raptor closure, please call The Access Fund. The Access Fund exists to help climbers and will be able to coordinate local meetings to take up issues on your behalf.

Nest sites and management considerations may vary from year to year; keep an eye out for signs at parking lots and trailheads which give current information, or call the responsible agency listed on our website: http://www.accessfund.org.

SOME ENVIRONMENTAL CONSIDERATIONS

To preserve the natural beauty and ecological integrity of our climbing environment, a few suggestions are offered (by the author): Use restrooms or outdoor toilets where possible. Otherwise, deposit solid human waste far from the cliffs and away from paths of approach and descent. Do not cover solid waste with a rock, but leave it exposed to the elements where it will deteriorate more quickly, or better, carry a small garden spade and bury it. Carry used toilet paper out in a plastic bag, or use a stick or Douglas-fir cone. Do not leave human-made riffraff lying about. If you pack it in, pack it out. Take care to preserve trees and other plants on approaches and climbs. While traveling in scree gullies and talus fields, seek sections that are more stable; thrashing up and down loose scree causes erosion and destroys plant life. Always use trails and footpaths where they have been developed and demonstrate conscientiousness by removing obstructions, stacking loose rocks along trail sides, and picking up trash. Dogs are best left at home, as they cannot be attended while one is climbing. Unattended dogs are often a nuisance or even a hazard to others, especially in high-use areas.

EQUIPMENT

Appropriate climbing hardware can vary drastically from one route to another, and what a climber chooses to carry is a matter of style and experience. So-called sport climbs obviously require only quickdraws unless otherwise noted. There is on other climbs an array of devices that most parties would want to carry. Thus, a "standard rack" (SR) for the Eldorado area might consist of the following gear:

A set of RPs
Wired Stoppers up to one inch
Various camming devices up to 2.5 inches
7 to 10 quick draws (QDs)
3 to 5 runners long enough to wear over the shoulder
1 double-length runner
6 to 8 unoccupied carabiners (usually with the runners)

Steve Muehlhauser on the fourth pitch of Point Break *(5.11a), Rincon Wall.*
RICHARD ROSSITER PHOTO

RATINGS

The system used for rating difficulty in this book is a streamlined version of the so-called Yosemite Decimal System. The Class 5 designation is assumed, so that 5.0 through 5.14 are written as 0 through 14, without the 5. prefix. The Welzenbach grades Class 3 and Class 4 have been retained. The Roman numeral grades I through VI for overall difficulty are not used.

The potential for a long leader fall is indicated by an S (serious) or VS (very serious) after the rating of difficulty. A climb rated S will have at least one notable runout and the potential for a scary fall. A climb rated VS typically will have poor protection for hard moves and the potential for a fatal or near-fatal fall. The absence of these letters indicates a relatively safe climb, providing it is within the leader's ability. However, because mistakes may exist, always exercise caution and judgment before starting up any route.

Remember that the rating of a climb is not absolute and represents an informal consensus of climbers' opinions. Some of the routes in this book may never have been repeated, which makes their ratings extremely subjective. But even the ratings of long-established routes are debatable—all of which should serve as a warning to not rely entirely on numbers. Look at the route up close and use your best judgment before proceeding.

ARRANGEMENT OF TEXT

All crags and routes in this book are catalogued from left to right, as they are normally viewed on approach. I have used this format simply because books published in western languages, such as English, are paginated from left to right. This lends a visual logic to the information as one leafs through the text and drawings. The guide is divided into south and north sections. Section I (Southern Crags) begins with Ralston Buttes (south of Coal Creek Canyon and Colorado 72) and finishes with Cryptic Crags just north of Mickey Mouse Wall. Section II (Eldorado Canyon) continues through Eldorado Canyon Sobo Buttress, the south ridge of South Boulder Peak, and including all crags normally appproached from Eldorado Canyon.

* * *

Classic Oxymoron: Wildlife Management.

The late, great Derek Hersey in the Land of Ra *(5.11a), Cadillac Crag.*
RICHARD ROSSITER PHOTO

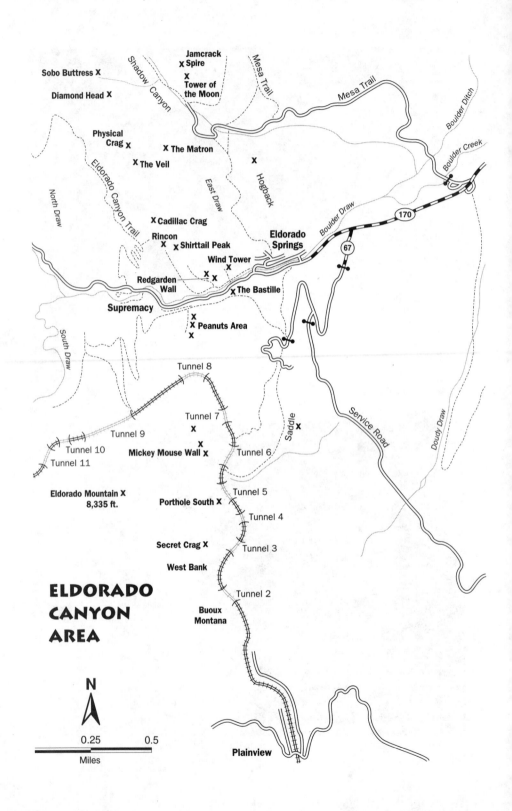

Sobo Buttress X

Diamond Head X

Jamcrack
X Spire
X
Tower of
the Moon

Shadow Canyon

Mesa Trail

Mesa Trail

Boulder Ditch

Boulder Creek

Physical
Crag X

X The Matron

X The Veil

X

Hogback

Eldorado Canyon Trail

North Draw

East Draw

Boulder Draw

170

X Cadillac Crag

Rincon
X X Shirttail Peak

Eldorado
Springs

67

Wind Tower
X
Redgarden X X
Wall   X The Bastille

Supremacy

South Draw

X
X Peanuts Area
X

Tunnel 8

Service Road

Doudy Draw

Tunnel 7
X
X
Mickey Mouse Wall X Tunnel 6
Tunnel 9
Tunnel 10
Tunnel 11

Saddle
X

Eldorado Mountain X
8,335 ft.

Tunnel 5

Porthole South X

Tunnel 4

Secret Crag X Tunnel 3

West Bank

**ELDORADO
CANYON
AREA**

Tunnel 2

Buoux
Montana

N

Plainview

0.25   0.5

Miles

Buoux
Montana

West Bank
Area

Bull
Gulch

Secret
Crag

Eldorado
Mountain

Porthole
South

Mickey Mouse
Wall

Cryptic
Crag

Eldorado
Canyon

Shirttail
Peak

ELDORADO MOUNTAIN

RALSTON BUTTES

Bullwinkle's

Main Cliff Area

Combat Rock

Trad Acres

27

10

11

14

7

4

21

23

SOUTHERN CRAGS

This section of the book covers all climbing areas south of Eldorado Canyon and includes Ralston Buttes (Jefferson County Open Space), Buoux Montana (private land), The West Bank (private land), Porthole South (unknown), Mickey Mouse Wall (City of Boulder Mountain Parks/Open Space) and Cryptic Crags (unknown).

RALSTON BUTTES

Ralston Buttes, also known as Coors Crag, has seen sporadic climbing activity over the last 30 years. Access issues, lack of published route information, and changing landownership have kept Ralston Buttes from becoming a major climbing destination. Since Ralston Buttes faces west toward the foothills, it has been less visible to local climbers than other similar crags such as Mickey Mouse Wall.

There have been four phases of development. In the 1960s, Denver climbers, including Bill Forrest and Chris Walker, climbed here, nailing some of the most obvious lines. In the 1970s, Jim Erickson, Steve Wunsch, Roger Briggs, Earl Wiggins, Katy Cassidy, and others freed some of these climbs and established a few more of the most obvious lines. In the 1980s, Eric Doub, with various partners, developed many of the harder traditional lines. The climbs were not publicized, as access was somewhat fragile. The landowners at the time, due to concerns about liability, publicly did not allow climbing, while apparently not trying very hard to prevent access to the few climbers who actually visited the place. In the late 1980s and up until the mid-1990s, a new generation of climbers developed many new routes, mostly bolted sport climbs. Again, their climbs were not publicized, and have not been documented until now.

In 1995, Ralston Buttes was purchased by Jefferson County for $650,000. This should have alleviated the landownership issue; however, in 1997, county officials posted "No Trespassing" signs (Closed Open Space!) to this public property while they "study" the area. It has been claimed that this piece of rock is sensitive, irrespective of the active uranium mine just below the crag, and a climbing history stretching back at least 26 years. County officials have yet to provide any specific evidence to support their claim. It is hoped that, through this publication, grassroots climber advocacy can change this unfortunate situation. The Jefferson County Commissioners office can be reached at (303) 271-8525.

CRIMP TOWER

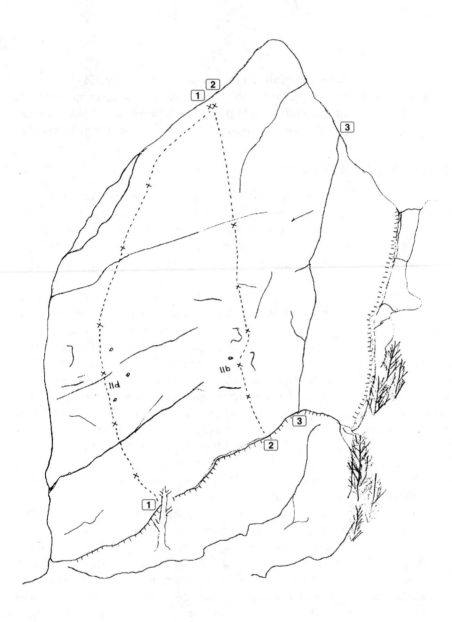

As a result of the somewhat clandestine new route activity in the past, which was never made public, and the unfortunate present access position, information about routes is incomplete. In addition to the usual guidebook compiler excuses for inaccuracy can be added the potential arrest and large fine for first-hand research. Apologies for errors and omissions. Topos courtesy of Tod Anderson.

CRIMP TOWER

Located on the extreme northern end of Ralston Buttes, possibly outside the parcel owned by Jefferson County. This crag would not be interesting except it is sheared off on the southeast aspect to present a vertical, red, isosceles-triangle-shaped wall 50 feet high. There are two bolt routes close together and a hand crack on this face. A nice view of the Blue Mountain Valley below provides a pastoral setting for the climbs on this formation.

1. **Chimp 11d** ★ Thin face climbing on edges and flakes on the left-hand arête. 6 bolts.

2. **Crimp 11b** ★ More edges and flakes. A pretty good, if short excursion, very thin and sequential. 5 bolts.

3. **Wise Crack 10a** FA: Jim Erickson, Art Higbee, 1972. Classic hand crack. A little bit more traffic or some specific cleaning will make this into a nice route.

NON-EMPIRICAL WALL

The first ascentionists started utilizing scientific route names. They and the concepts they designate are rather non-empirical (e.g. heliopause, phlogiston); ergo, this is the non-empirical wall. This is the largest formation at the northern end of the main ridge. The first three routes all end at a traverse line that leads off to the left and allows access to the anchors on these routes for toproping.

1. **Heliopause 11a** *Heliopause* is the leftmost route, behind a tree that obscures the crux. Pull up and right through an overhang; quite gymnastic. Slab it to the anchors (9). 4 bolts.

2. **Tardis 11c** ★ This is a good route: a bulge is battled, moving left across an overhanging traverse, pulling up on small sharp pockets (11c) to a steep slab. 6 bolts.

3. **Phlogiston 12b** ★ Fire conceived of as a physical substance. This route is a Ralston classic, especially when both pitches are done together. Steep, big, friendly pockets (10b) to a thin crack lieback crux (11b) on the first pitch. The second pitch pulls the strenuous bulge above. 11 bolts.

4. **Ralston Plasma 12a** Mainly handlebars, pockets, and wafer-thin steep tips. 4 bolts.

NON-EMPIRICAL WALL

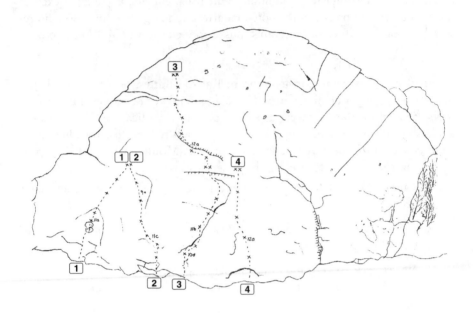

BULLWINKLE'S CRAG

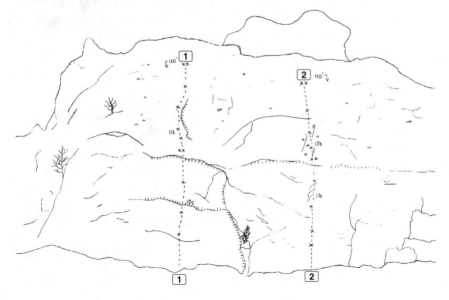

BULLWINKLE'S CRAG

Located about 100 yards south of the Non-empirical area. It is slightly before one gets to the chute or access gully through the cliff that is the standard approach to the top and back of Ralston. Routes are about 120 feet, done as one pitch, although two have intermediate stations.

1. **Boris 11b** ★ This is a good and very well camouflaged route. Start up a grey slab at the left end of the crag, below a roof. Go up to and over the roof (10c), then up easy (loose) rock to a pair of shuts; belay here or continue through the crux (11b), an overhanging flake/lieback facing left. 7 bolts.

2. **Natasha 11b** This route can be identified by the first bolt, which was tagged by the rangers, being one of the few they could reach. Not as good as *Boris*; the crux is a left-skirting, face-climbing sequence over a bulge below the main intermediate ledge, and it is a little bit decomposed. The upper part of this route is nice, steep, (9 or 10) thin hands and pockets. 8 bolts.

There is an easy gully next, referred to throughout as the means to get to the tops of the routes along the rest of the formation, all the way (east) to The Amphitheater. The next route is a little way farther, on a short slabby wall with an overhang at the bottom. Watch for a bolt below the overhang, somewhat hidden behind a tree.

3. **It's Miller Time 11a** ★ FA: Dale Goddard, Eric Doub, 1982. This lies on a small formation about 30 yards right of the descent gully. P1. Head up and right (7) to the edge of a flake, then angle back left (9) to a belay on a ledge. P2. Straight up past a short, left-facing corner, to the roof. Over this (11a), then easier to the top.

Somewhere to the right of *Miller Time* is a 20-foot, 10c route (no bolts) up black streaks on a slab to a tree. This was climbed by Eric Guokas et al. in 1982. About 100 yards right of the access gully lies the next route.

4. **Trippopotamus 10c** This route has one hard move at the start, a contorted roof-passing maneuver that is somewhat weight-dependent. Continue up the slab past 3 more bolts. 4 bolts.

TRAD ACRES (NO TOPO)

The name says it all. There are a few bolts on these routes but bring small wires up to a #3 Friend for *Thin Red Line*. This sector is about 200 yards past the access gully, and right before the trail funnels in close to the cliff before reaching the first part of the tallest portion of the cliff when approaching from the north. Look for the thin dihedral/pillar at the bottom of *Thin Red Line*, its distinctive crux. Trad Acres is right of that, leading up to an overhang behind a tree at the top of a moderate buttress.

1. **Thin Red Line 11b** ★ Start on a ledge below a shallow, tapering, right-facing corner about 40 feet high. Lowe balls and RPs work in the seam; it's 11b where the seam quits taking gear. Traverse left at the roof barrier to a crack leading through it (a new bolt was added at the beginning of the traverse, and there is a previously-installed bolt at the crack at the left end of the roof). Continue up interesting hand cracks, 9 or so, depending on the crack chosen, with ledges in between. Some serious rope drag to be avoided, double ropes help. Belay off the huge tree at the top, near the summit, which is known as "Ralston Boxcar," and is visible from miles away. Walk off toward Bullwinkle's and down, or find the 2-bolt anchor at the top of *Spartacus* (south 60 feet) and rappel. 2 bolts plus wires from RPs up and cams up to 3 feet, 150 feet total length.

2. **Trad Acres 10c** An obscure route with a high crux. A bit of a thrash because of the large conifer in the middle, not worth doing. Only 1 bolt, at the crux, and no fixed anchors at the top.

MAIN CLIFF

The majority of the climbs at Ralston lie on this section of the ridge, which is about 0.5-mile long and 250 feet high. Most of the routes in this section are two or three pitches long and require more than one 60-meter rope to rappel. The complex geometry of this cliff allows a wide variety of climbing experiences, from thin slabs to powerful overhangs. The routes here are comparable to the classics in Eldorado or Mickey Mouse and definitely worth a visit.

1. **Spartacus Smashes the Klan 11a/b** FA: Eric Doub, Jimmy Walker, 1982. Route was first climbed with no bolts. P1 now sports 3 bolts. P1. Medium Stoppers work for the runout past the dead tree to the first bolt. Continue up the slab after the crack ends 30 feet up. Very good grayish rock leads up to a two-coldshut anchor, 3 bolts, 90 feet. P2. Move right into a left-facing dihedral/crack which leads to a stratum with some loose blocks. Belay on a ledge on the right (55 feet). P3. Angle left (8) into the crack in the left side of an obvious ten-foot-wide "sentry box." Exiting this slot is the crux, 11a/b. Up to lower-off anchors, or continue to the ledge system above. Walk off to the left.

2. **Managed to Death 12b** ★ This route ascends the highly featured wall on thin, incut, and devious flakes and edges. 10 bolts.

3. **En Flagrante Bosch 11d** ★ This route starts in a crack left of *Reelin'*, then goes straight up the steep slab to a hanging spike that is surmounted into a hand crack. Continue up and right. 10 bolts. A second pitch has been partially completed.

4. **Reelin' in the Ears 12a** ★ Two ear-like flakes identify this steep line. Start under a dihedral that begins 10 feet up; yard over the roof below into it

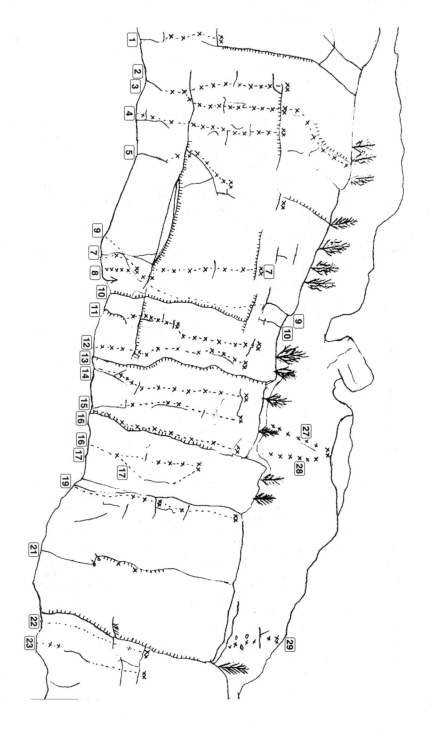

MAIN CLIFF OVERVIEW

MAIN CLIFF—NORTH END

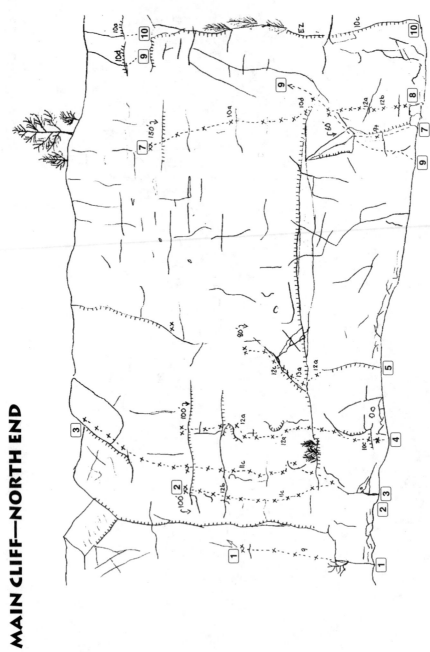

(10d, and height dependent—shorter is better). Continue up and right and blast through the steep crux bulge, playing it on the right. The next 60 feet is 10d/11a on good holds and fairly continuous. Highly recommended. 14 bolts.

5. **The Wishbone 12d/13a** ★ Follow a finger crack, then bolts up the apex above; very powerful. Early reports confirm a stout grade. 11 bolts.

6. **For Crying out Loud 9** Somewhere right of the large roof band is this pitch climbed by Doub et al.; it takes a 50-foot-long flake/crack. It may have been incorporated into *The Neighborhood* or *Wishbone*.

7. **The Neighborhood 10d** ★ Rack: P1, Gear to 3½ inches, 12 QDs for P2. This route goes up the left side of a pillar. P1. Up the pillar until it tops out just below the rightmost edge of the huge roof, 70 feet. P2. Head left along the brink of the roof and up the face 80 feet. The crux is getting onto the slab above the brink of the roof. A quality tour, probably the longest line at Ralston to date.

8. **Spanky 12b** ★ A hyper-thin excursion up the shield of rock on the face of the pillar, which *The Neighborhood* follows on its left margin. Crank over a small, steep overlap, then back slightly left (12b) on small pockets to a shallow offset that is ascended (11d, gradually easing) to the top of *Neighborhood* pillar. 7 bolts.

9. **Cassandra 6** FA: Steve Wunsch, Solo, 1972. FA: Direct Finish, Jim Erickson, Solo, 1973. A rather vague line. Start 20 feet to the left of the *The Neighborhood* and 50 feet left of *Rocky Mountain Springwater*. Climb up and right to an arête (crossing *The Neighborhood* near its belay), ascend cracks up this to a wide ledge (adjacent to *Rocky Mountain Springwater*). Traverse left, then up a crack, then crossing that line near the belay to finish on the ledge next to *Rocky Mountain Springwater*. **Variation:** The direct finish, Erickson's hardest free solo first ascent, takes the imposing 10d hand crack above the wide ledge.

10. **Rocky Mountain Springwater 10c** ★ FFA: Jim Erickson, Steve Wunsch, 1972. Rack: SR to 3½ inches. Occasional bushes, but a classic line. Takes the obvious, right-facing dihedral system. P1. Up the 10c dihedral 60 feet to a tiny ledge. P2. Mantel left onto a pinnacle, then up the dihedral (8) to a rocky ledge. P3. Ascend a thin crack line (10a) immediately to the right of the direct hand crack finish to *Cassandra*.

11. **Zook 11b** ★ Rack: to 3 inches. P1, 6 bolts + gear; P2, 9 bolts to the two-coldshut anchor. One of the best routes in the area. Begin in the left-facing dihedral 30 feet right of *Rocky Mountain Springwater*. P1. From the ledge above the corner, traverse left (8 S) past a bolt to below the big

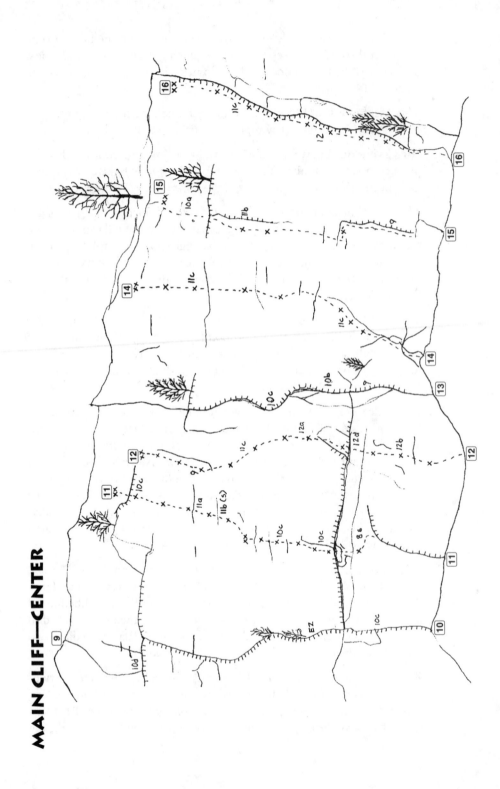

MAIN CLIFF—CENTER

overhang, then blast through it, going up right along the roof crack that turns into a vertical corner. Lieback past 2 bolts (10d) to the top of a small spike. Make a very thin (10c) traverse left past another bolt to a good ledge, then up past another bolt (9) to a triple-coldshut anchor. P2. Traverse down and right to a bolt, then straight up a disappearing offset to a monodoigt. The crux is a very thin, pocket-tweaking move up left into a small alcove (11b). Exit the alcove (10a) and weave up 50 feet of beautiful 9/10a face climbing to a bouldering-type move right below the anchors (10c). One 150-foot rappel back to the ground is possible if one raps eastward and down toward *Red Bullet.*

12. **Unknown 12d** A vague line ascends the face through the slot to the right of *Zook.* The roof is extremely thin, as is the face below.

13. **Miles from Nowhere 10c S** ★ FA: Jim Erickson, Roger Briggs, 1974. Rack: To 3 inches. This quality route follows the thin, left-facing dihedral system 30 feet right of *Rocky Mountain Springwater.* P1. Climb the 10a dihedral to a tiny ledge 40 feet up. P2. Continue over a bulge (10c) up to another small belay. P3. Easier (8) to the top.

14. **Red Bullet 11c** ★ Rack: 10 bolts and gear to 3 inches. The Red Bullet is a feature one can spot immediately right of the upper part of *Miles from Nowhere,* if standing at the bottom of *Zook.* The route on this tower is located on a 30-foot-wide, 120-foot-high plaque of rock, on its south side. Start at the left bottom of the plaque, going up a 20-foot stack of junk (big wires or mid-size cams will work). Reach up behind on the left for the first clip, then launch up right onto a very steep, narrowing, sliver-like ramp, chasing crisp, thin lieback edges (11c). Crank up to a good ledge where a #2 friend can be placed horizontally (retrobolt candidacy). Continue up a left-facing corner and face (10b) that is a little runout, then traverse right to the arête overlooking *Spent Brass.* Step up, back left, and go over a bolt-protected bulge (11a) to a very thin series of face climbing moves past 3 bolts (11b/c) to a hanging stance at 2 coldshuts.

15. **Blick Ins Chaos 11b/c** FA: Eric Doub, Andrew Nicodemus, Stefan Reitz, 1984. Rack: QDs, RPs to 3 inches. Now equipped with bolts at the crux and a lower-off anchor. Start near the east edge of the Red Bullet tower, below a "farmboy" hanger. Gain a nice dihedral on the right, which takes wires (9). Traverse left past the remains of a bonsai tree to a bolt at the bottom of the left-facing crux offset. Pass 2 bolts in the offset; many have complained of the bolt placement, which is too far left. This is ironic given that Doub first led this without bolts. "But those Crack 'n' Ups were bomber!" Do an 11b mantel followed by a tips move (10c/d) past an RP placement.

16. **Arête Already 12c** Follow the right-leaning arête to the ledge. 12 bolts.

17. **Closed Open Space 11d** ★ Rack: 6 bolts and gear to 3 inches. The first bolt on *Closed Open Space* can be seen close to the ground at an overhang below and left of a series of crisp flakes. The route follows a stepped arête leading up left of a brushy trough. Bolts on The Cobra can be seen 50 feet up. To begin, pass the first bolt at the overhang (10b), then use wires in the flakes above to a ledge left of the trough and below a steep step in the arête. Two bolts protect the desperate, thin scum-and mantel up the steep nose into a sinuous, shallow corner (The Cobra, 11d). As the crack begins to open, easier moves go up and right to a small stance below another steep small wall. Crank up and right on jugs (although some have disintegrated) across gymnastic moves protected by 3 bolts, and over the roof above to a slab (11c). Continue to the anchors.

18. **Tres Amigos 10c** Do the first 50 feet of *Closed Open Space*, but avoid The Cobra by continuing up the trough, which becomes good climbing above this point. The large overhang is channeled via a clean, overhanging hand crack (10c) easily identified from the ground. Traverse west to the coldshut anchors on *Closed Open Space*; rappel.

19. **Free Jeffco 11c** ★ Rack: QDs, gear to 3 inches. There is a very obvious tree on a ledge 70 feet off the ground, right of the trough on *Closed Open Space*. A system of flakes and an obvious, left-facing diagonal corner can be seen below the tree. P1. Flakes, then easy rock, can be followed to the corner, which has 2 bolts protecting moves up and out of the corner at its top (10a). This pitch ends at the tree, where a coldshut rap anchor is installed. P2. The crack above the tree takes good gear and is about 10a/b, into an alcove, then move out over a small arch at the top of the alcove (11b), protected by a bolt. More face climbing and another bolt lead to the top. Anchors can be found at the top of P2, on a very exposed slab in front of a tree on the edge of the clifftop.

20. **Fascism Is Brewing 9 S** FA: Eric Doub, Jimmy Walker, 1982. Location uncertain. Appears to take the face to the right of P1 of *Free Jeffco*. Pass a tree a little way up, join *Jeffco* about 80 feet up.

THE AMPHITHEATER

Farther right, a huge bulging section of the cliff is encountered. It is unknown if any routes have been done in this area; however, an obvious line splits the 250-foot-high, bulging wall. Just beyond the bulging wall is The Amphitheater. This contains some newer projects as well as routes done many years ago. One of the following lines may well be *Blind Boy Grunt*. This goes through a very prominent 17-foot roof. This was certainly climbed by Jeff Cristol and Eric Doub in 1982 at 10b A2, and possibly first done by Dave Breashears back in the 1970s.

21. **Unknown (Rating?)** An obvious line splits the bulging face to the right of *Free Jeffco*. Some fixed gear has been spotted.

22. **Teufelwader 11c** Begin immediately right of an overhanging chimney bearded with moss and usually seeping water. Power up and right to a bulge that is pulled up right, then back left to easier ground. This route may need more fixed protection to be a safe lead.

23. **Fin de Siecle 12d?** The most obvious line at The Amphitheater is a huge, right-facing dihedral that runs up the entire height of the cliff to its top. Details of this route are few, but the wall is seriously overhung and some fixed protection exists.

24. **Unknown Route 12c?** Located on the right side of The Amphitheater, a thin crack is supposedly mid-12. Two Lost Arrows can be seen about 40 feet up this system, which goes up right, then curves back left. This route, which overhangs the whole way, would be an excellent tour if converted to a modern sport climb.

25. **Limits of Hair 11b ★** The rock to the right of the previous route has a rotten band that widens as one proceeds east (right). Before the rot predominates, there is a good sport route that starts in a left-facing corner (obvious as a climbing target). An antique Star Dryvin bolt marks the start. P1. Clip this and launch up right (10b) onto an arête forming the right side of the corner. This section continues on good rock past 3 bolts to a small stance, before you make an exciting traverse to the left, above the roof at the top of the corner, with feet on the very brink of the slab above the roof. The crux is a face-climbing move up this slab to a right-slanting ledge. Another face-climbing move (10a/b) leads to a 2-coldshut anchor. P2. Up the vertical crack above. Protected with bolts and goes at about 10a. Pitch 1, 6 bolts, pitch 2, 4 bolts; rap from the coldshuts at the top of the crag.

The following routes lie on the upper tier of The Main Cliff as shown on the overview topo. They can best be reached by hiking up the access gully near Bullwinkle's Crag and following the ledge system above The Main Cliff. It is also possible to top out on one of the lower routes on The Main Cliff and do these routes as an aperitif.

26. **Rabid Rabbit 12a ★** FA: Eric Doub, Lars Henrikson, 1984. This follows an obvious crack angling up and left across the south face of a block at the top of the cliff, above *Blick Ins Chaos*—an unmistakable feature if one is hiking along the top of the cliff.

27. **Upper Crust 11c ★** Rack: QDs for 6 bolts. This fine route starts above the loose junk on the terrace, up a left-facing offset that curves into a roof. The first bolt was moved up and left after an early ascender got a

First ascent of Rabid Rabbit *(5.12a), Ralston Buttes.* PHOTO ERIC LIN DOUB COLLECTION

rope burn riding off the crux. Surmount this roof into a shallow, right-facing corner (11c), face climb the shallow corner above the roof, then move around left into a steep, gully-like feature (10b getting into it) and continue to the coldshuts.

28. **Unknown 12b** ★ Rack: QDs for 8 bolts. This route follows a distinctive, right-facing system of upside-down ledges in a dihedral 15 feet right of *Upper Crust*. Crank strenuously up this (11d), then yard out left onto the very steep wall, gaining a jug-like flake, followed by small divots and pockets to the top (12b).

29. **MRI 11d** ★ This route can best be reached by going up the access gully near Bullwinkle's Crag and traversing a long distance, past the top of *Closed Open Space*, to where a 6 move up a gully puts one near the west end of the barrier of rock. An unusual, deeply pocketed face leads into a strenuous horizontal roof that is pulled onto the summit (11d). This route was the scene of a neck-wrenching ascent that earned the first ascentionist an MRI and several weeks of physical therapy. 4 bolts.

COMBAT ROCK

Eric Doub reports about five routes on Combat Rock. This is a large cliff about 300 feet up and behind Coors Crag. This is best approached by skirting around the south end of Coors Crag. It would appear this is the same formation as the Upper Tier described above, but farther south. *Agent Orange* lies somewhere right of *MRI*.

30. **Agent Orange 9+** This route lies near the left end of the cliff and right of some huge roofs reminiscent of *Your Mother*.

31. **Surface to Air 11a** Right of *Agent Orange*.

32. **Air Raid 10 A1** FA: Eric Doub, Bill Doub, 1982. Start just right of an overhanging wall with a right-facing flake system. P1. Climb past a short, left-facing dihedral, to a 10a roof, over this and up 50 feet (8) to a strata band with buckets. Traverse right to a crack. Up this (A1) to a lip and belay. P2. Up the face (8) to the top.

33. **Behind Enemy Lines 9** FA: Eric Doub, Eric Guokas, Jimmy Walker, 1982. Start 125 feet right of *Air Raid*. P1. Up broken blocks. Climb past a bolt (8) right of a left-facing dihedral. Traverse right along the lip of an overhang (9) to a faint crack. Up the crack (past a bolt, 9) about 80 feet to a belay. P2. Climb up to a prominent, sharp, arête/fin. Past this to the top.

34. **Rock the Casbah 10d** This route takes a left-leaning dihedral/crack about 350 feet right of *Behind Enemy Lines*.

BUOUX MONTANA

BUOUX MONTANA

Buoux Montana is located in an unnamed draw about one mile north of Plainview and on the west side of the railroad tracks. The area features two relatively small outcrops near the bottom of the draw and a much larger buttress to the north. This area, like The West Bank, is private property. See Access Warning under The West Bank. Approach from Plainview as for The West Bank and Mickey Mouse Wall. Route information: David Light and Moe Hershoff.

BIG SKY MOTEL

This is the more westerly of the two big blocks in the draw, which features a single known route.

1. **Buffalo Girls 12a** ★ FA: David Light and John Gill, 1987. Follow bolts up the steep south face of the rock. Four (?) bolts to a 2-bolt anchor, 60 feet.

MAIN WALL

This is the large multi-tiered buttress on the north side of the draw. The following routes are located along the southeast wall, just above Big Sky Motel.

2. **Power Lounger 11b** ★ FA: Alison Sheets and Tim Hudgel, 1987. North of Big Sky Motel is a steep, pocketed south-facing wall. *Power Lounger* climbs this wall; the top anchors are visible from the railroad tracks. 4 bolts, one pin to a 2-bolt anchor.

3. **Tin Star 9** FA: John Gill and Alison Sheets, 1987. This line is located a short way down and right from *Power Lounger*. 3 bolts to a 2-bolt anchor.

4. **Howdy 10** FA: John Gill and Alison Sheets, 1987. This route is just right of *Tin Star*. 4 bolts to a 2-bolt anchor.

ACCESS WARNING! The following information is documented for historical purposes only. Neither Falcon Publishing nor the author assume any responsibility for individuals who enter The West Bank of their own volition. Though climbing in this area dates back at least 27 years, The West Bank is (according to The Access Fund) on private land and is not open to the public. There is also no way to reach the area without trespassing on railroad land. However, neither the railroad tracks nor The West Bank are posted "No Trespassing." Should you choose to enter this area—and we're not advocating that you do so—be quiet and discrete. If you are contacted by a landowner, please be polite and understanding of his position, and leave gracefully if asked.

THE WEST BANK

Three tunnels south of Mickey Mouse Wall and west of the railroad tracks is a splendid array of crags called The West Bank (also known as The Wild West). The area is remote and primitive, featuring mostly sport climbs with the odd

B	-	The Behemoth	RCR	-	Rock Cut Rock
R1	-	Ridge One	Secret Crag -		
R2	-	Ridge Two		TA	- Tier A
R3	-	Ridge Three		TB	- Tier B
V	-	The Virus		TC	- Tier C
UR4	-	Upper Ridge Four		TD	- Tier D
R4	-	Ridge Four	TW	-	Tunnel Wall
R5	-	Ridge Five	T3	-	Tunnel Three
SB	-	Sitting Bull	LR	-	Locomotive Rock

crack line here and there. The sport climbs were established primarily between 1987 and 1991. Some of these routes lack lowering anchors and leave a climber on the ridgecrest. Some of the hardware is outdated and potentially dangerous. Occasional fixed pins are missing, and on some routes, the bolt spacing is not so hot. Put another way, if this area had been developed a decade later, many of the routes would provide a different kind of experience (safer). With or without any technical improvements, however, The West Bank is big fun and well worth the walk. Bring a clip stick.

From south to north, there are four major ribs, several smaller features, and the multi-tiered Secret Crag forming the northern boundary. The highest and farthest west feature of the area is a giant free-standing block with a route called *Virus* on its overhanging south arête. This block is also on private land, near to a road, and the landowner has had unpleasant altercations with climbers. Climbers

B	-	The Behemoth	RCR	-	Rock Cut Rock
R1	-	Ridge One	Secret Crag -		
R2	-	Ridge Two		TA	- Tier A
R3	-	Ridge Three		TB	- Tier B
V	-	The Virus		TC	- Tier C
UR4	-	Upper Ridge Four		TD	- Tier D
R4	-	Ridge Four	TW	-	Tunnel Wall
R5	-	Ridge Five	T3	-	Tunnel Three
SB	-	Sitting Bull	LR	-	Locomotive Rock

are strongly advised to steer clear of this feature. In this guide, the long ribs are numbered from left to right (south to north). Secret Crag is not numbered at all, but described in tiers as it has been since the first routes were established there in 1972.

Approach as for Mickey Mouse Wall (see pages 73–77), but continue south along the tracks through three more tunnels. The West Bank lies west of the tracks between Tunnel Two and Tunnel Three (less than a mile from Plainview). About 200 feet north of Tunnel Two, a primitive trail climbs northwest from the tracks and leads up the slope toward Ridge Four and Secret Crag. After about 200 feet, a left branch (marked by cairns) leads south and west to Ridge One and Ridge Two. Please rebuild cairns if you find them in disarray.

Recently, people have been reaching The West Bank (and Mickey Mouse Wall) from Plainview without trouble. Keep in mind that this approach still involves trespassing on railroad land. If you choose this venue, park at pullouts

THE BEHEMOTH

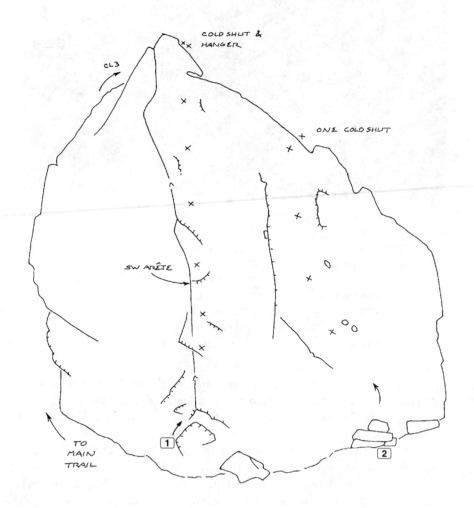

CL3

COLD SHUT &
HANGER

ONE COLD SHUT

SW ARÊTE

TO
MAIN
TRAIL

1

2

about 100 yards below the tracks at Plainview. Hike west through the pines (not up the road), step over a wire fence to the south of a white building, then walk north along the tracks. Pass through or around Tunnel Two and find the trail to The West Bank in about 200 feet.

THE BEHEMOTH

This large boulder is located 100 feet west of the railroad tracks and 200 feet south from the start to the main trail. To reach it, hike south from the start to the main trail or hike downhill to the east from a point (marked by a cairn) along the trail to Ridge One and Ridge Two. It is easy to scramble to the top of this 50-foot-high block from the north.

1. **Big Moe 13 A0 (Project)** FA: Moe Hershoff and Tripp Collins, 1989. This route tackles the steep southwest arête. 6 bolts to a 2-bolt anchor. The anchor consists of a coldshut and a non-threadable hanger.

2. **South Face 12d** This route ascends the middle of the south face. Stick-clip the first bolt, and step off a pile of rocks. 4 bolts to a single coldshut over the lip.

RIDGE ONE

This is the farthest south of the significant features in The West Bank, consisting of a long upper rib and a shorter lower rib separated by a notch. A bit of Class 4 is required to pass through the notch. Approach via the main trail. Branch left after 200 feet and contour south beneath some giant boulders, then follow the path as it curves around toward the west and eventually reaches the bottom of Ridge One. One may also approach as for Ridge Two, then break left across a grassy gully and traverse a ledge to the bottom of *Black President*. See map.

RIDGE ONE

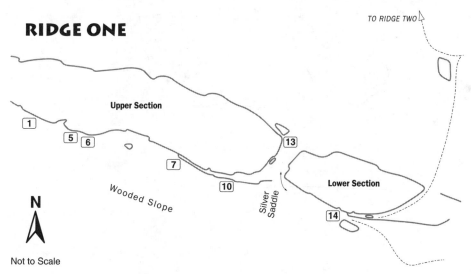

RIDGE ONE—UPPER AREA

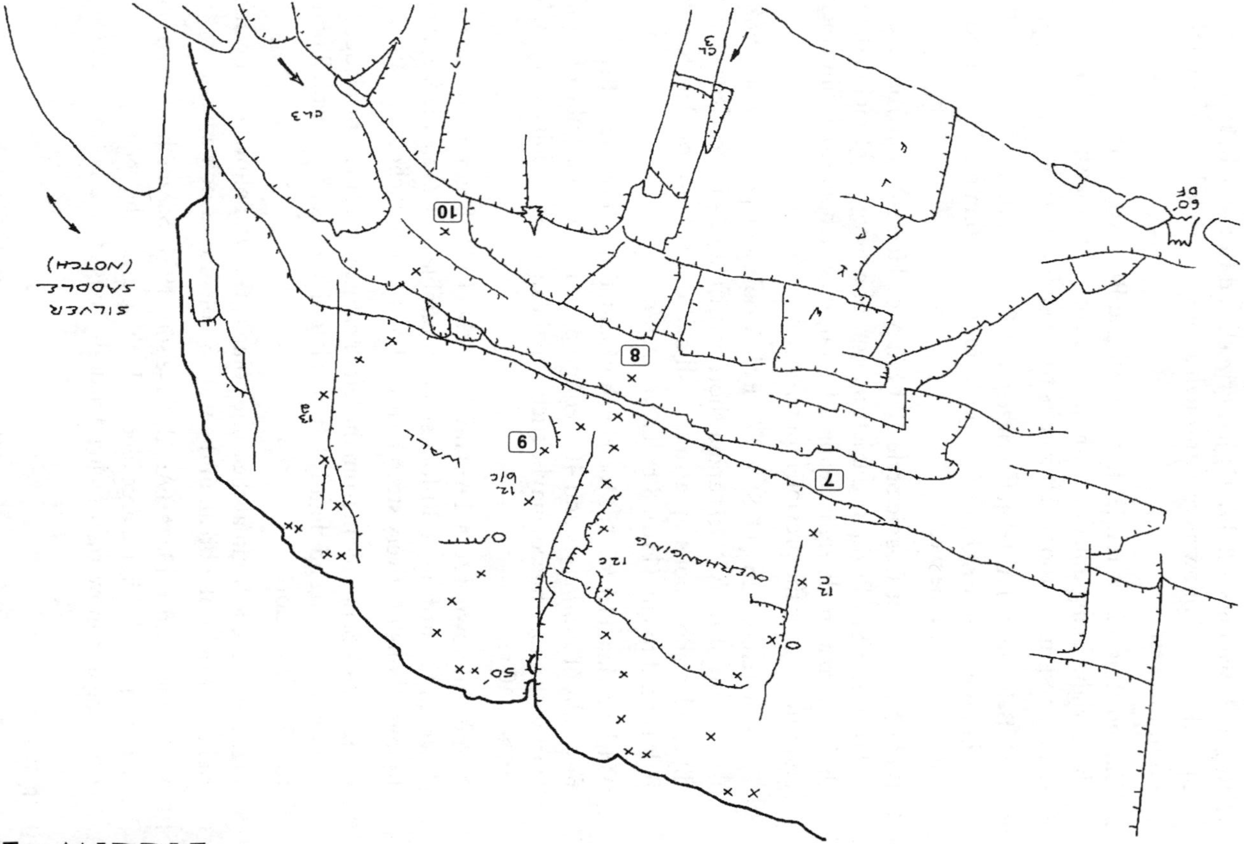

RIDGE ONE—MIDDLE

SILVER SADDLE (NOTCH)

CL 3

CL 3

FLAKE

OVERHANGING 12c

WALL

12 b/c

50'

13

7

8

9

10

GO DF

12c

O

1. **Raging Hormones 10b** FA: (?) Jeff Frizzell and Rob Woolf, 1988. Rack: up to 3 inches. Follow a crack through a roof. Gain a ledge and scramble off to the west.

2. **Casano Rojo 12a ★** FA: (?) Jeff Frizzell and Rob Woolf, 1988. Climb a short, right-facing dihedral with huecos, continue up a short steep wall (crux), and turn a roof (11). 3 bolts to a 2-bolt anchor.

3. **Ain't Behavin' 9** FA: (?) Jeff Frizzell and Rob Woolf, 1988. Rack: SR. Begin about 6 feet right of *Casano Rojo*. Follow thin cracks to a ledge and walk off to the west.

4. **Body Nazis Do It Doggie Style 10d** FA: Moe Hershoff and Tony Herr, 1990. Rack: SR. Begin at the left margin of a large, right-facing dihedral. Climb a small, right-facing dihedral, then step left to a thin crack and finish as for the previous route.

5. **The Adulteress 12b (11 S) ★** FA: Rob Woolf and Jeff Frizzell, 1988. Begin right of *Body Nazis* and a short way right of a large, right-facing dihedral. Follow bolts up a steep wall and through a roof. The fourth bolt is hard to clip (11d). 8 bolts, no anchor.

6. **Marked Man 11d ★** FA: Moe Hershoff and Tony Herr, 1990. Begin 50 feet right of *Adulteress* and 40 feet uphill from a 30-foot spike of rock. Start with a lone hueco, maybe stick-clip the first bolt. 3 bolts to a 2-bolt anchor, 40 feet.

7. **Name Unknown 12c ★** FA: Guy Lord (?), 1991. Begin about 50 feet down and right from a 30-foot spike. Scramble 50 feet to a ledge, then follow 5 bolts up a very steep headwall to a 2-bolt anchor.

8. **Ganas 12c ★** Scramble in from the left or right and begin from a ledge 50 feet up. Climb up and slightly left, just left of a break in the wall. 9 bolts to a 2-bolt anchor.

9. **Ejaculator 12c ★** Begin at the same point as *Ganas*. Follow bolts up and right, just right of a break in the wall. 8 bolts to a 2-bolt anchor.

10. **Wild Blue Yonder 13a ★** FA: Alan Nelson, 1991. Scramble in from the right and start behind a large block. Climb up and right, then up and back left along a shallow, right-facing dihedral. 7 bolts to a 2-bolt anchor.

SILVER SADDLE

This is a gap about 300 feet up from the bottom of Ridge One.

11. **Outlaw 12b** FA: Alan Nelson, 1991. This is the left of three short routes in the gap between the upper and lower sections of the ridge. Begin at a cluster of huecos. Climb up and left through a roof, then up a steep wall (crux). 5 bolts to a 2-bolt anchor.

RIDGE ONE—SILVER SADDLE

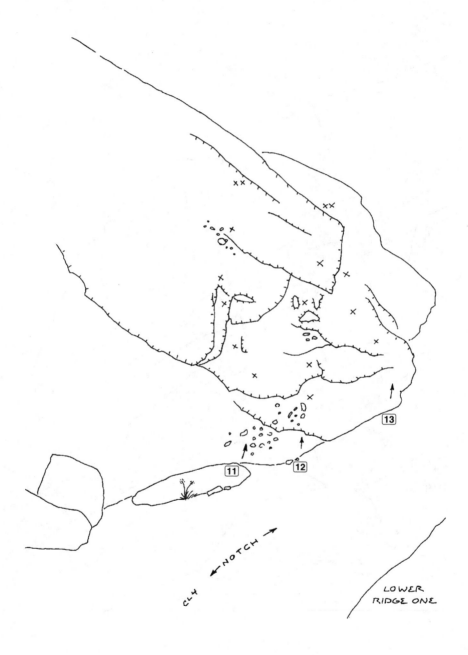

RIDGE ONE—LOWER SECTION

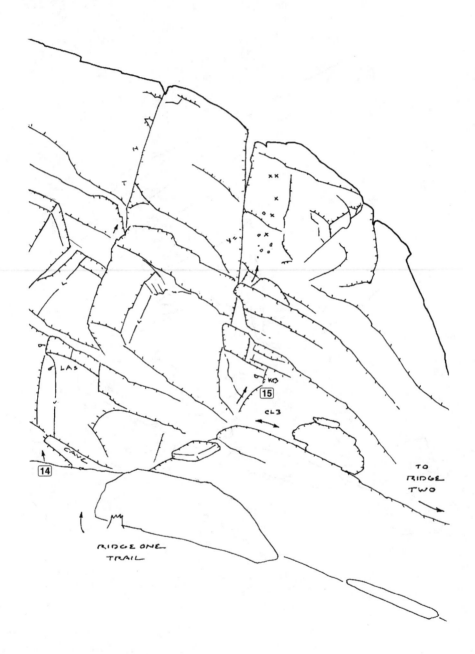

12. **Golden Shower 11d** FA: Alan Nelson, 1991. This is the middle of three short routes in the gap. 4 bolts to a 2-bolt anchor.

13. **Silver Saddle 9** FA: Guy Lord, 1990. This is the right of three short routes in the gap. 3 bolts to a 2-bolt anchor.

The following two routes are on the south face of the lower section of Ridge One.

14. **Black President 11a** ★ Rack: SR. Begin about 150 feet down and right from the gap. Climb a short, right-facing dihedral with two fixed pins (LAs in place, fall 1999). Move right and up to a belay in a blocky band. Climb a steep finger-and-hand crack in the headwall.

15. **Pebo Pockets 10d** ★ Begin 35 feet right from the preceding route. Scramble up onto a narrow ledge that is accessible from either end. Climb a short, left-facing dihedral with a fixed knifeblade, then tackle a bulging wall just right of a wide crack. One KB and 3 bolts to a 2-bolt anchor. The lower tier (beneath the traverse ledge) has two one-bolt anchors, apparently for toproping.

RIDGE TWO

Also known as The Vantage Wall. This long rib features a great variety of interesting routes. Approach as for Ridge One, but just before reaching the first big boulder (The Block Head), take a right branch in the trail as shown in The West Bank map.

1. **Little Face 7** This is the highest route on the ridge. Climb the right side of the south face just left of *Keegan's Bluff*. 4 bolts to a 2-bolt anchor, 60 feet. Real name of route not known.

2. **Keegan's Bluff 10b** FA: Tripp Collins, Dave Fortner, Keegan Schmidt, 1989. Start in a right-facing dihedral. Undercling/lieback up and left along flake. Lower off as for the preceding route.

3. **Arête Funicello 10c** FA: Dave Fortner, 1989. Begin a few feet right of the preceding route. Start with an overhang protected by an old pin, then climb the narrow rib above. One pin, 4 bolts, no anchor, 60 feet.

4. **Birthday Blow 8** FA: Tripp Collins and Dave Fortner, 1989. Rack: SR. Climb the big, right-facing dihedral just right of the preceding route.

5. **Pebbles and Bam Bam 10a** ★ FA: Tripp Collins and Dave Fortner, 1989. Climb the steep and beautiful wall just right of *Birthday Blow*. 3 bolts to a 2-bolt anchor. A wee bit runout it is.

6. **Wide Crack 7** FA: Unknown. Rack: SR. Climb the wide crack just right of *Bam Bam*.

RIDGE TWO

Main trail

Channel

Lower cliff band

29

26

24

22

18

15

9

4

1

N

Not to Scale

RIDGE TWO—TOP

LEFT OF MIDWAY

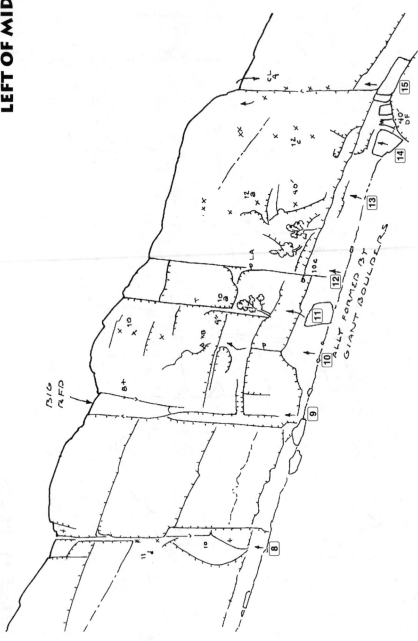

7. **Mouska Pipeline 9** FA: Joan Hooper, Stuart Sayah (sp?), 1989. Rack: gear to 1 inch. Start as for *Wide Crack*, then pull right and climb a thin crack to the top of the wall.

8. **Agent Orange 11d** FA: Jeff Frizzel (?), 1988. Rack: up to 4 inches. Begin in a right-facing dihedral, 30 feet right of *Mouska Pipeline*. Climb the corner/roof, then move right and continue up an arête. 3 bolts to a one-bolt anchor.

9. **Heave Ho 9** ★ FA: Dave Fortner and Tripp Collins, 1989. Begin just right of a large roof. Climb a crack in a right-facing dihedral.

10. **Haul Off and Heave 10b** ★ FA: Dave Fortner and Tripp Collins, 1989. Rack: QDs and SR. Begin 15 feet right of *Heave Ho*. Climb a thin crack with a fixed pin (missing), then go straight up the right side of an attractive face. 2 pins, 3 bolts, no anchor. One may also climb in from the right or left.

11. **Sleeping Digit 10b** FA: Dave Fortner and Tripp Collins, 1989. Rack: SR (5-inch piece optional). Step off a large block and follow a right-facing dihedral system to the ridgecrest. Escape as for *Sporting a Woody*.

12. **Hang 'em High 10c** FA: Dave Fortner and Tripp Collins, 1989. Rack: SR. Begin down in an alleyway formed by some giant blocks. Pull over a roof with an old pin (crux) and follow a right-facing corner system with another pin to the ridgecrest. Escape as for *Sporting a Woody*.

13. **Hooks Are for Kids 12a** Climb a shallow, right-facing flake, then continue over a small roof and up the face. 3 bolts to a 2-bolt anchor. The first bolt is 40 feet off the ground.

14. **Mrs. Coolie's Saloon 12c** FA: Guy Lord and Ken Trout, 1991. Begin from a large boulder, 15 feet right of the preceding route. 3 bolts to a 2-bolt anchor with slings. A faded redpoint tag was still on the first bolt as of October 1999.

Note: The following seven routes end on the ridgecrest and do not have rappel anchors; however, it is not difficult to downclimb the large, right-facing dihedral/ramp beneath *Sporting a Woody* (Class 4).

15. **Sporting a Woody 11c** FA: Dave Fortner and Tripp Collins, 1989. Climb up onto a ramp just right of a blunt arête. Maybe stick clip the first bolt, then climb up and left around the arête and continue to the top of the ridge. Fixed pin at the start is missing. 4 bolts, no anchor. Downclimb as shown in the topo (Class 4).

16. **Boner Boy 9 (TR)** Begin at the left side of a cave/overhang, 40 feet right of the preceding route. Climb through a V-shaped break in the roof and up the slab above.

MIDWAY

RIGHT OF MIDWAY

17. **Stray Route** There is a stray bolt out to the left from *Move Like a Stud*, about 40 feet up.

18. **Move Like a Stud 10c** ★ FA: Tripp Collins, Dave Fortner, Martin Birch, 1989. Pull through a roof and follow a beautiful crack up the steep wall.

19. **Dixie Rising 10d** FA: Tripp Collins, Dave Fortner, Martin Birch, 1989. Begin 5 feet right of the preceding route. Undercling a flake, then climb straight up past 2 bolts and join *Stud*.

20. **Mouth of the South 11b** FA: Tod Anderson and Richard Wright, c. 1990. Begin just right of a large pine and just left of a long, curving crack/flake. Face with 4 bolts. No anchor.

21. **South of the Mouth 5** Climb an obvious curving crack/flake. Gear.

22. **Friends in High Places 10c S** FA: Fortner, Birch, Collins, 1989. Rack: SR. Climb a right-facing dihedral around to the right from a low roof. Fixed pin on initial roof is missing.

23. **High Friends in Places 10b** ★ FA: Fortner, Birch, Collins, 1989. Rack: SR. Climb a steep, thin crack about 30 feet right of the preceding route.

24. **Slab Left 10a S** ★ FA: Fortner, Birch, Collins, 1989. Climb over some precarious blocks and continue up a nice slab. 3 bolts to a 2-bolt anchor with open coldshuts.

25. **Slab Right 9** ★ FA: Fortner, Birch, Collins, 1989. Begin 30 feet right of the preceding route and head up the slab. One pin and 3 bolts to the same anchor as the preceding route.

26. **Blade Runner 12a** ★ Begin beneath the right side a huge roof, about 300 feet east of the preceding route. Start up the left side of an arête, then pull around to the right and continue up a steep wall. 7 bolts to a 2-bolt anchor.

27. **Crack 9** Rack: SR. Begin as for the preceding route and clip the first bolt, then pull right to a crack in a right-facing corner.

28. **Small Animal Places 8** FA: Joan Hooper and Tripp Collins, 1989. Rack: SR to 6 inches. Climb a curved crack in the right wall of an alcove.

29. **Safe Cracker 12a** ★ FA: Alan Nelson, c. 1991. Begin 40 feet east of the preceding route. Climb a crack through a roof (crux above second bolt). 4 bolts to a 2-bolt anchor.

30. **Lipstick 12b** ★ FA: Alan Nelson, c. 1990. Begin just right of the preceding route. Pull up and right through a roof (crux). 4 bolts to a 2-bolt anchor.

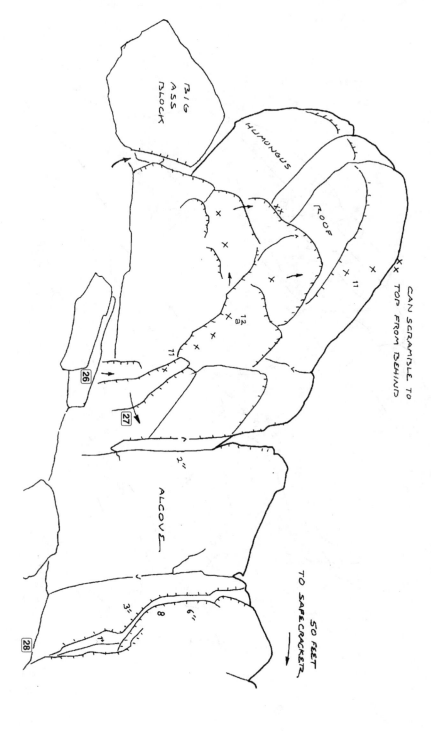

RIDGE TWO—LOWER RIGHT AREA

RIDGE TWO—BOTTOM

31. **Michelangelo's Worst Nightmare 10d** FA: Dave Fortner and Tripp Collins, 1989. Begin about 50 feet down and right from *Crackatoa*. Lieback around a left-facing flake, then hand-traverse out left beneath a roof.

32. **East Face ?** The east face just right of the big roof may have been climbed (toproped).

33. **East Pillar 9** A face down to the right from the preceding route has been toproped.

RIDGE THREE (NO MAP)

Ridge Three may be recognized from the bottom of the main trail by a stack of large blocks on its crest. Just three routes are recorded. Approach as for Ridge Two and hike until directly beneath Ridge Two. Follow a right branch in the trail north for 50 feet, then climb west up a boulder wash with small aspen. Scramble up a slab and gain a bench beneath a huge roof. It is easy to continue up beneath the south side of the ridge to where it fades and one may hike north to the gap at the top of Ridge Four.

1. **Great Roof 13(?)** ★ Locate a huge, southwest-facing roof about 400 feet up from the bottom of the ridge. 8 bolts to a 2-bolt anchor. Name of route uknown.

2. **Arête 11d** ★ Begin a short way right of the *Great Roof*. Climb short open-book, then step left and follow arête to a 2-bolt anchor on slab (60 feet).

3. **Field Test 11c/d** ★ FA: Moe Hershoff and Greg Hand, 1992. Rack: SR. Begin 250 feet down and right from the preceding routes, below the approach ramps. Climb up and left on slab to open-book dihedral, which leads to steep finish.

UPPER RIDGE FOUR

Ridge Four could be said to end (or begin) at a gap just west of *Festus*. However, the stratum continues westward from the gap for another 800 feet and reaches a high point with a colossal free-standing block called The Virus. The following routes are on an upper, western tier of this section, below The Virus and west of *Festus*.

1. **Cave Crack 9** Look for a large block that leans against the main rock and forms a cave. Climb a finger-and-hand crack just right of the southeast corner of the block (just left of the cave).

2. **When Men Were Men 11d** ★ FA: Tripp Collins and Dave Fortner, 1989. Redpoint: Moe Hershoff, 1991. Begin about 500 feet uphill from the gap in Ridge Four and 100 feet east of the preceding route. Climb a steep finger crack with an old ringed angle piton (originally had three or four pitons). 60 feet. Scramble off to the west. Name supplied by Bill DeMallie, thinking the fissure had been climbed in the early 1970s by Erickson, Wunsch, or the like.

RIDGE THREE FROM THE SOUTHWEST

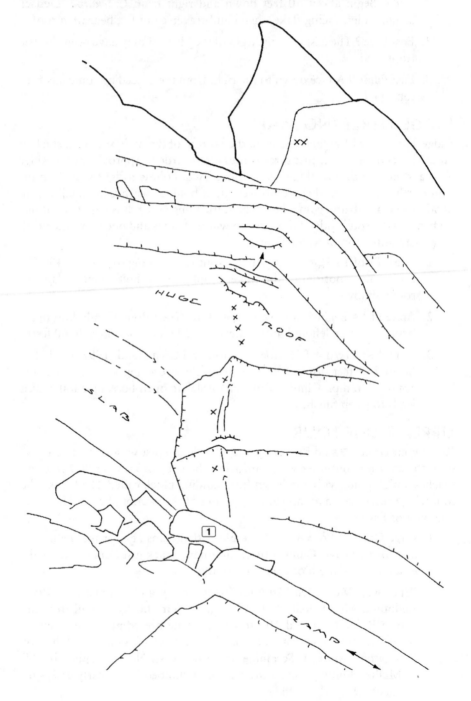

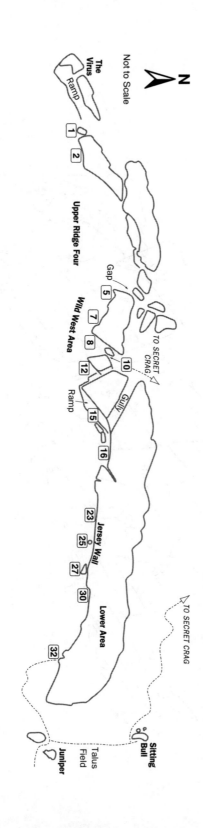

RIDGE FOUR

Not to Scale

N

The
Virus

Ramp

1

2

Upper Ridge Four

Gap

5

Wild West Area

7

8

12

10

TO SECRET
CRAG

Ramp

15

Gully

16

23

Jersey Wall

25

27

30

Lower Area

32

TO SECRET CRAG

Sitting
Bull

Talus
Field

Juniper

THE WILD WEST AREA

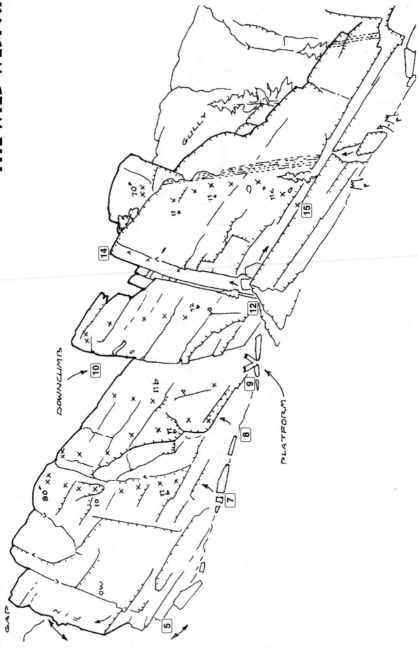

3. **Project 12?** A route was apparently begun 50 feet right of the preceding route along the east edge of the south face. An old battered rope still hangs over the line (September 1999).

RIDGE FOUR

Also known as The Wild West and The Jersey Wall. This is the farthest north of the long ribs at The West Bank, and features many excellent sport climbs. Hike the main trail about 200 feet to a junction with several cairns. Follow the right branch up into a talus field and head for the left side of a large juniper below Ridge Four. A primitive path (needing improvement) leads to the bottom of the south face near *Drive-By Shooting*.

4. **West Wall 9 (TR)** Begin beneath a west-facing wall at the very top of the main ridge. Climb up and right through stepped roofs. No bolts, no anchor.

5. **Festus 9 (TR)** FA: Bill DeMallie, 1989. Climb the sharp arête just right of the preceding route. Anchor holes were drilled, but bolts not placed.

6. **Wide Crack 8** Climb a wide crack in the dihedral just right of the arête of *Festus*.

7. **Rawhide 11c ★** FA: Dave Crawford and Bill DeMallie, 1989. Begin about 50 feet down and right from the top of the ridge. Pull over a low roof (crux) and continue up the steep wall. 7 bolts to a 2-bolt anchor, 80 feet.

8. **Little Joe 11c ★** FA: Bill DeMallie and Dave Crawford, 1989. Begin about 30 feet right of *Rawhide*, beneath an overhanging arête. Pull around onto the southeast face, clip a bolt, and continue up the steep and beautiful wall. Crux is along the left arête.

9. **Hoss 10d or 11b ★** FA: Dave Crawford and Bill DeMallie, 1989. Climb the steep wall just right of *Little Joe*. The crux can be avoided by moving out left from the second bolt. A pin and 4 bolts to the same anchor as *Little Joe*.

10. **Downclimb 5** Carefully downclimb the inside corner 10 feet right of *Hoss*.

11. **Loose Cannon 8** FA: R. Rossiter, solo, 1999. Begin just right of *Downclimb*. Work out right and follow a thin crack to the top of the buttress.

12. **Gunsmoke 12b ★** FA: Dave Crawford and Bill DeMallie, 1989. Climb the steep, southeast-facing wall around to the right from *Loose Cannon*. A pin and 4 bolts to a 2-bolt anchor. This fin/buttress is topped by a strange rock, shaped something like the head of the creature in *Alien*.

Scott Reynolds on Miss Kitty *(5.6), Ridge Four, The West Bank.* RICHARD ROSSITER PHOTO

13. **E-Z Corner 7** Climb a three-inch crack in the inside corner just right of *Gunsmoke*.

14. **Miss Kitty 6** ★ FA: Julie Erwin and Dave Crawford, 1989. Rack: QDs, and a wee bit of gear. Start with an easy crack just right of *E-Z Corner*, then move right and climb an easy arête to the top of the fin (3 bolts). No anchor.

15. **The Wild Wild West 12a** ★ FA: Dave Crawford and Fred Knapp, 1989. Or just *Wild West*. This is an impressive route on great rock. No single move is harder than 11c, but the climbing is fairly continuous. From the bottom of *Miss Kitty*, go right and down a ramp to a bolt with a gold-shut and belay. This point may also be reached from below. Climb the middle of a prominent reddish wall. Crux is near the bottom. 7 bolts to a 2-bolt anchor, 65 feet.

16. **Life During Wartime 13a** ★ FA: Keith Lenard and Moe Hershoff, 1991. Begin beneath a big roof down and right from *Wild West*. Climb through the big roof, followed by a smaller roof (12c), straight up through over-hanging face (crux). 6 bolts to a 2-bolt anchor, 60 feet.

17. **Name Unknown 11c** ★ Begin at a shallow, right-facing dihedral just right from the preceding route. 6 bolts to a 2-bolt anchor.

18. **Crack 6** Climb an easy crack/chimney a few feet right of the preceding route. This is roughly midway along the length of the ridge.

19. **Roof/Crack 11(?)** About 15 feet right of the preceding route, a good crack begins from the lip of a long, low roof.

20. **Honeymoon in Beirut 12b** ★ FA: Moe Hershoff, 1990. Climb a right-facing dihedral next to a big tree. Crux is at second bolt, but there is more hard climbing near the top. 7 bolts to a 2-bolt anchor. There is also a 2-bolt anchor at the fifth bolt.

21. **The Great Defender 13b (Project)** FA: Moe Hershoff, 1992. This route is located about 6 feet right of *Honeymoon in Beirut*.

22. **Moe Zone 13b (Project)** FA: Moe Hershoff, 1992. Locate 7 bolts just right of *The Great Defender*. Steep face, up over bulge to anchors.

23. **Occupied Territory 13a** ★ FA: Moe Hershoff, 1990. Start in a right-facing dihedral, then climb over a bulge and up an arête. The 13a is an overall rating; no single move is that hard. 9 bolts to a 2-bolt anchor. A lowering ring with slings has been fashioned at the sixth bolt.

24. **Mighty Mo 12c** ★ FA: Mike Downing, 1992. This is a short, hard route just right of *Occupied Territory*. 3 bolts to a 2-bolt anchor.

RIDGE FOUR—JERSEY WALL

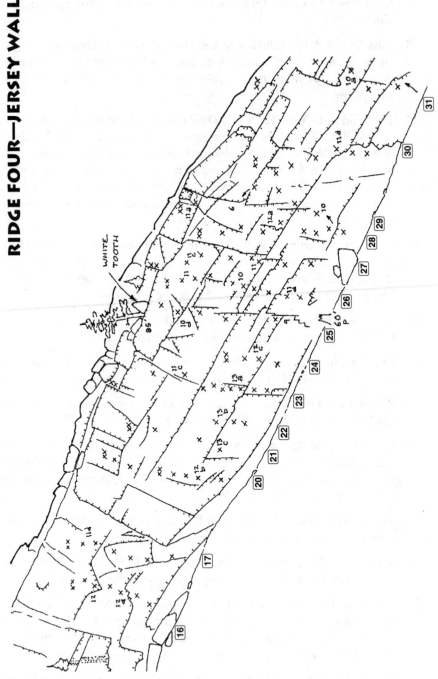

RIDGE FOUR—BOTTOM

25. **Mud Shark 10d** ★ FA: Dave Field, Dave Fortner, Ernie Moskovics, 1990. Begin about 15 feet right of *Occupied Territory*. This route climbs straight up to a strange white rock (shaped like a shark's tooth) at the top of the wall. The first bolt is 25 feet off the ground. 5 bolts to a tree with slings and a lowering ring. A #1.5 or #2 Friend may be used above the first bolt.

26. **L.G.H. (Lawyers Guns and Hiltis) 11d** ★ FA: Mark Rolofson and Ken Trout, 1994. Begin right of *Mud Shark* and a few feet right of a 60-foot pine. Crux is at second bolt, roof above is about 10b, final headwall is 11. 9 bolts to a 2-bolt anchor, 70 feet.

27. **Apostrophe 11d** ★ FA: Dave Field, Ernie Moskovics, 1990. Begin from a large block and climb a bulging wall. 8 bolts to a 2-bolt anchor.

28. **Dodge City 12a** ★ FA: Ken Trout and Rick Leitner, 1994. Begin with the previous route and stick-clip the first bolt; or (better) with the first 2 bolts of *Pandora's Bosch*, then climb straight up toward the left side of a high roof. 8 bolts to a 2-bolt anchor.

29. **Pandora's Bosch 11c** ★ FA: Tripp Collins and Dave Field, 1990. Begin just right of a large block. Climb up and right to an easy corner (#1.5 and #2 Friends), then turn the high roof with a long reach (80 feet). 7 bolts to a 2-bolt anchor.

30. **Killer Elite 11d** ★ Begin at a shallow, left-facing corner just right of a blunt arête. Very sustained. 6 bolts to a 2-bolt anchor.

31. **P.A.L. (Pinch a Loaf) 10b** ★ FA: Dave Field and Ernie Moskovics, 1989. Begin about 25 feet right of the preceding route. 4 bolts to a 2-bolt anchor (60 feet).

32. **Drive-By Shooting 12a** ★ FA: Will Niccolls and Keith Lenard, 1990. This route climbs a large roof near the bottom of Ridge Four. This is about 200 feet east of *P.A.L.* 5 bolts to a 2-bolt anchor.

RIDGE FIVE

This is a relatively small rib between the lower part of Ridge Four and Secret Crag. In spite of a large overhang along its southwest side, no routes have been recorded. On the southwest side of this rib and near its east end is a small block called Sitting Bull. Approach via the path to Secret Crag.

1. **Sitting Bull 12a (TR)** Anchor to a pine tree and hang a long sling over the lip above the concave east face. Climb the right side of the 20-foot wall. An easier line goes just left of center and finishes with a tiny, left-facing dihedral.

SECRET CRAG

Secret Crag forms the northern boundary of The West Bank and is by far the largest feature. The crag consists of several distinct tiers with most of the routes ascending the middle, Tier B. The west end of Tier B forms a beautiful square-cut pinnacle called The West Tower (in this guide). The lower, Tier A, in spite of having an incredible roof, has just two known routes. The next tier up (Tier C) has no recorded routes, but includes the summit of Secret Crag and is characterized by a gigantic promontory that resembles the head of an eagle. The farthest north section, which could be called Tier D, has three known routes.

Approach: Take the right branch of the main trail and cross the talus to a large juniper tree (as for Ridge Four), then break right and follow a footpath past Sitting Bull to the foot of Tier A. To reach Tier B, hike west and north around Tier A and walk out onto a spectacular terrace beneath The West Tower. From here a broad ramp descends beneath the south face of Tier B and provides access to several interesting routes. To reach the routes on Tier D, hike up the gully beneath Tunnel Wall, veer right and follow a faint path several hundred feet to the routes. Along the way is a cave with a natural arch.

TIER A

The following two routes are located right of a huge roof at the southwest corner of Secret Crag, about 1000 feet above the railroad tracks.

1. **Tir-A's Crack 5** FA: Bob Hritz and Steve Wunch, 1972. Climb a 3-inch crack and chimney, just right of a huge roof.

2. **Short Cut 9** FA: Bob Hritz, 1972 (toproped). Led: Steve Wunch and Jim Erickson, 1973. Begin about 50 feet right of *Tir-A's Crack*. Climb a short, right-facing dihedral (8), follow a crack up and left, and finish with a classic off-width.

TIER B

The following routes ascend the long "middle tier" and are easily reached by scrambling onto the terrace above Tier A from the west. It is worth mentioning that Tier B extends eastward all the way to the railroad tracks and that routes have been recorded on only the upper, western part.

3. **Left Headwall 12 (incomplete)** FA: Ken Trout. This route ascends the steep hanging wall just left of *Down Climb Gully* and is not complete. 6 bolts to a 2-bolt anchor. At least 1 bolt is missing.

4. **Downclimb Gully 4** The gully just north of the West Tower can be used to escape from the top of Tier B and the West Tower. Stay to the north side.

SECRET CRAG

Secret Crag

West Tower

Tier C

Tier B

Tier A

Tier D

Ridge Five

Ridge Four

Ridge Three

8

12

2

16

20

22

25

30

1

WEST TOWER

The following five routes ascend the beautiful square-cut tower at the west end of Tier B. This feature is also known as Black Tower (by DeMallie).

5. **Jack the Gripper 10 (TR)** FA: Rossiter and Effron, 1999. Begin in an alcove at the left side of West Tower. Undercling right beneath a roof, then hand-traverse right along a crack to join *Mind Control*.

6. **Mind Control 10d ★** FA: Bill DeMallie(?), 1988. A quality pitch. Start at the northwest corner of West Tower and pull around onto the west face. 8 bolts to a 2-bolt anchor.

7. **Bob's Arête 8 ★** FA: Bob Hritz and Steve Wunsch, 1972. Rack: SR. Climb a V-shaped corner just right of the southwest arête, then continue up the arête to the top.

8. **Peril-less Journey 8 ★** FA: Ken Trout and Marsha Trout, 1994. Climb the face just right of *Bob's Arête*. 6 bolts to a 2-bolt anchor, 65 feet. One may easily continue to the top of the tower via *Bob's Arête*.

9. **Opus 73 10a** FA: Jim Erickson and Steve Wunch, 1973. Climb the right-facing dihedral-and-crack system along the right margin of West Tower.

10. **Three-Stage Traverse 6** FA: R. Rossiter, solo, 1999. Begin at the same point as *Opus 73*. Break right and follow a ramp system out over empty space. Finish with a hand crack and gain the top of Tier B just west of the following route.

11. **Secret Agent 10 S A0** FA: Dan Hare and Scott Woodruff, 1982. Climb a red, right-leaning corner over a roof with a point of aid, then up another corner.

12. **Completion Backward Principle 11a ★** FA: Tod Anderson and Richard Wright, 1991. Begin about 100 feet down and right from *Opus 73*. 12 bolts to a 2-bolt anchor, 115 feet.

13. **Top-Down Design 12a ★** FA: Tod Anderson, Alan Nelson, Richard Wright, 1991. Begin at a shallow inset, about 40 feet down and right from the preceding route. 7 bolts to a 2-bolt anchor.

14. **Powder Finger 10c ★** Begin a few feet right of the preceding route, but left of a prominent, left-facing dihedral. 8 bolts to a 2-bolt anchor, 75 feet. A 10b move is required before the first bolt.

15. **Roof (Project)** FA: Tod Anderson and Richard Wright, 1991. Four bolts lead up and left from the anchors at the top of *Powder Finger* and onto a hanging slab.

SECRET CRAG FROM THE WEST

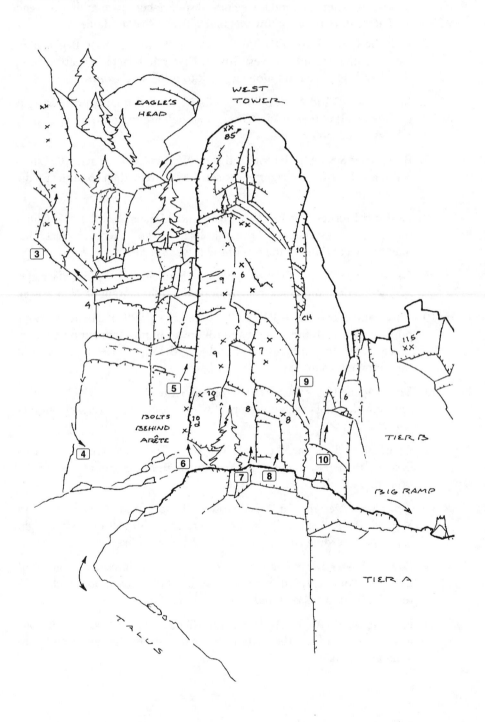

SECRET CRAG—SOUTH FACE

Willie Mein on Completion Backwards Principle *at the Secret Crag.*
RICHARD ROSSITER PHOTO

16. **Count Dracula 10c** ★ FA: Scott Woodruff and Dan Hare, 1977. Climb a prominent, left-facing dihedral to the top of a pinnacle and belay at the anchors for *Eldorado Gold*. Traverse down and right to a large, loose flake, then climb an impressive crack to the top of the wall.

17. **Eldorado Gold 11a** ★ FA: Ken Trout, Marsha Trout, Rick Leitner, 1994. This route ascends the right side of a prominent arête or pinnacle. Begin a few feet right of the preceding route. 8 bolts to a 2-bolt anchor, 85 feet.

18. **In Plain View 10** FA: Ken Trout, Marsha Trout, Rick Leitner, 1994. This route follows a right-facing dihedral system a few feet right of the preceding route. 5 bolts to a 2-bolt anchor.

19. **Deep Water 8** FA: Scott Woodruff and Dan Hare, 1976. Climb a small, right-facing dihedral to the right of *Count Dracula*.

20. **Book of Dreams 8** ★ Begin about 40 feet down and right from *Eldorado Gold*. Climb a shallow corner system with a fixed pin, past a pine to a ledge. Lieback up a hand-and-fist crack in a large, left-facing dihedral to gain the crest of Tier B.

21. **Promontory 6** FA: R. Rossiter, solo, 1999. Climb past the pine tree as for the preceding route, then move right and follow a rounded arête to the crest of Tier B.

22. **Riding with The King 9** ★ FA: Richard Rossiter and Serena Benson, 2000. The areas best 9. Begin at a shallow left-facing dihedral, 30 feet down and right from *Promontory*. P1. Climb up and right through a roof, then up a right-facing dihedral to a ramp with a 2-bolt anchor (5 bolts, 55 feet). P2. Ascend a beautiful green wall to the anchors atop *Promontory* (8 bolts, 85 feet).

23. **East Face 11?** Tier B ends with a steep, east-facing wall right beside the railroad tracks, a stone's throw south from Tunnel Three. Look for an old bolt about 20 feet up. No information.

TIER D

The following routes are located along the lower third of Tier D. Approach from the railroad tracks by hiking up the gully beneath Tunnel Rock. Veer right and follow a faint path up through ferns, past a surprising arch, and find the routes on either side of a small cave.

24. **Dancing on a Ceiling 12b/c** ★ Begin just left of a cave. Crank huecos up and left beneath a magnificent roof. 4 bolts to a 2-bolt anchor, 50 feet.

25. **Murmur 11b** ★ Begin a short way down and right from the cave. Lieback off a right-facing flake, then move left and up the wall. 6 bolts to a 2-bolt anchor, 55 feet.

SECRET CRAG—TIER D

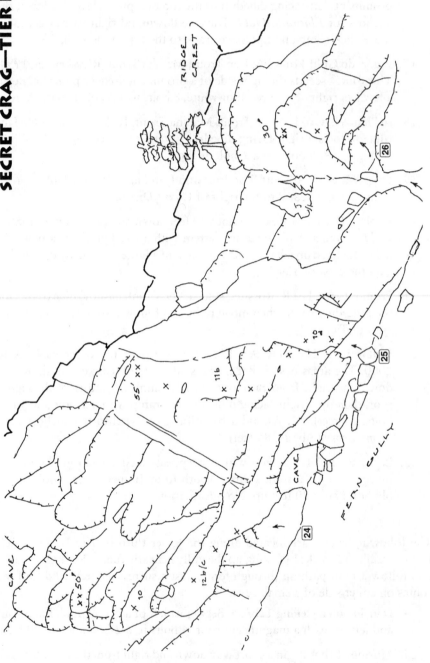

TUNNEL WALL

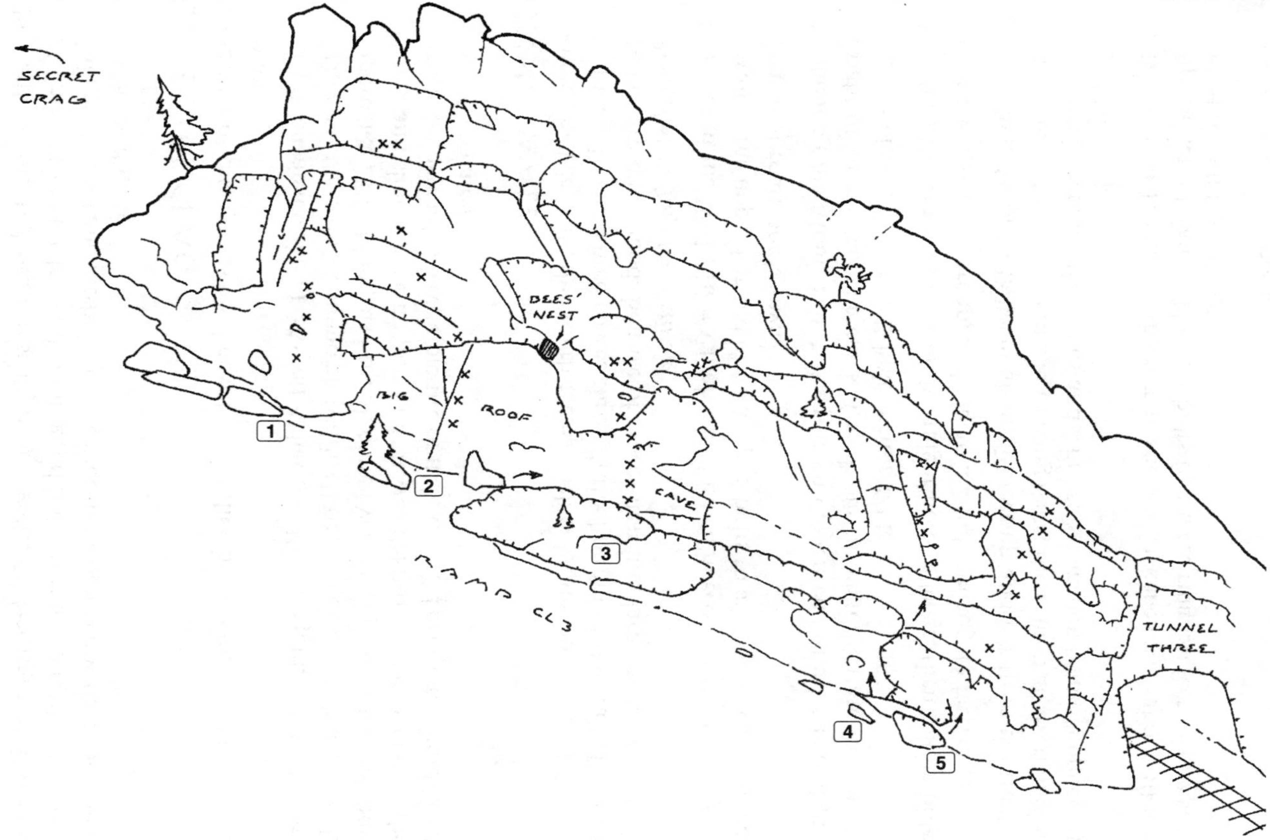

SECRET CRAG

BIG ROOF

RAMP CL3

DEES' NEST

CAVE

TUNNEL THREE.

1
2
3
4
5

26. **Little Route 10d** Begin just right of a gully, 40 feet right of *Murmur*. Climb in from the left and crank good holds through a roof. 1 bolt just above the roof and a 2-bolt anchor. One more bolt below the roof would be a good thing.

TOP SECRET CRAG

The location of this crag is not known. Jeff Achey has supplied the following description.

1. **Upside Down Cake 11** FA: Jeff Achey and Kent Lugbill, 1980. "*Upside Down Cake* is on a crag north (I think!) of Secret Crag. It (the route) is more like 25 feet long, as I recall, quite overhanging, at least at the bottom, and should have no pins in it. It was the most obvious line on the rock. Somewhere I have a picture of it, but. . . ." This route sounds a lot like *Crackatoa*.

TUNNEL WALL

Also known as Pile Wall, this south-facing rock is located just west of Tunnel Three; in fact, Tunnel Three passes through the bottom of the wall. The first three routes are quite good. Beware of a bees-nest in a large hueco 8 feet left from the top of *Pulling the Train*.

1. **Holes in the Wall 11d** ★ Climb well-formed huecos up an overhanging wall at the upper left end of the crag. 3 bolts to a 2-bolt anchor. Actual name of route not known.

2. **Shooting the Moon 12b** ★ Begin from the left end of a ledge and just right of an overhanging crack. Crank out through the roof, then work up and left. 6 bolts to a 2-bolt anchor, 60 feet.

3. **Pulling the Train 12a** ★ Climb straight up to a ledge, then follow bolts out the massive overhang. 5 bolts to a 2-bolt anchor, 45 feet.

4. **Sumthing Stupid 12?** Begin about 50 feet up and left from the tracks. Yard up and right around a left-facing flake, then climb an overhanging crack with a pin, 2 fixed nuts and 2 bolts. No anchor. Name supplied by Bill DeMallie.

5. **Brain Dead 12?** Climb the rotten, smoke-blackened wall about 30 feet up and left of Tunnel Three. 4 bolts to a large ring, 50 feet. Name supplied by Bill DeMallie.

LOCOMOTIVE ROCK

This small crag is located on the east side of the railroad tracks, across from the beginning to the main West Bank trail. It has a single hard route on its south side.

1. **Locomotive Breath 12d** ★ FA: Curt Fry, 1989. The easiest way to reach the beginning of this route is to leave the tracks north of the rock and

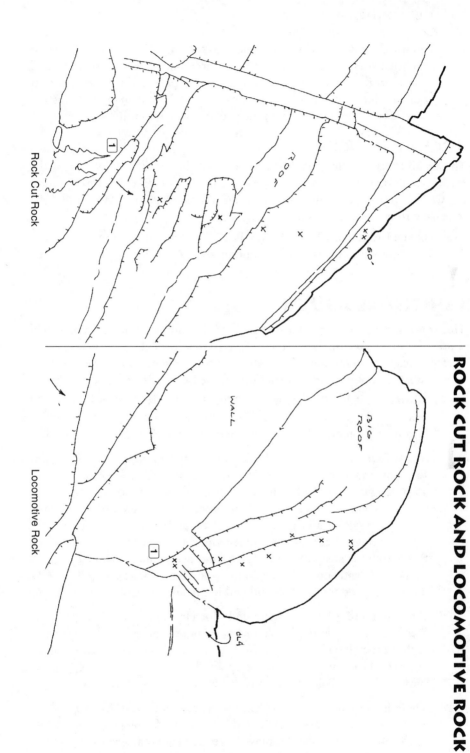

ROCK CUT ROCK AND LOCOMOTIVE ROCK

Rock Cut Rock

Locomotive Rock

ROOF

50'

WALL

BIG
ROOF

1

1

CL4

follow the edge of the rockcut south to the crag. Hike down to the east until it is easy to gain the east slab. Scramble 50 feet up the slab and move left to a crest where the anchors are apparent. Follow hand-holds out left along a crack in an overhanging wall. 5 bolts to a 2-bolt anchor. One may rappel 60 feet from the anchors at the bottom of the route.

ROCK CUT ROCK

This small buttress is located 160 feet north of the main trail and across the tracks from *Locomotive Breath*. Hike up the main trail for about 100 feet until a sawed-off tree appears up to the right. Head north past the tree and find the following route on a steep, south-facing wall.

1. **Name Unknown 12a** ★ FA: Guy Lord (?), 1991. Start from a ramp that slants down to the right and crank up over a roof (crux). 4 bolts to a 2-bolt anchor. Clip stick not needed.

PORTHOLE SOUTH

This south-facing buttress is located west of the railroad tracks, immediately south of Tunnel Five; in fact, Tunnel Five passes through the bottom of the crag. To escape from the summit, climb off to the west and south. A large block called Suburbia Boulder sits just south from the low point of the wall.

1. **Wasp 8** FA: Chip Ruckgaber and Mike Brooks, 1980. Begin about 200 feet up and left from the low point of the south face. Climb to the top of a short, left-facing dihedral, then angle up and left to the top of wall.

2. **South Face 10 S** FA: Larry Dalke and Cliff Jennings, 1967. FFA: Jim Erickson and Steve Wunch, 1976. FA: variation, FA: Jim Erickson, solo, 1976. Begin about 80 feet up and left from the low point of the south face. P1. Climb over a bulge with an old fixed pin and a bolt (10a), then up the left side of a large, detached flake and belay at 2 bolts (no descending rings). P2. Work up and left along a crack and ramp system (8), then climb the steep headwall (10 S) and belay on a small ledge. P3. A short pitch leads up and right to the ridgecrest. Variation: Follow a 9+ diagonal finger crack 30 feet up and left from the regular start.

3. **Borderline 12d** ★ FA: Eric Fedor and Moe Hershoff, c. 1990. Begin as for *South Face*. To gain the 2-bolt anchor without bringing crack gear, climb to the third bolt on *There Is No God*, then traverse left across the top of the big flake. From the anchor, move up and left, then follow 7 bolts up the steep wall to a 2-bolt anchor threaded with a sling (130 feet).

4. **There Is No God 10d** ★ FA: Darius Deavers and Dave McDermott, c. 1990. Begin as for *South Face* and belay behind a block about 35 feet up. There are 9 bolts and 2 pins above the belay (dangerous clip at second bolt). Rappel 135 feet from a 2-bolt anchor with slings.

PORTHOLE SOUTH

Suburbia
Boulder

Tunnel 5

PORTHOLE SOUTH—SOUTH FACE DETAIL

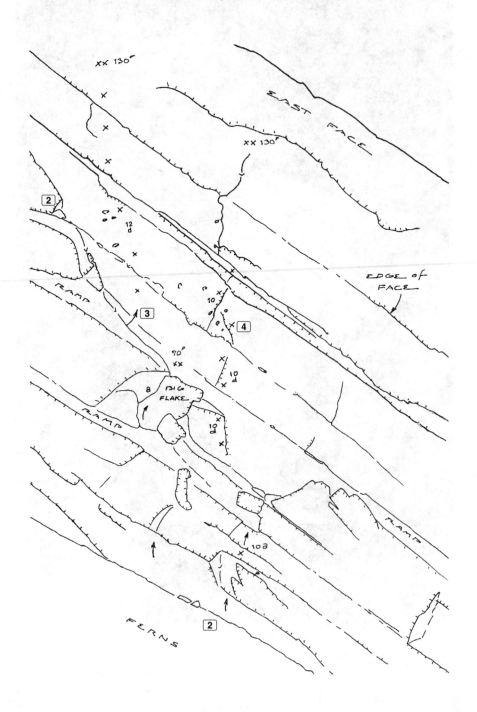

MICKEY MOUSE WALL

Mickey Mouse Wall is one of Boulder's premier climbing venues, but with its relatively long approach, it also is one of the least visited. It lies about an air-mile south of Eldorado Springs, high on the northeast shoulder of Eldorado Mountain. From Boulder, it may be recognized by the two huge knobs of rock at its summit that, in someone's mind, resembled a Mousketeer's beanie and lent the name. The crag consists of North, Central, and South Towers, which provide convenient divisions for identifying routes. A long ledge spans all three towers about one-third of the way up. The lower, more easterly part of the South Tower is known as Industrial Wall and features some very good sport climbs. There are also interesting spires and short walls on the ridgecrest above Industrial Wall. This area is called the East Ridge and has three small but distinct aspects: The Chamber, The Corridor, and The Garden of Stone, from left to right. Geologically, the rock is part of the Fountain Formation—the same, hard, conglomerate sandstone found in The Flatirons and Eldorado Canyon.

The main wall faces southwest, looking out across a secluded draw that forms a natural sanctuary—a place of serenity and rugged beauty. Stunted trees and bright lichens accent the steep faces that rise majestically above a "glacier" of giant talus. Eagles and falcons fly the local skies. In contrast to this primitive setting, the Denver and Rio Grande Railroad nearly circumnavigates Eldorado Mountain and runs through several long tunnels, one of which is blasted through the bottom of Mickey Mouse Wall. Other than the tracks and frequent trains, the area shows few signs of the usual human ravages—except for the many red and white closure signs posted by the City of Boulder all along the base of the wall.

RAPTOR CLOSURE: The City of Boulder Open Space and the Colorado Division of Wildlife have for the last several years (including 1999) closed the entire crag to climbing from February to August. Two peregrines appear to have a nest somewhere on the north side of the crag, or perhaps on the next crag to the north. Does the entire southwest face of Mickey Mouse Wall need to be closed to ensure the reproduction of these birds? Many times daily, freight trains roar through the bottom of the wall creating tremendous noise, billowing diesel fumes and practically shaking the rock. One wonders: if the trains don't bother the birds, how could a few climbers?

Approach One: This is the easiest approach to Mickey Mouse Wall, though it is no shorter than hiking in from Eldorado Springs. The advantage is that there is very little elevation gain. From Boulder, drive south on Colorado 93 (Broadway), past Rocky Flats, and turn west on Colorado 72. After about one mile, turn north on the dirt road to Plainview, drive for a couple of miles and park about 100 yards before reaching the railroad crossing. Hike northwest through the pines and gain the tracks just south of a white building. Walk about 2 miles north along the tracks and behold Mickey Mouse Wall after passing through the last of 4 tunnels.

Moe Hershoff on Asahi *(5.10c), Mickey Mouse Wall.* Richard Rossiter photo

Approach Two: This is the oldest and possibly the shortest approach to Mickey Mouse Wall. It's only fault is an elevation gain of 1200 feet between the trailhead and the railroad tracks. From Boulder, drive south on Colorado 93 and turn right on Colorado 170. Just before entering the town of Eldorado Springs, turn left on County Road 67 and park at a locked gate after 200 yards. This is the City of Boulder Open Space boundary. Hike up the maintained gravel road, avoiding a left after about 0.5 mile, and continue through a rockcut to a point where the road curves around to head north. Break south up a wash and follow a corridor through the woods to a good trail that climbs to the crest of a grassy ridge. One may also reach this trail at greater length by staying on the road.

From the crest the main trail drops down to the southeast. Instead, break right (southwest) and follow a footpath up the ridge to an old barbed-wire fence. Step over the fence and head south past a big boulder, then stay left of some trees and continue south into a wooded area. Follow the path through the trees to a broad, grassy shoulder. Hike west and pick up an old road grade that climbs to the railroad tracks. Hike 50 yards south along the tracks and pass through Tunnel Six, which goes through the bottom of Mickey Mouse Wall. South of the tunnel, an eroded footpath climbs northwest along the base of the wall. This path can be avoided by hiking up the more stable talus field to the left, reducing human impact and affording good views of the routes as one proceeds.

Tunnel Tips: Walk right up to the tunnel, then stop and listen. If you hear anything that sounds like a train . . . . DO NOT ENTER. If it is dead quiet, proceed, but be VERY QUICK. It is a real drag to be caught in a tunnel with a passing train. You are also trespassing, so you don't want to draw attention to yourself by alarming the engineers. Always carry a flashlight in case you return after sunset . . . you can't see a bloody thing once inside the tunnel. In fact a flashlight/headlamp during the day helps for a stress-free, rapid, tunnel experience.

Approach Three: The "main trail" mentioned above may also be used to reach Mickey Mouse Wall, but is somewhat longer. From the grassy ridge, follow the trail down, then east through a gate and up over a broad saddle. Eventually reach a fence posted "No Trespassing." Step over the fence and follow an old road grade up a brushy draw to the railroad tracks, just south of Tunnel Six. The path up the draw is well grown over and needs some serious pruning.

Approach Four: This is the more difficult of the three approaches to Mickey Mouse Wall, but it's a really nice walk. Begin in Eldorado Canyon and hike the Rattlesnake Gulch Trail all the way to the railroad tracks (about 2 miles; see map, page 10). Head east along the tracks toward a tunnel until it is easy to break south. Climb the forest slope to a high col at the top of the talus field that descends along the southwest face of Mickey Mouse Wall. A five-minute descent brings one to the Shield area and the highest routes on the crag. It is also possible to hike through the railroad tunnels, but this is not recommended as the first tunnel is quite long and curved, and one could get trapped inside by a train.

North Tower

Central Tower

South Tower

Gargoyle

Industrial Wall

Rappel route

3

10

16

18

24

23

23

32

36

MICKEY MOUSE WALL FROM THE SOUTHWEST

Descent: The easiest descent from the top of the wall is to traverse as needed to the notch between The North and Central Towers and make four half-rope rappels to the big block at the bottom of *Perversion*. Traverse a ledge to the northwest to reach the talus. From The South Tower, it is easy to scramble around the back side of The Central Tower to reach this notch. From other points, it is possible to rappel from trees, and there are bolt anchors atop most of the sport routes.

NORTH TOWER

The North Tower includes the summit of Mickey Mouse Wall and features the prominent "mouse ears" for which the crag is named. A Class-4 scramble up the steep north face may be used to reach or escape from the summit (the west "mouse ear"). The steep bulging wall at the right side of North Tower is called The Shield and features an array of excellent climbs.

1. **Roof 10** Begin near a large tree about 40 feet left of the first pitch of *Lifestream*. Climb a left-facing corner with fixed pin, turn a short roof, and gain a ledge.

2. **Eagle's Bier 9** FA: George Hurley and Bob Culp, 1965. This three-pitch route ascends the big, left-facing dihedral left of *Lifestream*. Begin in a left-facing dihedral a short way left of *Lifestream*.

3. **Lifestream 11a ★** FA: Richard Rossiter, Joyce Rossiter, Steve Ilg, 1987. Rack: up to one inch for P1; 9 QDs for P2. This route ascends the beautiful arête along the left edge of The Shield. Begin at the bottom of the wall, directly beneath the arête. Two pitches. Rappel 135 feet from a 2-bolt anchor to a big ledge, then 85 feet from a tree.

4. **Zen Effects 12b ★** FA: Richard Rossiter and George Watson, 1987. Redpoint: Joyce and Richard Rossiter, 1988. Sustained, difficult face climbing in spectacular position. From the top of P1 of *Lifestream* (10d), scramble up and right to a nice belay ledge just right from the bottom of the arête. 7 bolts to a 2-bolt anchor, 85 feet. It is also possible to continue this pitch up and left to the anchor on *Lifestream* (3 or 4 more bolts). The bolts on this route were placed with great difficulty on the lead (for no good reason whatever).

5. **Beagle's Ear 11a ★** FA: Dave Rearick and George Hurley, 1966. FFA: Chris Reveley and Jim Michael, 1975. Rack: up to a #4 Friend. This great climb follows a crack straight up to the right side of an overhanging square block called The Beagle's Ear. Climb P1 of *Lifestream*, then scramble up and right to a ledge at the base of the crack.

6. **Fake Right, Go Left 10c S ★** FA: Ken Trout and Mason Frichette, 1975. Rack: up to a #4 Friend. Only the beginning is difficult to protect. Climb

MICKEY MOUSE WALL: NORTH AND CENTRAL TOWERS

NORTH TOWER—THE SHIELD

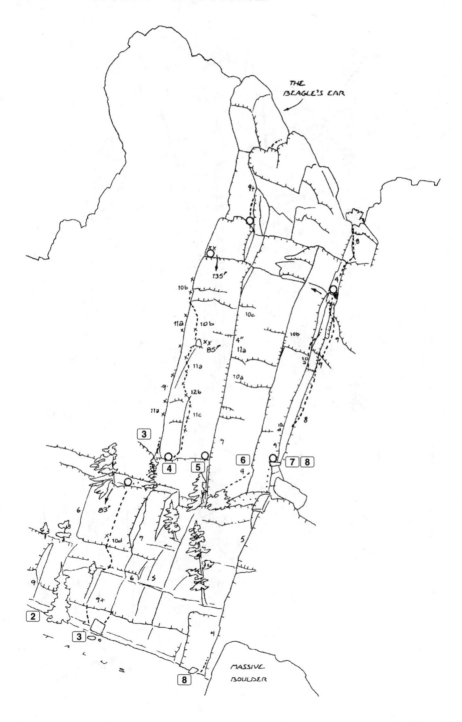

CENTRAL TOWER

straight up into the crack (10c S) or traverse in from the left (9 S). Near the top of the crack, traverse left to the anchors atop *Lifestream*. Name is from a subsequent ascent by David Breashears, Kevin Donald, Jeff Lowe, 1977.

7. **Don't Panic, It's Organic 10c ★** FA: Richard and Joyce Rosstier, 1986. Rack: up to a #3.5 Friend. The difficulty at the crux depends on how wide you can stem. Begin as for *Parallel Journey*, but climb the crack on the left.

8. **Parallel Journey 9 ★** FA: Richard Rossiter and Tom Sciolino, 1981. Rack: up to a #3.5 Friend. Along the right margin of The Shield, locate two parallel cracks about 6 feet apart. P1. Climb an easy, left-facing dihedral to a big ledge (85 feet). P2. Climb the crack on the right and finish at the top of the main rappel route (RR).

CENTRAL TOWER

The Central Tower is the massive, round-topped buttress down and right from the "Mouse Ears," featuring the classic routes *Perversion* and *Captain Beyond*.

9. **Zambezi 9+ ★ or 11c S ★** FA: George Hurley and Rick Medrick, 1960. FFA: Chris Reveley, 1978. Rack: SR. P1. Climb the first pitch of *Perversion* to the Main Ledge (9). P2. Traverse in from the left and belay on a ledge beneath 2 left-facing dihedrals. P3. Climb the left dihedral, then move right, climb past a bolt, and master the overhang (crux). Above the roof, an easy (8) crack leads to a ledge with a small Douglas-fir. P4. A short, easy pitch leads to the top of the wall. The main rappel route (RR) is just to the north. **Variation:** An excellent detour avoids the crux on the left (9+, see topo).

10. **Perversion 9 ★** FA of upper pitches: Layton Kor, Charles Kemp, Bob Bradley, Paul Mayrose, 1963. FA of P1: George Hurley and Bob Culp, 1965. Rack: SR. Classic. Traverse in from the left to gain the top of a huge boulder at the bottom of the Central Tower. P1. Climb a right-facing dihedral to the Main Ledge (9, 80 feet). P2. Step right, follow the immense open book up to a ledge (7, 150 feet). P3. Up the big corner to the top, 8, 70 feet.

10a. **Erickson's Dihedral 9+ ★** FA: Jim Erickson and John Behrens, 1977. Climb a clean, 90-degree, left-facing dihedral with a thin crack just right of the regular P2 and merge with the main line after 70 feet.

10b. **Vulcans Don't Lie 10b** FA: Greg Robinson and Tripp Collins, 1986. Climb out through the middle of the big roof near the top of the route.

11. **Vergin' on Perversion 11c ★** FA: Bill DeMallie and Dan Hare, 1989. Rack: up to 1 inch, plus 12 QDs. This four-pitch route mingles with

Perversion and gains the summit of Central Tower. Begin with a thin crack about 30 feet right of P1 of *Perversion*. Do *Erickson's Dihedral*, then follow the arête on the right all the way to the top.

12. **Scorpius 11a VS ★** FA: Jeff Achey and Robert Palais, 1981. A very scary face climb. Begin up a ramp about 30 feet to the left of *Better Red Than Dead*. Finish in a left-facing dihedral with a small tree.

13. **Rodent Lust 12d ★** FA: Colin Lantz and Chris Beh, 1989. Begin just right of *Scorpius*. Climb past 3 bolts (crux), then veer left through the initial traverse of *Scorpius*. Turn a roof, then work straight up the steep face to join *Vergin' On Perversion* (12 bolts in all). Rappel 100 feet from a tree.

14. **Better Red Than Dead 12b (10 S) ★** FA: Dan Michael and Mark Sonnenfeld, 1985. This is the earliest "sport climb" on Mickey Mouse Wall. Look for a line of 6 bolts a short way down and right from *Rodent Lust*. 25-foot runout to the first bolt (10 S), then very sustained in difficulty. There may be a 2-bolt anchor at the top. If not, traverse left and finish as for *Scorpius*.

15. **Beginner's Mind 12a S/VS** FA: Jeff Achey and Mark Sonnenfield, 1985. Rack: up to one inch, with a #4 Crack 'n' Up for the crux! Begin about 12 feet left of *Captain Beyond* and climb a beautiful, but poorly protected thin crack.

16. **Captain Beyond 10c ★** FA of P1 and P2: Layton Kor and Charles Kemp, 1963. FFA of P1 and P2: Roger Briggs and Larry Hamilton, 1974. FFA of entire route: Roger and Bill Briggs, 1974. Rack: up to a #4 Friend. This five-pitch classic offers a lot of crack climbing. Begin about 8 feet left of *Culp's Fault*. P1. Follow a left-facing dihedral through a small roof (10a) and belay at a piton after about 80 feet. P2. Traverse to the next crack on the left (*Scorpius*) and climb through a bulge (9+) to the main ledge that runs across the wall. Move the belay to the left. P3. Climb a short slab and belay beneath a right-facing dihedral with an overhanging off-width crack (8+). P4. Lieback or jam the off-width (10c) and continue up the easier chimney above. Gain a ledge and belay as for the last pitch of *Perversion*. P5. Cross *Perversion* and work up and left for 20 feet to a steep, right-facing dihedral. Climb the dihedral (10b) and belay on a small ledge near the top of Central Tower.

SOUTH TOWER

The South Tower includes the Red Dihedral area, Wall of Shiva's Dance, Industrial Wall, East Ridge, and is penetrated by Tunnel Six.

17. **Culp's Fault 8 ★** FA: Bob Culp, 1968. A good moderate route. Begin on a ledge 10 feet off the ground, between two left-facing corners. P1. Up

the left-facing corner to the main ledge, 8. P2. Climb the right of 2 dihedrals that face each other, turn the roof on the right (7), or left (9), then easier to the big notch between the two towers.

18. **Three Mousketeers 11c** ★ FA: Fred Knapp, Bill DeMallie, and Will Niccols, 1989. Begin 30 feet right of *Culp's Fault* and right of a left-facing dihedral. Crux is between the last 2 bolts. Beware of a loose block near the top of the pitch. Two pins and 6 bolts to a 2-pin anchor, 70 feet.

19. **Mighty Mouse 12b** ★ FA: Bill DeMallie and Dave Crawford, 1989. Begin 10 feet right of *Three Mousketeers*. 8 bolts to a 2-bolt anchor, 70 feet.

20. **Simian's Way 11a** ★ FA: George Hurley and Mike Yokel, 1970. FFA: Steve Wunsch and Scott Stewart, 1972. Rack: up to a #4 Friend. The route features a fine finger crack and an overhanging off-width slot. Begin to the right of a small tree, about 30 feet left of The Red Dihedral. P1. Up the compelling finger crack, 9+. P2. Move left and up (6) to the main ledge. P3. Up to and through the obvious, steep, off-width slot, 11a. P4. Up the crack system, into a right-facing dihedral, out right round an 8 roof, and back left to a ledge and belay. Scramble to the top. Most folks only climb the first pitch.

20a. **Dead Bird Crack 11a** FA: Jim Erickson and Art Higbee, 1975. Avoid the flared, off-width section of *Simian's Way* by climbing out to the right around a huge flake.

21. **Leap of Faith 12b S** FA: Jeff Achey and Roger Briggs, 1983. Climb the very thin crack to the left of *Plane Geometry*, then veer left to join *Simian's Way*.

22. **Plane Geometry 12b** ★ FA: Richard and Joyce Rossiter, 1989. Rack: include 7 QDs, a couple of mid-size TCUs, and a #3 Friend; 7 QDs only for P1. Formerly known as *Greenspace*. Two pitches of difficult face climbing on beautiful rock. Climb the first 20 feet of *The Red Dihedral*, then move left into the line.

23. **The Red Dihedral 12d (12a VS)** ★ FA: Layton Kor, Paul Mayrose, Larry Dalke, 1964. FFA: Christian Griffith, Eric Doub, 1985. Rack: SR. This was a coveted aid climb for two decades before it was climbed free. Begin in the large, left-facing dihedral to the left of *Krystal Klyr*, or climb any route that leads to the ledge beneath the enormous, overhanging corner for which the route is named. *Asahi* provides an excellent start. The state of the fixed pro on P2 is not known, but chances are, it will be discouraging. P4. Climb a dihedral to a ledge with a 2-bolt anchor (6, 75 feet). P2. Move right and climb P2 of *Asahi* (10b) or a wide crack to the right (8+). P3. Climb the stunning left-facing dihedral past several fixed

SOUTH TOWER

SOUTH TOWER AND WALL OF SHIVA'S DANCE

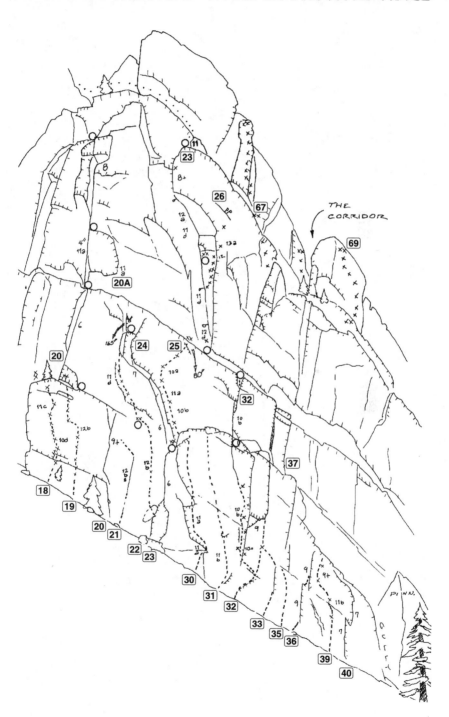

SOUTH TOWER DETAIL

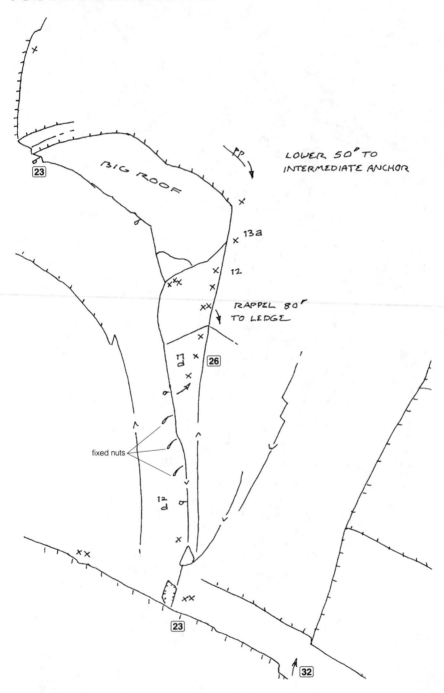

pins and Stoppers, then belay at some old bolts (12d, 85 feet). P4. Work up and left beneath a large roof (two fixed RURPs), then climb a crack to a good ledge (12a VS, 85 feet).

24. **The Green Dihedral 7** ★ FA: Unknown. Rack: up to a #4 Friend. Begin with P1 of *The Red Dihedral* (7), then continue up the obvious, left-arching corner. Two pitches.

25. **Boxcar Willie 11a (10 S)** ★ FA: Mike Clinton and Bill DeMallie, 1988. Rack: QDs, plus small wires. Climb P1 of *The Red Dihedral* and belay. Boldly ascend the smooth wall just right of *The Green Dihedral*. Ledge fall potential above first bolt. 5 bolts.

26. **Stigmata 13b** ★ FA: George Squibb, 1991. Climb through the crux of *The Red Dihedral* (12d), then break right and follow 3 bolts (11d) to a 2-bolt anchor on the arête. Lower off (70 feet) or continue up the arête, step around to the right and climb up the very steep wall (13a) to a 2-bolt anchor at 130 feet. Lower off to the anchor on the arête and re-thread the rope, then lower 70 feet to the belay ledge.

WALL OF SHIVA'S DANCE

Beneath the center of South Tower is a minor wall of exceptionally fine rock having several good, one-pitch climbs. The western part of the wall forms a buttress that is capped by a ledge. Rappel 75 feet from bolts at the west end of the ledge, or downclimb a ramp from the lower, eastern side of the wall.

27. **Fluffy Bunny 10a** FA: (?) Tom Leith, 1994. Hop up the shallow, right-facing dihedral just right of P1 of *The Red Dihedral*, then traverse right and climb a steep crack past a tree. Step left to a 2-bolt anchor on *The Red Dihedral*.

28. **Unamed 12a/b** VS FA: Jeff Frizzel and Tod Anderson, 1988. Begin just right of the preceding route. Climb to a bolt and continue up the narrow wall to the bolt anchor atop P1 of *The Red Dihedral*.

29. **Have Mercy 11b/c** VS FA: Charlie Fowler, c. 1985. This route may follow the arête just left of *Krystal Klyr*.

30. **Krystal Klyr 11b** VS ★ FA: David Beashears, Steve Mammen, Jim Collins, 1975. Begin about 15 feet left of *Perilous Journey*, just left of a blunt arête. Climb up and right around the roof/arête using a flat "krystal." "Klyr" the "krystal," then climb the steep, unprotected face just right of the arête. Bring #2 and #2.5 Friends for a horizontal groove just above the "krystal."

31. **Perilous Journey 11d** VS ★ FA: David Breashears and Steve Mammen, 1975. The notorious no-pro classic. Begin about 15 feet left of *Asahi*. Climb the peerless face up and left past some pockets. The first 40 feet are the most difficult. 125 feet in all.

32. **Asahi 10c** ★ FA: Richard and Joyce Rossiter, 1988. Begin down and right from *Perilous Journey*, beneath a right-facing dihedral. Climb steep rock to a bolt on the right side of an arête. Move left beneath the bolt, then climb straight up to a big ledge. 6 bolts, 130 feet. Scramble left and rappel 75 feet to the ground or climb a thin crack to a higher ledge (10b, 75 feet) and make two rappels.

33. **Linga Line 8 A2** FA: Bob Culp and George Hurley, 1966. FA; variation, Jim Erickson and Duncan Ferguson, 1974. Begin as for *Asahi* or farther down to the right. P1. Climb past an old bolt to a stance beneath a substantial roof. Traverse right and climb past the roof, then follow a right-facing dihedral to a big ledge (8, 130 feet). P2. Climbs "pockets" to a big ledge beneath a roof. Nail through the roof as for *Shiva's Dance* and continue to the top of the wall. **Variation:** Climb through the left side of the initial roof on P1 (9+).

34. **Moth 10a VS** FA: David Breashears, Steve Mammen, Art Higbee, c. 1975. Begin a few feet left of *Duncan's Doughnut*. Climb straight up to the horn on *Duncan's Doughnut*, then continue straight up to the top of the wall.

35. **Duncan's Doughnut 10a S** ★ FA: Duncan Ferguson and Jim Erickson, 1974. This is a beauty. Begin 7 feet left of *Offset*. Climb 40 feet up and slightly left to a horn, traverse 10 feet right, then climb straight up past a shallow, right-facing dihedral that is 10 feet long, and continue to the top of the wall. 120 feet. Scramble off to the east.

36. **The Offset 9 S** ★ FA: George Hurley and Mike Yokel, 1970. Rack: SR, emphasis on thin. Climb clean, offset, left-facing corners in the middle of the wall between *Linga Line* and *Shiva's Dance*. 100 feet.

37. **Turnabout 10a** FA: Dudley Chelton and Bob Culp, 1972.variation FA: Chris Reveley and Bruce Adams, 1974. From the top of *Offset*, climb a squeeze chimney in a right-facing dihedral. **Variation:** A third pitch turns a roof by a difficult reach and continues to the top of the next tier (10).

38. **Skink's Lip 10 VS** FA: Rob Candelaria, 1976. Begin just left of *Shiva's Dance*. Climb up and left along a faint crack, step right and head for the top of the wall.

39. **Monks in the Gym 11c** ★ FA: Mike Clinton and Bill DeMallie, 1988. Rack: mid-sized Stoppers, QDs, and a #3 Friend for the belay. Climb a clean face with 4 bolts just left of *Shiva's Dance*.

40. **Shiva's Dance 8 A2** FA: George Hurley and Bob Culp, 1966. Climb a flake and short corner at the lower-right side of the wall to a prominent ledge (7). Most parties climb off here; however, the route continues.

Traverse 10 feet left along the ledge. Climb a steep crack, then traverse up and left to the base of a very steep red wall. Climb a shallow dihedral several feet right of the wall and belay on a good ledge beneath a big roof. Nail out through the roof and continue to the top of the next tier. Downclimb to the east.

THE PROW

This small pinnacle with a sharp southwest arête is located between Wall of Shiva's Dance and Industrial Wall and serves as a landmark in locating routes.

41. **Flakes 8** FA: Rob Candelaria, 1996. Begin near the first large tree along the base of the wall from the tracks. Climb double cracks in the right side of The Prow and continue to the top. Scramble off to the northwest.

42. **Oblique Streak 9** FA: Bob Wade and Bob Culp, 1975. This route ascends a crack system in a smooth, green wall about 150 feet right of The Prow. Climb to a ledge with a small Douglas-fir tree. Step left and climb a left-facing dihedral and subsequent crack to a rotten band and belay (100 feet). Climb through a bulge with poor pro, then continue up buckets to the top of the tier.

43. **Mausoleum 11d ★** FA: Eric Guokas and Eric Doub, 1980. Rack: SR. Climb *Oblique Streak* and belay on a ledge with a 2-bolt anchor. Move left and climb a prominent overhanging arête with solution holes (11d, 90 feet). 3 bolts to a 2-bolt anchor (coldshuts).

INDUSTRIAL WALL

The following routes are located on the very steep south face, just above the railroad tracks. The routes range from 11d to 14a in difficulty and are all protected by bolts and the occasional pin. Most of these routes overhang for their entire length and will not be attractive to the average climber; but for those with the requisite skill and strength, Industrial Wall is big fun. The wall is divided into two sections by an easy, left-facing dihedral called *The Approach Pitch*. Left of this corner, the wall overhangs at an impressive angle above an incut cave/ramp. To the right, the wall is shorter, but is capped by a huge roof with the route *TGV*. Just below and east of the roof is another recessed area with *Soul Train* and *Tunnel Vision*.

44. **The Auctioneer 11d ★** FA: Jim Hall and Colin Lantz, 1992. Begin from the upper left end of the ramp and stick clip the first bolt. Crux is getting started. Continue up a wavy groove, then a steep face to a 2-bolt anchor. 6 bolts, 50 feet.

45. **Coltrane 12b ★** FA: Jim Hall and Colin Lantz, 1992. Begin about 40 feet down and right from the top of the ramp. Follow bolts up and left along

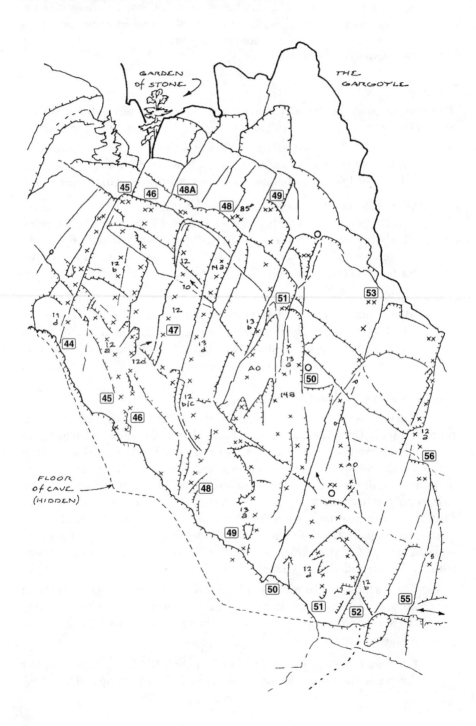

SOUTH TOWER, EAST RIDGE AREA AND INDUSTRIAL WALL

the lip of a long roof, then go straight up past a second roof to a 2-bolt bolt anchor. The first bolt hanger is upside down and can be reached from the ramp (12 bolts plus anchor, 75 feet).

46. **Driver Eight 12d** ★ FA: Jim Hall and Colin Lantz, 1992. Climb past the first 2 bolts of the preceding route, then continue straight up the very steep wall, past a second roof, to a 2-bolt anchor (11 bolts plus anchor).

47. **Prana 12d** ★ FA: Don Welsh, c. 1995. Climb to the fifth bolt on *Driver Eight*, then traverse right, climb past 3 bolts (12b/c), and finish with the *Alternate Finish* to *Vogue* (three original bolts, 10 bolts in all).

48. **Vogue 14b** ★ FA: George Squibb, 1991. Redpoint: Tommy Caldwell, 1999. Begin down and right from the preceding route and below a bolt placed on the ramp. The first protection bolt can be reached from the ramp. Climb up and right past three coldshuts, up and left along a dark red streak, then more or less straight up to a three-bolt anchor (12 bolts plus anchor, 85 feet).

48a. **Alternate Finish 12b/c** FA: George Squibb, 1991. Climb to the ninth bolt on *Vogue* (13d), then traverse up and left (10) and finish along the right edge of a flared crack. 2 bolts to a 2-bolt anchor.

49. **Jumping Someone Else's Train 13a (Project)** ★ FA: Colin Lantz, 1992. Redpoint of "first pitch": Lantz, 1992. Also known as *Jump*. Begin 12 feet left of *Rene* and stick-clip the first bolt. Climb about 6 feet up on the ramp, turn around, and jump for two good holds. This route was originally one long pitch ending at the anchor for upper *Terminal* (after 13 bolts), but now has a 2-bolt anchor after the sixth bolt. The "first pitch" is rated 13a. The "second pitch" continues past the anchor on upper *Terminal* to an anchor higher on the headwall (13b A0, 9 bolts).

50. **Rene A5** FA: Larry and Roger Dalke, 1967. Begin near the bottom of the ramp at a seam that still (1999) has an old copperhead bashed into the crack. Aid up to the copperhead, then switch to a seam on the left and nail up the bulging wall. Step right to belay in a niche as for *Terminal* and *Railings* (original bolt anchor is at right). Move left and aid up to a roof, then work up and left and belay in an alcove. There is an old bolt on the wall around to the left. Traverse left past the bolt to a crack system that leads to the top of the wall.

50a. **Deu Doe Finish A4** FA: Chris Kalous and Bob GoBell(sp?). This is a direct finish proceeding from P1 of *Rene*. "Continue up crack and seam until under roof. Over roof and up thin cracks to heinous off-width. Continue to top."

51. **Terminal 14a** ★ FA: Colin Lantz, 1991. Redpoint of P1: Lantz. P2: Tommy Caldwell, 1999. Begin to the right of *Rene*. Climb an extremely over-

hanging wall past 6 bolts (12d), then pull right to the anchors on *Railing*, or continue up and left past 7 more bolts to a 2-bolt anchor (14a, 13 bolts in all).

52. **Railing 12b** ★ FA: Jim Hall and Colin Lantz, 1991. A very popular pitch. Begin just right of *Terminal*. 5 bolts to a 2-bolt anchor, 40 feet.

53. **Railslide 12c** ★ FA: Jim Hall and Colin Lantz, 1992. This is more or less a second pitch to *Railing*. From the bolt anchor on *Railing*, climb straight up past 2 bolts and a pin, turn a roof just left of a slot, and gain a 2-bolt anchor on a hanging slab (5 bolts and two fixed pins).

54. **Transcontinental Railway 12b/c** ★ FA: George Squibb, 1994. This inventive route makes a diagonal traverse of Industrial Wall. Climb through the fifth bolt on *Railing*, then work up and left along a prominent rock stratum to the fourth bolt on *Auctioneer* and lower off. The crux is at the intersection with *Vogue*. 20 QDs, 130 feet.

55. **Approach Pitch 4** A left-facing dihedral with a single bolt leads to the initial anchors on *Spike* and *Anti-Des*.

56. **Spike 12a** ★ FA: Jim Hall and Colin Lantz, 1992. Climb *Approach Pitch* to a 2-bolt anchor and belay, or continue up the edge of an overhanging, right-facing dihedral and gain a 2-bolt anchor on a hanging slab. 8 bolts if done in one pitch.

57. **Anti-Des 13a** ★ FA: Colin Lantz, 1992. *Anti-Desdishado*, that is. Climb *Approach Pitch* and step right to a 2-bolt anchor. Climb the left side of a huge roof. 5 bolts to a 2-bolt anchor.

58. **TGV 13d** ★ FA: Matt Samet. Redpoint: George Squibb, 1992. To reach the bottom of this singular route, climb a rope ladder located down and right from *Tunnel Vision* (*Weenie Wagger*), then scramble back up the ridge to a notch just east of the anchor. Follow a right-facing flake system to the lip of the massive roof. Look for a difficult stem at the fifth bolt. 7 bolts to a 2-bolt anchor.

59. **Soul Train 12b** ★ FA: Jim Hall and Will Niccolls, 1991. A very popular pitch. Looks like your basic jug haul, but is less "cooperative" on close inspection. Begin in a deep recess down and right from the previous routes. Follow bolts up an overhanging arête to finish with a bomber solution hole. 6 bolts to a 2-bolt anchor.

60. **Tracktion 12d** ★ FA: Jim Hall and Colin Lantz, 1992. Begin just right of *Soul Train*. Climb past 2 bolts and up a left-facing dihedral with 4 fixed pins (all missing) and a final bolt to a 2-bolt anchor. A second pitch follows the arête along the right edge of the big roof, just right of *TGV*. Climb past 3 bolts on the left side of the arête, then pull around to the right. 7 bolts to a 2-bolt anchor. P2 may be approached as for *TGV*.

61. **Fraction 11c** FA: George Squibb, date unknown. Begin from a rounded ledge, just right of the second pitch of *Tracktion*. 4 bolts to a 2-bolt anchor, 45 feet. A redpoint tag is still on the first bolt. A bolt with no hanger is just to the right of the start.

62. **Tunnel Vision 13b ★** FA: Jim Hall. Redpoint: Colin Lantz, 1991. Begin a short way down and right from *Soul Train*. Climb a radically overhanging wall to a 2-bolt anchor. Crux is getting into an undercling halfway up. 6 bolts to a 2-bolt anchor, 40 feet.

63. **Weenie Wagger 6** FA: Art Higbee, solo, 1975. Begin about 50 feet east of *Tunnel Vision*. Climb a crack in the right wall of a V-shaped dihedral. A rope ladder normally hangs from a tree in this crack, which is used as the approach to *TGV* and upper *Tracktion*.

64. **A Rose for Andrea A2** FA: Delaney, Brooks, Tedli, 1986. Begin in an alcove 70 feet above the tracks. Aid up a seam to a chimney.

65. **Fiddle Sticks A1+** FA: Delaney, Brooks, Tedli, 1986. Begin in a cave near the tracks. Aid up the right side, then go left 10 feet above the roof.

66. **Charlie's Dihedral 7** FA: Pat Ament and Van Freeman, 1973. From the top of *Weenie Wagger*, scramble up and right to the bottom of an obtuse, right-facing dihedral. Climb the dihedral and scramble off to the right.

George Squibb on TGV *(5.13d), Industrial Wall.* DAN HARE PHOTO

INDUSTRIAL WALL—RIGHT SIDE

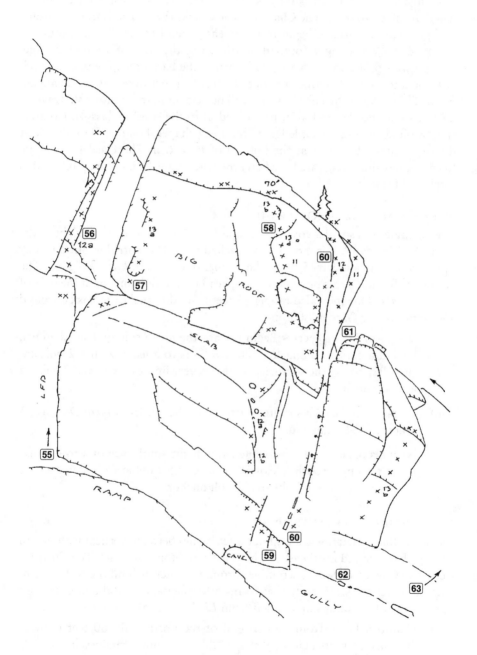

EAST RIDGE

This is the complex ridgecrest above Industrial Wall, between the top of The Red Dihedral and the railroad tracks. The ridge has three distinct areas designated (from left to right) The Chamber, The Corridor, and The Garden of Stone. To approach East Ridge, begin from the east side of the tracks, just south of Tunnel 6. Follow a vague footpath northeast to the crest of a wooded ridge, then go west past a cairn to a second cairn at the base of a spire with an arch near the top. Go left (south) for about 100 feet to a rocky crest above a hanging basin. The back side of The Gargoyle will be evident to the southwest. Traverse 25 feet right and descend a 20-foot dihedral to the south (Class 4). Contour right around the basin to a ledge with an egg-shaped boulder. Scramble west through a slot and arrive at the bottom of *R.N.R.* in The Garden of Stone. Route names and ratings are based on topos drawn by Alvino Pon, published in *Rock and Ice* #54.

THE CHAMBER (SEE PHOTO P. 91)

The Chamber is a small alcove at the top of The Corridor, 100 feet right of the upper *Red Dihedral*. It is most easily reached from The Corridor, but one may also scramble up and left (5) from the juniper tree beneath *Little King* (see The Garden of Stone). If this pitch is belayed, head for a 2-bolt anchor at the base of *New Damage*. One may also rappel 75 feet from this anchor to easier ground and return to the Garden of Stone.

67. **Wargasm 12 (Project)** ★ Begin toward the north side of The Chamber, behind a curious pinnacle. Follow 6 bolts to a ledge with a 2-bolt anchor. P2 follows the southeast arête of a very impressive tower. 7 bolts to a 2-bolt anchor.

68. **Promiscuity 12a** This route is around to the left from *New Damage*. 5 bolts to a 2-bolt anchor.

69. **New Damage 12a** ★ This route ascends the south face of a tower that forms the upper south side of The Corridor. Scramble around to a 2-bolt anchor at its base. 6 bolts to a 2-bolt anchor.

THE CORRIDOR (SEE PHOTO P. 91)

The Corridor is a narrow cleft (about 8 feet wide) between vertical walls south of The Chamber and northeast of The Garden of Stone. To reach The Corridor from The Garden of Stone, scramble through a notch behind the *R.N.R.* pinnacle and climb a steep gully that forms a left-facing dihedral along its right side (2), or follow ramps up and left from *Little King* (5).

70. **Catnip 8** Begin from the left end of the north wall, 60 feet right of *Wargasm*. Climb a clean, V-shaped dihedral with a thin crack.

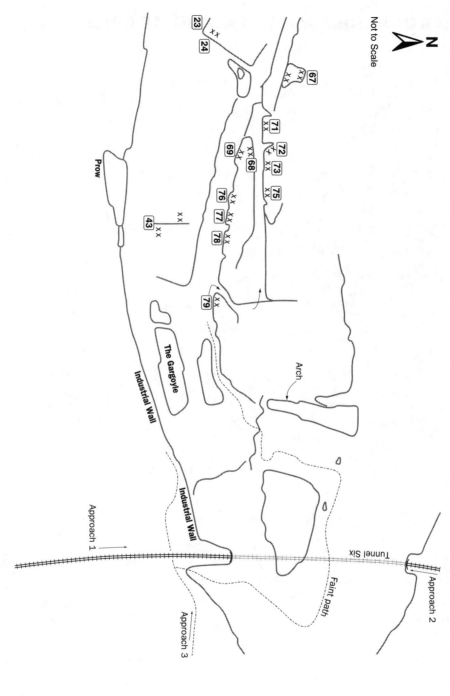

Prow

43
x x
x x

The Gargoyle

Industrial Wall

Industrial Wall

Approach 1

Approach 3

Tunnel Six

Faint path

Approach 2

Arch

23
x x
24

67
x x
x x

71
x x

72
73
x x

68
x x

69

75

76
x x

77
x x

78
x x

79
x x

EAST RIDGE AREA

MICKEY MOUSE WALL—EAST RIDGE AREA

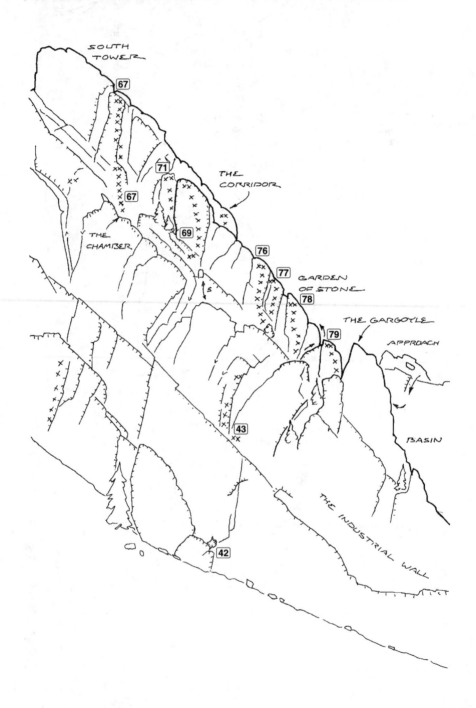

71. **Chastity 11a** ★ This is the leftmost bolt-protected face climb on the north wall of The Corridor. 4 bolts to a 2-bolt anchor.

72. **The Scourge 11d** ★ Begin just left of a large block in the middle of The Corridor. Pull over a roof at a white pebble. 5 bolts to a 2-bolt anchor.

73. **Storm Bringer 10d** ★ Begin just right of a large block, midway along The Corridor. 5 bolts to a 2-bolt anchor.

74. **Satin Crack 10** Climb a crack system between *Storm Bringer* and *The Tease*. Gear only.

75. **The Tease 9+** ★ Farthest right bolt route in The Corridor. Begin a short way up and left from a large Douglas-fir. 5 bolts to a 2-bolt anchor.

THE GARDEN OF STONE (SEE PHOTO P. 91)

The Garden of Stone is a series of south-facing pinnacles (or small buttresses) located along a ramp to the north and west of a prominent tower called The Gargoyle.

76. **Little King 10a** ★ From the alcove behind The Gargoyle, scramble 150 feet up and left along a steep ramp (Class 4) to a ledge with an old juniper tree. The first bolt is about 15 feet above the ledge. 7 bolts to a 2-bolt anchor with chains.

77. **P.B.S. 9** ★ Scramble up and right from the juniper beneath the preceding route. Follow 4 bolts up a steep face and lower off from a 2-bolt anchor.

78. **L.O.O.P. 11a** ★ Begin just left of a narrow ramp that slants up and right behind the *R.N.R.* pinnacle. Follow 6 bolts up and left to a 2-bolt anchor with chains.

79. **R.N.R. 9+** ★ Begin from a sandy ledge behind The Gargoyle. Climb up on a flake and follow 5 bolts up and left to a 2-bolt anchor.

EAST SIDE OF TRACKS

Just south of Tunnel Six and several hundred feet east of the tracks (along Approach Three) are two crags of a lesser God. Both are on private land.

CAVE ROCK

This rock could, it appears, have several routes of vague interest. One route is known. Cave Rock is located about 200 feet east of the tracks along Approach Three.

1. **Up and Left 12a (?)** FA: Alvino Pon (?). Begin just right of a shallow cave at the southwest side of the rock. Follow 8 bolts up and left above the cave to a 2-bolt anchor. Actual name unknown.

THE CORRIDOR—NORTH SIDE

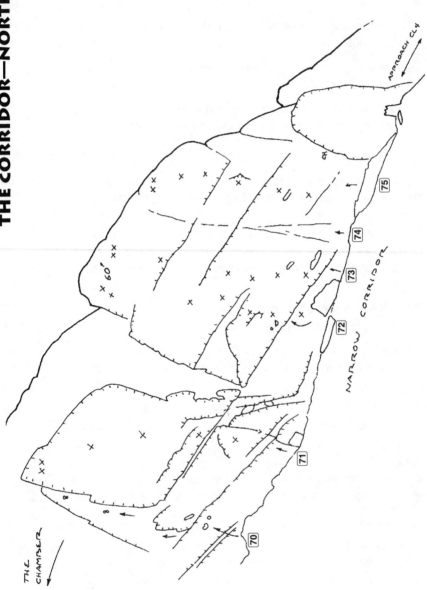

EAST SIDE OF TRACKS—UPPER: WARM UP ROCK; LOWER: CAVE ROCK

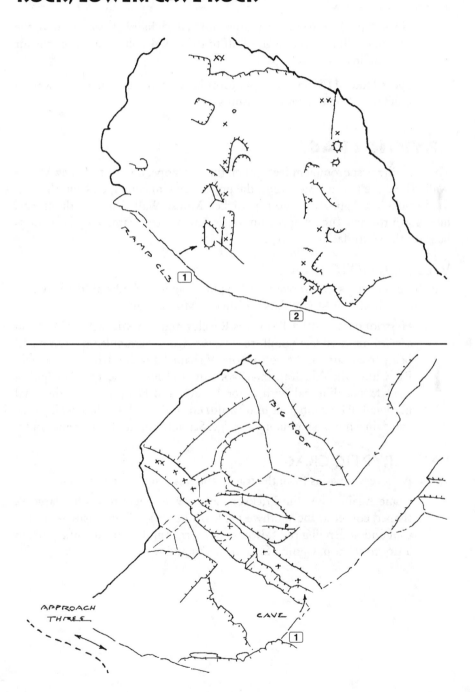

WARM UP ROCK

This south-facing rock is located up and behind the east side of Cave Rock. Two routes are known.

1. **Warm Up 10b** Start up on a ramp and make a hairy traverse right to the first bolt. Climb steep, juggy stuff to the top. 4 bolts to a 2-bolt anchor with chains.

2. **Sport Hiker 11b** Start at a platform beneath the middle of the wall. 6 bolts to a 2-bolt anchor (coldshuts).

CRYPTIC CRAGS

These are the first prominent features on the east slope, north of Mickey Mouse Wall. There are two distinct crags, the upper being much larger. Gain the railroad tracks via Approach Two for Mickey Mouse Wall. Once on the tracks, hike north toward Tunnel Seven until it is obvious to scramble up large talus beneath the south face of the rocks.

WEST CRYPTIC CRAG

This buttress begins just above East Cryptic Crag and climbs all the way to a summit north of The Mouse Ears on Mickey Mouse Wall.

1. **Hystrionoxobus 10 ★** FA: Chris Reveley and Jim Michael, 1974. Begin several hundred feet uphill from *Come Again*. Scramble up a ramp and belay from cams at the bottom of a V-shaped dihedral with a thin crack. P1. Climb the dihedral, then work up and left to belay. P2. Climb a right-facing dihedral with a good crack and belay beneath the final headwall. P3. Climb a clean offwidth crack through the headwall (crux) and gain a minor summit in the ridge. Scramble off to the west and south.

EAST CRYPTIC CRAG

This rock is very obvious from the tracks and has a single known route.

2. **Come Again 9** FA: Jim Erickson, solo, 1976. Begin beneath a large V-shaped corner at the southwest side of the rock. Climb easily up to big roof and undercling right. Round the corner and follow a hand crack in a slot to the top. Climb off to the north and west.

West Cryptic Crag

Toprope

1

East
Cryptic Crag

CRYPTIC CRAGS FROM
THE SOUTHEAST

ELDORADO CANYON

Note: This section of the book includes all the crags within Eldorado Canyon State Park and all adjacent crags beyond the park boundaries that are normally accessed from Eldorado Canyon.

Since the middle of the century Eldorado Canyon has been the central arena and seat of power for Colorado climbing and has given rise to some of the finest and most difficult routes in North America. Always a hub of activity, climbers from every state in the union and the far corners of the globe are found here amidst anglers, tourists, picnickers, sunbathers, hikers, bikers, outdoor clubs, and stray dogs. Eldorado Canyon is a state park and on more than one occasion people have been turned away at the entrance station for lack of available parking. Popular routes such as *Bastille Crack* will sometimes have a climbing party on each pitch, and waiting in line to begin a route is not unusual. But at times, in the off season, you might be the only one in the canyon. The Indians knew Eldorado as a place of great power, and indeed it is. If you haven't climbed on Redgarden Wall, The Bastille, or Rincon wall, you haven't been cragging in Colorado.

Eldorado has something for every climber. Superb rock, awe-inspiring verticality with Tower Two soaring 800 feet above South Boulder Creek, more than 600 routes ranging in difficulty from 5.0 to 5.14, easy access, and some of the most famous crags in America. Even true scenic solitude can still be had by visiting some of the more outlying features. Nearby Boulder, chic and New Age, offers every conceivable facility and amusement. Here one can work-out at an ultra-modern health club, take a steam and a tan, buy a pair of tights and a set of RPs, and get a new mantra, all within fifteen minutes of Eldorado.

The rock in Eldorado Canyon is a very hard conglomerate sandstone, predominantly dark red in color, that is common to all the crags from Flagstaff Mountain south to Mickey Mouse Wall. It is generally solid, holds protection well, and affords excellent climbing. As with The Flatirons, the east faces of most features lean back at an angle of about 50 degrees, are slabby, crackless, and sprinkled with stunted trees. The north, south, and west faces tend to be very steep and are typically interrupted by ledges, ramps, and overhangs. Discontinuous crack systems, which could hardly be described as abundant, are found on these steeper faces and tend to be finger-size or smaller. Thus, RPs and small camming devices are frequently useful. Many routes are protected by bolts, but most of these require additional gear. A typical rack should include

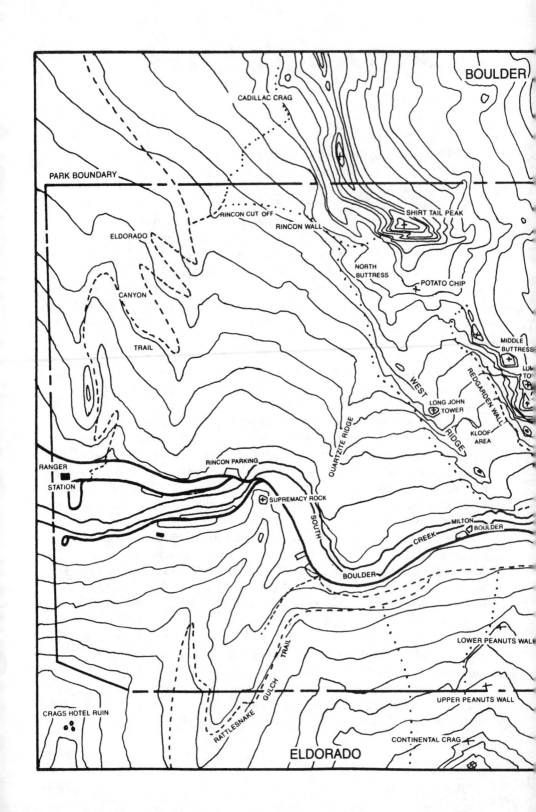

BOULDER

CADILLAC CRAG

PARK BOUNDARY

RINCON CUT OFF

RINCON WALL

SHIRT TAIL PEAK

ELDORADO

NORTH BUTTRESS

POTATO CHIP

CANYON

MIDDLE BUTTRESS

TRAIL

WEST

REDGARDEN WALL

LONG JOHN TOWER

QUARTZITE RIDGE

RIDGE

KLOOF AREA

RANGER STATION

RINCON PARKING

SUPREMACY ROCK

SOUTH

MILTON BOULDER

CREEK

BOULDER

LOWER PEANUTS WALL

RATTLESNAKE GULCH TRAIL

UPPER PEANUTS WALL

CRAGS HOTEL RUIN

CONTINENTAL CRAG

ELDORADO

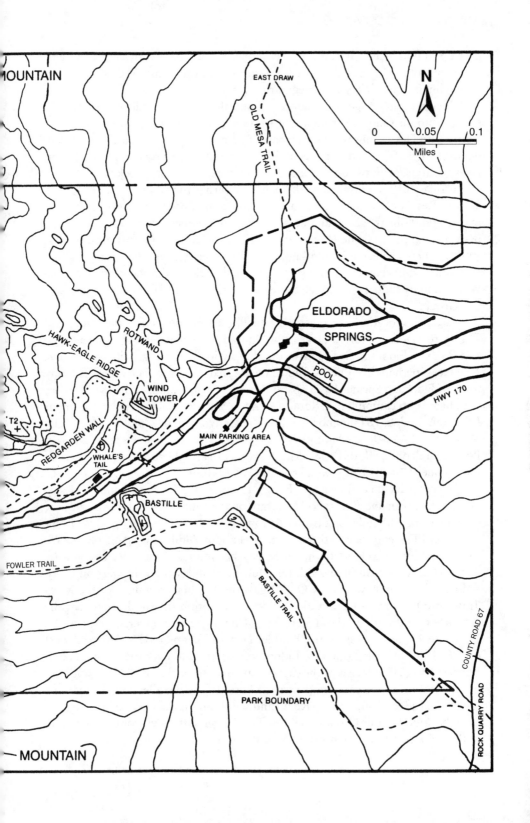

gear up to two inches. In terms of technique, the climbing varies from route to route, but is characterized by intricate face work, thin jams, and liebacks and underclings along flakes and irregularities.

Though Front Range granodiorite is found along the west side of the park, it is set off from the sandstone formations by a long quartzite dike that runs exposed from South Draw (southwest of the park) to a point about two-thirds of the way up West Ridge. This dike consists of the oldest and hardest rock in Eldorado and gives rise to a small, pyramidal buttress known as Supremacy Rock.

Just east of the entrance to the canyon, during the summer, the Eldorado Springs Resort offers swimming in its Olympic-sized pool. Information, books, maps, and T-shirts, are available at the visitor center at the west end of the park. Also at the west end is a popular picnic area featuring graffiti-proof tables, yellowjackets protected by the Endangered Species Act and the Saudi Arabian endurance volleyball championships. Full-scale, televised rescues are available year-round by Eldorado Canyon State Park staff and the Rocky Mountain Rescue Group.

Gasoline, groceries, beverages, and the like are not avilable at the state park. The nearest facility is three miles east of Eldorado at the junction of highways 170 and 93. The Eldorado Springs Resort, along with swimming, sells soft drinks, Twinkies—perhaps even beer—and of course, excellent artesian water. The tiny town of Eldorado Springs has a post office, horse concession, and a cafe.

There is no camping in Eldorado Canyon State Park. One venue is Boulder Mountain Lodge, 12 miles north in Boulder Canyon, along Colorado 119. Telephone: (303) 444-0882. Another is the American Youth Hostel 8 miles north in Boulder. Telephone: (303) 442-0522. For other overnight accommodations, call the Boulder Chamber of Commerce: (303) 442-1044.

The steep and colorful walls of Eldorado Canyon lie between Boulder Mountain on the north and Eldorado Mountain on the south. The narrow part of the canyon is only 0.5 mile long from east to west and is cut deeply by South Boulder Creek. The entrance to the state park is about 7 miles by road from downtown Boulder. Traveling south, Broadway becomes Colorado 93 beyond the Table Mesa area. Continue south for a few more miles and turn west on Colorado 170. Continue west on CO 170 past the southern terminus of the Mesa Trail, into the town of Eldorado Springs, and within 0.25 mile, arrive at the entrance to Eldorado Canyon State Park. Coming from Denver, head north on Interstate 25, northwest on the Boulder-Denver Turnpike (U.S. 36), and west on CO 170 (take the Louisville-Eldorado exit, up and over the turnpike, and right on CO 170). Once past the east entrance to the park, a dirt road continues up the bottom of the canyon, passes the base of The Bastille, cuts through the Quartzite Ridge at Supremacy Rock, and winds about the west end of the park on either side of South Boulder Creek. The ranger station/visitor center resides at the far west end of the north fork of this road.

Most of the crags described in this chapter are within the boundary of Eldorado Canyon State Park. This means that you will be a "park visitor" when you come here to climb, and that you will be subject to the rules and regulations of the park. **These include keeping dogs on their leashes.** This is often ignored by climbers venturing beyond the valley floor. Don't forget to pick up a parks pass! And yes, the rangers are there in the winter.

TRAILS

A trail system for Eldorado Canyon State Park was first designed and approved in 1980. With the YCC (Youth Conservation Corps), trails to all major crags were begun. However, Federal funding for this program was eliminated under the Reagan Administration, and by 1982, trail building was all but stopped. During the 1990s, great efforts were made to improve the trail system. Perhaps $200,000 has been spent on trail construction and maintenance, and crews of volunteers have put in huge amounts of time and effort. As a result, trails within the park are in great shape, and access to almost all the crags has become far easier and safer. This is an ongoing project. Climbers, who of course are the main beneficiaries of these efforts, are encouraged to help.

1. **Volunteer for trail crew work.** This can be done through the State Park, or through ACE.

2. **Please use the trails!** Many of the trails travel up and down marginally stable slopes. Cutting across these slopes off-trail prevents the growth of soil-stabilizing plants. This is ever more important with the increasing numbers of park visitors/climbers. In particular, the trail on the West Face of Redgarden Wall skirts a very unstable talus slope, where soil and plants are struggling.

3. **Dogs must be kept on leashes.** Climbers' dogs will wander off trails, damage plant life, frighten wildlife, and have on occasion menaced or even bitten other Park users.

The Fowler Trail: Also known as The Bastille Trail, this very scenic path begins on the left (south) side of the road circa 0.3 mile west of The Bastille and shares its first 100 yards or so with the Rattlesnake Gulch Trail. After heading east for about 200 yards, the trail crosses an open talus slope below Lower Peanuts Wall, with great views of Redgarden Wall. It passes through a notch that was blasted in the back of The Bastille, then curves around into a brushy draw and eventually intersects County Road 67 and the trail to Mickey Mouse Wall. Just before this intersection, another trail heads down the gulch to the north and comes out near the post office in Eldorado Springs. This is not within the current boundaries of the state park, but crosses land owned by the Artesian Water Company. Please respect their rights as landowners. The steep path beneath the west face of The Bastille also intersects The Fowler Trail.

Rattlesnake Gulch Trail: This fine hiking trail begins with The Fowler Trail, then breaks off to the southwest after about 100 yards. It winds its way up a V-shaped draw through beautiful, wooded terrain with compelling views of Redgarden Wall and West Ridge. The only climbing feature that is accessed by Rattlesnake Gulch Trail is Continental Crag, and only the first 150 yards of the trail are used. It is possible to reach Mickey Mouse Wall by hiking from the railroad tracks up over the northeast ridge of Eldorado Mountain and then dropping down to the top of the crag.

Eldorado Canyon Trail: Though it is possible to begin at Walker Ranch and hike down to Eldorado, most people do just the opposite. The four-mile trail begins at the west extreme of the state park and climbs northwest through rugged, primitive terrain, eventually arriving at Walker Ranch (county open space). To find the beginning to this superb trail, walk 50 yards west on the "main road" from the small "Rincon Parking Area" just north of Supremacy Rock and find the trail on the right (north). This point may also be reached by picking up a short connecting trail just east of the visitor center that leads up to the road. The Eldorado Canyon Trail accesses the Rincon Wall area, and all other features along the west side of the South Ridge of South Boulder Peak.

Streamside Trail: Streamside Trail begins at the footbridge that crosses South Boulder Creek just east of The Bastille. Once on the north side of the creek, at the base of the Whale's Tail, the trail can be followed either east or west. To the east, the path becomes indistinct and ends at a dam at the park boundary. To the west, the trail has been developed and is generally easy to walk, but comes to an abrupt end where the south buttress of the West Ridge drops into South Boulder Creek. The West Ridge Trail may be reached by a short scramble around the bottom of this buttress.

Redgarden Wall Trail: This trail begins from the Streamside Trail just west of Pickpocket Wall and climbs the steep slope beneath the west face of Redgarden Wall.

West Ridge Trail: This useful path begins just across South Boulder Creek from the Milton boulder and climbs via switchbacks and stone steps all the way beneath the southwest face of the West Ridge to Rincon Wall. It may be reached by crossing the creek just west of the Milton boulder or by scrambling around the bottom of the West Ridge from the Streamside Trail.

Rincon Cutoff: This is the route of choice for reaching Rincon Wall, Shirt-tail Peak, the upper West Ridge, and Cadillac Crag. Begin on the Eldorado Canyon Trail. Within the first 0.5 mile, the trail contours around a draw and heads southeast onto a sparsely wooded ridge. About 150 feet beyond the third switchback on this ridge, the trail begins to descend. Just at the high point, a signed footpath goes straight up the grassy slope on the right (east) and leads up to the broad talus field below Rincon Wall. To reach Cadillac Crag, follow the path up the ridge into the trees and out onto the next talus field to the north.

Old South Mesa Trail: WARNING ABOUT PARKING: There is no place to park a car in Eldorado Springs that is not on private land. Unless you like to gamble, drive through the entrance and park inside Eldorado Canyon State Park. Note that a pass is required and that you are likely to be cited if you don't get one. The best bet is to buy an annual pass. The southern end of the Old Mesa Trail provides access to the crags listed under East Draw.

The beginning of the Old Mesa Trail in Eldorado Springs is difficult to find, and with a degree of consistency, is mismarked on the official Boulder Mountain Parks trail map. From the entrance to the state park, walk about 50 feet to the east, cross the wooden bridge to the north, and follow the road back around to the east behind the swimming pool. Where the road branches in three directions, take the middle option and walk about 50 yards. Turn left, then right up a dirt driveway, and after a few paces, climb up a rutted trail on the right. If fate is on your side, you should now be on the Old Mesa Trail. Follow the path around very private property (on the left), then up a broad, grassy draw to a saddle that overlooks Shadow Canyon. Drop down north to a service road, go right, and find the Mesa Trail just on the other side of a stream crossing. A map is helpful in this area as there are three ways to get onto the main Mesa Trail.

Joyce Rossiter on the Northwest Corner *route (5.10d/11a), The Bastille.*
RICHARD ROSSITER PHOTO

ELDORADO CANYON SOUTH

ROTWAND SOUTH

Immediately above the parking lot is a rambling cliff with few lines and many tottering loose blocks. Four obscure routes have been recorded here by Jim Stuberg and Chip Ruckgaber around 1980, though they may well have been done previously. These are not described here, and interested parties are referred to Pat Ament's book *High Over Boulder* for more details.

THE BASTILLE

Two hundred yards west from the parking lot, the vertical buttress of The Bastille soars 300 feet directly over the road. The Bastille contains some of the finest pitches in Eldorado and the summit offers an incomparable panorama of the canyon.

Descent: There are fixed belay and rappel anchors at various locations on The Bastille (see topos). To descend from the top of the north face, cross a small chasm to the south and scramble up into a diagonal slot festooned with the remains of an ancient steel cable. (This is just above the finish to *Blind Faith*.) Follow the slot south as it becomes a ledge and continue along this west-facing ledge system via some ups and downs to the south end of the crag. Scoot down a short ramp to the old railroad grade that is now known as The Fowler Trail. Turn north and follow a steep path down along the west side of The Bastille to the road. The routes are listed from left to right, starting with the broken northeast section.

1. **Banzai Gardens 10b/c** FA: Jim Stuberg and Mike Brady, 1986. Begin about 60 feet left of *Northeast Corner*. P1. Climb broken rock to a pine tree and on up low angle rock to a left-facing dihedral. P2. Climb the dihedral and go right at a roof to a pine tree.

NORTH FACE

The March of Dimes Buttress is the 60-foot-high offset section of the north face about 50 feet east of *The Bastille Crack*. *Northeast Corner* ascends its left side. Its right margin forms a right-facing dihedral. There is a 2-bolt anchor atop this buttress.

THE BASTILLE FROM THE NORTHEAST

2. **Northeast Corner 9** FA: Stuberg and Tom Wilmering, 1980. Begin in the large, angling groove to the left of *March of Dimes* and climb 90 feet up to a tree. Go up to the right in a right-facing dihedral, past a large tree, and on to another tree. Go up a thin crack behind the tree, move right, and finish above. Or move farther right and climb the last pitch of *The Bastille Crack*.

3. **Lilliburlero 12a** FA: David Breashears, 1976. Start just right of *Northeast Corner*. Climb up about 10 feet and struggle up a thin, right-angling crack to easier ground.

4. **March of Dimes 10c ★** FA: Dudley Chelton and Duncan Ferguson, 1973. FA: variation start, Rob Candelaria, Richard Rossiter, toproped, 1988. Rack: up to a #3 Friend. This is a disjunct route with two good pitches and some mediocre rock in between. Begin just left of the right-facing dihedral about 50 feet left of *The Bastille Crack*, on the right side of the March of Dimes Buttress. P1. Climb either of two cracks (11a left, 9 right) for 15 feet, then up and left along a thin crack and finally up easier rock to a big ledge with 2 bolts. P2. Climb a left-facing dihedral, up and right via a face, and belay on the ledge near the top of *Werk Supp*. P3. Work up to the right and climb a thin, left-arching crack across a steep wall (crux). Scramble off to the east. **Variation:** Toprope the face above the first 15 feet (10d).

5. **Werk Supp 9+ ★** FA: Ralph Warsfield and Pat Ament, 1964. FFA: Dave Rearick and Pat Ament, 1964. Rack: up to a #4 Friend. There have been a few accidents on P1, with leader falls onto gear that has pulled. Be careful, particularly with the first 40 feet. Begin about 10 feet right of the right-facing dihedral that is about 50 feet left of *The Bastille Crack*. P1. Climb a superb 150-foot crack and flake system to a large ledge (with chains) that slopes down to the east (8+). P2. Move the belay down to the east and climb the obvious, right-angling squeeze chimney, offwidth, and hand crack to a ledge (crux). Climb the last pitch of *March of Dimes*, or climb off to the east (be careful of loose rock). Note: If rappelling with two ropes from the chains atop P1, be careful with the ropes. Any wind may cause them to catch around the loose blocks on top of the March of Dimes Buttress. Better to do two short raps.

5a. **Coach's Demise 9+** FA: Ed Body and Mike Brooks, 1985. This pitch parallels the upper half of P1 of *Werk Supp* on the left (9+ S).

6. **Nexus 10b/c S** FA: Jim McMillan and Larry Bruce, 1968. FFA: Ed Webster, Steve Mammon, Brad Gilbert, 1975. Climb the first 60 feet of *Werk Supp* and belay on the left. Go back to the right and cross *Werk Supp* at a flake, then follow the ascending strata for about 70 feet to the second pitch of *The Bastille Crack*.

THE BASTILLE—NORTH FACE

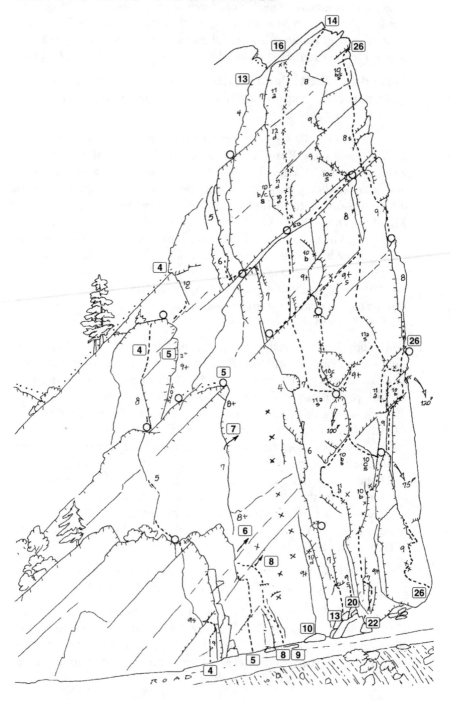

7. **Model Citizen 11b/c S** ★ FA: Mike Brooks and Melissa Ettelstein, 1984. Begin from the top of March of Dimes Buttress or climb into the line via *Werk Supp*. Angle up and right along an obvious series of steps past a bolt to a small, left-facing dihedral with yellow streaks. Move up about 6 feet, then right to *The Bastille Crack*.

8. **Marie Antoinette 9 VS** ★ FA: Roger Briggs, 1967. FFA: Billy Roos and John Ruger, 1973. A nice face pitch, little gear. Begin about 25 feet left of *Bastille Crack*. Climb up and left via finger cracks, straight up to a mantel (crux, no pro), then up and right past a bolt (9) to *The Bastille Crack*. One may also climb off to the left after the mantel.

9. **Madame de Guillotine 12c** FA: Rob Candelaria, Erik Fedor, 1989. Start as for *Marie Antoinette*, but move right just below the mantel to reach much harder climbing and the first of 9 bolts leading up the face (cutting across *Marie Antoinette* again), to the top of P2 of *The Bastille Crack*. **Variation:** Follow *Marie Antoinette* to her final encounter with the *Guillotine*. This avoids the crux of *Guillotine* and accesses the nice 11b upper section.

10. **Northcutt Start 10d** ★ FA: Led by Ray Northcutt, 1959, after he'd been sandbagged into thinking Layton Kor had already done it. Climb the steep, obtuse, left-facing dihedral just left of *The Bastille Crack*. Near the top, pull right along a thin crack with a piton, around to the right side of the arête, and up to the bolt anchor atop the first pitch of *The Bastille Crack*.

11. **DF Direct 11b VS** ★ FA: Duncan Ferguson, c. 1975. Climb *Northcutt Start* and continue straight up, very close to *The Bastille Crack*, until level with where P2 of *The Bastille Crack* jogs right. Here ascend a crack, then continue up the face to a ledge 160 feet up.

12. **Derek-tissima 12** ★ FA: Derek Hersey, 1984. Toprope the arête just right of *Northcutt Start*.

13. **The Bastille Crack 7** ★ FA: Two U.S. Army climbers, 1954. FFA: Allen Bergen and Stan Shepard, 1957. FA: of 8 finish, Layton Kor and Dave Dornan, 1959. Speed ascent: 7 minutes, 58.3 seconds (to the summit of The Bastille) Mic Fairchild. Rack: up to a #4 Friend. This is one of the most popular rock climbs in the world, and the second most popular in Eldorado for accidents, particularly on P1. Technically 7, but sustained, strenuous, steep, and now a little polished. Begin from the top of a pile of broken flakes, just right of an obtuse, left-facing dihedral. The crack is obvious from the road. P1. Climb up beside a left-facing flake, stem across to the crack, and place pro BEFORE committing to the jams. Swing left into the crack and jam up to a good stance with a 2-bolt anchor (65 feet, 7). P2. Climb up to a flake, move right, and continue up

the crack to a sloping stance beneath a short, double section of crack (95 feet, 6). P3. Climb the double crack and the steep, awkward section above to a wide, sloping ramp (50 feet, 7). P4. Traverse left 15 feet to gain the bottom of a steep, blocky, left-facing system that is followed to another broad, sloping ramp (75 feet, 6). P5. Climb a shallow chimney above the belay to the summit area (4); The first two pitches can be done as one 165-foot lead, though this can present communication difficulties; one's partner will be out of sight—and earshot if the creek is high. **Variation A:** Near the top of P2, lieback the short 8 flake on the right instead of taking the easier crack up and left. **Variation B:** At the start of P5, move 20 feet up the ramp and climb the steep face just left of a wide crack in the big dihedral formed by the summit block and the wall to the right (8).

UPPER NORTH FACE

14. **Outer Space 10c S ★** FA: Layton Kor and Steve Komito. FFA: of P1, Jim Erickson and Pat Ament, 1971; of P2, Erickson and Diana Hunter, 1971. Rack: up to a #3 Friend. This high-flying tour goes directly up the center of the north face from the second pitch of *The Bastille Crack*. X-M combines well with *Outer Space*. P1. Climb the first two pitches of *Bastille Crack* (165 feet, 7). P2. Move up and right along the ramp, around a prow, and up an obtuse, left-facing dihedral to a belay on a wide, sloping ramp (80 feet, 10b). P3. Climb up and left across overhanging rock to an obvious undercling (10c S), pull around to the left and climb a left-facing dihedral (9) to where it fades at a sloping stance. Move up and then left along a crack with a fixed pin, then up and right via pockets to the top of the north face.

14a. **Lost in Space 9 S** FA: Kevin Donald and Charlie Fowler, 1979. From the sloping stance halfway up the last pitch of *Outer Space*, go right, up a flake system and on to the top.

The next four routes all start more or less off the large ledge angling up and right high up on the north face. This may be approached via *Outer Space*, which belays here before its final pitch.

15. **Hairstyles and Attitudes 12c/d ★** FA: Dan Michael and Roger Briggs, 1988. Rack: 10 QDs. Spectacular. Begin about 12 feet down and left of the left-facing dihedral at the top of the first pitch of *Outer Space*, along the same stratum as the belay ramp. A sling belay is possible here from the first bolt, 3 feet left from the top of the second pitch of *Wide Country*; or belay from the ramp up and right from the top of the fourth pitch of *The Bastille Crack*. Follow a line of ring bolts up the left (east) side of the face and join the last section (3 bolts) of *Space Invaders*. The first crux (11c/d) is at the fourth bolt, followed by a no-hands knee lock. The second crux (12c/d) is at the seventh bolt, near the top of a shield-like formation.

16. **Space Invaders 11a** FA: Greg Brooks and Randy Spears, 1988. Rack: should include 7 or 8 QDs. This is the original version of *Hairstyles and Attitudes*, included for completeness. Begin with the second pitch of *Outer Space* and climb about 35 feet to the second piton in the left-facing dihedral. Traverse left to a ledge with a bolt, up over a flake (mid-range TCU), and on to the top of the face past three more bolts. There is a 2-bolt anchor at the top of this route.

17. **Saturnalia 11b S** FA: Steve Dieckhoff, Michael Gilbert, 1998. This pitch takes the face to the right of the top pitch of *Outer Space*. Climb up and left on steep huecos to the obvious bolt, crank left, then up past a horizontal crack to a second bolt. From here continue straight up past 11b moves to join the *Lost in Space* variation to *Outer Space* (9 S).

18. **Outer Face 10c S ★** FA: Rob Candelaria and Roger Briggs, 1976. Variation: Kevin Donald and John Baldwin, 1978. Start as for *Saturnalia*, but head straight up overhanging pockets for about 30 feet, up a smooth face, then up a finger crack to the left (crux). **Variation:** (10) climb up to the smooth wall, make a difficult mantel, and go right at the roof.

NORTH FACE: ROUTES TO RIGHT OF THE BASTILLE CRACK

19. **Crossfire 11d ★** FA: Rob Candelaria, Mic Fairchild, and Matt Baruch, 1988. Rack: wires, #2.5 Friend. Begin with *Bastille Crack* and climb up through the left-facing flake. Continue straight up past a bolt (crux), up past another bolt, then right into *Wide Country*. The original line continued straight up the face right of *Bastille Crack* (12a/b) and joined P2 of *Wide Country*. A fourth bolt on the upper section of the pitch has been removed.

20. **Wide Country 11a S ★** FA: Roger Briggs and Neil Foster, 1967. FFA: Of first pitch, Jim Erickson, 1972; of entire route, Duncan Ferguson and Don Peterson, 1972. Rack: up to a #3 Friend. Begin atop the pile of broken flakes just right of *Bastille Crack*. P1. Make unprotected 9 moves up into a shallow, left-facing dihedral, then upward with meager pro to a piton and bolt. Move up and left past the bolt to a sloping ledge (11a), straight up to a downward-pointing flake system, then head up and right up the flake (10c) to join *X-M*. P2. From the bolt belay, climb up and left to a point very near *Bastille Crack* (11a S), then straight up across the initial traverse of *Outer Space* past 2 short, left-facing dihedrals (10b), and left to belay. P3. Climb a funky and poorly protected groove and crack system up the east side of the summit block (10b/c S).

21. **Times Square 12d/13a** FA: Rob Candelaria and Mic Fairchild, 1988. Climb straight up from the first bolt on the first pitch of *Wide Country* and rejoin the route just left of where it joins *X-M*. Two bolts.

THE BASTILLE FROM THE NORTHWEST

THE BASTILLE—NORTH FACE RIGHT

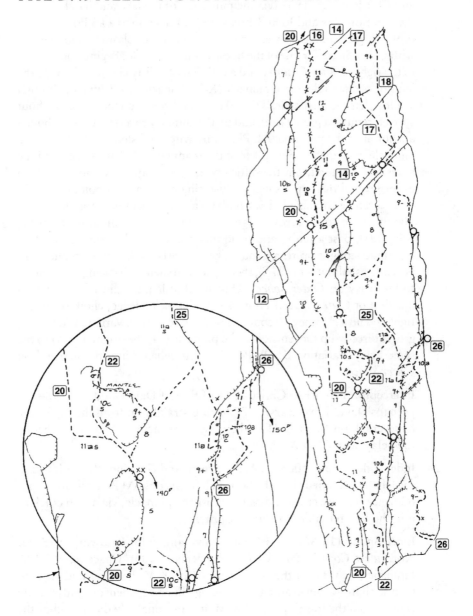

22. **X-M 10c S (7 VS)** FA: Layton Kor and Pat Ament, 1962. FFA: Larry Dalke and Cliff Jennings, 1967 (via the pinnacle); of the face and hand crack to the left, Ron Cox and John Behrens, 1968. Rack: up to a #3 Friend. Bring offwidth gear and shop-vac for the original start. Classic. Combine this with *Outer Space* for one of the finest 10s in Colorado. Begin about 10 feet to the right of *Wide Country* and a little left of a dirty chimney forming the left side of a semi-detached pinnacle (X-M Pinnacle). P1. Climb up through shallow, left-facing dihedrals (7 VS) to a hand crack, up the crack for about 15 feet, right at a piton (10b), and up the chimney to a stance with a bolted anchor atop the pinnacle. P2. Place tiny wires and step off the top of the pinnacle onto the steep wall left of the seam (10c S). This is thin, and the wires are not great, but the difficulty eases rapidly. Move up and left to easier ground then up a small, right-facing dihedral to a bolt anchor (P1 and P2 can be combined). P3. Climb up and left past two pitons to a scary 10c move up to a narrow ledge. Otherwise climb straight up from the belay (9+), past a piton, and hand-traverse left on the same ledge (9 S). Continue straight up to a good ledge and belay. P4. Angle up and right beneath a shallow roof (9+ S), then up a prominent, left-facing dihedral (8) to the belay on *Outer Space*. (This dihedral is just right of the obvious dihedral of *Outer Space*.) From the sloping belay ledge, climb off to the right and up a chimney, or continue with *Outer Space*. **Variation A:** For P1, grovel directly up the left side of the pinnacle (9+, the original start) to the same belay. **Variation B:** On P4, climb straight up into the dihedral on *Outer Space*.

23. **Interceptor 11b S** FA: Christian Griffith and Dale Goddard, 1984; or perhaps David Breashears, 1977. Climb straight up from the top of the hand crack on P1 of *X-M* to the easy, right-facing dihedral just below the belay atop P2 of *X-M*.

24. **Independent Study 10c S ★** FA: Pat Ament and Greg Finoff, 1984. Climb the left-facing dihedral at the bottom left side of X-M Pinnacle for about 60 feet, then power up and right across the pinnacle, via a thin crack to join the first pitch of *Northwest Corner*.

25. **Inner Space 11a S/VS ★** FA: Jeff Lowe and John Baldwin, 1978. Of *Northwest Corner* start: Charlie Fowler and Chip Chace, c. 1978. A fantastic pitch. From the belay atop P2 of *X-M*, head up and right to gain a shallow, left-leaning, left-facing dihedral, then up and slightly right to join the fourth pitch of *X-M*. It is optional whether one clips the obvious bolt (apparently part of *Trial by Existence*) near the start. This pitch may also be started from the second pitch of *Northwest Corner* by climbing up to the shallow dihedral from the top of the piton crack.

26. **Northwest Corner 11a** ★ FA: Layton Kor and Peter Lev, 1959. FFA: Pat Ament, 1966. Classic. This is popular when the pitons protecting the crux headwall are in place (currently they are in, summer 2000). Begin below and a bit right of X-M Pinnacle, about 15 feet from the road. P1. Undercling up and left across a slab, into a small, left-facing dihedral, right into the crack along the right side of X-M Pinnacle (9), and up the wide crack to a bolt belay on the top of the pinnacle. P2. Climb the left-facing dihedral behind the pinnacle to its top, then pull over a roof onto the headwall (9+). There are at least four ways of doing the crux section. **A:** Step left and climb the blunt arête just left of the piton crack to a bolt (11a), then move right and down slightly (9+), up a shallow dihedral, and right to a bolt belay on the arête. **B:** Climb straight up the piton crack (11b), then go right. **C:** Pull up and right from the first pin and arrive on top of the mantel shelf (10d). **D:** The original free ascent line: Clip the first couple of pins in the headwall crack, step back down and up a tiny ramp to the right, make a committing mantel to a bolt (10d), then climb up and right to the 2-bolt anchor. P3. Climb a crack and left-facing dihedral (8) up to a belay behind a flake. P4. Up a crack to a piton, left beneath a roof (9), then up the face to a belay at the top of the ramp just above the finish to *X-M*. See topo for choice of finishes.

27. **Trial by Existence 9+** FA: Pat Ament, Eric Doub, 1978. Begin from the stance on the headwall, just above the overhang on P2 of *Northwest Corner*. Move left and down slightly around the arête, up and left to a bolt, up and right to another bolt, then right (9+) to the bolt above the crux.

28. **Lost in the Ozone 11b/c S** FA: Roger Briggs and Kirk Dufty, 1981. Begin from the top of the piton crack in the headwall on P2 of *Northwest Corner*. Move up and left past a bolt, straight up for 30 feet, make a difficult traverse right to a crack in a roof. Follow it to a stance on the third pitch of *Northwest Corner*.

29. **This is Only a Test 11a VS** FA: Derek Hersey, Keith Ainsworth 1987. Begin as for *Northwest Corner* and climb up to where it enters the crack along the right side of X-M Pinnacle. Climb up and right into a left-facing flake system that is followed up and left (Friends and TCUs), straight up into a scoop, up another 30 feet (crux, no pro), then traverse right to the top of *Rain*.

30. **Chance of Rain 10b/c S** FA: Mike Brooks and Dan McQuade, 1985. This climbs the flake system between *Northwest Corner* and the first half of *Rain*. Turn a short roof with 2 pitons, then up underclings to the second roof on *Rain*.

31. **Rain 10d S ★** FA: Pat Ament and Tom Ruwitch, 1967. FFA: Roger Briggs and Mark Hesse, 1973; of modern line, David Breashears and Ajax Greene, 1975. Rack: sparingly up to a #3 Friend. Begin right of *Northwest Corner*. Climb straight up the red slab, past some overlaps to a roof with 2-inch crack beneath it. Undercling left and crank over the roof (10d), angle right, then up, passing 2 bolts (10d S). Move left and pull over a roof (10b S), then work straight up (8 S) and left to a 2-bolt anchor. Double-rope rappel or join *West Buttress*. **Variation:** On the FFA, Briggs and Hesse started up *Northwest Corner* to where it joins the crack along the right side of X-M Pinnacle, then traversed right (9) to the first bolt on *Rain*.

32. **Rain and Shine 11c VS** FA: Rob Candelaria, rope solo (tying off 40 feet of rope to the bolts atop *Rain*), 1977. This climbs the face directly above the 2-bolt anchor atop the first pitch of *Rain*. From the anchors atop *Rain*, head up for 15 to 20 feet, past obvious jugs. Place some small RPs, then head up and slightly right (crux). **Variation:** After placing the RPs, step left, then up.

WEST FACE

All routes to the right of *Rain* begin from the talus that rises steeply along the west side of The Bastille. A good landmark is the Giant Flake, about 160 feet up, which has a beautiful flat ledge with 2-bolt rappel anchor at its top.

33. **West Buttress 9 ★** FA: Layton Kor and Carl Pfiffner, 1959. FFA: Kor and Larry Dalke, 1964. Direct Start, Layton Kor, 1965. Rack: up to a #3 Friend. Beautiful and popular. Begin at a level area in the talus blocks, about 50 feet above the road and 12 feet below a huge boulder. P1. Place pro in a shallow corner, hand-traverse left (8), go up a vertical crack past two pitons (crux), hand-traverse left for 6 feet, then straight up the face (6 S) to a belay niche at the left side of The Giant Flake. P2. Climb the wide crack in the left-facing dihedral past a bolt, crank into the chimney, squeeze to the top of the flake, and belay on the perfect ledge (two ropes needed to rappel from here). P3. Move up to the left and climb a chimney (7) or, more exciting, climb the *Hair City* overhang (9) just to the right, and arrive on a big ledge. P4. Climb the deep chimney (0) or the wall to the right (4). **Variation A:** Direct Start (9+ S): Climb straight up to the piton crack and past a bolt, though very difficult if you are shorter than Layton (6'3" or so). **Variation B:** Climb straight up the thin crack above the piton on the first pitch (10b/c) all the way to the belay. Superb. **Variation C:** From the belay on P2, launch out right onto the arête of The Giant Flake and up (8+).

34. **Butt Hair 9+ VS** FA: Rob Candelaria and Dave Bowers, 1974. Climb the very narrow strip of face between *West Buttress* and *Hair City*. Don't mistake this for a pile.

THE BASTILLE—WEST FACE

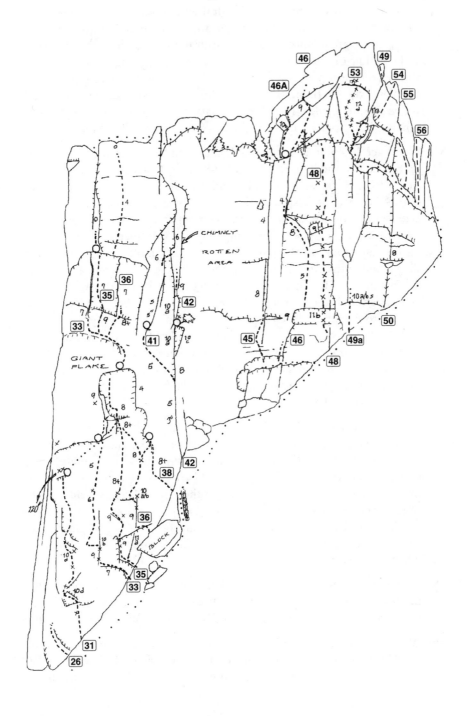

35. **Hair City 9 S ★** FA: Jim Erickson, John Behrens, Stan Badgett, 1969. Classic. Begin about 10 feet up and right from *West Buttress*. P1. Climb up into a shallow, right-facing dihedral with a piton and mantel onto a narrow shelf (8+). Clip a bolt overhead, move up and left to the arête (8), up and right to another bolt, then straight up (8+ S) to the overhang in the middle of the Giant Flake. Power up overhanging buckets, go left, and up to the top of the flake (8+). P2. Go easily up and left to the middle of the overhang, turn the exciting roof (9), and climb the wall above (7 S) to a ledge. P3. Climb the face to the right of a deep chimney (4). The last 2 pitches may be done as a single 160-foot lead.

36. **West Face 10a S or 11b ★** FA: Bob Culp and Stan Shepard, 1961. FFA: John Behrens and Jim Erickson, 1968. Thin Crack FA: Roger Briggs, circa 1972. Rack: up to a #3 Friend. This fine route ascends the right side of the west buttress, parallel to *Hair City*. Begin in the narrow trough between the huge talus block and the main wall, about 12 feet up and right from *Hair City*. P1. Climb up and left to a stance at the bottom of the obvious crack, work up to a bulge (9), clip an old, bent piton with a sling, then crank up and left (10a) to a stance on a steep slab. Make delicate moves (10b) up the slab and pull back right into the crack. Climb up and left to join *Hair City* (8 S) or up and right to belay in a chimney, then up to the top of the Giant Flake. P2. Climb up to the *Hair City* roof and climb the right-facing dihedral on the right (8), belay if desired, then continue up to the summit area (4). **Variation A:** Climb the brief initial crack from the bottom (11a). **Variation B:** Climb up to the 10 bulge on the first pitch, but instead of pulling up and left at the bulge, continue up the thin crack (11b).

37. **Polynesian Concepts 11a VS** FA: Kevin Donald and Duncan Ferguson, c. 1980. Begin this bold journey in the trough behind the huge talus block, up a bit from *West Face* and left of *West Arête*. P1. Climb up the middle of the wall (10d VS) to join *West Face* above its crux and belay at the bottom of the chimney. P2. Climb the unprotected, outside, south edge of the Giant Flake (10? VS) and belay at its top. P3. Climb the overhang to the right of the *West Face* right-facing dihedral, up past an "ear of rock," and belay on a ledge. P4. Climb a crack and right-facing dihedral to the top.

38. **West Arête 8+ S ★** FA: Unknown. FFA: Duncan Ferguson, solo, 1984. Begin about 20 feet up and right from *West Face*. Angle up and left along a crack and over steep pockets to join the *West Face* or *West Chimney* routes.

39. **Western Union 10d S** FA: Ed Webster, Lauren Husted, Chester Dreiman, 1984. A good second pitch. Start about 20 feet right of *West Arête*. P1. Zig-zag up the face to an alcove and belay (65 feet, 8). P2. Continue up

the rounded arête just right of the flake/chimney to a bulge 20-foot right of the *West Face* undercling. Surge up this bulge, past two fixed pins in a very thin crack, to a good ledge (100 feet, 10d). P3. A vertical crack system (6) gains the top after 100 feet.

40. **Slow Finger 8+** FA: Pat Ament and Cam John, 1980. Climb the steep wall to the right of *West Arête*, past a hole to a ledge. Join *West Chimney,* or climb off to the right.

41. **West Chimney 7** ★ Begin with the first 50 feet of *Blind Faith*. P1. Break off to the left before the crack steepens, angle up and left, and belay at the base of a right-leaning, right-facing dihedral with a wide crack (5). P2. Climb the offwidth and a left-facing dihedral until it is possible to traverse right beneath a fixed pin (6). Pull right into the chimney of *Blind Faith* (crux) and climb the huge chimney to the summit area (6).

42. **Blind Faith 10a** ★ FA: Jim Erickson, free solo, 1972. FA: Kevin Donald, c. 1975. Rack: up to a #4 Friend. Begin beneath an obvious, continuous crack about 40 feet up from the huge talus block. P1. Jam straight up the crack, which is wide and easy at first, then hand- size and difficult at the top (90 feet, 10a). Belay on a good ledge. P2. Power up through a blocky overhang (9) and up a big chimney to belay at the summit area. **Variation:** Climb the crack on the right about 20 feet before the belay on the first pitch (10c).

43. **Cream 10b S** ★ FA: Derek Hersey and Robb Cadwell, 1987. This takes the upper section of the left arête on the second pitch of *West Chimney*. Start where the climbing in the chimney eases. Move out left past two small sloping ledges to the arête, up this, then up the face above, veering left to finally surmount a very exposed pinnacle.

UPPER WEST FACE

Right of *Blind Faith*, there is a loose steep bowl, then the cliff faces west and there are a few more good routes.

44. **Overhanging Talus 10d S** FA: Derek Hersey, Robb Cadwell. Start left of *Breakfast in Bed*. Look for a fixed pin about 10 feet up. Climb over a steep bulge, then up for about 30 feet. Traverse right and go to *Bed*.

45. **Breakfast in Bed 8** ★ FA: Roger Briggs and Rob Candelaria, 1975. Begin from a ledge about 40 feet up from *Blind Faith*. Climb a steep, left-facing dihedral to the walk-off ledge (8).

45a. **The Early Riser 9** FA: Jim Erickson and Muriel Sharp, 1981. Below the start and a little left is a short, left-facing corner (9).

46. **Out to Lunge 9** ★ FA: Bob Culp, Alan Clark, John Link, 1968. P2 variation: FA: Jim Erickson, 1978. Rack: up to a #3 Friend. Begin as for *Breakfast in Bed*. P1. Climb up and right up a left-facing flake, and make a difficult mantel onto its top (9). Continue up the steep face, left under a roof, and up a left-facing dihedral to the walk-off ledge (8). P2. Climb up the middle of the clean slab and turn a roof (9). **Variation:** On P2, go up the left side of the slab and through the roof (10d/11a).

The next three routes all start in the same spot: under a wide crack just left of a left-facing dihedral. This is about 15 feet right of *Out to Lunge*.

47. **New Chautauqua 10c S** FA: Ed Webster and Chester Dreiman, 1984. Start up the wide crack, then angle left past a pin and over a roof (crux, pin). Traverse left to *Out to Lunge*, follow this for 50 feet, then go out the overhang on the right on huge pockets (9, pin) and climb up to the walk-off ledge. Double ropes are desirable.

48. **Sunset Boulevard 11b/c** ★ FA: Chris Archer, Eric Reynolds, Chris Blackmon, Keith Gotschall, Rick Thompson, Al Torrisi, Jordan Campbell, 1997. Rack: QDs, optional light rack. Start as for *New Chautauqua*, pass the first pin, then step right. Over the roof at a bolt (crux) and up the steep but easier face above, past six more bolts. Continue to the walk-off ledge.

49. **Neon Lights 11a S** ★ FA: Art Higbee, Jim Erickson, John Ruger, Ed Webster, 1975. Rack: up to a #3 Friend. P2 is popular, P1 somewhat neglected. P1. Climb up the wide crack for about 30 feet, over an unprotected roof (10c/d), then up easier terrain to the walk-off ledge. P2. Work in from the left and climb the broad, rounded overhang via an obvious crack system (11a).

49a. **Implied Consent 9** FA: Erickson, solo, 1980. Climb the bulge and crack just to the right of P1 of *Neon Lights*.

50. **Voodoo 8** ★ FA: Harrison, Stuberg, Brooks, 1981. Begin about 15 feet above *Neon Lights* and 80 feet down from the trail. P1. Climb a V-shaped corner up under a chockstone, then a right-facing dihedral up to the walk-off ledge. P2. Pull over a bulge just left of the belay and follow a crack system up to the ridgetop.

SUMMIT TOWER

This is the blunt pinnacle that rises above the walk-off ledge. Its west and south sides are very steep and have produced several routes of merit. The following routes ascend this feature. To descend from the top, scramble north, then west to the walk-off ledge.

51. **Pasta Point of No Return** 9 FA: Steve Bartlett, solo, 1985. Start up P2 of *Out to Lunge*, to the roof. Traverse right under the roof to the arête, then up and slightly left to the top.

52. **Serengetti Spaghetti** 10b/c FA: Mike Brooks and Dennis Smith, 1982. Begin on the right side of the arête to the right of P2 of *Out to Lunge*. Climb a crack up the southwest-facing wall to a small bowl, then go left and up rotten rock.

53. **Your Mother** 12d ★ FA: Colin Lantz and Greg Robinson, 1988. Rack: 8 QDs. Begin from the walk-off ledge and climb the broad overhang to the left of P2 of *Neon Lights*. There are 7 bolts leading to a 2-bolt anchor. The crux is near the top.

54. **Nursery Crhyme** 10d FA: Bob Horan and Skip Guerin, 1981. Begin to the right of *Neon Lights*. Work straight up to the right side of a flake, then undercling up and left.

55. **Tarzan** 10d FA: Harrison, Brooks, Stuberg, 1981. Begin just right of *Nursery Crhyme*. Climb the strenuous, overhanging, pocketed wall to a flake, then up and left to join *Voodoo* at its crux.

56. **Bridge-it Bardot** 8 FA: Jim Erickson, solo, 1980. To the right of *Tarzan*, stem up to a big hold, then up a crack in rotten rock.

57. **Hat Trick** 8+ FA: Stuberg, Harrison, Brooks, 1981. Begin from the road by a pine tree at the southwest corner of The Bastille. Climb a gully through a series of bulges, step right and finish in a hand crack.

58. **Bunny Fluff** 10d FA: Mike Brooks, toproped, 1982. Begin from the old railroad cut at the south side of The Bastille. Climb the south face of a small tower and up a hand crack to the top.

LE PETIT BASTILLE

This is the long, low ridge, just south of the old railroad cut/Fowler Trail, behind The Bastille. It was actually continuous with The Bastille until it was attacked by dynamite and bulldozers back in the 1930s. The following routes are on the north end of this feature, just above the cut.

1. **Bricklayer's Spite** 6 FA: Jim Stuberg and Carl Harrison, 1981. Begin from the roadcut 10 feet left of a boulder. Climb the bulging wall and a chimney.

2. **Scimitar** 10b/c FA: Stuberg, Harrison, Brooks, 1981. Begin just right of a boulder in the roadcut. Work up and through a curving dihedral, move right and follow a crack to the top

Hidetaka Suzuki on Your Mother *(5.12b), Summit Tower of The Bastille.*
BOB HORAN PHOTO

3. **Plankton Stew 8+** FA: Harrison, Stuberg, Brooks, 1981. Begin about 25 feet right of *Scimitar*. Climb a shallow, right-facing dihedral, up a thin crack, through a bulge, and beyond.

4. **Two-Tone Dihedral 8** FA: Harrison and Stuberg, 1981. Climb the large, right-facing dihedral about 20 feet up from *Plankton Stew* and turn a roof to the left.

5. **Sourpuss 8** FA: Stuberg, Harrison, Brooks, 1981. Begin beneath a short crack about 30 feet up from *Two-Tone Dihedral*. Make some face moves, jam the hand crack, and turn a roof.

PEANUTS WALL

Lower and Upper Peanuts Wall actually comprise two crags connected by a notch. The steep, north- and west-facing buttresses, though somewhat dark and gloomy, offer a number of excellent routes. The walls are located about 0.25 mile west of The Bastille, above the old railroad cut. Approach via The Fowler Trail, hike about 200 feet beyond the cutoff to the Rattlesnake Gulch Trail, and head straight south up giant talus to the base of Lower Peanuts Wall. To reach Upper Peanuts Wall, hike southwest along the base of the Lower Wall, past the gully between them, and voilà. Recognizable paths have been formed along the bases of both walls.

Descent: To descend from the summit ridge of Lower Peanuts Wall, either scramble down easy slabs to the east, or traverse northwest to the notch, thence

LOWER AND UPPER PEANUTS WALL

PEANUTS WALL—NORTHWEST FACE OVERVIEW

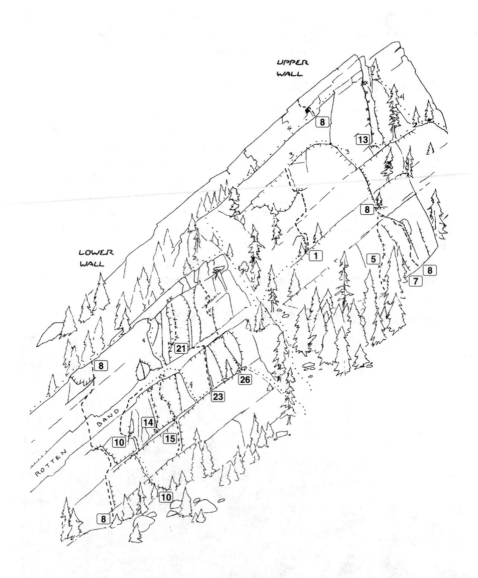

down to the west, whichever is closer. To descend from the summit ridge of the upper wall, scramble northeast down slabs and ramps to the notch, thence down to the west. Otherwise downclimb to the west (topo, q.v.), south on a ledge system, then back along the base of the wall. One may also reach the ledge system on the west face by rappelling 80 feet from the bolt anchor atop *Sunrider*.

LOWER PEANUTS WALL—NORTH FACE

1. **Easy Off 9** FA: Mike Brooks, 1981. Rack: thin only. Begin at the far east corner of the north face. Go up and right on a ramp, up and left to a ledge, then up and right to the ridge.

2. **Jackson Browne 11b** FA: Brooks and Joe Huggins, 1982. Begin 10 feet right of *Easy Off*. P1. Climb a right-leaning, right-facing dihedral for 60 feet, then belay on a ledge at a pin. P2. Traverse left round the corner to a bolt, then up and left into a right-facing dihedral.

3. **More Nerve than Verve 10d S** FA: Keith Ainsworth, Brad White, Mary Reidmiller, Steve Levin, 1993. Start at the low point of the wall, 15 feet right of *Jackson Browne*, and 10 feet below a tiny bush. Climb a 10a move over a small bulge, then straight up (10d) to the belay ledge on *Jackson Browne*. Continue up and left over the bulge past an obvious jug/spike, then up to a small, right-leaning dihedral capped by a triangular roof. Climb this (9) and up the easier slab above.

4. **Let's Jet 10d** FA: Charlie Fowler, Dan McGee, Marc Hirt, 1987. Begin from the low point of the wall. Climb along a lichen streak with 2 bolts.

5. **No Visible Means of Support 10b S** FA: Mike Brooks and Todd Montgomery, 1982. Rack: up to a #3 Friend. Begin about 100 feet right of the northeast corner of the rock near a conspicuous stump. P1. Wander up the wall (8+ S) and belay by a small tree. P2. Go up past a bolt, then up and left through a notch.

5a. **Easter Island 9 A2** FA: Jan Delaney and Mike Brooks, 1987. Go up and right from the top of P1 of *No Visible. . .* along an overhanging, right-facing dihedral and wide crack.

6. **Young, Blonde, and Easy 11b S/VS** ★ FA: Mike Brooks and Lynn Smith, 1983. Rack: pitons and nuts up to 1.5 inches. Begin to the right of a large block, 100 feet right of *No Visible*. Climb up and left across a slab to a bolt, up a thin crack/seam with poor fixed pins to a worse anchor. Rappel 80 feet.

7. **The Shield 11b/c S** ★ FA: Mike Brooks and Andrea Azoff, 1986. FFA: Ken Black. Note: Mike Brooks and Andrea Azoff, after attempting the crux second pitch, retreated leaving their gear in place. Later the same day, Ken Black (who enjoyed the nickname Psycho Kenny) successfully

LOWER PEANUTS WALL

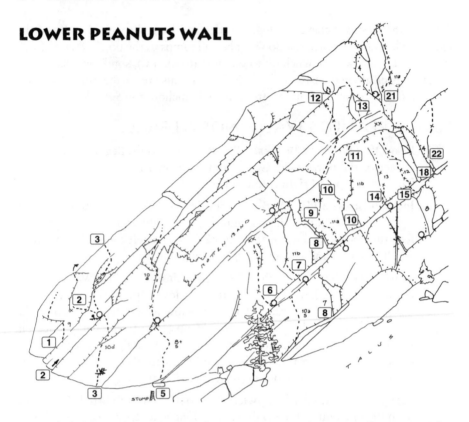

led this pitch (with an unknown partner), clipping Mike's gear. After collecting all the gear from this pitch, he then fell to his death from the third pitch, after pulling off a very sharp, large block, which severed his rope. Begin as for *Young, Blonde, and Easy.* P1. Climb up a ramp to the right, then up a blank slab (10a S) and belay on a ramp. P2. Climb a seam to a bolt, then follow the seam/crack up to a ledge with a large block and a poor anchor. The third pitch is loose and very dangerous, and it was never completed.

8. **Left Side 10b/c S** FA: Larry Dalke and Cliff Jennings, 1967. FFA: Chris Reveley and John Ruger, 1974. Begin as for *The Shield*. P1. Continue up the ramp, climb a left-facing dihedral (7), and belay at the bottom of a huge, left-leaning, left-facing dihedral with a wide crack. P2. Climb the left-facing dihedral and belay as for *The Shield* (crux). Climb straight up to a large ceiling, right 20 feet, and up a shallow dihedral.

9. **Blows Against the Empire 11a** ★ FA: Charlie Fowler, Dan McGee, Marc Hirt, 1987. Rack: up to one inch and QDs. Short and reachy crux. Harder for the short. Begin up and right from *The Shield*, where the wall begins to bend around to the southwest. Scramble up a ramp and right-facing

Joyce Rossiter on Home Free *(5.11b), Lower Peanuts Wall.* RICHARD ROSSITER PHOTO

LOWER PEANUTS WALL FROM THE NORTHWEST

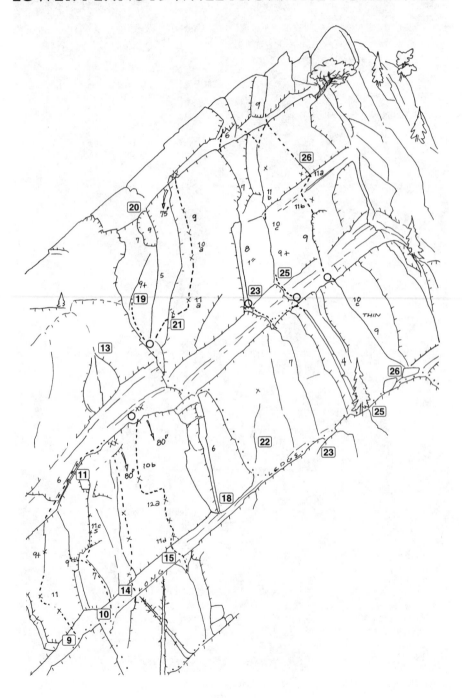

dihedral to a large, sloping ledge with a poor anchor. Climb the clean slab past a couple of bolts and a pin, then up and right along a brown band to the anchor at the top of *Girl's Climb*. It is also possible to lower from fixed nuts at the top of the slab.

10. **Peanuts 9 ★** FA: Layton Kor and Charles Roskosz, 1961. FFA: Jim Erickson and Henry Barber, 1973. Rack: up to a #2 Friend. Begin as for *Blows. . .* and belay on the ramp beneath an overhanging flake. Climb up to the flake, crank to the left, and follow a steep crack up to a brown band of rock (9). Work up and right (8+) to a ledge and belay, or continue to the bolt anchor atop *Girl's Climb*. Climb off to the southwest or do one of the upper pitches.

11. **Scorpions 11c S** FA: Fowler and McGee, 1987. Climb straight up the crack at the right side of the overhanging flake on *Peanuts*. 2 bolts and a pin.

11a. **Scorpions Direct Start 9** FA: Jim Stuberg, Carl Lemke, Carl Harrison, Mike Brooks, 1981. Begin by a small tree 30 feet left of the regular start. Climb up past two diagonal bands and up an obtuse dihedral.

12. **Air Guitar 11c ★** FA: Steve Dieckhoff, Kathy Lenz, 1993. Rack: QDs and some nuts for the diagonal break between first and second bolt. Takes the curving arête on the face left of *Aspenleaf Dihedral*. Start at the bolts atop *Scorpions*. Kind of a direct finish to that route. Climb straight up past 3 bolts to a tree on the ledge left of the top of *Aspenleaf Dihedral*.

13. **Aspenleaf Dihedral 10b** FA: Mike Brooks, free solo. Rack: thin. Begin from the ledge at the finishes to *Blows Against the Empire* and *Peanuts*. Climb an aesthetic dihedral to the summit ridge. Crux is low down.

14. **The Sacred and the Profane 12d/13a S ★** FA: Dale Goddard, 1987. Rack: 3 QDs. This superb and extremely thin route has rather long expanses between bolts. Begin as for *Peanuts*, but belay up and right along the ramp. Pull over a roof at a bolt and climb the right side of a blunt arête to a 2-bolt anchor. Lower off.

15. **Just Another Girl's Climb 12a/b S ★** FA: Andrea Azoff and Charlie Fowler, 1987. Rack: 4 QDs. A superb and difficult route. Begin at a large, left-facing dihedral 75 feet up and right from *Peanuts*. Climb up the corner (8) to an incut ledge, stretch up to clip the first bolt, pull over a roof (11d), and work up the face past 4 bolts. The runouts between bolts are a bit "sporting."

16. **Trouble and Strife 10d** FA: Harrison and Lemke, 1981. Hike up along the base of the wall past *Girl's Climb* to a short, north-facing wall. Climb the obvious crack up and right to the top.

17. **Tracer 8** FA: Carl Harrison, 1981. Climb the short, north-facing wall around the corner to the right of *Trouble and Strife*.

LOWER PEANUTS WALL—UPPER WEST FACE

18. **Your Basic Lieback 6** ★ FA: Richard Rossiter, solo, 1980, or Ruckgaber and Brooks, 1980. This is a good pitch. Begin on the lower of the long ledges that run across the wall, down and left of *Star Wars*. Climb a clean crack in a right-facing dihedral.

Directly above *Your Basic Lieback* is a recess with the following three routes. To descend, downclimb the chimney on the left, then down a slot just south of *Your Basic Lieback*.

19. **Wired 9+** ★ FA: Pat Ellinwood and David Rice, 1977. Short but sweet. Climb a thin crack up and right across the smooth slab to the top of the large, left-facing dihedral.

20. **Dihedral 9-** ★ FA: Jim Erickson, solo, 1978. Variation: R. Rossiter, 1980. Begin at the bottom of the recess, about 25 feet above the top of *Your Basic Lieback*. Climb the inside corner up and around the left side of a flake. One may also continue straight up (9).

21. **Forbidden Planet 11a/b** ★ FA: Erik Johnson and Andrea Azoff, 1987. Superb—one of the best routes on the crag. Belay as for *Wired* and *Dihedral*. Climb around to the right side of the arête at the right side of the recess and straight up the face past 5 bolts. There is a 2-bolt anchor at the top.

22. **Star Track 8** FA: Mike Brooks, Chip Ruckgaber, 1980. Begin to the right of *Your Basic Lieback* and the downclimb slot and from the same ledge. Climb a flake and crack system and the face above past a bolt. Finish just north of the dihedral of *Star Wars*.

23. **Star Wars 8** ★ FA: P1, R. Rossiter, solo, 1980; P2, Kevin Donald and partners, 1977. Rack: up to a #4 Friend. Sort of a classic. Scramble up toward the right side of the crag and cut back left along the lower of two diagonal ledges that run across the face. Begin at the bottom of a large, obtuse, left-facing dihedral. P1. Climb the dihedral for 60 feet to the next ledge and belay at base of a prominent, right-facing dihedral (7). P2. Climb the right-facing dihedral for 50 feet (8), power up a deep slot (6), then crank over a roof into another slot (6) and belay on the summit ridge.

23a. **Double Cracks 5** This is likely the original first pitch. Climb a pair of cracks from behind a tree just right of the obtuse, left-facing dihedral of the first pitch.

23b. **Nova 7 S** FA: Mike Brooks and Chip Ruckgaber, 1980. Climb the shallow, left-facing dihedral to the right of *Double Cracks*.

23c. **Jawa 7** FA: David Hague and Tom Wilmering, 1980. Climb the left-facing dihedral to the right of *Star Wars* (*Jawa* and *Nova* may well be the same pitch).

24. **Whiskey Gala 9** FA: Chip Ruckgaber and Mike Brooks, 1980. Climb a very flared, obtuse dihedral 20 feet to the right of the first pitch of *Star Wars*.

25. **The Empire Strikes Back 11b VS ★** FA: Dan Michael and Debbie Middleton, 1979. Rack: include a double set of RPs. This is a great pitch, but there is almost no protection other than a stray bolt near the top. Begin with one of the variations to *Star Wars* and belay on a ledge. Climb the very wide, obtuse dihedral to the right of the *Star Wars* dihedral, then go left and through a notch at the top. The bolt was placed later by a different party, and with its addition it is maybe more obvious to climb up and right in the upper section of the pitch.

26. **Home Free 11b ★** FA: Of entire route, R. and J. Rossiter, 1987. P1 was climbed by R. Rossiter and Mary Riedmiller, 1980. Rack: up to a #2 Friend. Superb mixed. P1. Climb the large, obtuse, left-facing dihedral at the right side of the west face area to a ledge and belay (10c). The difficulties can be reduced by stepping left to a flake, then up and right into the top of the corner (10a). P2. Climb a crack along the left side of a flake, up the face past a bolt (11b), over a small roof with a second bolt (11b), up to the top of the slab, and up a steep, right-facing dihedral (9) to the summit ridge.

27. **Off the Cuff 6** FA: Brooks, Pierce, Stuberg, Harrison, 1981. Begin 30 feet right of *Home Free*. Climb up left of a gully and belay on a ledge. Climb a 10-inch crack behind a flake and continue to the summit.

28. **Fickle Finger of Eight 8** FA: Carl Lemke, solo, 1981. Climb the short, but nice, left-facing dihedral to the right of *Off the Cuff*.

29. **Sickle 8** FA: Jim Stuberg, solo, 1981. Climb a shallow, right-facing dihedral just right of *Fickle Finger*, then move around the corner and finish in a hand crack.

30. **Strolling 8** FA: Carl Harrison, solo, 1981. To the right of the west face area is a slabby, discontinuous face with many trees. Climb a finger crack up the slabs, pass an overlap, and continue to the top of the wall.

31. **Live for the Moment 9** FA: Brooks, Azoff, Stuberg, 1987. ". . .between Upper and Lower Peanuts. . . a north-facing wall. . .a crack that angles up right to a slot. 40 feet (Not bad.)"

UPPER PEANUTS WALL

The Upper Wall is distinguished by its flat, lichen streaked, upper northwest face. The right edge of this face forms a sheer, smooth skyline arête that is visible from many points in the canyon. *Sunrider* ascends this arête. Note: Upper Peanuts Wall and Continental Crag are outside Eldorado Canyon State Park, and are unfortunately owned by the City of Boulder...a cruel twist of fate.

UPPER PEANUTS WALL—NORTH FACE

This is the shady, lichenous face to the right of the notch between the Lower and Upper Walls.

1. **Cardinal Richelieu 8+** ★ FA: Stuberg and Brooks, 1981. Begin 50 feet down and right from the notch. P1. Climb the right side of a clean flake (7), head up and right and belay on a ledge beneath a roof. P2. Climb through the roof (crux), then up a left-facing dihedral to a broad ramp. Downclimb to the left or choose an upper pitch.

2. **Through and Through 8+** FA: Andrea Azoff and Mike Brooks, 1987. Begin 200 feet down and left of *Sky King* (i.e., up and left from the top of *Cardinal Richelieu*). Climb a 30-foot pitch through the upper band of rock.

3. **Winnebago Warrior 10a/b S** FA: R. Rossiter and Linda Willing, 1980. Incomplete. Begin at a large tilted block toward the right side of the north face. Climb up and left in a junky, right-facing dihedral and belay on a ledge by a small tree. Work up and right over unprotected rock, up a seam into a pod. . . .

4. **Pleasure Trailer A1** FA: Brooks, Tedli, Delaney, c. 1987. Begin up and left from the top of *Advanced Rockcraft* and aid up a left-angling seam. This begins above where *Winnebago Warrior* leaves off (look for a RURP).

UPPER PEANUTS WALL—NORTHWEST BUTTRESS

This buttress forms the right margin of the north face and features some of the best rock on the crag.

5. **Gravity's Angel 11b** ★ FA: Erik Johnson and Andy Archer, 1987. Rack: QDs, a #1.5 Friend between the first and second bolts. Begin between the leaning block and a detached flake just right of *Winnabago Warrior*. Just right of *Winnbago Warrior* between the leaning block and a detached flake. Climb up and right past 5 bolts. Belay at the large tree on *Heavy Weather*.

6. **Ace of Spades 10** FA: Andy Archer and Eric Johnson, 1988. Rack: include a #2.5 Friend and RPs. Start as for *Gravity's Angel*. Go up and left from the second bolt and through a roof at an apex. Belay at the large tree on *Heavy Weather*.

7. **Advanced Rockcraft 12b VS** ★ FA: Of initial dihedral, Charlie Fowler and Kyle Copeland, 1986; upper section, Bob Horan and Mark Rolofson, 1986. This pitch ascends a beautiful, obtuse, left-facing dihedral, but funky fixed pro has kept traffic to a minimum. Begin just right of a dead tree that leans against a large detached flake. Climb straight up the corner past fixed pins and a bolt to a 2-pin anchor on the right. The crux is above the bolt. Lower off, or continue up the dihedral (10b/c VS) and belay at the big tree as for *Heavy Weather.*

8. **Heavy Weather 9** ★ FA: P1, R. Rossiter and Tim Hogan, 1980; P2, Rossiter and Dave Reidmiller, 1981; P3, (The Upper Wall Route), Layton and Kordell Kor, 1968; P4, *Sky King*, Rossiter and Reidmiller, 1981. Rack: up to a #4 Friend. A varied and interesting route that climbs all the way to the summit ridge in 4 pitches. Begin from a pedestal just right of *Advanced Rockcraft*. P1. Climb a crack system (7) and a short, left-facing dihedral (9), then belay at a large tree. P2. Climb up and left of the tree, up a flip-flop dihedral (9), and left up a ramp to the bottom a steep crack. P3. Jam up the wide crack (8+) and belay on a broad ramp. P4 *Sky King*. Move left to a square cave and climb a left-arching crack to the summit ridge (8+).

9. **Downstairs 6** FA: R. Rossiter and Linda Willing, 1980. Begin in an obtuse, left-facing dihedral just right of *Heavy Weather*. Climb up to a landing in the corner, then up a steep "stairwell" behind and right of a block. Join *Heavy Weather* at the tree belay.

10. **Upstairs 6** FA: Larry Dalke and Bill Chase, 1965. This route is said to ascend the right margin of Upper Peanuts Wall. Its exact location is unknown. It may have begun with *Downstairs* or *Twilight*.

11. **Twilight 7** FA: Linda Willing and R. Rossiter, 1980. Begin 30 feet up and right from *Downstairs*, then climb a left-facing dihedral and a squeeze chimney.

Note: The following three routes are most easily reached by hiking up the primitive trail beneath the west face until it is obvious to cut back left along a ledge system that continues out to the northwest arête. One may also reach this area from *Heavy Weather*.

12. **Northwest Face 12b** FA: Joyce and Richard Rossiter, toproped, 1987. Begin down to the left from *Sunrider*. Climb straight up the vertical wall a bit right of center to finish on a narrow ledge at the top of Sunrider Arête.

13. **Sunrider 11d** ★ FA: Joyce and Richard Rossiter, Karren Kuddes, Dan Hare, 1987. Classic. The sheer northwest arête of the Upper Wall catches the afternoon sun, even in the dead of winter. Begin from the flat ledge at the base of the arête. Climb directly up past a bolt to a stance (9+), make

difficult moves just left of the edge past 2 more bolts (crux), switch to the right side of the arête at the fourth bolt, and continue on the right to a bolt anchor at the top. 5 bolts, 80 feet. A #4 or 5 RP may be used above the first bolt. The crux moves are height-dependent.

14. **Upstairs Dihedral 9 ★** FA: R. Rossiter and Tim Hogan, 1980. Rack: up to a #4 Friend. Climb the offwith, fist, and hand crack up the massive dihedral between *Sunrider* and *The Cruise*. It is possible that this is the upper pitch of *Upstairs*, but the rating (6) is rather far off the mark.

15. **The Cruise 9 ★** FA: R. and J. Rossiter, 1987. Rack: up to a #3 Friend. A nice, steep pitch. Begin just down and right from the ledge at the start to *Sunrider*. Pull over a bulge and jam up a curving hand crack, pull around to the right side of the arête, climb up past a bolt (crux), up and right to a shallow corner, then up and left to the bolt anchor at the top of *Sunrider*.

CONTINENTAL CRAG

Continental Crag is above and south of Upper Peanuts Wall and is easily viewed from the Rattlesnake Gulch Trailhead. Approach from Rattlesnake Gulch Trail. Branch off to the right after about 200 feet at an opening in the trees and hike straight uphill to the right end of the crag via a long talus slope. Hike back left along a ledge system to access the bases of the climbs. The easiest descent is to rappel 80 feet from a horn, as shown in the topos.

CONTINENTAL CRAG FROM THE WEST

CONTINENTAL CRAG

1. **Paradise Lost 9+** FA: Richard and Joyce Rossiter, 1986. Rack: up to #4 Friend. Begin near the northeast end of the crag, behind a tall pine. P1. Climb an easy, right-facing dihedral and traverse left to a belay ledge. P2. Climb a crack up and right (9) then up a wide crack in the middle of a flat, yellow face.

2. **Continental Drift 10d** ★ FA: Richard and Joyce Rossiter, 1986. Rack: up to #4 Friend. Start along the big ledge about 50 feet right of *Paradise Lost*. Climb into a blocky, right-facing dihedral, traverse right beneath a clean slab, then up a thin crack with a pin (crux) to a tiny ledge at the top.

FAR RIGHT BUTTRESS

The obvious promontory at the southwest end of the ridge. Approach by scrambling straight up to the ledge at the base.

3. **Primal Scream 12a** ★ FA: Joyce and Richard Rossiter, 1986. Rack: SR. The best route hereabouts. Flashed on-sight, and the first 12 in Colorado led and established by a woman. Begin near a fallen tree beneath the northwest face of the buttress. Climb the right side of a flake, up and right onto the face, and into a left-arching, left-facing corner. Jam this corner (9) and a finger crack to a stance beneath a small roof. Place RPs here, then move up and right to a jug (crux). Pull into a wide slot and head for the top.

4. **Whymper 9** FA: Richard and Joyce Rossiter, 1986. Rack: SR. Follow *Primal Scream* to the top of the left-facing corner. Move up and right along a crack, climb a few feet of *On-Slot*, then move right and climb a right-facing corner to the top.

5. **On-Slot 11c** ★ FA: Richard and Joyce Rossiter, 1986. Rack: up to #4 Friend. This takes the impressive slot at the right side of the northwest face. Begin as for *Primal Scream*. Climb up and right in a left-facing dihedral to a prominent, overhanging, flared slot. Crank past a bolt (crux), and gain the top of the slot. Good jams (10b) lead to a 10a off-width section. Belay on a ledge with a bolt just below the summit.

6. **View through a Cracked Lens 11d (not pictured)** FA: Stuart and Bret Ruckman. Rack: SR. This route is located on an isolated feature 200 feet north (east side) of Tunnel Eight and above Continental Crag. Tunnel Six runs through the bottom of Mickey Mouse Wall. 3 bolts and 1 pin on a south-facing, overhanging wall. 65 feet.

SUPREMACY ROCK

This popular outcrop is located beside the road just before it crosses South Boulder Creek. The rock is part of the Quartzite Ridge, which reappears across the creek, then angles up the hill toward the West Ridge, intersecting with it near *Positively Fourth Street*. Supremacy Rock, thought to be a precambrian beach, is the only bit of quartzite in the park with worthy climbing. The routes here are very good, and the rock an interesting change from the sandstone. There is little friction, and gear is usually sparse. The slab routes are low-angle and slippery, and are most often toproped. Descent is usually from bolts at the summit.

To the southeast of Supremacy Rock, the quartzite continues as Cartoon Crag, though more shattered and vegetated. At least a dozen routes have been done here, mostly involving Jim Stuberg, and usually around 7 or 8 in difficulty. Interested parties are referred to Ament and McCarty's *High Over Boulder*.

UPPER NORTH FACE

1. **Northeast Arête 7 S ★** FA: Unknown. Climb the clean 80-foot arête to the summit.

2. **Supremacy Slab 9+ S ★** FA: Unknown. Begin at the bottom of the upper north-facing slab, just left of a fir tree. Angle up and left along a slippery, shallow groove, then up and right to the arête. The route is usually toproped. **Variations:** Harder variations can be found to left and right of the main line.

3. **Overhanging Arête 9+ VS** FA: Pete Cleveland, Pat Ament, 1966. Climb the steep face just left of the west arête of the summit block.

THE PYRAMID

This is the lower, more westerly buttress, right by the road. There is no fixed anchor on top, but there ought to be. Meanwhile, a large Douglas-fir tree 15 feet south of the summit can be used to set a toprope.

4. **Simple Simon Slab 6 S ★** FA: Unknown. Climb a crack up the middle of the north face of The Pyramid.

5. **Northwest Arête 8+ VS** FA: Pat Ament, 1967. Climb the right edge of the north face of The Pyramid.

6. **West Face 10a/b VS ★** FA: Pat Ament, 1967. Climb the narrow, triangular face right of *Northwest Arête*.

SOUTHWEST FACE

This very steep face is just round the corner from *Overhanging Arête*.

7. **Cold War 12c** FA: JB Tribout. Bolts just left of *The Web*.

8. **The Web 13b ★** FA: Chris Hill, Christian Griffith, 1987. Up the obvious, steep bolt line.

SUPREMACY ROCK—NORTHWEST FACE

9. **Supremacy Crack 11b ★** FA: Pat Ament, toproped, 1965; Led, Pat Ament, 1966. An Eldorado classic, and one of the first 11s established in the country. Short, but very strenuous. Up the obvious handcrack to a tricky finish.

QUARTZITE CRAG

On the north side of the creek, the quartzite reappears. It is shattered and loose and lacking in definite lines. One of the better routes (*Nerves of Steel*, 9) was done in the 1960s by Larry Dalke. This starts where the hillside meets the creekbed, heads for the obvious, right-facing dihedral above, and traverses out right at its top. A handful more routes was done in the early 1980s by Carl Harrison and Jim Stuberg. Interested parties are referred to Ament and McCarty's *High Over Boulder*.

BOULDER MOUNTAIN SOUTH RIDGE AND ELDORADO CANYON FROM THE WEST

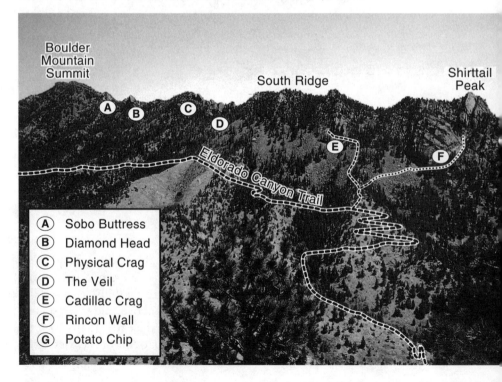

Boulder Mountain Summit

South Ridge

Shirttail Peak

Eldorado Canyon Trail

- Ⓐ Sobo Buttress
- Ⓑ Diamond Head
- Ⓒ Physical Crag
- Ⓓ The Veil
- Ⓔ Cadillac Crag
- Ⓕ Rincon Wall
- Ⓖ Potato Chip

SOUTH RIDGE AREA

SOBO BUTTRESS

SOuth BOulder Peak Buttress. One mile north of Rincon Wall and 0.1 mile north of Diamond Head is a steep, south-facing buttress, characterized by two steep cracks on either side of a narrow, nose-like flake. Both cracks are good climbs. Approach via The Eldorado Canyon Trail and hike cross-country to the northeast, where the trail crosses a tiny stream in North Draw. Otherwise, hike Shadow Canyon Trail about 0.2 mile past a cabin at a spring to a point roughly beneath Jamcrack Spire, break off to the northwest, and scramble up a broad vale of house-sized boulders directly to the base of Sobo Buttress. This broad gully is called Chaos Canyon after its big sister in Rocky Mountain National Park.

(E)	Cadillac Crag
(F)	Rincon Wall
(G)	Potato Chip
(H)	The West Ridge
(RP)	Rincon Parking

SOBO BUTTRESS

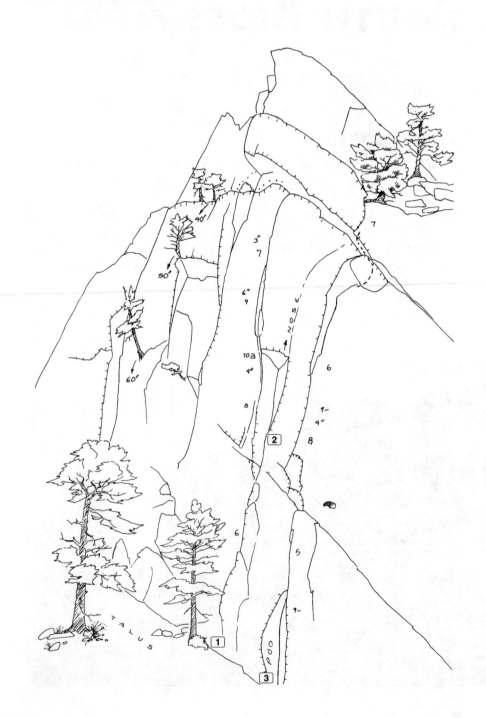

1. **Cruisin' for Bulgar 10a** ★ FA: Tim Hogan and Richard Rossiter, 1981. Rack: up to a #4 Friend. Begin behind a tree about 10 feet left of *Good Cleavage* and climb the obvious crack up past the left side of the "nose." Descend as for *Good Cleavage*.

2. **Sick and Wrong 10c S-** ★ FA: Tony Bubb and Mark Spieker, 1999. Rack: up to a #4 Camalot. Begin as for *Cruisin' for Bulgar*, then break right and follow a crack through a roof.

3. **Good Cleavage 9** ★ FA: Richard Rossiter and Tim Hogan, 1981. Rack: up to a #4 Friend. Just right of the obvious "nose" is a wide crack in a right-facing dihedral. Climb a "pod" and crack (9-) up to the bottom of the dihedral and belay. Lieback or jam the 4-inch crack (9-), climb to the top of the dihedral, up over a short bulge (7), and belay by an ancient tree. To descend, scramble to the north and rappel from trees as shown in the topo.

DIAMOND HEAD

Just under a mile north from Rincon Wall is a large pyramidal spire called Diamond Head. It is easily seen to the north of The Veil, and is characterized by a smooth, southwest-facing summit slab and a broad, overhanging wall along the lower west face. Approach via The Eldorado Canyon Trail and hike cross-country to the northeast from the stream crossing in North Draw. Alternatively, hike up Chaos Canyon as described for Sobo Buttress and cut back to the south

DIAMOND HEAD FROM THE WEST

DIAMOND HEAD

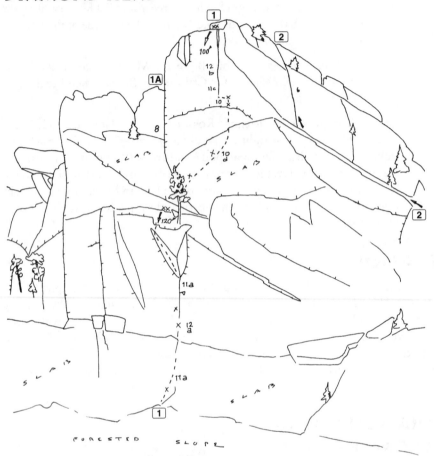

once on the west side of the ridge. To descend from the summit, downclimb to the south, then west, or rappel from bolts 100 feet west to a ledge, and again from bolts, 120 feet to the ground.

1. **Shibumi 12b** ★ FA (P2): Bill Gibson and Marco Cornacchione, à vue, 1988. FA (P1): Bret Ruckman, Bill Gibson, Marco Cornacchione, 1989. Rack: up to a #3 Friend with extra small- to mid-size Rocks, 8 QDs. Double ropes. Begin from the summit and rappel 100 feet west to a ledge with a pine tree and a 2-bolt anchor. A second 120-foot rappel reaches the base. One may also walk to the base from the west. P1. Climb up a 30-foot slab past 2 bolts (11a). Pass over a roof, then clip two more bolts (12a) and a fixed pin (11a) in a seam. Head up and left (10a) under a roof to the large ledge with the bolt anchor. P2. Climb up into the bottom of a dihedral, up to a bolt on the right (10), right past

another bolt, up and left at a flake and two pitons, then up a very steep and very thin finger crack to the summit (crux). **Variation A:** The dihedral continues to the top (8).

2. **Let it Rock 6** FA: R. Rossiter, solo, 1980. Begin at the lower south end of the summit slab. Angle up and left along a band of brown rock, then climb the higher of two thin cracks up and right to the summit.

SPLIT BLOCK

Immediately northwest of Physical Crag is a small, west-facing buttress that is split by an obvious hand crack (*Ohmer's Odyssey*).

1. **Perry Meson 8 ★** FA: Chuck Fitch, solo, 1980. Follow cracks and flakes up the left side of the wall.

2. **Nuts and Volts 10b S ★** FA: Alan Nelson, Alan Bartlett. Follow 4 bolts up the face between *Perry Meson* and *Ohmer's Odyssey*. Runout to second bolt.

3. **Ohmer's Odyssey 9 ★** FA: Alec Sharp, solo, 1980. Crank over a small roof and climb the excellent hand crack that splits the block.

4. **Ah Wish Anode the Real Name 10b S ★** Three bolts up face. Crux before first bolt.

5. **Escergot 7** FA: Alec Sharp, solo, 1980. Begin toward the right side of the buttress. Climb in from the left and jam a crack through a bulge, then up to the top via flakes.

SPLIT BLOCK AND PHYSICAL CRAG FROM THE WEST

SPLIT BLOCK AND PHYSICAL CRAG FROM THE WEST

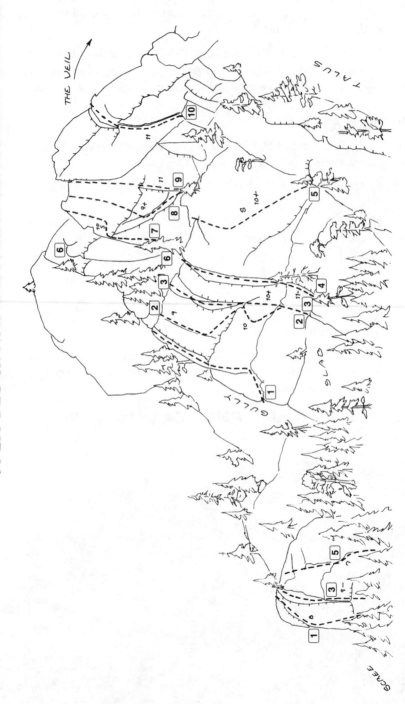

PHYSICAL CRAG

Just north from The Veil is a compact, bulky crag. It has a massive overhang at its right side that is split by a black offwidth crack. Down to the northwest of Physical Crag is the smaller but interesting Split Block. Approach as for The Veil via The Eldorado Canyon Trail. Hike until directly beneath the objective, then cut straight up the slope to the bottom of the crag. To descend from the routes, scramble off to either side or rappel from trees.

The first five routes are on the lower tier of rock.

1. **Watts for Supper? 10b/c** FA: Fitch and Sharp, 1980. Begin at the left side of the lower tier. From a ledge, climb up and right, then power straight up the right of two left-facing dihedrals. **Variation:** The climb becomes 8 by climbing out to the left of the crux dihedral.

2. **Quark of Nature 10b/c S** FA: Sharp and Fitch, 1980. Climb out left around the initial bulge on *Earthquark*, then back right to the optional belay. Traverse left across the wall to a crack and up to the top of the wall.

3. **Earthquark 10d S** FA: Sharp and Fitch, 1980. Begin near the center of the wall. Ascend a bulge with a thin crack and flake (10d), then continue up a slot to the top of the wall. There is an optional belay at the base of the slot.

4. **Fission Chips 11b ★** FA: Sharp and Fitch, 1980. Climb the crack and right-facing dihedral at the left margin of the slab with *Hertz of Gold*.

5. **Hertz of Gold 10d S ★** FA: Fitch and Sharp, 1980. Begin at the right side of the wall and make a rising traverse up to the left. The crux is near the middle of the slab.

The next five routes are on the upper tier of the crag.

6. **Pole Vault 9 ★** FA: Alec Sharp, solo, 1980. Begin to the left of *Ohm on the Range*. Climb a large, low-angled, left-facing dihedral with the crux at the bottom.

7. **Ohm on the Range 10b/c S ★** FA: Fitch and Sharp, 1980. Begin behind a large tree to the left of *Dyne and Dash*. Climb a left-facing dihedral to a flake crack, traverse right to a large foothold in dramatic position, and move upward (crux S) to easier ground.

8. **Dyne and Dash 9+** FA: Fitch and Sharp, 1980. Make a long reach and climb left-leaning grooves to the slab above.

9. **Crown Joules 11b/c ★** FA: Alec Sharp and Chuck Fitch, 1980. Begin at a large flake to the left of *Bacon and Ergs*. Climb a slightly overhanging, right-facing dihedral from a wide crack.

10. **Bacon and Ergs 11b/c ★** FA: Alec Sharp, 1980. This is quite an impressive line. Climb the offwidth crack through the huge roof at the right side of the crag.

THE VEIL FROM THE WEST

THE VEIL

About 500 yards north of Rincon Wall is a broad, serrated crag with a smooth slab at its center. Though the approach is arduous, The Veil presents provocative views of the Front Range and has several excellent routes. Alec Sharp, with a couple of different partners, visited the crag between 1980 and 1982 and made very bold leads of the most obvious lines.

Approach: Approach The Veil from The Eldorado Canyon Trail. Do not take The Rincon Trail, but continue on the main trail to a high point above an old burn. From here The Veil is visible to the northeast. Continue north until due west of the objective and hike cross-country to the bottom of the wall. To descend from the summit ridge, scramble off to the north or south (Class 4) or rappel from trees. From the top of The Veil Slab, rappel west from the belay anchor, 150 feet to a tree, then 75 feet to the ground.

1. **Wanderlust 6 ★** FA: Alec Sharp and Chuck Fitch, 1980. Variation: Tony Bubb and Mark Spieker, 1996. Begin directly beneath The Veil Slab. Climb an easy slab and a square chimney, up and left in a crack, up a left-facing dihedral, and belay beneath the bottom left corner of The Veil Slab. Move left and climb the large, left-facing dihedral at the left side of the slab. **Variation:** Near the top of the route, climb an offwidth crack through a roof on the left (9+).

2. **Way Honed and Gnarly 11b/c VS ★** FA: Alec Sharp with Howard Carter, 1982. This is the bold route on The Veil. This continuously difficult pitch was led using skyhooks for "protection." Begin with *Forever* and climb the left side of The Veil Slab about 8 feet in from the left margin.

THE VEIL

3. **The Flat Earth 11a** ★ FA: Richard and Joyce Rossiter, toproped, 1989. Begin with *Forever* and climb the center of The Veil Slab between that route and the following.

4. **Forever 10c VS** ★ FA: Sharp and Fitch, 1981. An exquisite line. Begin directly beneath The Veil Slab. P1. Climb an easy slab and a square chimney, then belay in a crack. P2. Move up and right and climb small, right-facing dihedrals (10b/c), up and over a bulge (9+ S), then traverse right along the bottom of The Veil Slab to a "piton and nut" belay. P3. Climb the slab past a "pocket break" and up to the top (crux VS).

5. **Kindness 9+ VS** ★ FA: Chuck Fitch and Alec Sharp, 1980. To the left of the steep slab of *Silver Threads*, climb a corner and belay on a slab beneath a groove. Climb the groove, then go up and right over a bulge to a belay (9). Work up and left to the edge of The Veil Slab and up its right margin (9+ VS).

6. **Silver Threads 8 S** ★ FA: Dan Hare and Katy Cassidy, 1982. Begin just left of *Zabrina*. Climb the slab and a shallow, right-facing dihedral with a tree to a ledge and belay tree (8 S). Work directly up the face via a thin, steep crack to another ledge with a ponderosa pine.

7. **West Arête 11c** ★ FA: Richard and Joyce Rossiter, toproped, 1989. This route climbs the west arête of Veil Spire on steep, beautiful rock.

8. **Zabrina 9+ or 10b/c S** ★ FA: Mark Rolofson and Alfredo Len, 1980. This was the first route on The Veil. Begin directly beneath Veil Spire. Climb a steep slab past a bolt (10b/c), up to a ledge beneath an overhang and belay. Climb a crack on the right (9+), then follow a crack and shallow dihedral (8) up the right side of the arête and belay on a ledge. Climb easily to the summit. **Variation:** The crux may be avoided by climbing a crack to the right (7).

CADILLAC CRAG

Four hundred feet north-northwest from Rincon Wall stand four dramatic fins of rock. The arêtes are extremely narrow with steep, clean faces to either side. The second fin is the tallest, with its arête rising 180 feet above the talus.

Approach: Take The Eldorado Canyon Trail and The Rincon Cutoff. Shortly before reaching the talus field across from Rincon, branch left and follow a footpath a little farther up the ridge to the north. After about 200 feet, enter a broad talus field and hike straight up the fall line. Pass between two tall dead trees, then contour north on a footpath to the base of the crag. Please avoid thrashing up and down the loose talus slope nearer the crag. One may also reach Cadillac Crag via a path that leads up and left from the north end of Rincon Wall.

The fins are named One, Two, Three, and Four, from right to left, as in the previous guide. The descents vary and are described separately for each fin.

CADILLAC CRAG FROM THE WEST

CADILLAC CRAG FROM THE NORTHWEST

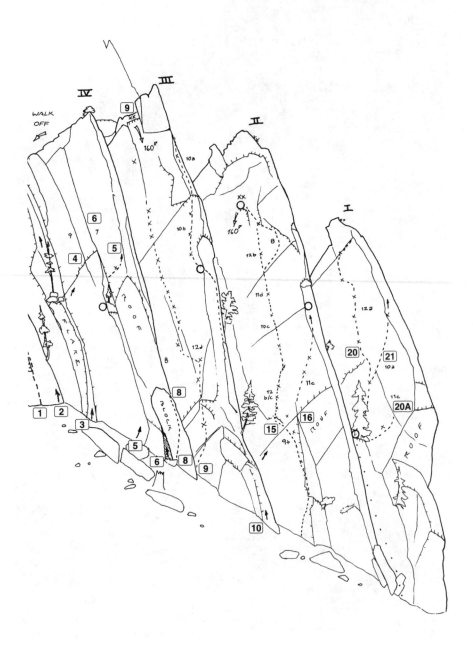

Note: Cadillac Crag, and the other cliffs to the north, are not within Eldorado Canyon State Park, but are owned by the City of Boulder Open Space. Placement of bolts is prohibited.

FIN FOUR

This is the farthest left of the four fins and has the easiest walk-off: follow a good ledge to the north, down to the west, then back along the base of the cliff to the southwest. To descend via rappel, use the 2-bolt anchor at the top of *Trail of Tears*.

1. **Shallow Dihedral 11 (?)** FA: Unknown. On the short wall to the left of Fin Four is a shallow, right-facing dihedral capped by a bulge with a bolt.

2. **Let It Vee 7** FA: David Hague and Ray Reichart, 1981. Climb the dihedral that forms the left margin of the north face of Fin Four. 75 feet.

3. **You're Ugly and Your Mother Dresses You Funny 8 ★** FA: Jim Stuberg and Chip Ruckgaber, 1981. This is the crack system to the left of *Deviant*. Begin at the bottom of the north face. Climb up along a left-leaning flake, past a tree, then up into a hand crack along the right side of a slot. 110 feet.

4. **Deviant 9+ ★** FA: Larry Hamilton, 1975. This climbs the thin crack to the left of P2 of *Gonzo*. Approach from P1 of *Gonzo*, or from the tree of *You're Ugly*. . . .

5. **Emission Control 10d ★** FA: Greg Davis and Dan Hare, 1984. Rack: up to a #2.5 Friend. A good route. Most people start this route with *Gonzo,* but the original line takes the arête on the left (7 S). In either case, belay below the small tree as for *Gonzo*. Climb up just above the tree, go right past a bolt to the arête (crux), and straight up to the top (7 S).

6. **Gonzo 8 ★** FA: Larry Hamilton and Roger Briggs, 1974. This has become one of the classic routes on the crag. Begin at the left side of the big block between Fins Four and Three, arc up and left in the dihedral (8), and belay at a stance below a small tree. Shoot up the wide crack directly above the tree (7).

7. **Heartbreaker 11b ★** FA: Richard and Joyce Rossiter, Elaine Chandler, and Mark Rolofson, 1988. Rack: 8 QDs and a few pieces up to one-half inch to protect the lower part of *V3*. Previously known as *Never Cry Wolf*, a pun on Rob Woolf. This is a fine route up the narrow southwest face. Begin with *V3*, but once above the roof on the left, move out to a bolt in mid-face. Follow a line of bolts to the top of the face. The crux is between the first and third bolts. (8). Some holds have broken off near the third and fourth bolts, extending the crux and making one of the bolts difficult to clip. 7 bolts. Belay from a single bolt on the summit and walk off to the north.

FIN THREE

To descend from the summit, hike off to the north, go down to the west, then back along the base of the cliff, or rappel from the 2-bolt anchor at the top of *Trail of Tears*.

8. **V3 8** ★ FA: John Ruger, Billy Roos, Bob Carmichael, 1972. Rack: up to a #4 Friend. Quality. Climb to the top of the huge block that rests in the trough between Fin Four and Fin Three, then up the steep, clean, V-shaped trough above. Finish up to the right and belay from the 2-bolt anchor at the top of *Trail of Tears*. One may also climb a nice finger crack (9) just left of the mid-section of the dihedral.

9. **Trail of Tears 12d** ★ FA: Larry Harris, 1988. Begin in the alcove between the arête and a fallen block to the north. Climb up and over a bulge and up the arête to a Metolius bolt. Move up and left and follow a line of bolts up the middle of the face to the notch behind the summit. There is a crux at 30 feet and another at 80 feet. 13 bolts to a 2-bolt anchor, 160 feet.

10. **Moonlight Drive 10b** ★ FA: Greg Davis and Dan Hare, 1984. Begin at the same point as the next two routes. P1. Head up a left-facing flake in the middle of the lower south face, then angle up and left beneath a roof to a belay on the arête. P2. Shift around to the left, climb up past 3 bolts (10b), swing back to the right, and drive straight up past another bolt (10a) enroute to the summit.

11. **Star Gate 11d** ★ FA: Richard and Joyce Rossiter, 1989. Rack: up to a #3.5 Friend, QDs. An aesthetic journey up the steep southwest face. P1. Climb the first pitch of *Auburn Lane* (10d) and belay in the cozy niche. P2. Move left onto the main face, work up and left past 3 bolts (11d), pull over a small roof, then up and left past two more bolts (11a). Climb a short crack and the face above (9) to a narrow ramp, up and left along the ramp, up a crack (#3.5 Friend), hand-traverse right (8), and belay in a niche beside the summit. **Variation:** Move right from the fifth bolt (10b) and follow a right-facing dihedral system (9) to the narrow ramp. 6 bolts, no anchor at the top.

12. **Auburn Lane 10d** FA: Mike Brooks and Carl Harrison, 1981. This route climbs a crack that runs all the way up the right side of the southwest face. Begin in the alcove at the bottom of the face. Climb an irregular crack to the left of a tree, then up a vertical finger crack (crux) to a perfect belay niche at the right side of the main face. P2. Continue in a crack in a right-facing corner and surmount a roof via a finger crack (9). Each pitch is about 80 feet long.

CADILLAC CRAG FROM THE WEST

13. **Midnight Trundler 10b** FA: Alec Sharp and Doug Madara, 1980. In the alcove above and between the second and third fins, find a short hand crack through a bulge.

14. **Garbage Pile 1** FA: Unclaimed. This is the messy trough between the second and third fins.

FIN TWO

This, the tallest of the fins, has four fine routes. It is possible to downclimb from the summit over nasty, loose rock and descend to the north or south, but it is much easier to rappel 50 meters down the south face from 2 bolts.

15. **The Black Face 12d** ★ FA: Joyce and Richard Rossiter, 1988. Rack: RPs, #0.5 Friend, and 11 QDs. This route ascends the north side of Fin Two. Begin with the left of two arêtes. Climb up past 2 bolts (10a), and move left into the middle of the face. The formidable crux begins here and continues past 3 bolts. Above this, a reprieve of beautiful 10 face is followed by two more difficult sections (12a) that lead to the alcove formed by the summit overhang. Escape from the top of the face via a thin crack and slot that lead up and right to the arête. 11 bolts, to a 2-bolt anchor, 50 meters. **Variation A:** To start, scramble up the gully and hand-traverse out right to the third bolt. **Variation B:** The difficult moves at the last bolt may be avoided by climbing off to the right.

16. **Brand New Cadillac 11c S** FA: Kirk Peterson and David Houston, 1986. The lower section of the 50-meter west arête begins as two smaller arêtes that climb to meet the lateral points of a unique, diamond-shaped roof. This steep route ascends the left arête to the left corner of the roof (short, one-inch crack here), then swerves up the slightly runout face past 2 bolts to join *Highway of Diamonds* at its belay.

17. **Highway of Diamonds 9+ S** ★ FA: Steve Wunsch, Bob Hritz, Jim Logan, 1973. FA: variation, Ed Webster, early 1980s. Begin in the trough between Fin Two and Fin One, scramble up about 30 feet and hand-traverse out left in a wide crack (#3.5 or #4 Friend). Angle up and left across the face (8 S), up a thin crack into a shallow, left-facing corner, then out left to a belay on the arête. Climb up to a roof, skirt around it on the right (crux), and continue up the arête to the top. **Variation:** Just above the middle of the hand-traverse is a short, left-facing dihedral with a tiny fir tree about halfway up. Climb this, then traverse up and left to the belay on the arête.

18. **Land of Ra 11a** ★ FA: Richard and Joyce Rossiter, 1988. Rack: up to a #1 Friend plus a #3.5 or #4 Friend. This superb and sustained pitch ascends the middle of the south face beginning with the first 40 feet of

Highway of Diamonds. Climb up to a wide crack that angles up to the left. Follow this a few feet, then go straight up on good holds (8 S) to the first bolt. Master a thin face (crux), then climb up and slightly left (10c) to a finger crack (9+) and finish with a bit of steep face. 5 bolts in all to a 2-bolt anchor, 180 feet.

FIN ONE

The first (farthest right) fin forms something of a free-standing tower and has a beautiful, flat-topped summit of solid rock. It is the only one of the four fins that does not offer an easy unroped descent. Rappel 50 meters down the north face or make two shorter rappels utilizing a tree in the gully. **Note:** There is a good, 2-bolt belay anchor on the summit, but without the addition of a long runner, it is difficult to retrieve the rappel ropes. A 2-bolt anchor is needed at the top of *The Untitled*.

19. **First Route 3** Climb the trough between Fin Two and Fin One.

20. **The Untitled 12a** ★ FA: Richard Rossiter, Joyce Rossiter, Jack Roberts, Bret Ruckman, 1988. A beautiful route up the vertical north face. Scramble up to the tree as for *Ichiban Arête*. Climb up to the first bolt of that route, then follow a line of bolts up the middle of the wall to the summit. The crux is in the vicinity of the fifth bolt. 5 bolts, one pin to a 2-bolt anchor, 160 feet from the ground.

20a. **Flash Cadillac 11c/d** FA: Jack Roberts, Bret Ruckman, 1988. A sort of direct start to *The Untitled*. Head right from the tree past a bolt, to a finger crack. Up this to join *The Untitled*.

21. **Ichiban Arête 10b** ★ FA: Richard and Joyce Rossiter, 1988. Scramble up the trough between Fin One and Fin Two to a ledge with a 20-foot Douglas-fir tree and belay. Climb the face behind the tree, past a bolt, out to the arête to another bolt, and go straight up the arête to the summit.

22. **Ghetto Cruiser 7** FA: Kent Taylor, Dave Garland, Steve Deickhoff, 1988. Rack: up to #4 Friend. Climb in from the talus slope on the south side and take a left-facing dihedral up to *Easy Street*.

23. **Easy Street 3** FA: Unknown. The easiest route to the summit. Begin at the southeast corner of the fin and traverse out across the upper south face on a broad ramp to the southwest arête, then straight up to the top.

RINCON WALL

Some of the finest routes in Eldorado, combined with lots of sun, make this a favorite location for a fair winter day . . . or any day. Approach via The Eldorado

RINCON WALL FROM THE SOUTHWEST

RINCON WALL FROM THE WEST

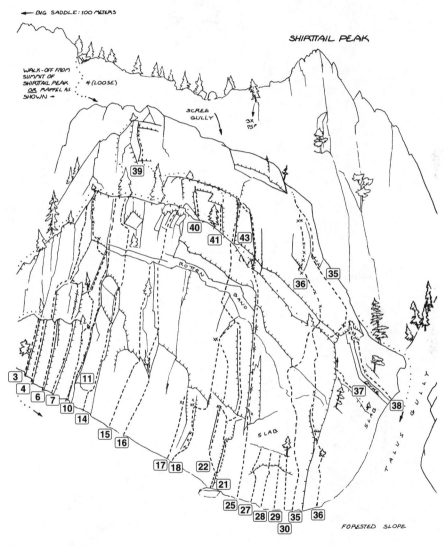

SHIRTTAIL PEAK

← BIG SADDLE : 100 METERS

WALK-OFF FROM
SUMMIT OF
SHIRTTAIL PEAK
OR RAPPEL AS
SHOWN →

4 (LOOSE)

SCREE
GULLY

3X
75'

ROTTEN
BAND

SLAB

SLAB

TALUS GULLY

FORESTED SLOPE

ELDORADO CANYON ·7 KM →

SCENIC ROUTE BUTTRESS

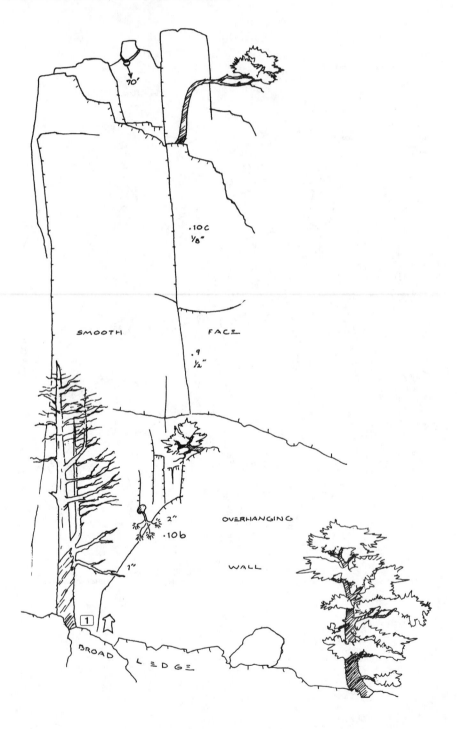

Canyon Trail and The Rincon Cutoff, which lead directly to the bottom of the west face. To descend from the shorter routes, rappel from obvious bolt anchors or trees with slings and rappel rings. Most of the longer routes finish on a broad ledge, high on the wall, that spans nearly the entire crag. Rappel 160 feet from a tree at the south end of this ledge, or walk off to the north. A few routes finish along the summit ridge; to descend from here, scramble north until it is easy to downclimb into the gully between Rincon and Shirttail Peak, then hike down to the south and west. It is also possible to downclimb west from the summit and gain the walk-off ledge. The talus along the upper west side of the wall has been eroded by climbers, destroying plants and exposing tree roots. Please hike on the trail where it exists.

1. **Scenic Route 10c** ★ FA: Richard and Joyce Rossiter, 1986. FA: variation, Peter Hunt and Steve Ilg, toproped, 1986. Rack: up to a #3 Friend. In the upper center of the large broken area just left of Rincon Wall, find a clean, rectangular buttress split by a thin crack. Approach from the north side or from the summit of Rincon Wall and hike to the base along a good ledge. Climb an overhanging, diagonal crack up to the main face (10a), then climb a thin crack and right-facing dihedral up the vertical slab (crux) to a scenic belay niche. Rappel 70 feet back to the ledge. **Variation:** The arête on the left can be climbed by traversing left above the diagonal crack (10d).

OVER THE HILL DIHEDRAL AREA

The northwest side of Rincon Wall is characterized by a series of exceptionally well-formed, left-facing dihedrals and arêtes. These are shady in the morning as they face north and west. To descend from the shorter routes, rappel from trees or bolts. To descend from the top of the wall, walk off to the north along a ledge system.

2. **Kaisho 7** FA: R. Rossiter and Dan Hare, tandem solo, 1987. Easy Victory. Climb the short arête left of *N.I.C.*

3. **N.I.C. 5** ★ FA: Unknown. The Next Inside Corner, that is the fifth from the right, has a tree in it. Short but sweet. Walk off to the left.

4. **Emerald City 9** ★ FA: Ed Webster and Doug White, 1976. Rack: up to 1 inch. This excellent route climbs the fourth left-facing dihedral left of *Aerospace*. Begin from a ledge just above the talus. The crux is about 25 feet up the 75-foot dihedral. This combines well with the upper 9 pitch of *Over the Hill*.

5. **Faulty Logic 10a** ★ FA: Chris Archer and Keith Gotschall, 1987. FA: variation, Chris Archer, Eric Reynolds. Rack: up to 1 inch. This pitch takes the arête between *Emerald City* and *Over and Out*. Begin from the

OVER THE HILL DIHEDRAL AREA DETAIL

ledge at the base of *Emerald City*. Move up and right to the arête and pull around the corner, shoot up the face past 2 bolts (crux), and up a shallow, right-facing dihedral. **Variation:** Toprope the narrow face right of *Faulty Logic*. Start up *Over and Out*, then up the face to the ledge (11b).

6. **Over and Out 8** ★ FA: Duncan Ferguson and Chris Reveley, 1974. Rack: up to a #3 Friend. An under-climbed route of good quality. Climb the nice dihedral left of *Over the Hill* (8) to an incut, hand-traverse left and pull up onto a ledge (optional belay). Climb the very clean corner above via a double crack (6), then move up and right to the big, loose ledge beneath the final pitch of *Over the Hill* and belay. Climb the crack up the middle of the face (9) or the dihedral to the left (8).

7. **Over the Hill 10b** ★ FA: Pat Ament, Jim Erickson, Bill Putnam, 1972. Rack: up to a #2 Friend. One of the all-time classics of Eldorado. Begin at the bottom of the second dihedral from the right, which may be identified by a narrow, detached flake about 10 feet up, and a fixed pin a bit higher. P1. Climb the peerless, left-facing dihedral to a ledge beside a small tree (10a). (Optional belay.) Stem the short but thin crux upper section of the dihedral past three pins (Erickson led this on first ascent with just 1 pin), up a short wall (7), and left to a large belay ledge with loose rock (careful!). P2. Climb the corner at the left and move right, or better, climb angling holds up to the bottom of the beautiful crack that splits the slab. Up this (9) to the top. **Variation:** Scuttle up the dihedral left of P2 (8).

8. **Bachar Yer Aryan 11c/d** ★ FA: Mike Clinton and Bill DeMallie, 1988. Rack: RPs and HBs and QDs. This line zigzags up the lower right side of the flat northwest face to the right of the third pitch of *Over the Hill* and connects with *Aeronaut* at its second bolt. It was intended that people would finish the pitch staying on the left side of the arête, and 2 bolts were placed within arm's reach of the bolts on *Aeronaut* to force the issue. But after the first couple of moves along the arête, it is easier to switch to the right side. The route is otherwise good. Climb up to the bottom of the crack on *Over the Hill* and place a wire, move right and up past a fixed pin, then up and right via exciting moves to the arête.

9. **Aerial Bondage 11c (9 VS)** ★ FA: Chris Archer and Keith Gotschall, 1987. Begin at the bottom of *Aerial Book*. Move up and left across a vertical yellow face (10b/c), clip a bolt, pull up and left onto the arête (crux), straight up (10a) past another bolt at about 60 feet (10d), and on to the belay ledge atop the first pitch of *Over the Hill*. A ground fall is possible before reaching either bolt.

10. **Aerial Book 11a** ★ FA: Pat Ament and Fred Pfahler, 1965. FFA: Wendell Nuss and Michael Gilbert, 1975. Rack: up to 1 inch. Another Rincon

OVER THE HILL DIHEDRAL AREA

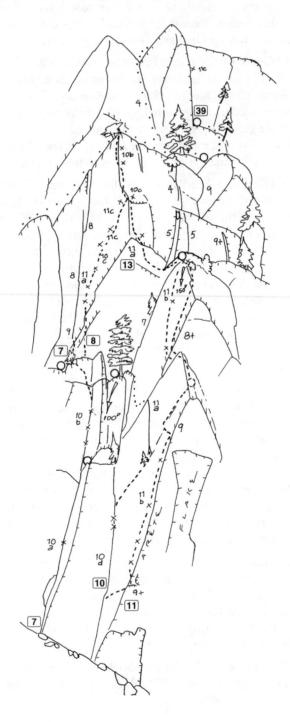

classic. Begin in the farthest right of the dihedrals. P1. Stem (thin) straight up to a piton belay (10d, Crack 'n' Ups and/or tiny RPs). 70 feet. P2. Move up and right past a small tree, jam a peerless fingertip crack (crux) to a diagonal ledge, and up a ramp left to a big tree. Rappel 100 feet to the talus or climb up and right to join *Aeronaut*. One may also traverse left from the tree to *Bachar Yer Aryan* or *Over the Hill*.

11. **Aerospace 11b S ★** FA: Ed Webster, Bill Feiges, and Leonard Coyne, 1979. Classic. One of the finest routes in Eldorado. Begin as for *Aerial Book*. P1. Climb up the corner for about 20 feet, move right beneath a small, thick flake, swing around to the right side of the arête (10b, #9 Stopper), and move up to the first of 4 bolts (9). Make delicate moves up the face and arête (crux) to a stance, climb up past the fourth bolt to a tiny stance on the now overhanging arête (10c), place an RP, move left to a crack, hand traverse up to the arête, and belay. 100 feet. P2. Climb straight up the arête to an overhang, move left and turn the roof (8+), up and right to the arête, and up to a bolt anchor on a ledge. (The first two pitches of *Aerospace* may be combined into one 155-foot lead to the bolt anchor). P3. Climb easy cracks (5) straight up from the belay to the walk-off ledge. **Variation:** From the stance beneath the fourth bolt, the original line traversed right and climbed the left side of a large, over-hanging flake (9+), then regained the arête higher up.

12. **Aerohead 11b ★** FA: Bill Gibson and Stephen DeWet, 1988. A direct finish to *Aerospace*. From the roof on P2, climb the center of the face past 2 bolts.

13. **Aeronaut 11b ★** FA: Richard and Joyce Rossiter, 1987. A continuation of *Aerospace*. Begin from the bolt anchor atop P2. Traverse left on a sloping ramp, crank over a roof at a bolt (crux) and climb the exposed arête past 3 more bolts and two 10 sections to the walk-off ledge.

14. **Windy 11a/b S ★** FA: John Behrens and Rob Culbertson, 1969. FFA: Reveley, Higbee, Erickson, 1974. FA: variation, Erickson and Reveley, 1974. Rack: include some large cams/BigBros for the crux. This route covers some beautiful terrain to the right of *Aerospace*, but sees little action. Begin just right of the arête of *Aerospace*. P1. Climb in from the side (easy) or climb the west face of a large block (9 S) and belay. P2. Crank up into a steep, left-facing dihedral (11a/b S) and belay at the bottom of a chimney. It is perhaps better to combine P1 and P2. P3. Climb the chimney (9), up a dihedral, and belay up and right of a large roof. P4. Climb straight up the wall and shallow corner to a big ledge (10a). Climb a shallow, left-facing dihedral (10a S), left under a roof, and lieback around a bulge (8). **Variation:** Climb a right-facing dihedral formed by the right side of the block at the bottom (9+).

Climb of the Century *(5.11c)*, *Rincon Wall.* RICHARD ROSSITER PHOTO

15. **Trident 10b/c S** FA: Chris Reveley and Greg Davis, 1974. A lonely route. Begin a few feet right of the preceding route. P1. Climb a shallow, funky, left-facing dihedral (9), left into another one, jam a crack through a roof (9), up a wall, and belay in a gully. P2. Climb up the gully, under a cool chockstone, and belay on a big ledge beneath a roof with three cracks. Climb one of the cracks (crux).

16. **Variation V 10b/c S** FA: Chris Reveley and Bill Briggs, 1974. Some loose rock here. Begin about 30 feet(?) left of *Wendego*. P1. Climb a hazardous-looking, left-facing dihedral up to a large, V-shaped gully with a small tree. P2. Just above the tree, climb a crack up to the right (9), and up a dihedral to a good ledge beneath an overhang with three cracks. P3. Climb one of the cracks (10b/c) through the roof to the walk-off ledge.

17. **Climb of the Century 11c S ★** FA: Alec Sharp, Casey Newman, Jeff Butterfield, 1980. Free Solo: Derek Hersey. Begin a few feet left of *Wendego*. Work up onto a small pedestal, past a pin, (crux), then power straight up the overhanging, left-facing dihedral, to a 2-bolt anchor. Lower off (80 feet).

18. **Wendego 12a S ★** FA: Pat Ament and Larry Dalke, 1964. FFA: Jeff Achey, Kevin Bein, Barbara Devine, 1980. Led barefoot by Skip Guerin. Rack: up to a #2 Friend. Classic. Beautiful first pitch, protected by some old upward-driven pins. Begin beneath a massive, overhanging, left-facing dihedral that leads to a vertical, left-facing dihedral. The right wall of the dihedral is covered by smeared chalk. P1. Climb up a short corner, clip the first of three disheartening pitons, and start a series of very thin moves up the dihedral (medium Friend below top pin). Crank around the right end (11c), and climb straight up (10d) to a 2-bolt anchor. Lower off (70 feet) or continue. P2. Traverse 8 feet right to a crack, climb up through a bulge (10d), and on up to a bolt anchor. Rappel 150 feet to the ground or climb the last pitch of *Center Route* to the walk-off ledge.

19. **Surf's Up A2 (or free?) ★** FA: Charlie Fowler and Patrick Meek, 1986. Rack: SR plus LAs and KBs. Begin with the first 15 feet of *Aid Line*, then crank left toward a bolt above a jug. Turn the left side of the roof (12c/d), climb a double crack (9), and move left to the anchor on *Wendego*. Rappel or climb upper *Wendego* (10d). This pitch may have been freed by Fowler.

20. **Aid Line 9+ A3 ★** FA: Ron Olevsky, 1970s. FFA: of second pitch, Chris Reveley, 1976. Begin at an overhanging, left-facing dihedral about 12 feet left of *Center Route*. Climb straight up on aid to a pin or bolt. Where the crack fizzles out, move up and right past a bolt, then climb a right-facing dihedral (*Evictor*) to the bolt belay. P2. Climb the bulge

RINCON WALL—LOWER SOUTHWEST FACE

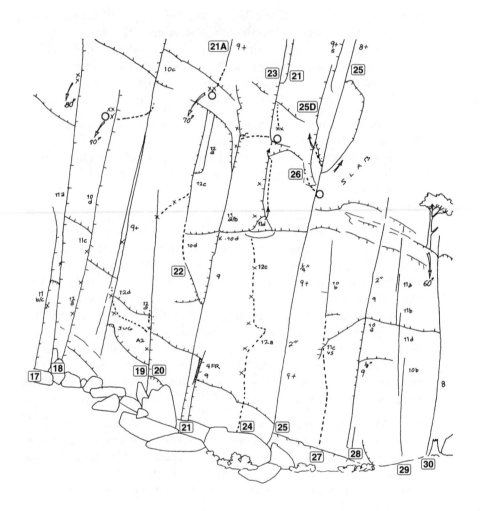

Richard Rossiter on the Center Route *(5.11a/b), Rincon Wall.* GREG EPPERSON PHOTO—ROSSITER COLLECTION

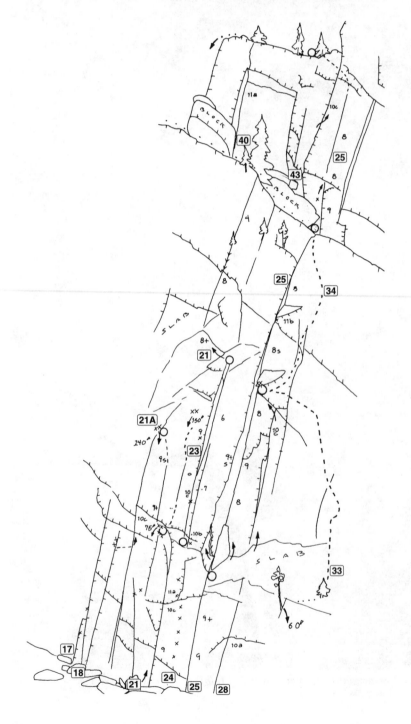

(10a) and thin crack directly above the belay and veer left to upper *Wendego* or right to the 2-bolt anchor on *Arête Bandits* (9 S). P2 is also listed as a variation (21A) to *Center Route*.

21. **Center Route 11a/b** ★ FA: Larry and Roger Dalke, 1965; FFA: Chris Revely, Scott Woodruff, Dan Hare, 1976. Rack: up to a #4 Friend. Classic. P1 is great and popular, but the upper section and its variations are also good. Begin atop a large, flat boulder beneath a flip-flop dihedral about 20 feet left of *Rincon*. P1. Climb over a roof (9), up the dihedral to another roof. Power up the strenuous crux crack, then go left at the top to a bolt anchor and lower 70 feet. To continue, move right to belay beneath a right-facing dihedral. P2. Climb a thin crack over a bulge (10b) and up a right-facing dihedral for about 100 feet. P3. Angle up to the left on a steep, south-facing wall (8+), straight up for 25 feet, through a roof at a V-slot (8), and up the face on the left to a belay along the walk-off ledge.

21a. **The Olevsky Variation 10a** FA: Ron Olevsky. FFA: Chris Reveley, 1976. Climb the bulge and thin crack above the bolt belay up to the left from the first pitch.

22. **Evictor 12c/d S** ★ FA: R. Olevsky; FFA: Dale Goddard, 1986. Rack: up to a #2 Friend. Classic. A very strenuous and difficult lead. Climb the first 25 feet of *Center Route* to a downward-pointing flake, angle up and left into a thin crack and shallow, right-facing dihedral, then power up to the 2-bolt anchor on *Center Route*. Rappel or lower off, 70 feet.

23. **Arête Bandits 10d S** ★ FA: Toproped by R. and J. Rossiter, 1986; led by Bill DeMallie and Mike Clinton, 1988(?). This pitch parallels the second pitch of *Center Route* a few feet to the left. Climb the bulge (10b) at the start of the second pitch, then pick up a thin crack, just left of the shallow, right-facing dihedral. Continue upward past a piton (crux) to a horizontal break, step down and left, then climb straight up the arête of the upper right-facing dihedral, past a bolt, to a 2-bolt anchor (9 S). Rappel 150 feet to the base of the first pitch of *Rincon*, or climb the third pitch of *Center Route* and walk off to the north.

24. **Camouflage 12c** ★ FA: Dan Michael, Bill Meyers, and Paul Piana, 1987. Rack: 9 QDs. High quality. Takes the thin face between *Center Route* and *Rincon*. Pull an overhang, then follow a line of bolts up the face, over a roof, and up an arête to a 2-bolt anchor. Very thin and sustained.

SOUTHWEST FACE

The southwest side of Rincon Wall is offset by a massive, 200-foot, right-facing dihedral that is home to the original line on the crag, named *Rincon*. To the right of *Rincon*, above a once grassy alcove, is a short wall with a series of very popular cracks.

25. **Rincon 11a/b** ★ FA: Layton Kor and Jack Turner, 1962. FFA: Jim Erickson and Dave Meyers, 1969. FA: of P4, Richard and Joyce Rossiter, 1986. Rack: up to a #3 Friend. Classic line, very sunny, excellent rock. Four pitches with direct finish. P1. Begin at the left side of the alcove and climb a clean finger and hand crack straight up to the base of the massive, right-facing dihedral (9+). P2. Climb up the corner or around the right side of a flake and up the right-facing dihedral for about 100 feet to a belay from bolts in a brown band (9). P3. Stem up the steep, right-facing dihedral with little protection and increasing difficulty, clip a lone piton at the lip of the overhang, and crank onto a slab (crux). Continue up the corner for another 30 feet and belay at a tree on the left. Cross the walk-off ledge and belay beneath a huge boulder (or walk off to the south). P4. Climb a steep, shallow, left-facing dihedral past a bolt (9), turn the roof (8), up the beautiful slab via a finger crack (8), and left at the top to belay on a big ledge.

25a. **Briggs Variation 10c S** FA: Roger and Bill Briggs, 1973. Climb the right-facing dihedral just right of P2 of *Rincon* and make a difficult traverse back left to the piton belay (10c S).

25b. **Reveley-Hunter 10** FA: Chris Reveley and Diana Hunter, 1975. Begin with the *Briggs Variation*, then hand-traverse left, pull over a roof, and climb a finger crack (10).

25c. **Reveley-Adams 10** FA: Chris Reveley and Bruce Adams, 1974. From the top of P1 of *Rincon*, make a dramatic hand traverse out left and mantel up to join the second pitch of *Center Route* (10).

25d. **On the Crest 11b/c** ★ FA: Skip Guerin and Rufus Miller, c. 1980. Excellent. Begins from the top of P1 of *Rincon*. From the belay, climb up and left across the left wall of the dihedral via short corners (11b/c), then up the arête (9+ S), and back right to the regular piton belay.

26. **No 'Arm in It 10d S** ★ FA: Pieced together by Alec Sharp and Casey Newman, 1980. A pretty weird route. P1. Climb the first pitch of *Rincon* (9+). P2 Traverse left to the top of P1 of *Center Route* (10). P3. Move down and traverse left to the top of first pitch of *Wendego* (10), turn the overhang, angle up and left to gain a crack, and belay. P4. Climb a left-facing dihedral and finish with *Trident* (10) or *Windy* (9).

27. **Mind over Matter 11c S/VS** ★ FA: Toproped by Jim and Dan Michael, 1979; led by Ed Webster, 1983. Begin between *Rincon* and *Five-Ten Crack*. Angle up and left to the left side of an arching roof, gain a thin crack, and climb to the ledge.

28. **Five-Ten Crack 10a** ★ FA: Roger and Bill Briggs, 1973. Rack: wires and a #3 Friend. Nice. Begin with a short 2-inch crack, up a shallow, right-facing dihedral, pull over a roof (crux), and up a fine finger crack to a ledge.

Andy Donson on Camouflage *(5.12c), Rincon Wall.* STEVE BARTLETT PHOTO

29. **Thunderbolt 11d S/VS** ★ FA: Ken Duncan and Scott Blunk, 1977. Climb discontinuous thin cracks and face to finish a few feet left of the rappel tree. Often toproped. A.k.a. *Raccoon Soup.*

30. **Five-Eight Crack 8+** ★ FA: Bob Culp and Bob LaGrange, 1962. Climb the crack that finishes just right of the rappel tree (slings).

31. **Outer Limbits 11b** FA: Bill DeMallie and Mike Clinton, 1988. Climb the face directly behind the large pine tree to the right of the 8 crack. Sling the tree for protection.

32. **Neato 8** FA: Jim Stuberg and Mike Brooks, 1980. Climb the first crack left of *Rinodina* to a tree.

SOUTHWEST ARÊTE

33. **White Death 10a S** FA: Derek Hersey, Barry Brolley, 1990. Start from the tree atop *Five-Eight Crack*. Climb the face above, then the face just right of a vertical crack, keeping left of *Rinodina*. Angle left along the rotten band into *Rincon* at the belay below the crux.

34. **Rincon Dink 10 S** FA: Derek Hersey. Start at the belay below the crux of *Rincon*. Move out right, then up the face above (see topo) to rejoin *Rincon* at the big ledge.

35. **Rinodina 9 S** ★ FA: George Hurley and Bob Culp, 1965. FFA: of both finishes, Jim Erickson and Jim Walsh, 1970. Rack: up to a #4 Friend. Begin about 20 feet left of *Point Break*, just left of a black-lichened, right-facing dihedral. P1. Scramble up an easy crack for 100 feet and belay beneath a rotten band. P2. Climb through the band (7), then angle up and right to the tree at the south end of the walk-off ledge. P3. Move down the ledge about 25 feet to the south, pull over a bulge (8 S), climb the south edge of the great slab past a bolt, then up to a belay ledge. P4. Angle left toward the bottom of the overhanging prow, then climb a right-facing dihedral (9) to the 2-bolt anchor on *Point Break*. **Variation:** The original route continued left beneath the prow (9) and climbed a grungy crack up to the final slab.

36. **Point Break 11a** ★ FA: Richard and Joyce Rossiter, 1986. Rack: up to a #2 Friend. Classic. Begin about 15 right of a lichenous, right-facing di-hedral, just where the wall begins to curve up to the east. P1. Climb a slab up over a bulge (6) and belay from a 2-bolt anchor near a small tree. P2. Power up a strenuous, overhanging, right-facing dihedral past a bolt and fixed pin (10d), up a bulging, black wall past 2 more bolts (10c), up a slab, and belay at a tree at the south end of the walk-off ledge. P3. Step right and pull over the roof (8+), then climb straight up the clean slab

RINCON WALL—SOUTH FACE

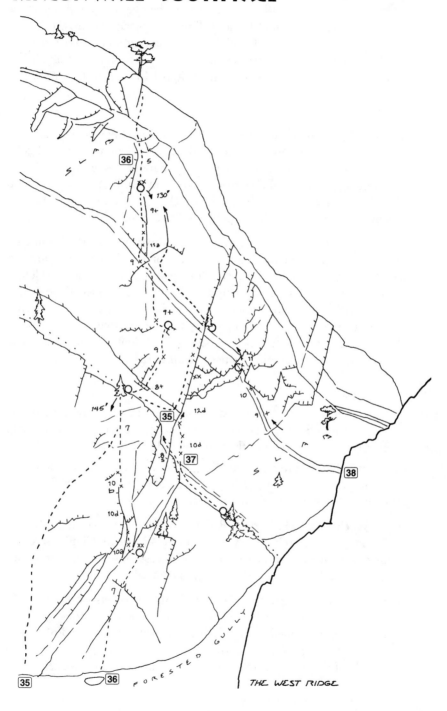

past a bolt (9) to a belay at a left-facing flake. P4. Move left and clip a bolt, climb straight up (9+) to the base of the overhanging prow, move left, crank over the roof (10c), and climb straight up the prow (crux) to a 2-bolt anchor on a slab. Climb a shallow corner and slab (6) to a tree on the summit ridge. Otherwise, rappel 130 feet from the 2-bolt anchor to the tree on the walk-off ledge, then rappel 145 feet to the ground.

SOUTH FACE

37. **(Another) Pipeline Bone Crusher 12c ★** FA: Joe Huggins and partners, 1986. From the southwest corner of Rincon, hike up the forested gully between the West Ridge and Rincon Wall for about 100 feet and scramble left up a grassy ramp. Belay from a tree and climb up a knobby (and slightly loose) wall past 3 bolts, then tackle the radical finger crack in the overhanging dihedral. Rappel from fixed gear.

38. **Tsunami 11b/c S/VS** FA: Jim Morrison and partners, c. 1981. Hike up the gully between the West Ridge and Rincon to where a dike slants up across a slab to a double roof. P1. Climb just right of the dike and left of a tree, past a bolt (9), straight up to a flake (10), turn the flake on the left, and belay on a sloping ledge from a fixed pin. P2. Climb the roof above past two pitons (crux), up slabs, and left to a tree in a long corner. The third and fourth pitches are those of *Rinodina* (9). One could also finish with the overhanging arête of *Point Break* (11a).

UPPER CLIFF

The following routes begin from the walk-off ledge between the tops of the *Rincon* dihedral and *Aerospace*. Descend from any of the routes by scrambling off to the north and back down to the walk-off ledge (Class 4).

39. **Brevitata 11c ★** FA: R. and J. Rossiter, 1986. Rack: up to 0.5 inch. Climb the conspicous, yellow, right-facing dihedral up and left from *Bat's Ass Dihedral*. There is a fixed pin at the crux.

40. **Bat's Ass Dihedral 11a/b ★** FA: Rob Candelaria, Pat Adams, Bill Briggs, 1976. Free solo, Derek Hersey. Rack: up to #3 Friend. Climb the steep, right-facing dihedral at the left side of the recess, power over a strenuous bulge (crux), then up and left through a roof (also hard).

41. **Kangaroo Tail 9 S ★** FA: Scott Woodruff and Chris Peisker, 1978. Rack: up to 2 inches. To the left of *Ventura Highway*, a 60-foot-high, box-shaped recess is formed by two facing dihedrals at either end of a roof. Make difficult moves to get started, climb the left-facing dihedral at the right side of the recess, crank over a roof, and up to a big ledge.

42. **Cuban Bluegrass 12b S** ★ FA: Steve Levin, Bruce Miller, 1999. Rack: up to #2.5 Friend, heavy on the smaller Aliens/TCUs/RPs. Climb straight up into the tight, right-facing corner between *Kangaroo Tail* and *Ventura Highway*. The thin crux is encountered shortly after gaining the dihedral. ~

43. **Ventura Highway 10c** ★ FA: R. and J. Rossiter, 1986. Rack: up to a #2 Friend. This ascends a black flip-flop dihedral about 20 feet left of the *Direct Finish* to *Rincon*. Climb easily up the left-facing dihedral, swing around to the right side as it changes face, climb the smooth corner (10c), crank over a roof (9, #2 Friend), and up left to a big ledge.

SHIRTTAIL PEAK

To the north of The Potato Chip, and up and east from Rincon Wall, towers Shirttail Peak. It is the highest point within Eldorado Canyon State Park. The summit, with its 360-degree vista, is a worthy objective by any of its routes. The peak has an expansive, flat, southwest face and two steep, west-facing arêtes. Tiger Balm Buttress, the more northerly, leads straight to the summit, while the Giuoco Piano Arête climbs to the right of the southwest face and terminates at a secondary (false) summit. Approach all routes via The Rincon Trail and the forested talus gully between Rincon Wall and the North Buttress of the West Ridge.

Descent: To descend from the summit, scramble north to a large fir tree about 20 feet below the ridgecrest on the west side and make three 75-foot rappels to the gully between Shirttail Peak and the summit ridge of Rincon Wall. Be careful of loose rock. Alternatively, scramble north to a rotten, red buttress, just east of the ridgecrest, downclimb to the west (loose Class 4), then down the gully to the base of the crag. The safest descent is to scramble north along the crest about 200 yards to the broad saddle between and above Cadillac Crag and Rincon Wall, and hike easily back to the base of Rincon. This is most practical if you do not leave gear at the bottom of your route on Shirttail.

TIGER BALM BUTTRESS

The first two pitches of *Tiger Balm Arête* ascend a steep, blunt buttress that yields several excellent one- and two-pitch climbs. There is a spacious ledge with a 30-foot pine tree at the top of this feature. To descend without climbing the upper half of *Tiger Balm Arête* or *Gambit*, rappel north 150 feet to the gully or make two shorter rappels tree to tree. There is a 3-bolt anchor at the top of the north face of the buttress.

1. **Sunstroke 9** FA: Carl Harrison and Carl Lempke, 1982. Begin with a right-facing dihedral left of *Tiger Balm Arête*. Work up through a couple of bulges, up a red dihedral with a hand crack, up over a roof and onward. . . .

SHIRTTAIL PEAK OVERVIEW

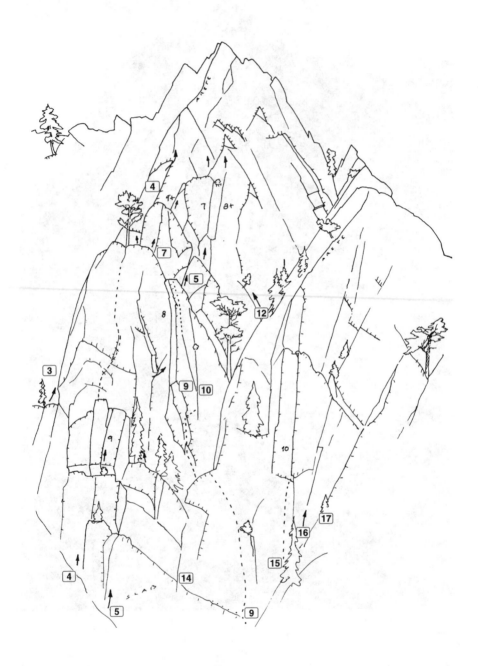

2. **King of Pain 12a** ★ FA: Toproped by R. and J. Rossiter, 1986; bolted and led by Mike Clinton and Bill DeMallie, 1988? Rack: up to a #3 Friend plus 10 QDs. This and the following route ascend the superb face left of *Tiger Balm Arête*. Climb up to the first bolt on *Mrs. Clean* (use long slings) and follow the line of bolts to the top of the face.

3. **Mrs. Clean Gets Down 11a** ★ FA: Joyce and Richard Rossiter and Karen Kuddes, 1986. Rack: SR. Scramble 75 feet up the gully on the north side of Tiger Balm Buttress and belay on a ledge with a pine tree. Climb up around the left side of a small fir tree, up a left-facing dihedral to a roof (9, #3 Friend), up and right past a bolt, and up to a flake (crux, tiny wire). Work up and left of a pine tree (9+), pull over the arête near its top, and belay on a big ledge.

4. **Tiger Balm Arête 11b VS** ★ FA: George Hurley and Bob Culp, 1965. FFA: Jim Erickson, 1971. FA: variation, Tobin Sorenson, 1975. A fine, hairy route. The 9 section above the crux is runout. At least two climbers have taken ledge falls from above the bolt. P1. Climb up the center of the buttress to an overhang, or begin with *Gambit* and traverse in from the right. Climb a shallow corner up to an inset ledge beside a stunted tree (7), and up the steep crack behind it (9) to a large, inward-sloping ledge. A crack and chimney just to the left may also be climbed (8). P2. Work up past a bolt in the tiered roof (crux), crank up and right into a shallow, right-facing dihedral (10b), then straight up (9) to the tree atop the buttress. P3. Climb over a bulge behind the tree (9), up a V-shaped dihedral, out right around a roof, and belay on the arête. P4. Climb the arête to the summit (4). **Variation:** Climb the crack to the right of the chimney on P1.

5. **Gambit 8** ★ FA: George Hurley and Bob Culp, 1965. FA: variation, Richard Rossiter, and Linda Willing, 1979. Classic. A grand summit route but beware of loose rock in a few places. Begin at the bottom right side of Tiger Balm Buttress. P1. Climb the right-facing dihedral just left of a clean slab and follow it for about 100 feet to a big ledge with some trees (6). P2. Climb the steep corner and crack system behind the tallest tree (7), up to a roof that diagonals up to the left (optional belay here), then move right and climb a superb, left-facing dihedral (8) up to a big ledge with much loose rock. P3. Climb an awkward slot (pin) up to the next ledge (7). P4. Climb over a bulge to gain a crack, then up parallel cracks (7) to a ledge with a bush. Climb up and right through two small overhangs (6), then up cracks and blocks to the summit (4). **Variation A:** The steep crack system just right of P4 may be ascended to the ledge with a bush (8+). **Variation B:** From the top of P2, climb *Ginseng Junkie*.

TIGER BALM BUTTRESS—NORTH SIDE

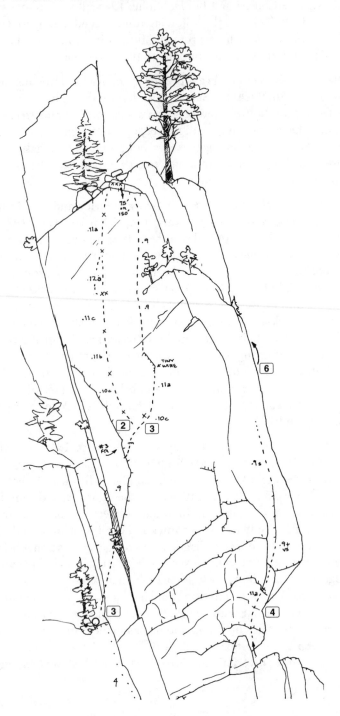

TIGER BALM BUTTRESS FROM THE SOUTHWEST

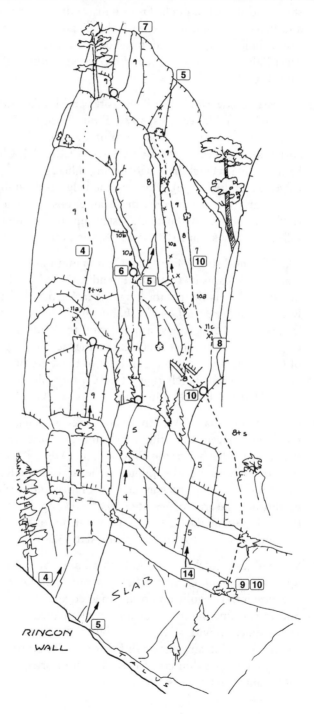

6. **Missing Link 10c ★** FA: Jim Erickson, 1980. Rack: up to a #4 Friend. A steep and dramatic pitch. From halfway up P2 of *Gambit*, undercling and lieback up and left beneath the diagonal overhang (10c), pull up over a bulge (10b), and continue upward (easier) to the pine tree atop Tiger Balm Buttress. Connect with *Ginseng Junkie, Tiger Balm Arête*, or rappel to the north.

7. **Ginseng Junkie 10a ★** FA: R. Rossiter and Linda Willing, 1979; of P3, R. Rossiter and Steve Ross, 1979. From the top of P2 of *Gambit*, belay on top of a chockstone, just south of the pine tree. P3. Climb a vertical corner and fist crack (8/9) up to the next ledge. P4. Climb a short, overhanging finger crack in a right-facing dihedral (10a) to a long, blocky ledge (Yosemite Ledge). Move up the ledge and climb a thin crack that shoots up toward the arête, make an exposed finger traverse above a roof (7), and follow the crack system up to the summit. One may also follow the crack out to the arête (8), then up to the top.

8. **The Throne 11b/c ★** FA: Mike Clinton and Bill DeMallie, 1988. Rack: many wires, cams up to a #0.5 Friend and "at least 12 QDs." Takes the face immediately right of the long, left-facing dihedral of *Gambit*. 5 bolts. Begin as for *Serrated Jam Crack,* but climb the slab up to the right via a thin crack (11b), left past a bolt (crux) to *Serrated Jam Crack*, and up through the crux of that route. Climb the face just left of the finger crack of *Cro-Magnon* past a bolt, and out to the arête on the left (11b), then up the arête immediately right of the *Gambit* dihedral to a 3-bolt anchor (10a). Descent: Rappel 150 feet.

9. **Cro-Magnon 10a ★** FA: Richard and Joyce Rossiter, 1986. Rack: up to a #3 Friend. Ascends the thin crack and face just right of *The Throne*. Begin on a ledge below the Giuoco Piano Arête. P1. Climb a slab to the right of a left-facing dihedral, up to the left of a small tree (8), and belay as for *Serrated Jam Crack* in the gully of *Mountaineer's Route*. P2. Work up through the crux of *Serrated Jam Crack*, up the clean finger crack to the left (9), on up the face to the 3-bolt anchor of The Throne and rappel, or continue to the top of the licheny slab (5).

10. **Serrated Jam Crack 10a ★** FA: Richard and Joyce Rossiter, 1983. Rack: up to a #4 Friend. Climb the first pitch of *Mountaineer's Route* or *Cro - Magnon* into the gully and belay on a ledge about 60 feet below the big pine tree. Climb out to the left and crank up through a roof (8), up a left-facing dihedral with a large loose block, and move right into an incipient crack. Climb straight up difficult rock (crux) to a stance where one may go left up a thin crack (*Cro-Magnon*) or right, up the wider *Serrated Jam Crack* (7).

UPPER SOUTHWEST FACE

The following routes are most easily reached by climbing *Mountaineer's Route* up to the "Hasegawa" pine tree, then up the gully beneath the face as appropriate.

11. **The Tail 9+** FA: Hurley and Culp, 1965. FFA: Roger Briggs and Larry Hamilton, 1974. The location of this route is not known. Begin in the gully near the large pine tree. . .join *Gambit* near the top of the face.

12. **Moriarty's Revenge 9+** ★ FA: Tim Beaman and Scott Woodruff, 1975. Begin about 60 up the big gully from the large pine. P1. Traverse left to a small tree out on the face, step right, up a zigzag crack for 35 feet, up broken rock to another crack that is followed to the right end of a tapering roof. Cross left beneath the roof and belay. P2. Turn the left end of the roof, up and left for about 20 feet, then up and right to the summit.

12a. **Moriarty's Mistake 9** FA: Scott Woodruff and Dan Hare, 1976. Go up and right from the right end of the roof (9).

13. **Windlass 9+** FA: Roger Briggs and Larry Hamilton, 1974. Exact location is not known. Climb a wandering crack up to join the last pitch of *Gambit*.

14. **Mountaineer's Route 5** ★ FA: George and Jean Hurley, 1965. This ascends the prominent gully separating the two summits of Shirttail. Begin about 30 feet right of the bottom of the big gully, just left of the Giuoco Piano Arête. P1. Work up and left to a tall and graceful "Hasegawa" pine tree. P2. Climb straight up the gully to the arête. P3. Climb northward to the summit.

15. **Giuoco Piano Direct 10b/c S** ★ FA: George Hurley and Bob Culp, 1965. FFA: Chris Reveley, Mark Norden, Joe Zimmerman, 1974. An alluring line. Belay as high as possible. P1. Climb the steep face up to the obvious, left-facing dihedral and work up the vertical corner (crux) to a belay on an incut ledge. P2. Climb the upper dihedral and belay on the arête. P3. Climb the arête to the summit. Rappel the gully, or continue to the summit.

16. **Double Life 9+** ★ FA: Carl Harrison, Jim Stuberg, Mike Brooks, 1981. This line climbs the face to the right of the GP Arête. Begin between *Giuoco Piano Direct* and *Future Primitive*, near a large tree. P1. Climb up to a crack and lieback past two pitons and a tree to a good ledge (crux). P2. Follow right-angling cracks for 130 feet. P3. Work up and left to the false summit.

17. **Future Primitive 6** ★ FA: R. Rossiter, solo, 1978. This is the easiest route up the Giuoco Piano Arête. Scramble up and right past the vertical lower section of the arête. P1. Climb the face to the left of a left-facing dihedral and move left along a diagonal ledge to a tree. P2. Climb up into a crack

and work up to the arête on the left. P3. Climb straight up the GP Arête to the false summit on the east ridge. P4. Climb the southeast arête to the summit.

18. **Jabberwalk 6** FA: Bob and Jane Culp, 1965. Begin up to the right of the GP Arête. Climb a trashy, left-facing dihedral, then up and left to a ledge with trees. Climb cracks to the right of the arête all the way to the false summit, then up the southeast arête to the summit.

THE POTATO CHIP

The Potato Chip is a dramatic blade of orange rock standing on the skyline over the North Buttress of the West Ridge, a little down and south from Shirttail Peak. Approach as for Shirttail. Take the Rincon Trail to Rincon Wall and hike up the talus gully on the south toward Shirttail Peak. Veer off to the southeast and arrive presently at the base of the spire.

To the left (?) of The Potato Chip are two routes on a west-facing wall:

1. **Baby Giraffe 9** FA: Harrison and Stuberg, 1981. Climb a short, overhanging, offwidth crack left of *Sour Cream*.

2. **Sour Cream 8** FA: Stuberg, Brooks, Harrison, 1981. Climb a 75-foot dihedral at the right side of the wall.

Pat Adams on the second ascent of French Fry *(5.12b), The Potato Chip.* BOB HORAN PHOTO

3. **Potato Chip Route 10b/c S ★** FA: Scott Woodruff and Dan Hare, 1975. FA: variation, Glenn Randall, date unknown. P1. Climb a decomposed couloir to a tree and belay. P2. Ascend a diagonal crack up across the sheer north face to the west arête and belay. P3. Traverse about 30 feet across the south face and up to the summit. **Variation:** Climb directly up the west edge from the belay (10a S).

4. **French Fry 12b ★** FA: Bob Horan and Pat Adams, 1987. A classic face route in a grandiose setting. Climb straight up the middle of the south face past 4 bolts to a 2-bolt anchor.

5. **Mr. Potato Head 11d** FA: Steve Levin, Dan Hare. Climb the face right of *French Fry*. 6 bolts to same anchor as *French Fry*.

WEST RIDGE AND UPPER REDGARDEN WALL
FROM THE SOUTH

ELDORADO CANYON NORTH

THE WEST RIDGE

This is the long, diagonal ridge west of Redgarden Wall. It arises from the waters of South Boulder Creek and climbs some 2000 feet to the northwest, where it terminates across a narrow gully from Rincon Wall. The low point of the ridge is about 0.3 mile west of The Bastille and across the stream from the Milton Boulder. The West Ridge has more than 150 routes—many of exceptional quality—that range in length from 25-foot mini-routes to five-pitch classics like *Long John Wall*. Nearly all routes ascend south- and west-facing features. Descents can usually be made back down the west side of the ridge via downclimb or rappel. In a few cases, it is easier to scramble down the east slabs. Descent information is given where appropriate.

Approaches: When South Boulder Creek is low or frozen over, cross from the dirt road just above the Milton Boulder. Otherwise, hike The Streamside Trail from the footbridge west to where a sign claims the trail ends. Scramble up a short, slippery ramp and jump/downclimb to a boulder on the west side. Continue west 25 feet along the north side of the creek, then climb up the bank and pick up the West Ridge Trail. There is a sign about 20 feet above the creek marking the start of this trail.

NORTH BUTTRESS

This southwest-facing, 300-foot-wide buttress is the grand finale of the West Ridge. Isolated by a deep cleft on the south and a forested gully on the north, it is practically an independent crag. It has numerous vertical cracks and dihedrals and hosts some of the finest short routes in Eldorado. The North Buttress is most easily approached via The Eldorado Canyon Trail and the Rincon Cutoff. From the west face of Rincon Wall, hike south about 100 feet to reach the northwest corner of the crag.

The North Buttress of the West Ridge terminates with a steep, triangular wall about 60 feet high. The west edge of the wall is about 15 feet left of Bushwhack Crack.

THE WEST RIDGE—NORTH BUTTRESS OVERVIEW

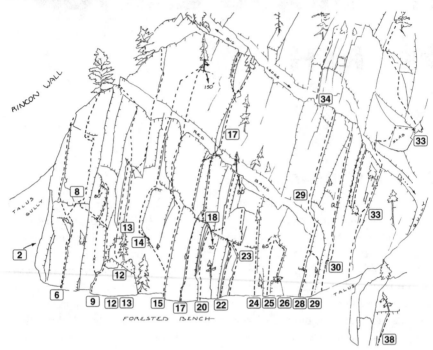

1. **Tales of Ulysses 7** FA: Dave Bohn and Ken Duncan, 1976. Start some distance up the gully, beyond *Prince of Darkness*. Climb a crack and corner just above the finish to *Laughing at the Moon*.

2. **Prince of Darkness 11a** ★ FA: Chris Archer, Stephan DeWet, Cris Ann Crysdale, 1988. Rack: #3, #4 Rocks, #2.5 Friend, and QDs. This is an excellent short route with good protection. From the beginning of the hand traverse on *Sirens of Titan*, climb straight up the wall past 4 bolts to the apex.

3. **Sirens of Titan 9** ★ FA: Rob Candelaria and Pat Ament, 1975. P1. Climb up into a recess in the middle of the face and hand-traverse a diagonal crack out to the arête on the right (9). P2. Ascend the narrow face, or move right and climb the last pitch of *Bushwhack Crack* (6).

3a. **Sylvia's Bush 8** FA: Paula Munger and Pat Ament, 1975. From the belay on the arête on *Sirens of Titan*, move up a little, then traverse a crack back left across the face.

4. **Ice Nine 6** ★ FA: Carl Harrison, solo, 1981. Begin at the lower west side of the face at an offwidth crack. Climb the crack and crank up onto the arête, hand traverse right, and climb the face or dihedral.

THE WEST RIDGE—NORTH BUTTRESS FROM THE NORTHWEST

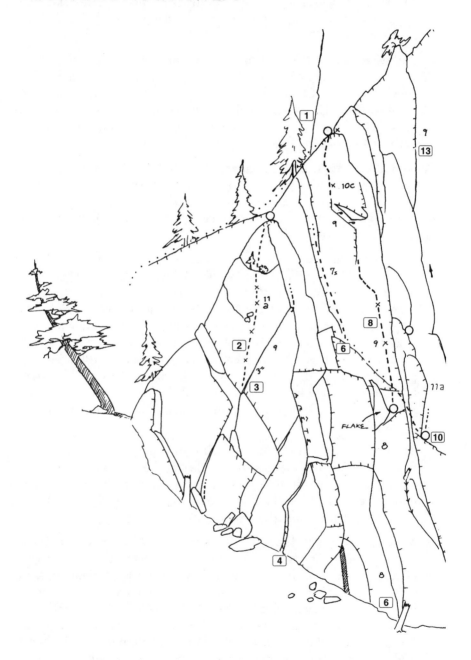

5. **Rambo Drop Test 10b** FA: Bill DeMallie, free solo, 1988. All but a few feet have been climbed previously. Climb the upper pitch of *Bushwhack Crack* into the left-facing dihedral, reverse the *Laughing. . .traverse*, pull up around the right side of a roof, and up the face just left of a right-facing dihedral.

6. **Bushwhack Crack 8 S** FA: Chris Reveley and John Serles, 1974. Begin about 18 feet left of *Muscular Dystrophy* at a clean, left-facing dihedral behind a tree. P1. Climb up and around the right side of a very precarious flake (8) and belay. P2. Climb the left side of the slab for 50 feet (6 S) into a left-facing dihedral and finish along the back side of the arête. Belay at a bolt as for *Laughing....*

7. **Speakeasy 7 S** FA: Brooks, Stuberg, Harrison, 1981. Some loose rock here. Begin behind a tree at a flop-flop corner, 6 feet left of *Muscular Dystrophy*. Work up a groove past precarious flakes, up a chimney, and belay on a ledge at the right. Continue up the chimney and finish as for *Muscular Dystrophy*.

8. **Laughing at the Moon 10b ★** FA: Richard and Joyce Rossiter, 1986. Rack: depends on approach; only QDs are needed for *Laughing at the Moon*. P1. Begin with the P1 of *Muscular Dystrophy* and belay beneath the crux dihedral. P2. Traverse up and left along a ledge, pull up onto a higher ledge at the base of a slab and belay (0). P3. Climb straight up the clean face past 2 bolts (9), up and left into a tiny, right-facing dihedral, hand-traverse left past 2 pins, then mantel up to a stance (10b), climb up past a bolt (10b), then up and right to the top of the wall. **Variation:** Climb up and right from the beginning of the hand traverse and climb the face just left of a right-facing dihedral. (This was the first version of this route.)

9. **The Bat 10b S ★** FA: Jim Stuberg and Carl Harrison, 1981. Climb the first 10 feet of *Muscular Dystrophy*, then pull left into a seam with a fixed pin and climb straight up (crux) to a ledge and belay. Move left into a crack system and climb straight up to join *Laughing at the Moon* or the last pitch of *Muscular Dystrophy*.

10. **Muscular Dystrophy 11a ★** FA: Tim Beaman and Dan Hare, 1974. Begin at a clean, right-angling crack at the left side of a fallen block, about 50 feet left of *Chockstone*. P1. Climb the finger crack to a stance (9-), up a right-facing dihedral to a left-facing dihedral, then to a belay niche beneath a right-facing, right-leaning dihedral with a tapering crack. P2. Climb the imposing dihedral to a ledge with some blocks (crux). P3. Move up and left into a crack and gully and climb to the top. Follow a ledge system around into the gully to the north to descend.

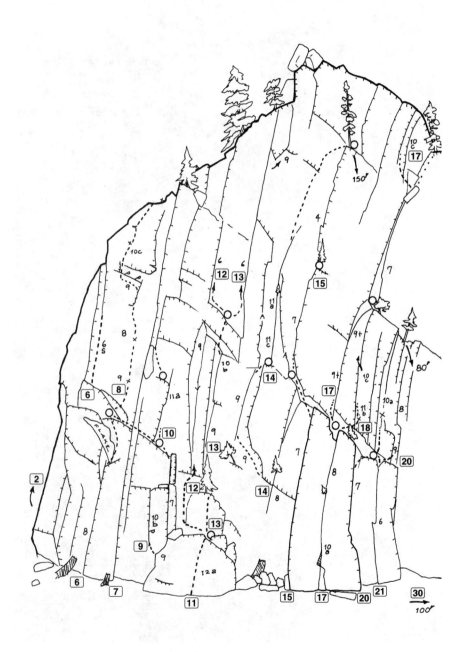

NORTH BUTTRESS

11. **A Cut Above 12a (TR)** FA: Pat Ament and Gray Ringsby, 1983. Climb the center of the fallen block to the left of the bigger block of *Chockstone*. Thin.

12. **Fading Light 10a ★** FA: Dan Hare and Alan Bradley, 1979. Approach as for *Blackout*. P1. Climb up through a roof into the left of two right-facing dihedrals, jam up the steep corner via a good crack, and turn the roof at the top to the same belay ledge as *Blackout* (9?). P2. Climb up a short, right-facing dihedral and continue on poor rock to the walk-off ledge.

13. **Blackout 10b ★** FA: Richard and Joyce Rossiter, 1986. Rack: up to a #4 Friend plus extra RPs. Also known as *Byobu*. Climb up onto the above-mentioned block from the south and belay beneath a fir tree, or climb the first part of *Muscular Dystrophy* and move right to the tree. P1. Climb directly up from the tree into the right-hand, right-facing dihedral of two for 40 feet (10a), jam the slightly overhanging crack in the left wall (9), then crank up and right through an overhang (10b), and belay on a ledge. P2. Move right into a crack, up through a groove, and an overhang in a short, right-facing dihedral to a big ledge (9). **Variation:** Climb a 9+ S seam out to the right of the crack and roof of P1.

14. **Jericho 11c (9 S) ★** FA: Chris Reveley and George Hurley, 1976. Classic. P1. Climb the first 15 feet of *Knight's Move*, work out left along a crack to an arête just left of a right-facing dihedral (9 S), and up the arête to an awkward belay (9+ S). P2. Climb a flared, overhanging dihedral (11c) up past a tree (11b), up steep slabs, and finally right to a large tree. Rappel 160 feet to the ground.

14a. **The Road to Jericho 9** FA: Doug McAuliffe, Jim Morrison, 1981. This variation start begins below the *Jericho* dihedral. Climb a thin crack, over a 9- bulge to a foot ledge. Move left to a small pine, (optional belay). Climb the face to two cracks that lead (9) to the *Jericho* dihedral.

15. **Knight's Move 7 ★** FA: Hurley and Culp, 1966. A worthy route. P1. Climb the dihedral to the left of *Chockstone* and belay at its top (7). P2. Move up and left, then climb a steep V-slot and dihedral to a belay at its top (7). P3. Climb an easier pitch up to a big tree. Scramble off via the ledge above, or rappel 160 feet to the ground.

16. **Cornerstone 11c (TR)** FA: Peter Hunt, toproped, 1986. Led with 2 bolts by Mark Tarrant (rope solo), 1986. Climb the first 10 feet of *Chockstone*, then work left and up the left arête of the block. The bolts were removed in 1987. A second pitch was bolted and led, but these bolts were also removed. **Variation:** Start P1 direct (12 TR).

NORTH BUTTRESS—CHOCKSTONE AREA

The route *Chockstone* follows a crack up the center of a large, rectangular block that leans against the wall near the middle of the North Buttress. The block is about 70 feet high and provides a reference for locating adjacent routes.

17. **Chockstone 10a (9+ S)** ★ FA: George Hurley and Bob Culp, 1966. FFA: Jim Erickson and Jim Walsh, 1970. Rack: up to a #3 Friend. Classic. P1. Climb the obvious crack up the middle of the huge block to the ledge at its top (10a). P2. Step left and climb a thin crack into a shallow, left-facing dihedral, pull around to the right (9+ S; the S stands for sandbag), and belay at a small tree. Alternatively, climb *Superstone* as a second pitch. P3. Climb a red, right-facing dihedral (8), and an easy gully to a big, diagonal ledge that may be descended (Class 3) to the north (easier) or the south. One may also descend via rappel from trees (see topo).

17a. **Chock Suey 10d** FA: Richard and Joyce Rossiter, 1983. Climb a shallow, right-facing dihedral to the left of the easy gully.

18. **Superstone 11b/c** ★ FA: Joyce and Richard Rossiter, 1986. Rack: up to a #3 Friend. Quality. Approach via the first pitch of *Chockstone* or *Purple Haze*. From the small tree atop the right side of the huge rectangular block, pull up and right to clip a bolt, make crux moves to get started, and climb straight up the right-facing dihedral that becomes left-facing at the top. It is possible to avoid a second crux by moving right a short way, then pulling back left as the dihedral begins to face left.

19. **Joke Crack 11c** FA: Alec Sharp and Leonard Coyne, 1981. Climb the finger-and-hand crack in the overhanging wall a few feet left of *Purple Haze*.

20. **Purple Haze 9** ★ FA: Dan Hare and Jim Michael, 1975. Classic. P1. Climb the dihedral at the right side of *Chockstone* (7) and belay on a ledge to the right. P2. Move right, climb a shallow corner (crux), and a hand crack to a tree. Rappel 80 feet to the ground.

21. **Friends in High Places 10a** ★ FA: Bruce Hildenbrand and Robert Mueller, 1986. Quality. To the right of the *Purple Haze* dihedral, climb a crack up a slab, past a tree, and belay as for *Purple Haze*. Climb the crux of *Purple Haze*, then take the right-facing dihedral on the left (10a).

22. **Born Under Punches 10a** FA: Joel Schiavone and Dan Grandusky, 1981. Begin just left of *Ministry of Fear* and climb the right-facing dihedral to a rotten roof with a block, then crank up and left to finish.

23. **Ministry of Fear 11d VS** ★ FA: Alec Sharp and Matt Lavender, 1981. In a magazine article entitled "Bolder Boulder," Sharp wrote that he couldn't sleep the night before he climbed this route so great was his anxiety. Begin about 25 feet to the right of *Chockstone*, just right of a grungy,

THE WEST RIDGE—NORTH BUTTRESS

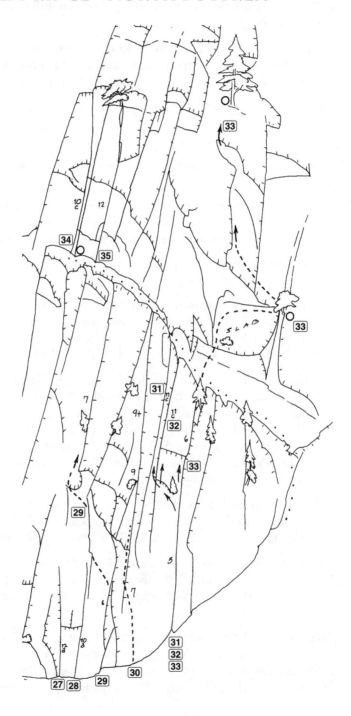

right-facing dihedral. Climb up to the overhang, hand-traverse right, pull over the roof, and climb a seam up the steep wall to a ledge below the rotten band.

24. **Halo 9** FA: Brooks and Lynn Smith, 1982. Begin just left of a short, left-facing dihedral with a tree, about midway between *Xanadu* and *Chockstone*. Climb a 70-foot, left-facing dihedral to a tree.

25. **Jeep 9+** FA: Brooks and Lynn Smith, 1982. Climb the wide crack just right of *Halo*.

26. **Android Tilt 10b/c** ★ FA: Mike Brooks and Joe Huggins, 1982. Begin at a tree, climb a left-facing dihedral to a roof, and go left to a bolt. Rappel 60 feet.

27. **Dead Teachers in Space 12b** FA: Charlie Fowler and Kyle Copeland, 1986. Climb a short, thin seam just left of *As We Liked It*. This has become more challenging since the fixed knifeblade fell out.

28. **As We Liked It 10a** ★ FA: Pat Ament and Gray Ringsby, 1980. Climb a thin crack straight up to *S&M*.

29. **S&M 7** ★ FA: Carl Harrison and Scott Kimball, 1981. Begin just left of *Xanadu*. Climb a left-facing dihedral for 25 feet, move left into another left-facing dihedral, around the left side of a roof, and up a larger, left-facing dihedral to a rotten ledge. 150 feet. Downclimb to the south.

30. **Xanadu 10a** ★ FA: Brad Gilbert, Jim Michael, Dan Hare, 1974. Rack: up to a #2 Friend. Classic. Begin at a small buttress at the south end of the face just before the wall bends around into a gully. Climb the buttress (8) into a long, left-facing dihedral with a thin crack. The crux is the upper third of the route. **Variation A:** The right-facing dihedral on the left (9+). **Variation B:** The face to the right can be toproped—bearhug techniques recommended—at 11a.

31. **Kubla Khan 11b/c S** ★ FA: Alec Sharp and Matt Lavender, 1981. Begin with *Tryptich* and climb the left of two right-facing dihedrals. Move down and left from the ledge at the bottom of *Tanquerey* to enter the dihedral.

32. **Tanquerey 11c S** ★ FA: Kurt Gray and Charly Oliver, 1980. FFA: Alec Sharp and Matt Lavender, 1981. Begin as for *Tryptich*, but cut left at a tree and climb the right of two right-facing dihedrals. Downclimb a rotten ledge to the right.

33. **Tryptich 10b/c VS** FA: Scott Woodruff and Dan Hare, 1976. A wandering route. Begin about 20 feet right of *Xanadu*. P1. Climb a crack and a left-facing dihedral to a rotten ledge (6). P2. Work up onto the left side of a slab, undercling right beneath a roof, and belay at a tree. P3. Move

left past the bottom an arching crack to a dihedral (crux), up and left over a roof to a belay at a tree. P4. Scramble up a slab, climb a tiny dihedral, then a short headwall.

Up to the left along the rotten ledge from the top of the first pitch of *Tryptich* is a large roof with the following two routes.

34. **Whiplash 10c ★** FA: Dan Hare and Scott Woodruff, 1976. Quality. Climb the hand crack a few feet left of *Parlez Vouz*.

35. **Parlez Vous Hangdog 12 ★** FA: Charlie Fowler, 1986. Rack: up to a #3 Friend. Quality. Just left from the top of *S&M* climb a crack through the massive roof.

KASHMIR AREA

There is a large, steep gully right of *Tryptich*. Between here and Cirque of Cracks is a less popular section of cliff. The rock is discontinuous, somewhat forested, and presents no cohesive line of any length.

36. **Hang Ten 8** FA: Carl Harrison, solo, 1981. About 15 feet left of *Kashmir*, climb a finger crack that turns into a hand crack in a clean little corner. This is the last route before the end of the buttress.

37. **Srinagar 7** FA: Harrison, Stuberg. Climb a crack to the left of *Kashmir*.

38. **Kashmir 11b ★** FA: Christian Griffith, 1979. A fine little pitch. Perhaps 150 feet north of Cirque of Cracks is a short wall with a tree on a ledge about 30 feet up. Climb a thin crack up and right to the tree. Rappel, or downclimb *Srinagar*.

39. **Coffee Break with Joe 8** FA: Joe Huggins and Mike Brooks, 1982. Begin by a small, skinny tree right of *Kashmir*. Lieback up a crack and avoid an easy gully. A crack just to the left (6) was also climbed by Brooks, 1982.

40. **Rhadamanthus 10** FA: Brooks and Jennifer Martin, 1982. Begin about 50 feet right of *Kashmir* and climb a blackish, 50-foot, left-facing dihedral.

41. **Willow World 8** FA: Brooks, 1982. Begin at a large tree about 25 feet left of *The Formula*. Ascend parallel cracks for 30 feet, then up a hand crack to a big tree.

CIRQUE OF CRACKS

This is a broad alcove about 150 feet north from the top of the Quartzite Ridge and perhaps 500 feet from the north end of the West Ridge. The south edge is not very well defined, but at the north it is demarcated by an overhanging buttress containing the route *The Formula*. The wide crack *Duh Dihedral* is a good landmark. The middle of the cirque is interrupted by a section of broken cliffs.

THE WEST RIDGE—CIRQUE OF CRACKS

42. **Early Bird Special 6** FA: Brooks, 1982. Begin 2 feet left of *The Formula* and climb a 50-foot crack system.

43. **The Formula 11d/12a** ★ FA: Mark Rolofson, 1980. Climb the overhanging dihedral on the arête left of *Pool of Blood*. Crux is entering the dihedral past a fixed pin.

44. **Pool of Blood 9** ★ FA: Pat Ament and Carl Diehl, 1975. Begin about 15 feet left of *Duh Dihedral* and climb the obvious, left-facing dihedral to a ledge. Finish with *Duh Dihedral* and rappel from a tree with slings.

45. **Tampon 7** FA: John Sherman, 1980. Pad carefully up the shallow, left-facing dihedral just right of *Pool of Blood*.

46. **Duh Dihedral 6** ★ FA: Jim Walsh and Ed Wright, 1970. Rack: Up to a #4 Friend. Popular. Climb the awkward, wide crack in the steep dihedral formed by the junction of two walls.

47. **Zap Snack 10a** FA: Eric Doub and James Epp, 1979. Begin a few feet right of *Duh Dihedral*. Climb straight up to good ledges and belay. Climb a 25-foot dihedral.

48. **Fine Line 9** ★ FA: Harrison and Brooks, 1981. Climb the crack and right-facing dihedral just left of *Terminal Velocity*.

49. **Terminal Velocity 11b/c S** ★ FA: Mark Rolofson and Alfredo Len, 1980. Start just left of *Hand Crack*. Climb a face, arête, and corner (crux, S/VS) up to a ledge, and stem up the nice left-facing dihedral (10d).

50. **Hand Crack 10b** ★ FA: Unknown. Rack: Up to #3 Friend. Climb the steep finger-and-hand crack between *Funeral March* and *Terminal Velocity*. The crux is about 20 feet up.

51. **Funeral March 9** FA: Erickson and Ferguson, 1970. Climb a 6-inch crack up through a roof.

52. **River of Darkness 7** FA: Dan Hare, solo, 1981. Climb a 40-foot, off-width crack in a left-facing dihedral just below *Lady Fingers*.

53. **Lady Fingers 7** FA: Lynn Smith and M. Brooks, 1982. Climb a short, left-facing dihedral about 80 feet up along the left side of the broken area.

54. **Mirage 9 (?)** FA: Harrison and Stacy Michaels, 1981. Begin about 15 feet left of *Foxtrot* at a tree. Climb discontinuous cracks up the right side of a slab, move left and up a steep groove, and belay at a tree. The relationship between this and the next route is not known.

55. **Clean Dan 10d** FA: Mike Brooks, roped solo, 1982. Climb a crack a few feet left of *Parallels* and descend from a bolt.

About 80 feet to the right of *The Formula* and 25 feet left of *Pins and Needles* is a steep wall with three thin cracks.

56. **Parallels 11c/d S ★** FA: Guerin and Horan, 1981. Climb the left of the three imposing cracks. Gear can be good, but strenuous to place.

57. **Foxtrot 11d S ★** FA: Guerin and Horan, 1981. Climb the center crack of three. Gear is better than it appears.

58. **Crazy Fingers 12a/b ★** FA: Bob Horan and Skip Guerin, 1981. Climb the right-hand crack. Traverse left and descend from a bolt for this and the preceeding three routes.

59. **Pins and Needles 11b** FA: Dan Hare and Dan Michael, 1980. Begin in a right-facing corner to the left of *Inverted Vee*. Climb straight up and crank over a bulge past 2 pitons (crux), up a shallow, left-facing dihedral, and right to belay at a tree. Climb up to a roof, turn it on the left (8), and continue up to a big Douglas-fir tree.

59a. **Eggshells 10** FA: Woodruff and Hare, 1981. Where *Pins and Needles* goes right, step left into a thin, right-facing dihedral and go up to a semi-sling belay. Continue straight up via rotten rock to a horn (9+), then right to rejoin the original line.

THE ROTTEN WALL

Above *Positively Fourth Street* the trail no longer hugs the cliff, which deteriorates into a mess of decomposed roofs, gullies, and dihedrals (The Rotten Wall). The trail goes over a miniature pass where the Quartzite Ridge intersects the West Ridge.

60. **Inverted Vee 8** FA: Stuberg and Harrison, 1981. Begin "roughly 100 feet" left of *Five Fang*, just right of *Pins and Needles*. Climb a deep dihedral up to a huge, V-shaped overhang (that appears inverted if you climb upside down) and belay. Climb around the left side of the roof and up a steep gully to a big tree.

61. **Five Fang Overhang 8** FA: Carl Harrison, solo, 1980. Climb up a red streak on a south-facing, overhanging wall.

POSITIVELY FOURTH STREET AREA

There is a small, vertical cliff about 60 feet northwest of the route *Pony Express*. It is about 75 feet south from the top of the Quartzite Ridge. The trail at this point hugs the cliff and climbs steeply up rock steps. Descent from these climbs is an easy scramble to the north along a ledge.

62. **Doc's Little Brother 6** FA: Stuberg, 1981. Climb the vegetated crack just left of *Michael Solar*.

63. **Doctor Michael Solar 7** ★ FA: Erickson and Walsh, 1970. Climb a crack about 20 feet left of *Positively Fourth Street*. Begin just left of a tree.

64. **Lunar Avenue 8 S** FA: Stuberg, Ruckgaber, Harrison, 1980. Climb the face between *Positively Fourth Street* and *Doctor Michael Solar.*

65. **Positively Fourth Street 9+** ★ FA: Jim Erickson and Jim Walsh, 1970. A nice, steep pitch on solid rock. Climb a crack near the right side of the wall. Move left near the top of the crack (9+) or climb straight up (10a).

66. **Coniferous Types 10** FA: Harrison, Brooks, 1982. Climb the arête just right (as in 3˚feet right) of *Positively Fourth Street.*

67. **Highway 61 9** FA: Hare, Gilbert, Woodruff, 1974. From the top of *Positively Fourth Street*, move right and climb a rotten dihedral to a tree. Scramble to a ledge and climb a blank face, left to a tree and belay. Climb a large block via a crack on its left side and finish in a dihedral.

68. **Working Class Hero 8** FA: Harrison, Stuberg, Ruckgaber, East, 1980. Climb the large, right-facing dihedral to the left of *Cold Turkey* and continue upward as needed.

69. **Shoeshine A1** FA: Brooks, 1982. Begin about 8 feet right of *Working Class Hero* and climb a thin crack above a small tree.

70. **January Bath 8+** FA: Brooks and Jim Hoffman, 1981. To the left of *Cold Turkey*, in an overhanging, rotten band, take the left of two cracks up to a right-facing dihedral, and belay at a small tree. Walk up and left to a dead tree and climb a crack at its left. Downclimb a gully to the northwest.

71. **Cold Turkey 9+** ★ FA: Jim Erickson and Jim Hofman, 1969. Climb a flared chimney into right-facing dihedral and crack system.

PONY EXPRESS AREA

This narrow section of cliff has some of the best climbing on the West Ridge. It is perhaps 1000 feet above the creek. As you reach this area, the trees thin out, exposing a clean sweep of wall all the way to *Positively Fourth Street*. This is where the rotten Quartzite Ridge comes into sight about 150 feet to the west. The big, right-facing dihedral of *Pony Express* is obvious, starting about 85 feet up. The longest routes are two pitches and do not exceed 150 feet in height. Descend by rappelling from trees.

72. **Air Mail 9+ S** ★ FA: Gary Issac, 1977. Just left of *Zip Code* is a right-facing dihedral.

73. **Zip Code 11b** ★ FA: Erickson, Woodruff, Hare, 1978. Begin about 20 feet left of *Pony Express*. Climb up to a huge flake, up a short, right-facing dihedral, over a bulge, and up a crack to the top.

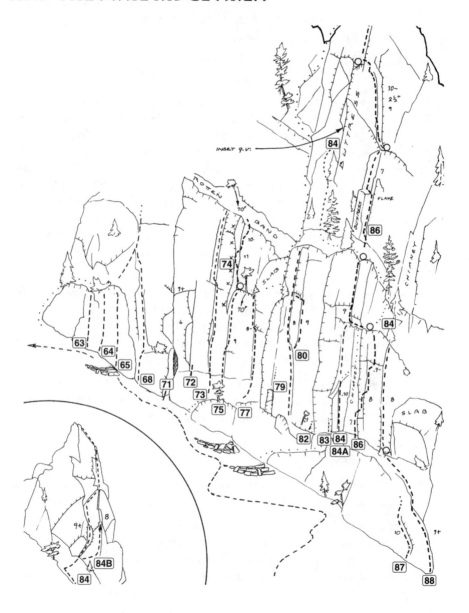

74. **Iron Pony 11d** ★ FA: Dan Hare and Mike Engle, 1989. Rack: up to #2 Friend. Climb *Pony Express* to the bottom of the right-facing dihedral (c. 20 feet below the belay ledge). Move left on a flake to a bolt, up and right (9) to a stance on the arête, then steam past 5 bolts, using holds on both sides of the arête, to the top.

74a. **Horse d'Oeuvre 8** FA: Chip Ruckgraber. A direct start to *Iron Horse*. Climb a crack about 15 to 20 feet left of *Pony Express*.

75. **Pony Express 11c** ★ FA: Larry and Roger Dalke, 1966. FFA: Duncan Ferguson, Steve Wunsch, John Bragg, 1974. Variation, FA: Roger Briggs, 1974. Free solo, Derek Hersey, 1991. Rack: up to a #1.5 Friend. One of the finest routes on the West Ridge. Gain a ledge with a pine tree 15 feet up, directly below the main dihedral. P1. Climb the left crack (the right being *Iron Horse*) into the bottom of the right-facing dihedral, then right to belay at the lone pine (9). P2. Climb the dihedral for about 30 feet, pull left, and make a very difficult move off the edge of the arête to a jug (crux), back right into the dihedral, up past another difficult section (10d), and belay on the left. **Variation:** Climb straight up the dihedral at the crux (11d).

76. **Iron Horse 11c S/VS** ★ FA: Dan Hare, Jim and Dan Michael, 1984. Rack: up to a #2 Friend. Climb the superb, very thin crack 7 feet right of *Pony Express*. Belay at the lone pine. This route has a second pitch that climbs the last 20 feet of the arête of the *Pony Express* dihedral, but this has been superseded by *Iron Pony*, which climbs the entire arête.

77. **Mesca-Line 7** ★ FA: Erickson and Hofman, 1969. A very good line. Climb the crack that leads up to the right edge of the ledge with the lone pine. The crux is maneuvering around a left-facing flake.

78. **Dandi-Line 7** FA: Brooks and Harrison, 1981. Climb the left-facing dihedral right of *Mesca-Line*.

79. **Sister Morphine 9** ★ FA: Harrison and Brooks, 1981. Ascend a pedestal, step onto the face, and climb the thin crack just right of *Dandi-Line*.

80. **Drug Abuse 9** FA: Stuberg, Hague, Harrison, Brooks, 1981. Begin 10 feet right of *Sister Morphine*. Climb the right side of a large block, straight up for 40 feet, up to the right side of a roof, undercling left beneath the roof, and up to a ledge. **Variation:** Ascend a crack (8) up to the left side of the roof.

81. **Seemingly Innocent 8** FA: Coy, Harrison, Stuberg, 1981. Begin about 4 feet right of *Drug Abuse*. This is about 6 feet from *Dead Letter Department*. Climb a bulge, then up past some trees for 100 feet.

THE MAIL RIDGE

About 150 or 200 feet northwest of Long John Tower is another (sort of) distinguishable summit and west-facing buttress. If by no other means, it may be recognized by a large, rotten chimney at the bottom and by the steep, reddish, south face of the summit block. To descend from the summit, downclimb to the notch on the north, down a steep gully to the southwest, north across a slab to the rappel tree on *Pony Express*, thence a 75-foot rappel to the talus.

82. **Dead Letter Department 8** FA: Duncan Ferguson, solo, 1971. Just left of the lower buttress of Mail Ridge, (about 25 feet right of *Sister Morphine*) climb a left-facing dihedral with an offwidth crack.

83. **Hyperspace Roundup 12c ★** FA: Mike Brooks, rope solo 1982. FFA: Fowler and J. Huggins, 1986. Rack: RPs to mid-range Rocks. Climb the thin, overhanging, right-facing dihedral about 20 feet left of the Mail Ridge chimney. 2 bolts.

84. **The Mail Ridge 9+** FA: Dalke and Ament, 1965. FA: Variation A; Woodruff and Brad Gilbert, 1974. P1. Climb the chimney to a ledge (6). P2. Move right and scramble up to a large tree. P3. Scramble up a ramp to the left to the north side of the buttress, up left around some trees, and back right on a ledge. P4. Ascend a steep, clean V-slot (9+), up and right to the arête, and up to the belay niche of *Handcracker Direct* (9). P5. Shoot straight for the top (0). **Variation A:** Climb a right-facing dihedral about 12 feet left of P1 (10b/c). **Variation B: The Lightning Bolt Crack 8+** FA: Ferguson and Erickson, 1971. Climb the obvious crack to the right of the V-slot.

85. **The Reckoning 12c/d ★** FA: Mark Tarrant with Richard Wright, 1987. Rack: up to a #2 Friend. Climb the first two pitches of *Handcracker Direct*. Go down a ramp to the right to a tree and belay beneath a finger crack. P3. Climb the crack to a small roof, left to the arête and up for 15 feet, pull left around the arête to easy rock, then up to the large ledge at the bottom of the south face of the summit tower of Mail Ridge (90 feet, 12a). P4. Climb the middle of the "great" south face, past 5 bolts and a pin to a 2-bolt anchor. (60 feet, 12c/d). P4 may also be reached via the West Face Trail along Redgarden Wall and the east slabs of the West Ridge. It is roughly west of *Grandmother's Challenge*.

86. **Handcracker Direct 10a ★** FA: of P1, Jim Garber and R. Rossiter, 1980; of P2, Dan Hare and Scott Woodruff, 1974; of P3, Rossiter and Garber, 1980; of P4, Erickson and Wunsch, 1971. FA: Variation A, Hare and Woodruff, 1974. Variation C, Mark Tarrant and Randy Wharton, 1989. A good summit route, a near-classic. Perhaps 75 feet left of the rock rib of *Chick on the Side*, scramble up to the right on a ramp and belay at the

THE WEST RIDGE—
BASE OF THE MAIL
RIDGE DETAIL

bottom of the Mail Ridge chimney. P1. Climb a clean, left-facing dihedral, pull right into another left-facing dihedral, up a short way, right again, up over two bulges, and left to belay on a ledge beneath a roof (8). P2. Climb the roof (9), then up a crack and corner to belay on a large ledge. P3. Climb a flake/chimney on the right side of the buttress, step left and climb the arête (7) to a big ledge at the base of the south face of the summit block. P4. Climb a slightly overhanging hand crack in a left-facing dihedral (crux), then pull left and belay at a good stance. P5. The last pitch is easy and goes straight to the summit. **Variation A:** Straight up the initial dihedral on P1 (8). **Variation B: Sundial 8 FA:** Brooks and Lynn Smith, 1981. Climb a crack with a chockstone 10 feet (?) right of the fourth (?) pitch. **Variation C:** About halfway up P5, move right into a right-facing dihedral and straight up to the dihedral at the top, 11b S. Bring Stoppers and small cams.

87. **Chick on the Side 10b/c** ★ FA: Erickson and Wunsch, 1976. Takes an obvious steep, left-leaning, left-facing dihedral. Climb up to a fixed pin, then power up the corner to a ledge. Walk off to the left or continue with *Bloke*.

88. **Bloke on the Side 9+ S** FA: Harrison, Brooks, Stuberg, 1981. Begin about 10 feet right of *Chick on the Side*. Climb a short bulge (crux) onto a south-facing rib of rock. Climb this to a belay at the base of a shallow, right-facing dihedral (9+). Climb the dihedral and subsequent crack system to a ledge (8).

THE NEDERLANDS

This is a nondescript section of cliff, with nondescript routes, between the rotten chimney to the left of *Practice Climb 101* and Mail Ridge.

89. **Rope to Ruin 8** FA: Harrison, Brooks, Stuberg, 1981. Begin 20 feet right of *Chick on the Side*. Go up a short groove to a tree, then up and right through an overhanging headwall. Up a ramp, left to a sloping ledge, and up a series of short walls.

90. **Wind Tunnel 7** ★ FA: Jim Erickson and Dave Meyers, 1969. Good in parts. Begin about 50 feet left of the chimney of *Rhombohedral*, beneath an attractive slab. P1. Climb straight up the smooth slab to a small tree (7), continue up past a couple more trees and belay. P2. Climb straight up for 60 feet to rotten ledge, right 15 feet, up a dihedral, past a tree and belay 20 feet higher. P3. Climb a crack for about 50 feet.

91. **Bridget the Midget 8** FA: Harrison, Brooks, Stuberg, 1981. Begin a short way left of *Good Ship Venus*. Jam a crack to a pedestal and move right onto the face, up and right to a dihedral, and up past trees.

92. **The Good Ship Venus 8** FA: Harrison, Stuberg, Brooks, 1981. Start about 25 feet left of *Rhombohedral* and climb the obvious hand crack to a broken ledge. Climb twin finger cracks.

93. **The Rhombohedral 8+** FA: Pat Ament and Russ Oberg, 1965. Begin in the gully to the left of *Practice Climb 101*. P1. Climb an overhanging slot for 50 feet, up the chimney, and belay after about 120 feet. P2. Continue up the gully and belay at a leaning tree. P3. Go up an easy inside corner to a tree, then up right on ledges to the base of a north-facing wall with a wide crack. P4. Climb the crack/chimney and exit through a hole at the top.

SIDEWALL AREA

This is a steep area of dihedrals and cracks between *Sooberb* and a deep, rotten chimney on the left. There are thick trees along the base, and the trail, after going steeply up rock steps just below, suddenly makes a switchback by the rotten chimney. All routes begin from a large, pleasant bench about 25 feet above the talus. Reach the bench by climbing in from the chimney at the left.

94. **Warp Drive Overload 12b/c** ★ FA: Mark Rolofson and Dan McQuade, 1987. Climb the arête left of the first pitch of *Practice Climb 101*. 2 bolts, 60 feet.

95. **Practice Climb 101 12c S** ★ FA: Larry and Roger Dalke, 1966. FFA: of P1, Breashears, Erickson, Wunsch, 1976; of P2, John Allen, 1981. Begin from a pedestal to the left (north) of a bench. P1 is popular. P2 is very strenuous and committing. P1. Climb a bulge up into a shallow, right-facing dihedral, move up to the right, back left along a crack, and climb the upper part of the dihedral (strenuous 11a) to a good belay ledge, with 2 bolts, at the left. P2. Climb straight up the left side of the over-hang to an old piton in a thin crack, turn the roof (12c S), and climb the steep face above to the ledge with a juniper tree.

95a. **Practice Wall 11a** ★ An excellent combo. Ascend P1 of *Practice Climb 101* to the belay ledge, place a nut a little higher, then make a downward traverse right to the top of P1 of *Sidewall* and belay at 2 bolts. Stem the exquisite dihedral (11a) of *Sidewall*.

95b. **Muscle and Hate 11a** ★ FA: Bob Shire and Tony Bubb, 1997. From the top of *Practice Climb 101*, traverse left to a tree used for rappels and belay. Climb a roof with huecos and continue up the right of two cracks. Rappel 65 feet back to start from a tree at left.

96. **False Prophet 11c/d S** ★ FA: P2, Alec Sharp and Doug Madara, 1980. FA: P1, Doug Hall and Kim Carrigan, later in 1980. This is a stupen-dous route with poor protection. P1. Begin as for *Practice Climb 101*,

but veer off to the right after about 25 feet and climb a shallow dihedral just right of the arête to the belay on *Sidewall* (10d S). P2. Climb up a few feet, then pull left to gain a thin crack, crank over the bulge and ascend a clean, right-facing dihedral to a ledge with a juniper tree. Rappel 120 feet to the bench.

97. **Sidewall 11c VS** ★ FA: Pat Ament and Roger Briggs, 1966. FFA: Erickson, Wunsch, Bragg, 1974. First Free Solo, Derek Hersey. A classic route, but the first pitch is very poorly protected for the first 50 feet. P1. Climb the obvious, chalky, right-facing dihedral to a stance beneath the roof, then make crux moves to reach a jug on the left wall and clip a bolt above. Pull up left to a sling belay from 2 bolts. P2. Pull back right into the dihedral and climb with good pro (mostly RPs and a #3 Friend) up to a belay in a niche (11a). A third pitch climbed the wall above but is seldom done. Rappel 120 feet from a juniper tree back to the base of the route.

97a. **Unbroken Chain 11b/c VS** FA: Nathan Charlton and Steve Morris, 1984. Climb the first 20 feet of P1, then undercling to the left to the small dihedral of *False Prophet*.

97b. **Wild Side 12 (TR)** FA: Charlton and Morris, 1985. Pull right from the first belay and climb the steep dihedral to the right of P2.

98. **Quiet Desperation 11c S/VS** ★ FA: Sharp and Hare, 1980. Begin with a difficult bulge and climb the shallow, right-facing dihedral just left of *The Human Factor*.

99. **The Human Factor 11d S/VS** ★ FA: Alec Sharp and Dan Hare, 1980. Climb the overhanging, right-facing dihedral to the left of *Sooberb*.

100. **Court Jester 10c S** ★ FA: Alec Sharp and John Bremer, 1980. Climb a steep crack left of *Sooberb* and angle left after about 60 feet to join *The Human Factor*. Rappel 80 feet from a juniper tree.

101. **Sooberb 10c** ★ FA: Ament and Dalke, 1965. FFA: Jim Erickson, 1972. Somewhat junky, but the overhang on P3 is a classic. Begin from the south end of the bench. P1. Climb the near side of Sick Flake (a greenish, bent flake 20 feet high) and the dihedral above to a ledge (8). P2. Climb a bulge and a shallow, left-facing corner, then out left across a clean slab to a large ledge with a juniper tree. P3. Climb the widest part of the roof via a crack to a slot (10c), and continue up good rock to the summit. **Variation A:** The original line climbed up to the bench from below Sick Flake. **Variation B: Curving Dihedral 10** FA: Feiges, Athans, Lugbill, Bremer, 1979. Climb the right side of the roof on P3 (maybe the same as Variation D), then up into a curving dihedral. **Variation C: Happy Landing 10a/b** FA: Feiges, Athans, Lugbill, Bremer, 1979. Climb a left-facing,

overhanging dihedral just right of *Curving Dihedral*. **Variation D: The Erickson Variation 9+** FA: Jim and Dave Erickson, 1968. On P3, climb a crack through the roof 15 feet right of the original line, then rejoin the original line.

102. **Barrel of Monkeys 11c** FA: Mark and Scott Tarrant, 1994. Rack: two long slings, QDs. Start as for *Sooberb*. Angle up and right to Sick Flake (long sling around tree), climb the outside of the flake, and follow 7 bolts (long QD on first bolt), to a double-bolt anchor. Cruxes are by the second bolt (11c) and 11b/c by the sixth bolt. Rappel 82 feet to the bench from a two-bolt anchor.

103. **Quicksand 10** FA: Dan Hare and Scott Woodruff, 1978. Climb *Ignominity* to about 10 feet below the main roof, traverse straight right around a bulge, and belay in a corner (10). Start up P3 of *Long John Wall*, break right into a parallel crack and climb the right-hand slot through the roof.

104. **Ignominity 9 ★** FA: Erickson and Behrens, 1968. FA: variation, Jean Ruwitch and Richard Rossiter, 1980. A steep and worthy route. Begin about 20 feet left of *Long John Wall* at a right-facing dihedral. P1. Climb the dihedral and the face above, then belay at a small tree (7). P2. Climb the right side of Sick Flake (a greenish, bent flake), undercling right beneath a small roof (8), up through another roof (9), up a right-facing dihedral, and belay on a ledge. P3. Climb a slot through a bulge (8) and up the wall above to a large ledge beneath the roof of *Sooberb*. **Variation:** Climb through the roof on P3 via a thin crack farther right (10b).

LONG JOHN TOWER
The following two routes begin where the trail is formed by steep rock steps heading straight up the hill.

105. **Thin Ice 9+ S** FA: Eric Guokas and Mark Sheppard, 1980. Climb the arête just left of the start of *Long John Wall*.

106. **Long John Wall 8 ★** FA: Larry Dalke, Pat Ament, Wayne Goss, 1964. FFA: Original start, Rob Candelaria, 1973. Rack: up to a #4 Friend. Classic. This is the longest and one of the finest routes on the West Ridge. Begin about 60 feet left of The Unsaid Wall near a large pine tree. Watch for poison ivy at the base. P1. Climb the face to the right of a dark, right-facing dihedral, up left at its top, back right into a crack system (5), and up to belay on a ledge. P2. Climb a beautiful crack up to a roof (8), turn the roof on the left (7), up the corner, and left to belay along a rotten band. P3. Climb a V-slot through a bulge (5), then follow a right-facing dihedral to a roof with two large slots through it and belay. P4. Master

WEST RIDGE—MIDDLE SECTION

Red Garden Wall

Kloof
Alcove

1

97

106

108

115

119

THE WEST RIDGE—LONG JOHN TOWER AREA

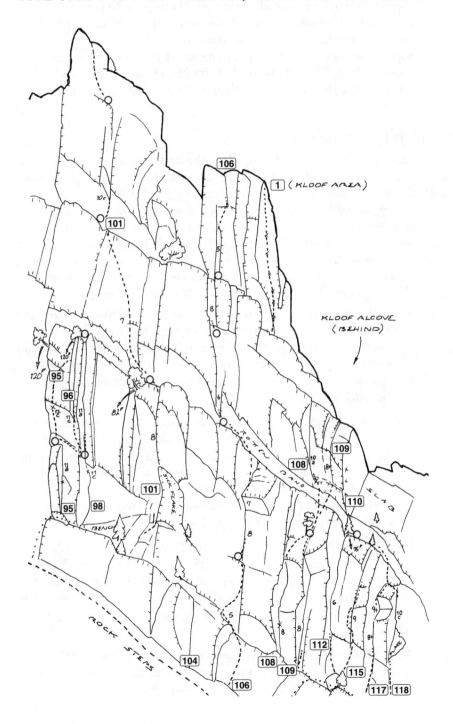

the overhanging slot on the left (crux). P5. Climb straight up a clean inset (5) and up to a U-notch at the top of Long John Tower. Descend the east slabs or downclimb a deep V-slot just to the north and rappel from juniper trees along the route *Sooberb* (two rappels with one 60-meter rope). **Variation A:** The original line aided the roof above the initial dihedral. **Variation B: Pluto 8** FA: Larry Hamilton and Dakers Gowans, 1974. Take a thin, hanging crack and dihedral right of the last pitch of *Long John Wall*.

THE UNSAID WALL

This popular area is about 400 feet up along the wall from the creek and begins just left of the *Verschneidung* slab. It has a series of clean, right-facing dihedrals. All of the routes begin from a deeply in-cut ledge that runs along the lower part of the wall, about 35 feet above the ground. This is accessed most easily by scrambling up from the trail, just down and left from *The Unsaid*. There are some nicely landscaped terraces around here for gearing up. Just past *Break on Through*, the trail ascends a series of steep rock steps up to the Sidewall Area. The easiest descent from any of the routes is to rappel 75 feet west from one of the bolted rappel anchors at the top of *Washington Irving*.

107. **Rock for Climbing Routes To 11b/c S** FA: Alec and Muriel Sharp and Matt Lavender, 1980. Climb an overhanging crack just left of *Break on Through*, up the arête, and belay on a slab. Climb a crack (6) just right of *Long John Wall* and belay near the bottom of the crux pitch of *Break on Through*. Traverse to the right and climb a steep crack to the right of the last pitch of *Chianti*.

108. **Break on Through 10b ★** FA: Jim Erickson and John Behrens, 1968. Rack: up to a #3 Friend. Classic. Begin about 25 feet left of the fallen block, beneath a steep, right-facing dihedral. Climb the blocky dihedral (8) for about 75 feet and belay at a tree on the right. Work up through a rotten band and tackle the clean, right-facing dihedral to the left of *Chianti* (crux). To descend, downclimb east, south, then west to the tree above *Washington Irving* and rappel 75 feet west.

109. **Chianti 8+ ★** FA: Erickson, Jim Hofman, Dave Meyers, 1970. About 15 feet left of the fallen block at the beginning of *The Unsaid*, climb an inset up a steep wall (8), pass the left side of a roof (7), then up a crack to a belay at a tree. Climb up through a rotten band, move right beneath an overhang, and climb a steep crack and corner system to the top of the ridge (8+).

110. **Atom Smasher 12c ★** FA: Erik Johnson and Shawn Ennis, 1987. Rack: wires, #2 Friend, QDs. Begin above the tree at the top of *Washington Irving* and climb the right side of the smooth arête past 3 bolts.

THE WEST RIDGE—THE UNSAID WALL

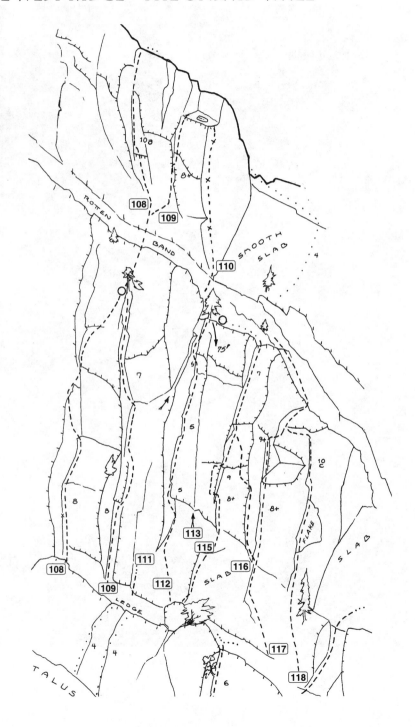

THE UNSAID WALL

111. **Sunshine Wall** 8 FA: Alec and Muriel Sharp, 1980. Begin about 5 feet right of *Chianti*. Climb a steep crack to a belay beneath an overhang. Climb a narrow ramp on the right to the top of *Washington Irving*.

112. **Washington Irving** 6 ★ FA: Erickson, Walsh, Wright, 1969. Rack: up to a #3 Friend. Classic. This is a popular "beginner route" with good pro. From the pedestal at the bottom of *The Unsaid*, climb up and left and power up the solid, right-facing dihedral about 15 feet left of that route.

113. **Next to Nearly** 9 ★ FA: Unknown. FFA: Rob Candelaria and Pat Ament, 1975. Climb the crack between *The Unsaid* and *Washington Irving*.

114. **The Unled** 11b FA: Jim Bodenheimer (?). Toprope the arête between *Next to Nearly* and *The Unsaid*.

115. **The Unsaid** 9 ★ FA: George Meyers and Roger Grette, 1970. Rack: up to #2 Friend. Classic. Very popular. Begin atop a distinct pedestal with a tree and a fallen block along the in-cut ledge. Climb a slab up to a steep crack and right-facing dihedral system, continue for about 12 feet, then crank left to a pothole on the face (8+). Move straight up to a narrow roof (9), pull back into the main crack and continue to the top.

116. **Shock of the New** 10d S/VS FA: Alec Sharp, Bob D'Antonio, Matt Lavender, 1981. Begin with *The Unsaid* and continue up the arête, first on the right, then on the left.

117. **Strawberry Shortcut** 9+ S ★ FA: George Hurley, Cindy Stanley, Chris Reveley, 1976. FA: Variation A, Hare and Woodruff, 1980. This fine pitch takes the dihedral to the left of *Cruisin'*. . . . From the talus, climb a right-facing dihedral with a tree up to a deeply in-cut ledge and belay (this is just south of the tree and pedestal at the base of *The Unsaid*). Climb the dihedral to a small slab beneath a roof (8+), up a shallow, left-facing corner, pull right above the overhang (9+), and finish as for *Cruisin'*. . . .

117a. **The Direct Finish** 8 Climb a short, right-facing dihedral through the headwall.

117b. **Baby Sitter** 8+ FA: Brooks and Foster, 1982. More of a boulder problem than a route. Take a horizontal crack near the ground, below *Strawberry Shortcut*.

118. **Cruisin' for Burgers** 10c ★ FA: Candelaria, Erickson, Ament, 1975. Excellent. This is first route left of the *Verschneidung* slab. Approach as for *Verschneidung*, but from the initial ledge, merge left into an obtuse, right-facing dihedral with a large, detached flake. The crux is the last 15 feet of the dihedral. Climb up to the left for 50 feet and rappel. The original line includes the rotten headwall up and right from the leftward traverse (9 S).

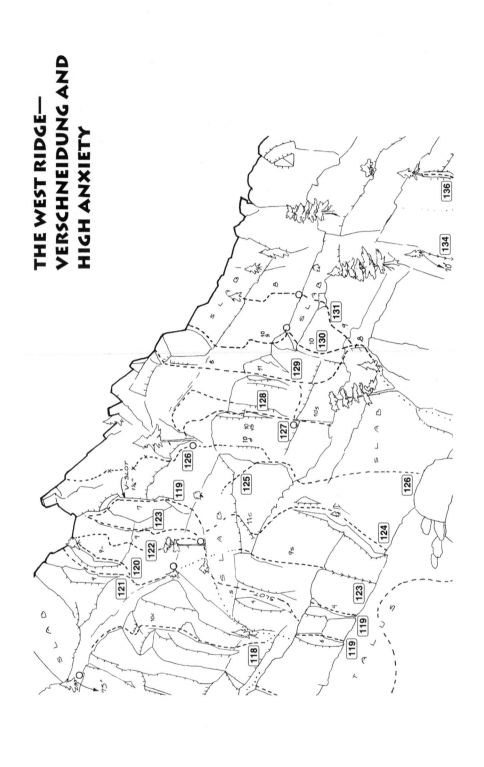

THE WEST RIDGE—
VERSCHNEIDUNG AND
HIGH ANXIETY

VERSCHNEIDUNG (VD) AREA

This area lies 50 feet or so above the two huge boulders and dead pine mentioned for the High Anxiety Area. It is characterized by a flat, tilted slab with a tall, thin tree at mid-face. The distinctive *Verschneidung* V-slot is just above the slab.

119. **Verschneidung 7** ★ FA: Jim Erickson and John Behrens, 1968. Classic. Begin below the left side of the tilted slab, perhaps 80 feet northwest of the huge boulder and dead pine, and just above where the trail passes over a notch chopped and sawn into a large fallen tree. P1. Climb either of two short, right-facing corners to a ledge, (6 left, 4 right), up a slot to the edge of the slab, and up right to belay at the tall thin tree. P2. Climb the obvious V-slot via a 1.5-inch crack (7) and exit left at the top.

120. **Ghetto Blaster 9** FA: Brooks and Jim Foster, 1982. Begin 20 feet right of a dead tree, and 5 feet right of an easy, wide crack. Climb the face above a large crystal that is about 3 feet off the ground (9 S), up to a block with a crack through it, then up the main slab to a small tree at the upper left corner and belay. Climb an overhanging wall and take the right of two dihedrals (9).

121. **White Rabbit 9** FA: Carl Harrison and Sandy East, 1980. Begin as for P2 of *Ghetto Blaster*, but climb the dihedral to the left.

122. **Toothsheaf Transfusion 11a S** FA: Derek Hersey, Keith Ainsworth, 1987. Ascend the steep upper face between *Ghetto Blaster* and *Clear-a-Sill*. Keith recalls long reaches between large holds.

123. **Clear-a-Sill 9** ★ FA: Chris Reveley and Ajax Green, 1976. Begin at a groove a short way right of the start of *Verschneidung*. Climb the groove and a crack past the left side of the overhanging headwall (9 S) and belay at the tall tree below the *Verschneidung* slot. Climb an overhanging, left-facing corner just left of the slot (9).

124. **Verschneidung Indirect Start 11b VS** FA: Chip Chace, Chris Archer, 1990 or 1991. This pitch takes the rather long, right-leaning undercling to the left of the *Verschneidung Direct Start* crux, to gain the slab below *Verschneidung*.

HIGH ANXIETY AREA

This is the nondescript section of wall between *Verschneidung* and The Amphitheater. The best landmark in this area is a pair of enormous, half-buried boulders that force the trail to make a detour to the west. A huge, dead ponderosa pine mentioned in the previous edition of this guide now lies in pieces atop these boulders. This is about 200 feet above the creek.

125. **Verschneidung Direct Start 10c VS** FA: Tobin Sorenson and Jim Erickson, 1975. Begin as for *Varieties of Religious Experience*. Where this route veers right, follow a short 10c undercling up and left to join the big slab and climb easily up to the tree below *Verschneidung*.

126. **Varieties of Religious Experience 11b ★** FA: Chris Archer and Cris Ann Crysdale, 1987. Rack: 2 sets RPs, Aliens, Friends #1-3, QDs. Recommended. Start at a small tree 20 feet off the ground, above the now recumbent dead pine tree. P1. Climb up and slightly left to the undercling. Climb out the undercling, (10a) over a small roof, up and right to a short, right-facing dihedral (10d), and up to the large tree on the right edge of the *Verschneidung* slab. P2. Work left to the arête and climb past 3 bolts (crux) to the top.

127. **The Foaming Cleanser 10b/c VS** FA: Chris Reveley and Ajax Greene, 1976. Begin above the large boulder, climb a slab, and belay on a ledge with a small pine tree. Climb a poorly protected seam over a bulge and up a shallow, right-facing dihedral that is capped by a roof. Veer off to the left and rappel from a tree.

128. **She's a Soft Scrubber 11a S** FA: Derek Hersey, Brad White, John Huffer. Quite good. Start as for *Foaming Cleanser* to the ledge, then gain the dihedral just to the right, and a 1- to 2.5-inch crack (11a). Cross a steep, rotten band above (9) by stepping right, then up to a ledge. Left, easier, to the tree atop *Varieties of Religious Experience*.

129. **High Anxiety 11b S ★** FA: Scott Woodruff and Dan Hare, 1977. Begin as for *Crow's Landing* or *Foaming Cleanser* and traverse into the bottom of the route. Climb over a bulge via thin crack (10 S) to a belay by a small pine tree. Go up the steep wall to the right-hand of two right-facing dihedrals, up the dihedral (crux), and belay above. An easier lead goes to the top of the wall.

130. **Crow's Landing 10 S** FA: Alec Sharp and Chris Dale, 1980. Begin atop the huge boulder as for *Auntie Perspirant*, then go up a blunt, out-leaning rib, and belay (8). Climb a short, right-facing corner to a small ledge, up a short, left-facing corner that changes to right-facing, and belay on a large slab. Climb broken rock right of a small tree.

131. **Auntie Perspirant 10 S** FA: Harrison and Stuberg, 1981. Begin from the top of the huge boulder. P1. Climb a dihedral (7) and walk right on the ledge to the red overhang, 6 feet left of *Odarodle*. P2. Up the overhang, left, and follow the crack up toward a water groove, then some hard moves out right onto a sloping ledge. P3. Climb an arête and up red rock to the top of the wall.

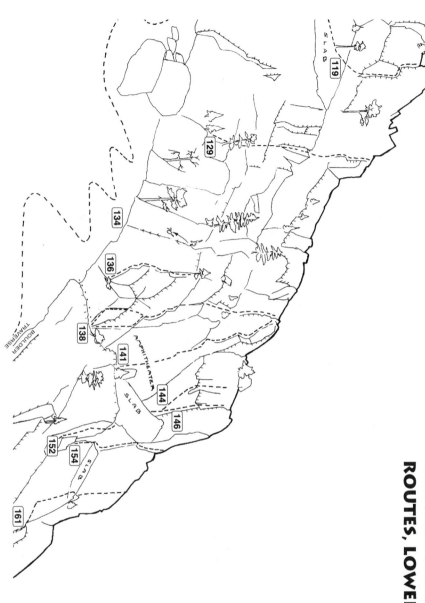

119
129
134
136
138
141
144
146
152
154
161
BOULDER TRAVERSE
AMPHITHEATER
SLAB
SLAB
SLAB
SLAB

THE WEST RIDGE—PRINCIPLE
ROUTES, LOWER SECTION

132. **Odarodle 9** FA: Harrison and Brooks, 1981. Climb a line 6 feet right of the huge boulder to a small ledge. Climb a bulging wall and go up the face just left of a small tree. Climb a groove in the red rock above.

133. **Quo Vadis 8** FA: Brooks and Lynn Smith, 1982. Climb up to the rappel tree mentioned in *Up the Downclimb* via a right-facing dihedral. Take the dihedral left of the rappel point, left 10 feet, over buckets, up a wide crack, mantel onto a slab, and climb a short wall.

134. **Up the Downclimb 8** FA: Stuberg and Harrison, 1981. About 75 feet northwest from the amphitheater is a groove/chimney with a tree that is used as a rappel anchor. Climb the groove.

135. **Arch Enemy 10 A1** FA: D. Smith and Brooks, 1982. Begin about 15 feet left of *Super Scooper*. Go up a left-facing dihedral to a ledge (6). Climb a right-facing dihedral, right to buckets, up and right via a thin crack at the top of a wall.

136. **Super Scooper 9+** FA: Mark Norden and Chris Reveley, 1974. Begin from the talus about 30 feet northwest of The Amphitheater. Climb a small dihedral that arches up and left into an overhang, and belay above. Climb an overhanging wall with a rotten flake (8).

137. **Runsholl Scrunch 9 A2** FA: Brooks and Copeland, 1983. Climb the arête to the right of *Super Scooper* and belay on the ledge to the left of *Initial Hangover* (8). Climb up and left to the right side of a pillar (A2) and up to a tree.

THE AMPHITHEATER

Just above and north of *Morning Thunder* is a large alcove or amphitheater with a large, sunny south-facing slab on the left and a severely overhanging wall on the right. Leave the trail just above an obvious, steep, bouldering traverse (this is right next to the trail). Scramble up and right to a ledge at the base or approach via the ramp that leads up to *Morning Thunder*.

138. **Initial Route 8** FA: Layton Kor and Herb Swedlund, 1963. Begin from the lower west corner of the amphitheater. P1. Work up and left into a blocky dihedral and belay on a ledge beneath a roof. P2. Climb a slot through the roof and work up to a ledge with a juniper tree (8+). P3. Work up into a left-facing corner and finish at the top of *Allosaur*.

138a. **Initial Hangover 10** Climb a roof to the left of P1 of *Initial Route*, then join it after about 20 feet.

139. **Territorial Integrity 10** FA: Chris Archer, D. C. Carr, 1987. Toprope the *Allosaur* face on the extreme left.

THE AMPHITHEATER

THE WEST RIDGE—TERMINUS AND
THE AMPHITHEATER FROM THE SOUTHWEST

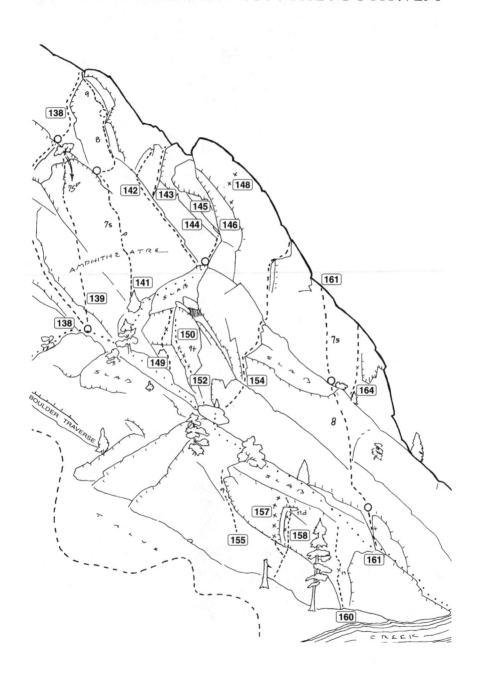

140. **Piece Easy 6** FA: Carl Harrison, 1981. Not to be confused with *Urine Trouble*. Climb the left side of the *Allosaur* wall.

141. **Allosaur 9 (7 S)** ★ FA: Larry Hamilton and Dakers Gowans, 1974. A fun route. Begin near a juniper tree. P1. Climb up the middle of the south-facing wall of The Amphitheater to a ledge on the left (7 S). P2. Move up and right, climb a left-facing dihedral (8), and belay on a ramp. P3. Climb up and left beneath the roof/dihedral and pop around the left end of the roof (9).

142. **Blind Mouse 8** FA: Stuberg, Harrison, Brooks, 1981. Climb up the ramp of *Something Blue* past the V-slot, then lieback up a crack on the right.

143. **Something Blue 9+** FA: Brooks and Lynn Smith, 1982. Climb a steep ramp to the left of *Blues Power* and cut right through a V-slot after about 30 feet.

144. **Blues Power 12b** ★ FA: Skip Guerin and Bob Horan, 1981. Rack: up to a #4 Friend. Climb the obvious, very steep, finger-and-hand crack to the left of *Office Girls*. **Note:** This is an expanding crack.

145. **Office Girls Walk the Plank 12d** ★ FA: Copeland and Brooks, 1983. FFA: C. Fowler, 1986. Rack: Friends up to #3.5. Climb the long, over-hanging hand-and-fist crack just left of *Wing Shot*. It begins with a slot.

146. **Wing Shot 11b** ★ FA: Chris Reveley and John Ruger, 1974. Rack: up to a #3 Friend. Scramble up beneath the gigantic roof and climb the hand crack on the right.

147. **Shot and a Chaser 11b** FA: Derek Hersey, Steve Dieckhoff, 1980. Start up *Wing Shot*, then take the left-facing dihedral on the right to finish.

148. **Thunder Construction (?)** There are 3 bolts and a lower-off anchor on the steep southwest arête right of *Shot and a Chaser* and above *Morning Thunder*. This is presumably an abandoned, unfinished project, as there appears to be a long runout to the first bolt.

MORNING THUNDER AREA

These routes climb the rib on the south side of The Amphitheater and the sunny face on its right. Leave the West Ridge Trail just below an obvious, steep, bouldering traverse (right above the trail) and scramble up and right to a ledge at the base. The climbs can also be accessed from the upper end of a large ramp that climbs directly up from The Streamside Trail. Belay from the top of a boulder beneath a clean, south-facing wall.

149. **Thunderworld 11a** FA: Steve Dieckhoff, Gray Ringsby. Rack: up to a #3 Friend. Climb the west-facing overhang around to the left from *Morning Thunder*. Launch up the large flake, then make a couple of thin moves

up and right past a bolt. Jeff Achey and Dan Hare previously climbed the flake and headed straight (?) up the face. **Variation:** Escaping left from the apex of the flake is rather easier.

150. **Thunderbolts from Hell 12a** ★ FA: Gray Ringsby and Steve Dieckhoff, 1988. Rack: 3 QDs and #3 Rock. Start up the initial few feet of *Morning Thunder*. Move left and sashay up the strenuous arête, using holds on both sides, past 3 bolts, to a double-bolt anchor.

151. **The Achievers 10d VS** FA: Guokas and Payne, 1986. Start as for *Morning Thunder*, then head straight up from the initial crack.

152. **Morning Thunder 9+** ★ FA: Pat Ament and Christian Griffith, 1979. Rack: up to a #3 Friend. A short, strenuous, pretty route. From the boulder at the base of the wall, climb up and right along a zigzag crack.

152a. **Jam Con 9** FA: Pat Ament and Cam Jon, 1980. Blast out the right side of the chockstone at the top of *Morning Thunder*.

153. **The Exterminator 11a S** FA: Guokas, Lester, Reynolds, 1986. Climb the thin, left-facing dihedral to the right of *Morning Thunder*.

154. **Flyback 9 S** FA: Harrison, Brooks, Stuberg, 1981. P1. From the boulder at the base of *Morning Thunder*, scramble up to the east, climb a steep dihedral (9 S), and traverse east to the top of a slab. P2. Climb straight up the headwall (9), right on a ledge, and up a crack to the top.

155. **First Unknown 8** FA: Carl Harrison and Sandy East, 1980. Location of this route is a little vague. Begin from a sloping ledge about 60 feet above the stream. Climb a dihedral with a hanging flake.

TERMINUS

This is the south end of the West Ridge, just above South Boulder Creek. The area is a little complex. The first few routes listed here start off the trail, which skirts the base of the West Ridge just above the river (*Water Line*, etc.). The last few routes listed begin from higher ledge systems best accessed by scrambling up one of the ramps beginning just before the end of The Streamside Trail.

156. **Trivial Pursuit A3** FA: Mike Brooks and Kyle Copeland, 1985. Begin about 10 feet left of *Mineral Maze*. Aid out the obvious crack to the lip of the roof, left to buckets, and up to a tree.

157. **Leggo My Ego 12a/b** FA: Larry Harris, Kent Kator. Start as for *Mineral Maze*, but climb the thin face left of the dihedral past 5 bolts. One can also toprope the same line directly, a little easier.

158. **Mineral Maze 11d** ★ FA: Bob Horan, 1984. Above a slab, up and left from *Water Line*, and directly above the sign marking the start of West Ridge Trail, climb a right-facing dihedral and pull over the roof at its top. 2 bolts.

159. **Suchasigha Bobba 10d S** FA: Brooks and Joe Huggins, 1982. Start just left of *Water Line*. Stem up a short, left-angling seam, move right, then straight up to potholes.

160. **Water Line 11a S ★** FA: Mike Brooks and Lynn Smith, 1982. There is a little scramble over a slippery ramp, just past the end of The Streamside Trail, and right above the river, which accesses the West Ridge. Fifteen feet past this is a narrow, south-facing wall with a diagonal grassy crack and bolt. Climb this (11a), and go straight up above the bolt (8).

161. **Roadside Attraction 11b S** FA: Chip Ruckgaber, Maurice Reed, Mike Benge, 1981. From the west end of The Streamside Trail, scramble up a large ramp until beneath an overhanging, left-facing dihedral with a fixed pin. P1. Climb the dihedral and belay at its top (crux). P2. Climb the beautiful face above (8 S) and belay behind a block. P3. Climb a steep, west-facing wall (7). The second pitch is probably the same as the first pitch of *Good Cling Fun*.

162. **Good Cling Fun 9+** FA: Eric Doub and Tony Asnicar, 1979. In the middle of the south-facing slabs at the bottom of the West Ridge, identify vertical stripes of black and yellow lichen. P1. Begin on a blocky ledge about 40 feet down to the right from the bottom of these stripes. Climb a clean, flat wall to a slab and belay about 30 feet up the slab. P2. Climb an overhang and finish on the east slabs.

163. **Leg of Ilg 9** FA: Doub and Griffith, 1980. Begin from a ramp below and east of *Earnest Stemmingway*. Climb an overhang off of the ramp (9), up 50 feet to a dead tree, and up a 20-foot, left-facing dihedral with a perfect 1.5-inch crack in it (7).

164. **Earnest Stemmingway 9 ★** FA: Pat Ament and Mark Shepard, 1980. The southernmost section of the West Ridge is transected by two diagonal ramps that slant up toward the west. Begin at a small tree about 75 feet up along the more easterly ramp. Climb up and right over a small roof, up a shallow, left-facing dihedral with a bolt, and up the east slabs to a tree.

165. **Warg 5 (?)** Christian Griffith, 1980. Down and to the right of *Earnest Stemmingway*, just left of the obvious tree, go up a short dihedral, right under a red roof, and up a groove to a tree.

166. **Gimli 7** FA: Eric Doub and Christian Griffith, 1980. This route climbs the south margin of the east slabs. Scramble up to a tree below and right of a roof. Climb moderate bulges and slabs for 130 feet to a tree.

KLOOF ALCOVE AREA

This clandestine area ajoins the West Ridge across from the West Face of Redgarden wall. Approach via the Redgarden Wall Trail. Hike up the trail and

KLOOF ROOF ALCOVE

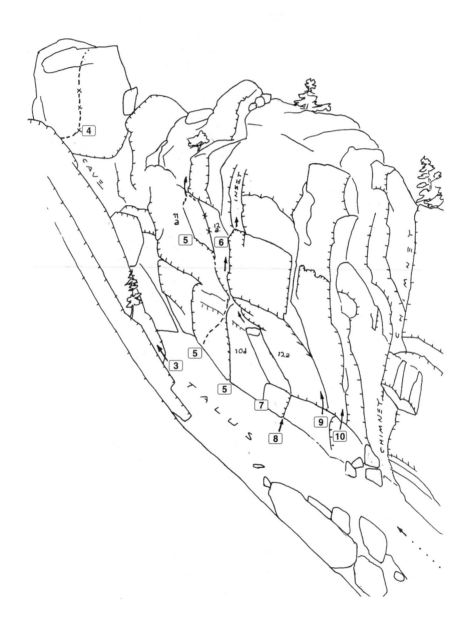

locate a sign (approximately under *Vertigo*) marking the access trail to Kloof Alcove. This is the only viable way to cross the steep, loose talus. As one approaches the alcove, the trail becomes less defined. Head up into a notch at the base of the alcove. Try to stay on the trail to avoid further erosion of this barely stable slope. This is a nice sheltered spot in winter, sunny and protected from the wind.

Routes are described left to right (clockwise), starting from the east side of the entrance to the alcove.

1. **Incarnation 13a** ★ FA: Bob Horan with Henry Lester and "Clean Dan" Grandusky. Toproped earlier by Mark Tarrant. Rack: include small Friends. This pitch takes the south face of Long John Tower on the West Ridge, but the easiest approach is from the Kloof Alcove. Hike up the ramp to the base of the tower. Start just left of *Weevil's Walk*. Climb up the overhanging wall past an initial rotten section, then 5 bolts (crux) to a small ledge at mid-face. Finish up a smooth slab past one more bolt and 2 pins (11b). This pitch is 90 feet long.

2. **Weevil's Walk 10c S** ★ FA: Pat Ament, Greg Jacobson, 1963. FFA: Jim Erickson, Duncan Ferguson, 1971. From the lower entrance to the alcove, scramble northwest up a broad slab to the bottom of a dead-vertical, south-facing wall with a conspicuous "U" shaped inset. P1. Climb up bad rock to a finger/hand crack (crux) that is climbed to a ledge. P2. Traverse right to the end of the ledge, then angle up and left to the top.

3. **The Wizard 10b/c** FA: Clean Dan Grandusky, Bill Rogers, Doug Kurtz, 1980. Start from two pine trees at the base of the slab west of Kloof. Wander up the slab (7) and belay at the last large pine. Traverse left around the corner 60 feet to an overhanging, right-facing dihedral. Climb halfway up this and step left into another corner and belay. Climb the short corner. This is just right of *Weevil's Walk*. **Variation A: Psycho-Killer 11a** FA: Clean Dan, Mary Clifford, 1983. Continue straight up the initial dihedral of *The Wizard* and angle left at the top.

4. **Non-Dairy Creamer 11c** FA: Scott Reynolds, John Payne, 1986. Climbs the south face of the huge chockstone. Start from the left, after scrambling up the slab, then up past 3 bolts.

The other routes here tackle the very steep west-facing wall. Descent from the ledge at the top is by a scramble to the south, or a rappel from the bolts at the top of *Sequential*.

5. **Kloof 11a** ★ FA: Scott Woodruff, Dan Hare 1976. Climb a short, steep wall up and right to the ledge just left of the *Polygap* dihedral, climb a crack up and left along a flake to a horn, then straight up the face to the top.

6. **Sequential 12a** ★ FA: Randy Leavitt, Dan Hare, 1981. Start as for *Kloof*, but where *Kloof* heads left, launch out across the roof (crux) into the very strenuous crack above (sometimes a fixed nut) to a two-bolt lower-off at the top.

7. **Space Neutralizer 12a** ★ FA: Bob Horan, Mark Rolofson, 1986. A little down and right from the start of *Kloof*, locate two short but very steep cracks leading to the ledge immediately below the dihedral. The left crack (less defined, with fixed pin) is *Space Neutralizer*. Pass the pin, then veer right at the flake.

8. **Polygap 12a** ★ FA: Skip Guerin, John Baldwin, 1981. The right crack, more defined, is *Polygap*. Up the crack, step left onto the ledge at the base of the dihedral. Belay. Up the dihedral (11a S) to the top. **Variation A: Extendogap 12c** FA: John Baldwin, 1996. The arête right of P2 of *Polygap* has been toproped.

Right of *Polygap* is a grossly overhanging blank face, with a ridiculous dead-end RURP seam. Just right of this are two wild lines, starting from the same spot. The left one arcs up and left into a dihedral, the right arcs up and right into a separate dihedral.

9. **Lycra-Clad Donkeys C2** FA: John Baldwin, Steve Sangdahl. This is the left line. One of the last great lines left in the Canyon still not freed at time of writing. Clean aid only.

10. **Superfly 12d S** ★ FA: Skip Guerin, with Chip Ruckgaber and Christian Griffith, 1983. Rack: mostly thin, #4 Friend. This takes the right line. Established ground-up over two or three days, as a pink point (gear left in, rope pulled). Still waiting for a second lead. (Christian reports being "really scared" belaying.)

11. **Lug's Crack 9+** FA: Mike Brooks, Andrea Azoff, 1987. Rack: Friends up to #4. Below *Kloof*, 75 to 100 feet, is a good ledge with a big tree. Start right of the tree, up to a left-angling crack, up to a tree belay.

RIVER BLOCK

In the riverbed below the gully between the West Ridge and Redgarden Wall sits a 25-foot-tall boulder. There are two routes.

12. **Eastern Priest 11 S** FA: Bob Horan, free solo. Start from the apex of the river-deposited rocks/gravel. Climb up and left. Start is the crux.

13. **Kiss of Life 12b/c** FA: Bob Horan. Rack: RPs. This takes the roof and face on the east side.

REDGARDEN WALL

Redgarden Wall rises to the north from the narrows of South Boulder Creek and is the largest crag in the Boulder area, reaching a height of 700 feet and featuring at least 283 routes.

Approaches: To reach the west face, take the footbridge across South Boulder Creek and hike west along the Streamside Trail until it climbs up above the creek and passes a small rib that overhangs to the west (Pickpocket Buttress). A trail branches right and wanders up along the west side of this buttress all the way to the *Hot Spur* area. To reach the South Buttress Roof routes and the Lower Ramp, hike The Streambank Trail past The Whale's Tail to a big cement slab and scramble up the talus to the base of the wall. To reach the southeast face (Bulge Wall), take the footbridge across South Boulder Creek and hike up the Wind Tower Trail until it is obvious to cut west beneath the southeast-facing wall.

Descents: There are several ways to descend from the upper reaches of Redgarden wall.

Use the *East Slabs Descent Route* to downclimb from the summits of Lumpe Tower, Tower One, Tower Two, and the South Buttress. From Tower One or Lumpe Tower, scramble down to the notch between the two and work southeast down a gully (Class 4) to the broad saddle between Towers One and Two. From here, scramble a short way into the wooded gully just east of Tower Two, hike down to the southeast about 100 feet until the gully drops off and it is easy to get up onto the rib on the left (northeast). Scramble south down this rib (the upper South Buttress) for 150 feet, cut back to the northeast, climb down (or around) a short overhang, and shoot down a prominent groove for about 100 feet. Stem down past a bulge, go left into another groove, descend 100 feet, and go down to the right (southeast) to a large, grassy ledge with some juniper trees. From here, step left into a V-slot and downclimb (Class 4) to the gully between the East Slabs and Hawkeagle Ridge. Follow a primitive footpath down the brushy gully until beneath *Cinch Crack*, then climb down around either side of the giant chockstone (east side if wet), and on to the Wind Tower Trail.

Note: If you are not familiar with this descent, do not try it in the dark, nor if it is covered with snow or ice. It is possible, though not convenient, to rappel from trees.

It is also possible to descend the gully to the west between Lumpe Tower and Tower One, if for example, you had left gear at the bottom of the West Face. Make two long rappels from the notch to the Red Ledge that runs across the west face and a third from a tree on that ledge (two 50-meter ropes needed).

To descend from the summit ridges of the Middle Buttress and The Hot Spur, that is from the tops of such routes as the *Great Zot*, *Rewritten*, *Green Slab Direct*, and *The Hot Spur*, scramble north along the east side of the ridgecrest to a notch. Beyond the notch, the terrain climbs up toward Shirttail Peak; to the

REDGARDEN WALL—EAST SLABS DESCENT AREA

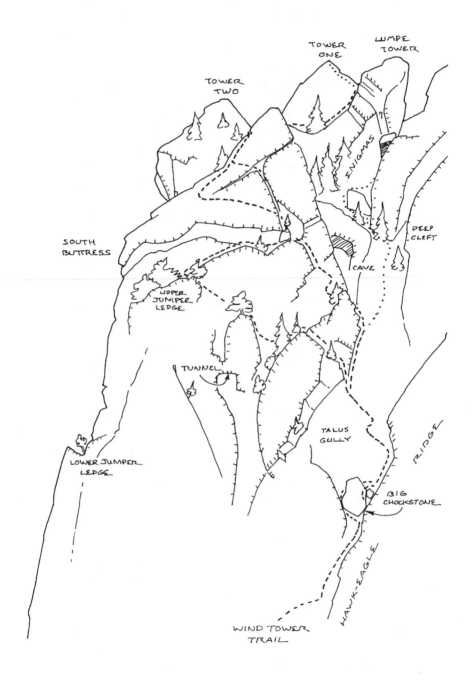

west a navigable gully descends to the main draw between Redgarden Wall and the West Ridge. Descend this loose gully (Class 3), then follow the West Face Trail back down toward South Boulder Creek.

The routes are listed from left to right, beginning with the upper end of the West Face.

THE HOT SPUR AREA

This is the highest and farthest northwest of the three large buttresses comprising the West Face of Redgarden Wall. It has a broad, steep, south-southwest-facing wall interrupted by square-cut roofs. A shattered, discontinuous west face meanders up past the Crag X area to finally merge with the West Ridge at a prominent spire called The Potato Chip.

If one continues northwest up the forested gully beyond The Hot Spur, a section of broken cliffs, which is the northern continuation of Redgarden Wall, will be encountered on the right. At the top (north end) of this formation is The Potato Chip, and just beyond, the south face of Shirttail Peak. The lower routes in this area are probably more easily reached via the West Face Trail and the upper gully, while The Potato Chip is typically accessed from The Rincon Cutoff.

1. **Crag X 9** FA: Jim Beyer, rope solo, 1979. Somewhere to the north of Redgarden Wall, locate a large pocketed wall (may be part of Shirttail Peak). Work up about 30 feet to a small juniper tree on the southwest corner of the wall, walk right, and belay. Go left 15 feet, turn a small roof (crux), follow a right-angling dihedral to a crack, et cetera.

2. **Doris Gets Her Oats 8** FA: Stuberg and Brooks, 1981. Circa 300 feet northwest from The Hot Spur is a south-facing wall with a prominent, left-angling ramp (*Hypothermia* area?). Begin from a ledge and climb an offwidth crack. Exit left.

3. **Heddie La Rue 9** FA: Brooks, Stuberg, Coy, 1981. Climb a crack system about 10 feet right of *Doris Gets Her Oats*.

4. **Hypothermia 9** FA: Tim Beaman, Scott Woodruff, Dan Hare, 1975. Locate the more westerly of two, short, south-facing walls 200 feet northwest from The Hot Spur. Climb over a small roof via a thin crack, move right, back up to the left, and belay on a ledge. Step left and follow a jam crack to the top. 70 feet.

The next four routes are situated on the scruffy west face of The Hot Spur.

5. **Gazette 6** FA: Brooks, 1981. Begin 30 feet left of *Jag* and follow a thin crack to a tree.

6. **Jag 8** FA: Brooks and Smith, 1981. Begin about 15 feet left of *The Hot Spur*. Go up to an undercling, follow a crack for 30 feet, and angle left to the left side of a loose flake. Climb the left of two left-facing dihedrals. Scramble off to the north.

REDGARDEN WALL—WEST FACE FROM THE SOUTHWEST

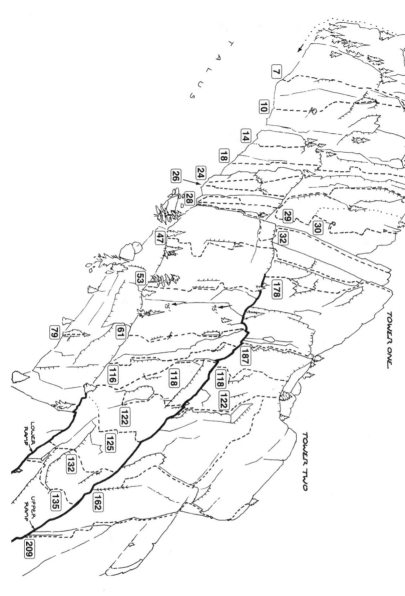

REDGARDEN WALL—
THE HOT SPUR TO TOWER TWO

REDGARDEN WALL—WEST FACE, THE HOT SPUR

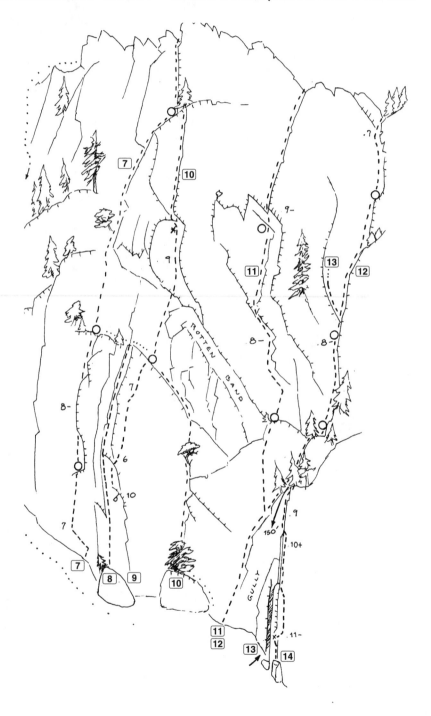

7. **The Hot Spur 8** FA: Bob Culp and Stan Shepard, 1961. Begin a short way left of a large fallen block. P1. Move up and left along a diagonal crack, then straight up to belay at the base of a chimney (6). P2. Climb the chimney, which narrows to a jam crack (8), and belay on a ledge beside a small tree. P3. Climb a long, undistinguished pitch to a ledge beneath a steep headwall (Class 4). P4. This is the best part of the route. . . climb the headwall via a slightly overhanging, left-facing corner to the top of the face (6).

8. **Waiting Room 7** FA: Unknown. Begin atop a fallen flake at the bottom of the west arête. Climb the arête via cracks and corners (7) to the belay ledge of *Northumberland Crack* and finish with the overhanging crack of that route (9).

9. **The Dull Men's Club 10 S** FA: Todd Bibler and Chris Archer, 1987. Climb the face and corner system between *Northumberland Crack* and *Waiting Room.*

10. **Northumberland Crack 9** FA: Bob Culp and George Hurley, 1965. A route of dramatic exposure and some loose rock. About 60 feet left of *Sunstar*, climb up onto a large block and belay behind a tree. P1. Climb cracks to a rotten ledge (6), traverse left, and belay beneath an awesome, overhanging crack at the left edge of the wall. P2. Climb rotten rock to a bolt beneath the roof and belay (optional). Climb through the overhang (9) and up the continuation of the crack to a ledge. P3. Move left and climb a steep, left-facing corner with jugs (6) to the top of the wall.

11. **Roof Wall 9** FA: Bob Culp and Stan Shepard, 1961. FFA: Erickson and Higbee, 1973. FA, Variation: Jim Erickson, 1973. The upper half of this route is pretty good, but getting there is not. P1. Begin as for *Lost in Space,* but angle up to the left and belay on a ledge by a small tree. P2. Climb a reddish V-slot (8) into a left-facing dihedral and belay beneath the main roof (or just above). P3. Master the roof (9) and finish with a shallow corner and crack. **Variation:** As an alternate start, climb a short undercling (10) and join the regular route.

THE MIDDLE BUTTRESS

This broad and rugged section of the West Face is home to a good number of fine routes. It extends to the north from the West Chimney to the steep gully of the route *Lost in Space.* In the middle of the upper wall stands a dramatic spire known as Rebuffat's Arête. It provides a fitting finish to a number of routes. To descend from any route that reaches the ridgecrest, scramble north along the east side of the crest to a notch, downclimb a gully to the west, then back along the base of the wall toward the south.

12. **Lost in Space 7/8** FA: Jim and Dave Erickson, 1970. Begin about 10 feet left of *Sunstar* and ascend indistinct terrain for a couple of hundred feet to the base of a huge dihedral. Climb directly up the dihedral for three pitches to the top of the wall. The crux is a bulge at about 75 feet, and there is a 7 move near the top.

13. **Sunstar 9** ★ FA: of first pitch, Dick Walker and Steve Gaskill, 1972; of entire route, Walker and Phil Raevsky, 1974. The first two pitches were previously published under the name *Ozone*. It is possible that Jim Erickson first climbed the chimney in 1970. An interesting route in a spectacular position. Begin in a distinct chimney immediately left of *Disappearing Act*. P1. Climb the chimney past two chockstones (6) and belay on top of the second one (optional). P2. Climb a crack in the back of a left-facing dihedral, stay to the right (9-), and belay on a big ledge. P3. Scramble up via easy terrain and belay at the base of a giant dihedral (*Lost in Space*). P4. Climb up over two bulges, then move up and left to a ledge that is about 20 feet right of a large tree (7). P5. Climb a clean, right-facing dihedral, pass a roof at its top, and follow the line of least resistance to the top of the face (150 feet, 8+).

14. **Disappearing Act 11a** ★ FA: Scott Woodruff and Dan Hare, 1975; FFA of P1; Roger Briggs, 1974. A Redgarden Wall classic. Begin about 5 feet right of a chimney and about 25 feet left of *The Grand Course*. P1. Climb onto a pedestal and pull right into the crack. Climb directly up the thin crack. When it veers left into a hand crack and steepens, step right (11a) into a right-facing corner that leads (9+) to a small stance. P2. Climb the crack just right of the edge of the face (10d), pull left around the corner, and climb the steep arête via a crack (9) to a big ledge.

14a. **Rabbits from Hats 11d** FA: Chris Archer, Todd Bibler, 1987. Where the P1 crack of *Disappearing Act* veers left, instead of stepping right, continue straight up past a short hand crack and two pins to the belay.

15. **Paris Girl 12d/13a (11a VS)** ★ FA: Christian Griffith, 1985. The cruxes are protected, but there is an 11 runout below the first bolt and a long 10 runout after the last bolt. Follow a line of bolts up the superb 95-degree wall between *The Grand Course* and *Disappearing Act*. 7 bolts, 140 feet.

16. **The Grand Course 10a or 11a** ★ FA: Layton Kor and Pat Ament, 1965. FFA: Jim Erickson and John Behrens, 1968. This was the first 11 pitch in Eldorado, climbed on-sight. FA: of 9 handcrack, Pat Ament, c.1965. Rack: up to a #4 Friend. Some serious birdshit on the first pitch does not keep this route from being rated a classic. Belay from the ground, or from the top of a pillar at the base of a chimney system at the right edge of the leftmost buttress on the west face of Redgarden Wall. P1. From the

REDGARDEN WALL—UPPER WEST FACE

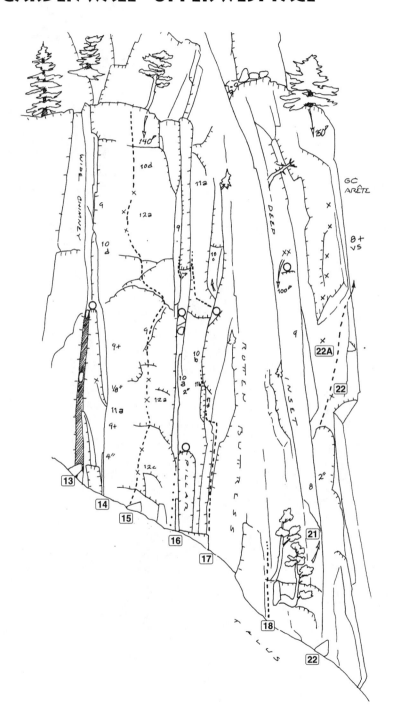

Joyce Rossiter on the fifth pitch of The Naked Edge *(5.11a/b), Redgarden Wall.*
RICHARD ROSSITER PHOTO

pillar, jam the obvious hand-and-fist crack (10a) up past some chockstones (optional belay). P2. Climb up to a roof and climb a handcrack on the left (9), or move right and climb a vertical dihedral (11a).

17. **Silver Raven 11d S** ★ FA: Dan Hare et al. (11 A2), 1977. FFA: Skip Guerin and Bob Horan, 1981. Rack: up to #2 Friend, #4 Friend for the chimney. The first pitch is superb and very strenuous. Begin about 10 feet right of *The Grand Course* in a rotten chimney. P1. Climb 20 feet up the chimney, move left into the bottom of a thin crack in a shallow, right-facing dihedral, and climb to its top (crux). Pull left under a bulge into a left-facing dihedral (11b), jam to its top (10b), and belay above a bulge at a minimal stance. P2. Climb up into a slot with loose rock, turn a roof on the left (10c), up a left-facing corner, and left to belay. The two pitches can be combined, or avoid the loose second pitch by traversing left about 8 feet and ascending the crux dihedral of *The Grand Course* (11a).

DARKNESS 'TIL DAWN ALCOVE

Maybe 600 feet up the West Face Trail, and about 60 feet right of *The Grand Course*, is a shady alcove, nicely landscaped and containing a tree stump, poking out horizontally about six feet off the big flat ledge. There is a steep, sharp-edged, 150-foot-high arête capped by a ledge, just right. The obvious, deep dihedral of *Darkness 'til Dawn* defines the back of the alcove.

About a ropelength above the talus is an intermittent ledge system (The Red Ledge). This appears in the Green Slab area, forms the summit of the sharp edged arête of *Color of Pomegranates* (GC arête), follows the strata rightwards past *Yellow Spur*, and almost intersects with the summit of the Upper Ramp. This serves as a useful feature in describing routes and sometimes also as a means of connecting better pitches on adjacent routes.

18. **Green Slab Direct 9** ★ FA: Bob Culp and Henry Huermann, 1961. FA: (4 arête) Bob Culp and Roger Raubach, 1961. Rack: up to a #3 Friend. The upper half of this route is superb and is frequently combined with *Darkness 'til Dawn*, *Grandmother's Challenge*, or *The Green Spur*. Begin a short way to the left of the horizontal tree stump. P1. Climb a steep slab, turn a roof on the left (8), and continue up cracks to belay by a small tree. P2. Climb another 50 feet to a good ledge (the north end of The Red Ledge). P3. Climb a steep finger crack about 65 feet to a fixed pin, traverse straight right to gain a left-angling ramp (9), or traverse left into a discontinuous crack (9+) and climb straight up to the ramp. Belay along the ramp where it is intersected by the second option. P4. Move up and slightly right along a steep crack to the top of the wall (6). **Variation A:** The original line followed the ramp up to the top. **Variation B:** The upper half of the route may be avoided by climbing the arête at the left side of the wall above the Red Ledge (4).

19. **Bits and Pieces 11a S** FA: Mike Clinton and Bill DeMallie, 1988. FA P4: Chris Archer, Chip Chace, 1987, who approached from *Lost in Space*. Rack: up to a #10 Stopper. Nice fourth pitch. P1. Climb the first pitch of *Green Slab Direct*. P2. Climb a crack and shallow, right-facing corners to the right of the regular second pitch of *Green Slab Direct* (9+ S). P3. Scramble up and left across The Red Ledge to the bottom of the arête that is north of the gully at the left side the upper face of *Green Slab Direct*. P4. Climb the arête and face to the left of the gully. There are three sections of slightly runout 10 with an 11a move at the top. "Save a #9 and #10 Stopper for the final hard moves."

20. **The Green Slab 8** FA: Bob Culp and Henry Huermann, 1961. This old route is seldom climbed. Begin just left of *Darkness 'til Dawn* beneath a steep slab. P1. Climb the slab to a left-facing corner and belay on a ledge at its top (8). P2. Up the gully (some loose rock) for a long pitch to a good ledge that runs across the face. This is the north end of The Red Ledge. P3. Climb up the gully for about 50 feet and follow a ramp that curves up and left to a tree (150 feet, 6). P4. Work straight up to the top of the wall (Class 4).

21. **Darkness 'til Dawn 10a** ★ FA: Jeff Sherman, Hunter Smith, John Ruger, 1974. Rack: up to a #4 Friend. This is a superb pitch, sustained, varied, and steep. Climb the crack in the shady alcove behind the *Grandmother's Challenge* arête, 140 feet to chains. A seldom-climbed 10a S second pitch follows the steep crack above to gain the expansive ledge above *Grandmother's Challenge* (part of The Red Ledge).

THE GRANDMOTHER'S CHALLENGE AREA

This area is defined by the dramatic, 150-foot, overhanging arête right of the *Darkness 'til Dawn* alcove, and the south-facing wall immediately right. *Grandmother's Challenge* takes the obvious, steep crack up this face to The Red Ledge. This area is located about 80 feet up along the base of the wall from West Chimney and about 600 feet above the foot of the ridge (Pickpocket Buttress).

22. **The Colour of Pomegranates 12d S** FA: Christian Griffith, 1985. The north-facing wall just right of *Darkness 'til Dawn* overhangs for 150 feet. Begin *Pomegranates* as for *Darkness 'til Dawn*. Climb up this route for 50 feet, then head out right on an obvious ledge system, up and right to the arête. Hard moves up the arête gain the bolt, from which 20 feet of hard climbing gains a second ledge system. The upper arête is runout "8+."

22a. **Project** There is a bolted project straight up the faultless face between *Darkness* and the upper section of *Pomegranates*. Bolted by Chris Hill in the 1980s.

23. **Spur of the Moment 11c S** ★ FA: Eric Doub, Jimmy Walker, "Clean Dan" Grandusky, 1985. This is a steep and poorly protected line up the right side of the dramatic arête. Step up from a block at the left side of the arête, work up around to the right side (left side of the face), go up the face (9+ S), then work right to the belay on *Grandmother's Challenge*. Traverse left under the roof (2 pins, 11c S), then straight up the face to the top of the prow (8).

24. **Grandmother's Challenge 10c** ★ FA: Layton Kor, Pat Ament, Dean Moore, 1963. FFA: Jim Erickson and John Behrens, 1968. FFA of original line: Chris Reveley and Mark Hesse, 1976. Rack: up to a #4 Friend. Classic. Begin about 6 feet left of *The Green Spur* and climb a crack (8, up to 4 inches) to a belay stance on a chockstone. Make some wild and strenuous moves up an overhanging offwidth crack under an intimidating roof (10c), pull right and lieback a flake past the lip (10c), then follow a crack straight up to the top of the face. **Variation:** The original line took a thin crack through the roof just left of the main crack (10d).

25. **Green Sleeves 10c/d S** ★ FA: Ed Webster, Henry Browning, 1987. Follow *The Green Spur* pitch two to its crux, then veer left into a corner and out a small roof to gain a good crack and easier climbing up to a ledge (9+, 150 feet). Continue to a large pine above, then traverse left past a gap to a ledge below and left of *Green Slab Direct*. The next pitch takes the finger crack left of *Green Slab Direct*. Up a short thin crack (9), then face-climb out right past a bolt into the start of the finger crack (10). Follow this to an easier arête and a large dead pine on the skyline (10, 140 feet). Descend *Paris Girl* (two ropes needed).

26. **The Green Spur 9** ★ FA: Dave Dornan and Dallas Jackson, 1960. FFA: Larry Dalke and John Lewis, 1964. Rack: up to a #2.5 Friend. Classic. Begin about 40 feet left of *West Chimney* and about 15 feet left of an arête (*Rewritten*). P1. Jam a short crack up the right side of an obvious pedestal and belay at the bottom of a chimney about 50 feet up (4). P2. Climb straight up the awkward, flared chimney (9, large Friends), up a crack into an overhanging, right-facing dihedral (9), step across to a crack on the right, then up more easily to the eyebolt on The Red Ledge, and belay as for *Rewritten*. P1 and P2 can be combined as one superb 200-foot pitch. P3. Move the belay up to the big ledge above *Grandmother's Challenge*. Climb to the top of a large block, up a crack, pull over a roof (9), and up to a belay on Rebuffat's Arête. P4. Climb to the top of the arête (8). P5. Step across and climb the face to the top of the wall (5). **Variation A:** P2: From the belay at the bottom of the chimney, step right, climb a crack through a roof (8), and continue upward

REDGARDEN WALL—
WEST FACE, MIDDLE BUTTRESS

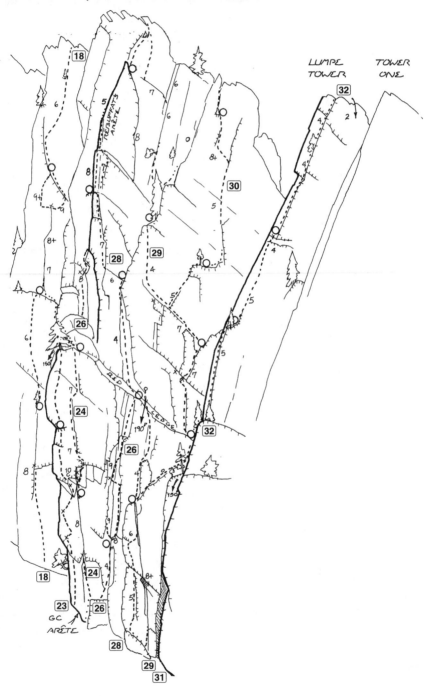

REDGARDEN WALL—WEST FACE

Middle Buttress

Rebuffat's Arete.

Lumpe Tower

14

18

24

28

31

32

36

West Ridge

until it is easy to stem left into the main line. **Variation B:** From the eyebolt, one may also finish with *Rewritten* or *Green Slab Direct*, either of which is recommended. From the same eyebolt, one may also rappel 200 feet to the ground.

27. **Burning Chrome 10** FA: Steve Dieckhoff, Ralph Burns, 1990. Climb the dihedral immediately right of the second pitch of *The Green Spur*, past a 10 bulge, rejoining *The Green Spur* where it steps right. Not very independent.

28. **Rewritten 7 or 8 S** ★ FA: George Hurley, Bob Culp, John Link, 1967. Rack: up to a #3 Friend. Classic. Begin at the alcove at the base of *West Chimney*. P1 is awkward to protect. The route has seen a few accidents; be careful with route-finding and gear placements. P1. Go up a ramp to the left, pull up onto a narrow ledge, and climb a shallow corner up to a small overhang near the arête. Pull up over the roof and hand traverse right (7) to finish in the crack of *The Great Zot*. P2. Climb a chimney behind a flake, continue up the face to The Red Ledge, and belay at a large, steel eyebolt (4). P3. Climb straight up a blocky, slightly loose, left-facing dihedral, squeeze into a chimney, and belay in a deep groove just above (5). Note that the face to the left of the short chimney can be climbed but is unprotected 9. P4. Make a fantastic, exposed hand traverse via a crack across the vertical wall on the left (6), climb straight up a hand crack for 50 feet (7), and exit left at the top. Climb directly up the arête (8) or up a shallow dihedral on the right (7) and belay just left of the edge. P5. Continue up the arête (6), put a sling around the pointed summit, and belay. P6. Stem across the headwall to a shallow dihedral and climb to the top of the wall (5). **Variation:** The original line climbed the gully at the left of Rebuffat's Arête from the top of the hand crack.

29. **The Great Zot 8+** ★ FA: Bob Culp and Stan Shepard, 1960. FA Variation A: Rob Candelaria and Lee Rozaklis, 1974. FA Variation B: R. Rossiter and Lynn Householder, 1978. FA Variation C: R. Rossiter and Linda Willing, 1979. FA Variation D: Rossiter and Willing, 1979. FA Variation E: unknown. FA Variation F: Joe O'Laughlin and Steve Turner, 1968. Classic. This is a popular route that can have heavy traffic on weekends. Beware of rockfall from overhead parties. *The Zot Face* is the recommended finish, as the upper section of the original line degenerates into fourth-class terrain. Begin in a small alcove at the bottom of *West Chimney*. P1. Climb a shallow corner and crack up to a small cave, jam out through the top of the cave via a hand crack (8+), and continue up the crack (7) to a belay ledge that is shared with *Rewritten*. P2. Climb a short, easy pitch up and right to a belay on The Red Ledge (0). P3. Climb shallow corners up to a roof (5), move left, pull over the roof at a left-facing dihedral (6), and go straight up to a belay ledge. P4. Move up and left to the top of a flake and follow a crack another 15 feet to a

REDGARDEN WALL—WEST FACE, MIDDLE BUTTRESS

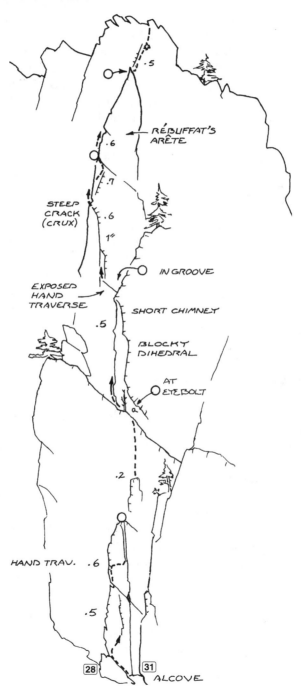

.5

RÉBUFFAT'S
ARÊTE

.6

.7

STEEP
CRACK
(CRUX)

.6

1"

IN GROOVE

EXPOSED
HAND
TRAVERSE

SHORT CHIMNEY

BLOCKY
DIHEDRAL

.5

AT
EYEBOLT

.2

HAND TRAV. .6

.5

28   31
ALCOVE

stance. From here, the original line goes up and left (2) to a belay at a large Douglas-fir tree. P5. Climb up and right to the ridgecrest (Class 4). **Variation A:** On P3, move left on The Red Ledge and climb straight up to the traverse on the fourth pitch. **Variation B:** On P5, climb a crack straight up from the tree. **Variation C:** On P5, move left from the tree and climb double cracks (6) to the skyline. **Variation D:** On P5, move left and climb a crack next to a right-facing dihedral, hand-traverse left (6), and finish above Rebuffat's Arête. **Variation E:** On P5, climb the wide crack (8+) in the right-facing dihedral formed by Rebuffat's Arête. **Variation F:** On P5, climb out onto Rebuffat's Arête via an inset ramp and fire up the arête (7).

30. **The Zot Face 8+ ★** FA: R. Rossiter and Ann Chernoff, 1980. This is the logical and direct finish to *The Great Zot*: exposed, sustained, and directly above the lower half of that route. P4. Climb the first 40 feet or so of the fourth pitch of *The Great Zot* to a small stance, then angle up and right along a narrow ramp (5) and belay atop a flake with a small tree. One may also climb straight up to this belay from the beginning of the traverse (10c S). P5. Step right and climb a dihedral and the face above to some left-facing flakes (5). Angle up and left along a thin crack to a small, right-facing dihedral (8+), up the dihedral (7), and slightly left to a perfect little belay ledge with a tiny tree. P6. Climb straight up to the ridgecrest in an easy groove.

LUMPE TOWER

Lumpe Tower is the narrow buttress and summit immediately north of Tower One. It becomes distinct above The Red Ledge and is distinguished by a clean, 300-foot west arête named for Jon Swanson, a climber who died in the Selkirk Mountains of Canada. To descend from the summit, downclimb to the south about 50 feet to the col between Lumpe Tower and Tower One. Rappel to the west, (down the Dirty Deed Chimney). Be aware that the last rappel from a large tree on The Red Ledge is overhanging and requires two 165-foot ropes. One can also downclimb from the summit, scramble to the south col as described above, then head east in a gully system. *The East Slabs Descent* becomes better defined above the saddle between Tower 1 and Tower 2.

31. **The West Chimney 5 S** This is the deep cleft between Lumpe Tower and the Middle Buttress of the West Face. It is about 450 feet high and runs from the talus to an isolated notch on the ridgecrest. The upper section is seldom climbed and should not be confused with the Dirty Deed Chimney, which is at the south side of Lumpe Tower. The lower 150-foot section can be used to access The Red Ledge, thence *The Dirty Deed* or *Swanson Arête*, but it is subject to rockfall, is distinctly unaesthetic, and

LUMPE TOWER AND TOWER ONE FROM THE WEST

LUMPE TOWER AND TOWER ONE FROM THE NORTHWEST

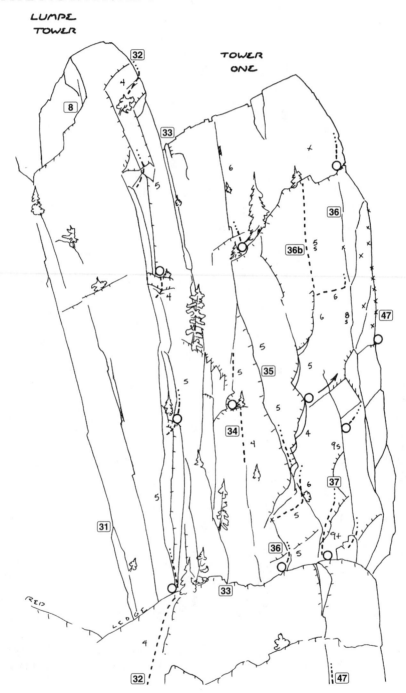

puts a party in direct conflict with a frequently used rappel route. It may be best not to think of it as a pitch and climb *Rewritten* or *The Great Zot* to reach The Red Ledge.

32. **Swanson Arête 5** ★ FA: Stan Shepard and party, 1960. Classic. This is one of the best moderate climbs in Eldorado. Climb the first pitch of *Rewritten* or *The Great Zot*, which of course makes the route 7 or 8+. From the belay niche, traverse up and right to *The West Chimney* and scramble up onto The Red Ledge. P1. From the high point on the ledge (behind a tree), climb a left-facing corner system to a belay at a tree (5). P2. Follow a crack system up the right side of the arête to a small roof (5), step right, pull over the roof (4), and belay on a ledge just above. P3. Climb a crack to the right of the arête, pull over a small roof into a clean dihedral (5), go up and right of a tree, and up a finger crack in a short corner to the summit (3). **Variation:** Climb part, or all, of the arête from the first belay to the tree near the summit (8). This yields a dramatic, exposed ascent on excellent rock, but there is little protection.

33. **The Dirty Deed 6** FA: Charles Alexander and Dean Moore, 1959. Not recommended. Often used as a rappel route. The traditional start is *The West Chimney*, but accessing The Red Ledge via the first pitch of *Rewritten* (7) or *The Great Zot* (8) is more pleasant. From here, traverse right along The Red Ledge to the bottom of the gully between Lumpe Tower and Tower One (the Dirty Deed Chimney). Follow this chimney to the top.

Right of the Dirty Deed Chimney is the large, well featured, airy Northwest Face of Tower One. This can be climbed by one of the four routes described below, or by many other variations and combinations.

34. **The Ytrid Deed 6** ★ FA: Pat Ament et al., c. 1965. Very nice. From The Red Ledge, climb up the Dirty Deed Chimney about 20 feet, then work up and right onto the face, and straight up to a ledge with small trees and optional belay (4). Climb a crack past the top of the *Daedalus* dihedral (5), then up a short way to a big ledge with several trees. Just left of the biggest tree, climb a crack and slot up the north arête of Tower One.

35. **Daedalus 5** FA: Soloed by R. Rossiter, 1981. Start 20 feet right of the base of the Dirty Deed Chimney. Start as for *Icarus*, then enter and follow a prominent, right-facing dihedral to the left (5). This leads to a large ledge with trees mentioned in *Yrtid Deed*. From here, finish with *Yrtid Deed* or one of the adjacent routes.

36. **Icarus 6 S** ★ FA: Route and variations soloed by R. Rossiter, 1981. Classic. This airy line achieves magnificent position on the northwest side of Tower One. Approach via *Rewritten*, *The Great Zot*, or *Yellow Spur* and begin from The Red Ledge about 20 feet right of the Dirty Deed

Chimney. P1. Climb over a bulge (5), traverse right across a slab, and climb a zigzag, right-facing dihedral to a belay just above an obvious crack that leads out to the arête (5). P2. Continue up the dihedral to where it fades into the face (5), make an exposed traverse out right to the arête (6 S), and climb straight up to a belay niche on the arête. P3. Climb the narrow arête above (6 S, last pitch of *Yellow Spur*) to the pointed summit of Tower One. **Variation A:** Traverse right at a crack below the first belay and follow *West Arête* to the summit (8 S). **Variation B:** Climb straight up the face from the top of the zigzag dihedral (5 S).

37. **West Arête 9 S ★** FA: Of entire arête, Steve Monk, solo, 1980. Classic. Climb the first three pitches of *The Yellow Spur* (or any nearby route that leads to The Red Ledge). From the top of the third pitch of *The Yellow Spur*, go up over a bulge (9) and up the very dramatic, clean arête to join *Icarus*, then up the last pitch of *The Yellow Spur*. The lower section of the arête is 9 and unprotected. The section beneath the traverse on Icarus is 8 and unprotected.

LUMPE TOWER—APPLE STRUDEL AREA

This is the clean, steep face about 165 feet high, between *The West Chimney* and *The Yellow Spur*. The top of this face forms part of The Red Ledge. The bottom of this face starts almost off the trail, a little way above the steel ladder.

38. **Blueberry Boodle 10d/11a** FA: Glen Randall, Joe Kaelin, 1977. Start up the right side of *The West Chimney*, belay. Traverse right under the roof to gain the beautiful upper slab of *Apple Strudel*. Follow this to The Red Ledge.

39. **Journey to Ithaca 10d S** FA: Archer and Hare, 1988. Rack: include Lowe Balls, or similar. P1. As for *Parting Shot*. P2. Go left just before the roof (10a), and take a thin crack and face just right of the arête, past a big flake, to the ledge.

40. **Parting Shot 11b/c ★** FA: Chris Archer and Dan Hare, 1988. Begin where a narrow ledge, which continues rightwards across the face to the base of *The Yellow Spur*, leaves the West Face trail. The right side of *The West Chimney* forms a small buttress that creates a right-facing dihedral at its right side. P1. Climb the dihedral past a couple of bolts (10d) to a pedestal. P2. Continue up the corner, out right to a bolt beneath a roof. Over the roof (crux) and follow more bolts to the ledge at the top of the face.

41. **Apple Strudel 12a/b S ★** FA: Pat Ament and Paul Hagan, 1969. FFA: Jeff Achey, Randy Leavitt, Dan Hare, c. 1981. Classic. About 75 feet left of *The Yellow Spur*, and just right of *Parting Shot*. P1. Climb straight up the face past 2 bolts (crux) to the right end of a roof, move right and

Fran Bagenal on Ruper (5.8 S), *Upper Southwest Face of Redgarden Wall.*
STEVE BARTLETT PHOTO

climb past another bolt, then up to a sling belay beneath a long, shallow roof. P2. Move left and turn the roof (11c), then follow more bolts up the steep wall to a small ledge about 25 feet beneath The Red Ledge.

42. **The Untouchables 12b/c ★** FA: Mark Tarrant and Dan Hare, 1988. Begin just right of *Apple Strudel* and climb up past 3 bolts to the two-bolt belay on that route, 60 feet up. Crux is very height dependent. A second pitch has been toproped, but due to a loose block, has not been led.

YELLOW SPUR/VERTIGO AREA

There is a narrow ledge which starts at the left end of the *Apple Strudel* face, below *Parting Shot*, and leads south (right) for 150 feet past the base of *The Yellow Spur*. At the right end of the face, directly under the start of *The Yellow Spur*, a second ledge begins, about 12 feet lower. This is the Vertigo Ledge. Access this ledge by hiking up the West Face Trail past the wooden and steel ladders, to any of several weak points where one can scramble up, or else continue a little farther up the trail to meet the north end of the ledge. Note that the northern part of the ledge has two levels: the upper level is at the base of *The Yellow Spur*, while the lower level accesses *Vertigo, Mickey Mouse Nailup*, etc.

43. **Ignition 12a (11 S) ★** Rack: up to a #3 Friend. The original version followed just the first 4 bolts then traversed right into *The Yellow Spur*; FA: Charlie Fowler, Dan Hare and Kris Hansen then led a pitch squeezed between this and *The Yellow Spur*, reversed the traverse, then led the upper section, as described, in 1988. The route described here combines the best of the two pitches. Climb past 4 bolts just left of *The Yellow Spur* (crux). Continue upward past another bolt and a left-leaning flake (11c) to a small roof, step left to a downward-pointing flake, up past a bolt and into a black, left-facing corner (10d), and up to a belay above a bulge. Finish as with *Over the Shoulder*. **Variation:** (The right-hand start). Start as for the direct start of *The Yellow Spur* and head up, over a bulge (bolt, 10d) to join main line.

44. **Over the Shoulder Stuff 10b S** FA: Scott Woodruff, Dan Hare, Chris Reveley, 1976. From the lip of the roof on *The Yellow Spur*, climb up and left into an overhanging slot (crux), move right at a dead tree, over the bulge and belay. Climb up through a left-facing dihedral and up to a ledge that is about 20 feet below The Red Ledge.

45. **One and a Half Hours of Power 11b S ★** FA: Derek Hersey, Janet Robinson, 1988. Start at *The Yellow Spur*, follow *Over the Shoulder Stuff*, and connect into *Ignition* to finish.

46. **Loose Living 10a S** FA: Dan Hare and Katy Cassidy, 1982. Begin with *The Yellow Spur*, veer left as for *Over the Shoulder*, go over a bulge, up

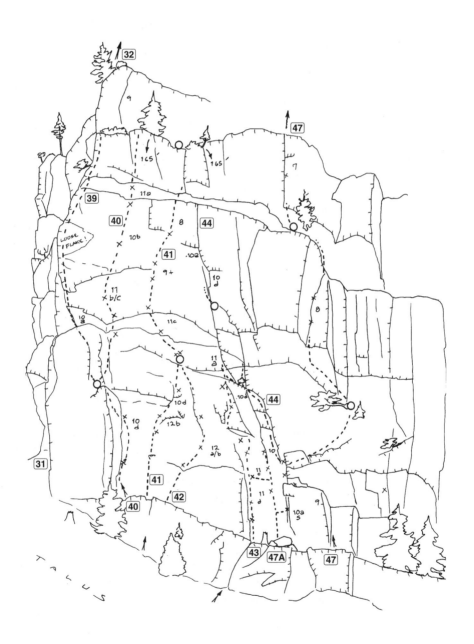

steep loose rock via a thin crack, over another bulge, and left to the belay on *Over the Shoulder*. Climb up and right to a crack and up to The Red Ledge beneath *The Dirty Deed*.

47. **The Yellow Spur 9** ★ FA: Layton Kor and Dave Dornan, 1959. FFA: Royal Robbins and Pat Ament, 1964. FFA Variation A: Rick Medrick, 1965. FA Variation B: Dalke and Ament, 1962. FA Variation C: Dalke and Ament, 1962. FA *Edge Game:* Ed Webster and Michael Dougherty, 1984. FA Variation E: Culp et al., 1965. FFA Variation F: Larry Dalke, 1967. Speed ascent: Michael Gilbert, 17 minutes. Rack: RPs to a #3 Friend. 6-7 QDs. One of the all-time classics of Eldorado. This is a long and sustained route, and difficult to retreat from. Allow plenty of time to top out and get back down. Hike up the West Face Trail past the steel ladder. Here a switchback brings one to the base of a 150-foot-high, smooth, bulging, face. This is the Apple Strudel Face. *The Yellow Spur* begins immediately right of this, off the upper Vertigo Ledge. Either traverse this ledge to the base, or scramble (4) 15 feet up a shallow, juggy dihedral to gain the upper ledge. There is a roof 25 feet up. *The Yellow Spur* follows a flake around its left end. The 10b direct start goes straight up to this flake, and the 9 start is in a shallow, right-facing corner 15 feet right.

P1. To do the 9 start, climb up the right-facing dihedral (9) and traverse left beneath the roof. Power over the left side of the roof (9), then up and right to a belay at a dwarfed tree. P2. Traverse up and left, up a clean, right-facing dihedral with fixed pins (8), and left to a belay on a good ledge. P3. Climb cracks and a shallow corner up to a stance beneath a bulge (7), over the bulge and up a V-slot (7) to a sizable ledge and belay. Be careful of loose rock on this ledge! P4. Traverse right and climb a huge dihedral to a belay stance beneath a roof (0). P5. Hand traverse out right beneath the roof, turn the corner (8), and climb up the steep, left-facing dihedral (8+) to a fantastic belay on a tiny triangular pedestal. P6. Climb a crack on the arête, step right, and follow a line of fixed pins (sustained 9) to a stance at a detached flake. From the flake, traverse left along the strata (The "Robbins Traverse"), then straight up past a piton to the top of the headwall and up the arête to a belay niche (8). P7. Climb straight up the exposed, classic arête to the summit (6 S). **Variation A: Direct Start** begin 15 feet left of the 9 start, directly below where P1 cranks through the roof. Make a few moves up and right on overhanging rock (10b) to a weird crack, straight up to the roof and join the 9 version. **Variation B:** Traverse left from the first belay and climb the nearer of two right-facing dihedrals (8). **Variation C:** Climb the steep wall above the dwarfed tree, then back left to belay atop P2 (8 S). **Variation D: Edge Game (9)** Climb a crack 20 feet left of P3. This leads directly to the base of the West Arête. **Variation E:** Climb out to the left

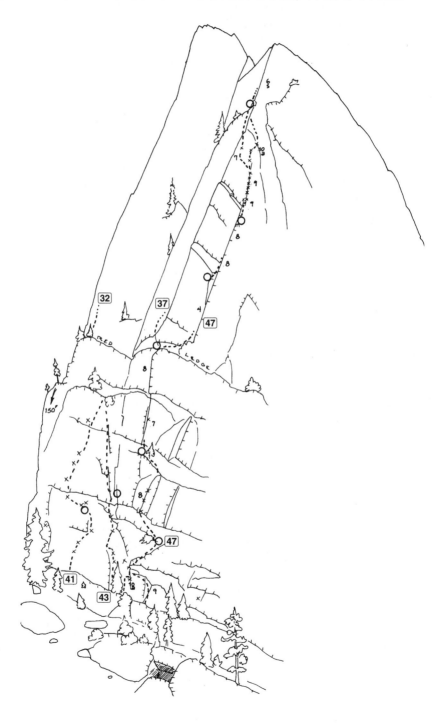

beneath the big roof on P5 and up the arête as for *Icarus* (8 S). **Variation F:** The popular free version of the original aid line on P6. Climb up and right past 2 bolts and a pin (10c), swing around to the right, then up and left to the belay on the arête.

48. **The Magic Roof A2** FA: Brooks, Magi Tedli, DeLaney, 1986. Begin about 20 feet right of *The Yellow Spur* and climb a hairline crack through a roof. Look for a bolt in the roof.

49. **Rocky Raccoon 9** ★ FA: Teena Wells and Ron Akin, 1981. Start 30 feet right of *The Yellow Spur*. Climb a tree to the lip of the large overhang and pull onto the wall (7) at a fist crack. Belay at a tree. Follow the same crack system, now finger-sized, for 50 feet to a ledge. Continue up parallel cracks (9) and step left to belay. One may also climb a nice, right-facing dihedral 15 feet to the left (7) to reach the belay. Climb an overhang "protected" by a #0 RP (8), then up and right to reach the Upper Ramp or left to *The Yellow Spur*.

50. **Fresh Garbage 9** FA: Jim Erickson and John Behrens, 1969. Climb an overhanging, rotten gully to the left of *Lower Mellow Yellow* for about 30 feet and belay. Begin with a short bulge (9), then straight up. One may also do a handjam to the right of this (10a). Climb a steep wall to a tree.

UPPER RAMP—WEST FACE

This is the narrow section of cliff that lies right of *The Yellow Spur* and below the summit of the Lower Ramp. Descent from here is normally by rappel down the face left of *Vertigo*. Locate a very large tree on the west face below the saddle behind Upper Ramp. Rap 70 feet to a bolted anchor at the top of *Song of the Dodo*, then 80 feet/25 meters to the ground. One can also rappel *Pigeon Crack* via a hard-to-see anchor at the top of this climb, then one or two more rappels from trees with slings—one rope is adequate, two faster—to regain the Vertigo Ledge.

51. **Lower Mellow Yellow 8** FA: Larry and Roger Dalke, 1968. This was the original start to *Mellow Yellow* (11d). Begin at a dead tree about midway between *Neurosis* and *The Yellow Spur*. Climb the overhang (6) and step left to belay. Climb the headwall (8), then up easier rock for 60 feet to a ledge. Climb an overhanging, left-facing dihedral to the top (7).

52. **Neurosis 10d S** FA: Layton Kor, 1965. FFA: Wunsch, Bragg, Higbee, 1974. FA of left start: Erickson, Behrens, 1978. Climb the overhang about 10 feet left of *Psychosis* (10d S) and belay above. Climb a thin crack through an obtuse, right-facing dihedral to the belay of *Psychosis* (9+). Climb straight up to a roof, traverse right (10d), and up to the top. The initial overhang may be climbed farther left (10).

REDGARDEN WALL—WEST FACE OF
UPPER RAMP FROM THE SOUTHWEST

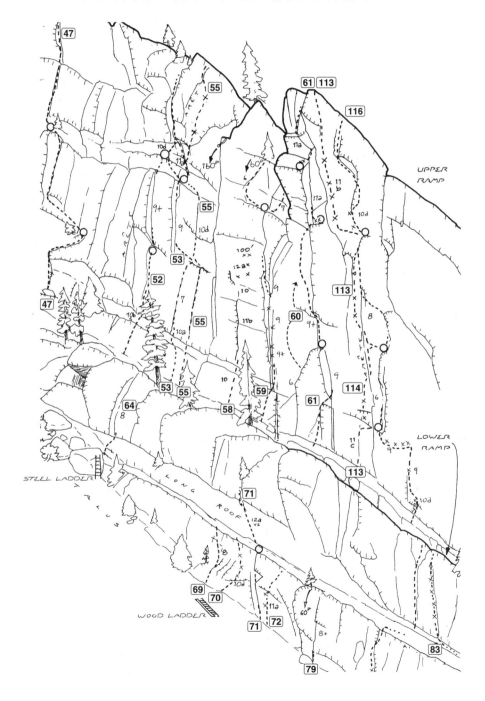

53. **Psychosis 10d S ★** FA: Layton Kor and John Lewis, 1965. FFA: Wunsch, Erickson, Marquardt, Reveley, 1973. FA Variation: Erickson, Fowler, 1978. An impressive and interesting route. Start behind a huge Douglas-fir tree near the top of *Schizophrenia*. P1. Climb up through a tricky roof with small pro (10c) and up the face to a stance (optional belay). Move left and climb a shallow, slightly rotten, right-facing dihedral to a rotten ledge, and move up to the left to belay (9). P2. Make a scary traverse to the right (10d S, harder for short climbers) to a hand crack and power to the top (10a). **Variation A:** The second pitch of *Old Farts* adds some quality to the route. **Variation B:** Skip the belay on the second pitch and climb the hand crack in the big overhang from the bottom (11a).

54. **Psycho Pigeon 11a ★** FA: Ed Webster, Henry Browning, 1987. Climbs the entire west face, via the top of the Upper Ramp, in seven pitches. Start 15 feet left of *Pigeon Crack*. (The three pitches above the Upper Ramp are very good. The first three pitches more or less follow *Old Farts*). P1. Climb a flake to roofs, gain a shallow, right-facing corner (9) just right of *Psychosis*. Belay 100 feet up *Psychosis* at a small stance. P2. Climb a vertical 10 crack on the left (black rock) over a small roof to another small belay stance on the right after 65 feet. P3. Angle right on strata past an unlikely bulge (9). Continue up a steep wall (bolt) to pockets on an exposed face. A short 9 headwall (bolt), gains easier ground and the upper end of the Upper Ramp. Walk left to a big juniper at the start of *Mellow Yellow*. P4. Climb just left of obvious cracks, up rather less obvious cracks, over a bulge and up a steep wall to a stance 80 feet up and just below a short flaring corner in a black face. Face climb out left (9) onto an arête and belay on a sloping stance. P5. Face-climb up an 8 arête forming the right side of *The Yellow Spur*, past a bolt, to a rest on the right. Climb out right, make 10+ moves past a bolt onto an exposed arête above an overhang. Up this past 3 more bolts to a shallow corner that gains the *Yellow Spur* arête belay. P6. Up *The Yellow Spur* a few feet, then veer left up a thin crack, then past 2 bolts to rejoin *The Yellow Spur* at The Robbins Traverse (11a). P7. Finish with the slab 40 feet left of the last pitch of *The Yellow Spur*, past 1 bolt (8).

55. **Three Old Farts Young at Heart 10d (9 VS) ★** FA: Jeff Lowe, Mike Wiess, Jim Donini, 1977. Start between *Psychosis* and *Pigeon Crack*. P1. Climb a 9+ flake (no gear) and continue up a finger crack through a roof (crux) to a belay stance on a rotten ledge, just right of *Psychosis*. P2. Step right around the corner and climb the steep, south-facing wall past 2 bolts (10a S).

56. **Pigeon Crack 8** FA: Dave Dornan and Peter Lev, 1960. This is seldom done as a climb but affords a rappel route from the top of the Upper Ramp. It is a grungy chimney about 50 feet north of *Vertigo*.

57. **In Between 11a S** FA: Layton Kor and Cliff Jennings, 1966. FFA: Jim Erickson and John Ruger, 1975. Just left of *Mickey Mouse Nailup*, climb the left of two inside corners (10d) to a semi-sling belay. Climb a headwall past three sections of 9, to a stance, continue near to *Pigeon Crack* for 12 feet, move back right to the original aid cracks, and finish on a ledge below the top of the Upper Ramp.

58. **Song of the Dodo 12a S** FA: Jack and Pam Roberts, 1998. Start up a crack system (11b S) in between *In Between* and *Mickey Mouse Nailup*. Where this becomes a right-facing flake, traverse right past a bolt (9) to another bolt, then up past a third bolt (12a). Watch for rope drag. This 25-meter pitch ends at a bolted rappel anchor on the rappel route from the Upper Ramp.

59. **Mickey Mouse Nailup 9+ S ★** FA: Dave Dornan, Joe Oliger, 1960. FFA: Jim Erickson and Jim Walsh, 1968. This is a good, steep route. Perhaps begin with *Schizophrenia* and finish with *Italian Arête* to *Smoke and Mirrors*. Begin behind a large tree about 20 feet left of *Vertigo*. Climb up a slab and follow the poorly protected crack past a number of old, rusty pins to a fin, go left as shown in the topo and finish at the top of the Upper Ramp.

60. **Magic Carpet Ride 11c/d** FA: Alan Bartlett, John Aughinbaugh, Jack Roberts, 1998. Rack: QDs. Begin left of *Vertigo*. Follow the steep face past 9 bolts to the *Vertigo* belay below the dihedral. Double ropes or a couple of long slings recommended.

61. **Vertigo 11b ★** FA: Dave Dornan and Peter Lev, 1961. FFA: Pat Ament and Roger Briggs, 1966. FA of roof: Henry Barber and John Stannard, 1973. Rack: up to a #3 Friend. Excellent. Begin at the south end of the Yellow Spur Ledge, just before it drops down toward the top of the Lower Ramp. P1. Climb the right side of a flake via a left-facing to right-facing dihedral (9) and belay on a good ledge, or start behind a large tree about 15 feet to the left and climb an easy (6) left-facing corner to the same ledge. P2. Climb an awkward bulge (9+), out left on easy ground, and back to the right to a bolted belay ledge at the top of a left-facing dihedral. P3. Pull up and left into an overhanging, right-facing dihedral (once equipped with as many as six fixed pins!) and power up to a belay ledge at the left (11b). P4. Move out to the right and climb a juggy crack through the massive roof, then jam a one-inch crack to the top of the Upper Ramp (11a). **Variations to P4: 61a.** Traverse way left and then up (8+) as shown in the topo. **61b. For the Birds 8** FA: Rob Candelaria and Misa Giesey, 1977. Go right to join *Dubious Graffiti* (8 for the traverse, harder once *Dubious Graffiti* is gained). **61c. Nervous in Suburbia (Project)** This is the working title of a bolted and long abandoned project

(two or 3 bolts, a pin; may possibly need another bolt) up the arête left of the dihedral pitch on *Vertigo*. Bolted by Dan Michael, (a.k.a. *Dan's Arête*) but never redpointed, this should be about 13b.

REDGARDEN WALL—LOWER WEST FACE
These short routes ascend directly from the West Face Trail and climb to the Vertigo Ledge.

62. **Senora 9** FA: Brooks and Leslie Dillion, 1982. Begin about 25 feet left of *Schizophrenia*. Climb a short, overhanging hand crack, then move up and right to an overhanging lieback.

63. **Bitter Route 9** FA: Brooks and Lisa Wilson, 1982. Begin about 5 feet left of *Schizophrenia*. Go up a rotten pillar, over "a roof thingy," a little left, and up to the big tree at the base of *Psychosis*.

64. **Schizophrenia 8 ★** FA: Doug McAuliffe, Jim Morrison. Begin in a niche between a huge boulder and the main wall, behind the steel ladder, and beneath a right-facing dihedral. Climb in from the left, turn a modest roof, and power up the dihedral past a solution hole. Finish on the big ledge beneath *Psychosis*.

65. **Arcane Saw 7** FA: Mike Brooks, 1982. Six feet right of *Schizophrenia*, climb straight up through a "type of roof thing."

66. **Flower Quarter 6** FA: Mike Brooks, 1982. Climb up to and over a square roof.

67. **Shadow 7 or 10** FA: Mike Brooks and Lynn Smith, 1982. Begin at a small juniper tree just left of the start of *Day Dream*. Climb up and over a roof just left of a large, left-facing, obtuse dihedral. An easier version takes the roof a bit farther to the left.

68. **Day Dream 10d** FA: Mike Brooks, 1982. Begin about 50 feet beyond the wooden ladder. Climb up a short slab and turn a 5-foot roof.

69. **Strangle Hold 10b/c** FA: Mike Brooks(?), 1981(?). Climb the clean face by the wooden ladder, and just right of two small trees at the north end of the smooth wall. Locate a bolt on the upper part of the face

70. **Unknown 10c ★** FA: Charlie Fowler (?), 1986. Begin just left of the right-facing dihedral of *Mickey Mouse Die-Rect*. Move up and right over a bulge (crux), then up the face past 2 bolts and a piton.

71. **Mickey Mouse Die-Rect 12a S** FA: of P1, Duncan Ferguson, 1974; of roof, Rob Candelaria, roped solo (tying off 30 feet of slack) 1978. Climb a pretty, right-facing dihedral (9 S) and belay on a ledge beneath a rotten band. Look for slings, then climb the large roof past a fixed nut to a conspicuous notch and pull over.

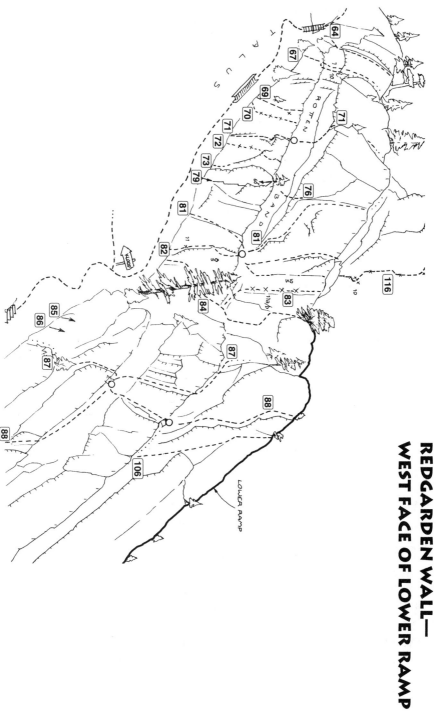

REDGARDEN WALL—
WEST FACE OF LOWER RAMP

72. **Toys for Tots 11a/b ★** FA: Charlie Fowler, 1986. Climb the vertical face past 2 bolts between *Phee Nix* and *Mickey Mouse Die-Rect.*

73. **Phee Nix 11d VS ★** FA: Mike Brooks, toproped?, 1981. Begin just left of *Flakey Floont* and angle left along a shallow, left-leaning, left-facing corner. The crux is in the first few moves. This was a commentary on the park entrance fee.

74. **Flakey Floont 7** FA: Unknown. Only flippant flakes flap their flukes flouncing on such effluent. Climb the chimney at the left of the buttress.

75. **Rough Roof 12b S/VS** FA: John Arran, Lidija Painkiher, Jennifer Martin, 1987. Rack: #1.5 Friend at base of roof and mid-range Rock after crux. From the tree above *Mr. Natural*, walk left to end of ledge. Climb up past old pins, up and right across roof, pull over the lip at a knifeblade, then up and left to finish.

76. **Over 'ed Power Line 12a S/VS** FA: John Aaran, Jennifer Martin 1986. Climb the massive roof behind and to the right of the tree at the top of *Mr. Natural*. Look for a bolt or pin. And yes, there was a guy called Ed standing at the base at the time.

77. **Captain 4Q 9 S** FA: Unknown. This nice pitch climbs the face left of *Mr. Natural* and near to the arête.

78. **Little Fish that Die Abruptly 12a** FA: Peter Hunt and Wayne Burleson, toproped, 1986. Climb the narrow face between *Mr. Natural* and *Captain 4Q.*

79. **Mr. Natural 8+ ★** FA: Robert Crumb. Perhaps 150 feet up the path beyond the big Douglas-fir tree, a 60-foot-high buttress protrudes to the west. A lightning bolt-shaped crack shoots up the south face to a ledge with a small tree. Climb the crack, then power around a flake and up to the tree.

80. **Nagulous Point 10b/c S** FA: Mike Brooks and Lynn Smith, 1982. Just right of *Mr. Natural*, turn a roof and climb a thin crack up to a ledge.

WEST FACE OF LOWER RAMP

The next few climbs start from near the trail and finish on top of the Lower Ramp. Some starts are described relative to features on the trail. There are two sets of railroad tie stairs. The lower has 7 steps, and the upper has 9 steps. Descend by scrambling down the Lower Ramp.

81. **Blow Hard 10** FA: Chris Reveley, Scott Woodruff, and Dan Hare, 1976. Begin a short way left of *Super Slab Direct Start*. Climb a very steep, flared chimney, then face climb up and left to the ledge at the base of *Dubious Graffiti.*

82. **Super Slab Direct Start 11c** FA: Pat Ament and Larry Dalke, 1963. FFA: Larry Marquardt and Art Higbee, 1973. FA of variation: Larry Marquardt and Chris Reveley, 1973. Begin under the left-facing dihedral with a fixed pin, about 40 feet up the path from the big Douglas-fir tree. P1. Up the dihedral (crux, highly reach dependent), move right after about 40 feet, and climb up to a ledge. P2. Go up and left into a chimney, and up to the ledge at the base of *Super Slab*. **Variation:** On P2, follow a harder thin crack to the right (10c S, the original aid line).

83. **Suparête 11a/b** ★ FA: Mark Tarrant and Dan Hare, 1988. This is an attractive route. Start a little way up from the "Kloof Alcove" sign. Immediately right of the variation P2 of *Super Slab Direct Start*, climb the face and arête past 4 bolts.

84. **West Face of Lower Ramp 0** From *The Slimy Spoon* et al., continue up the path beneath the west face of the Lower Ramp. About 30 feet north of a large Douglas-fir tree, climb a short corner up onto a bench, traverse right, then angle up to the left to the large juniper tree at the top of the Lower Ramp.

85. **Premonition 7** FA: Stuberg and Brooks, 1981. Begin about 15 feet left of *Velvet Hammer*. Climb a chimney system and dihedrals to the top of the Lower Ramp.

86. **Remention 8** FA: Gary Bratton, Curt Fry, Stuberg, 1986. Between *Premonition* and *Velvet Hammer*. Make tricky moves up to a dihedral and continue up to a ledge. Climb a dihedral to a steep, red-and-black wall.

87. **Velvet Hammer 10a/b** FA: Dan Hare and Dan Michael, 1978. Perhaps 50 feet left from *The Slimy Spoon*, and 20 feet right from the higher set of (9) railroad tie stairs, climb an overhanging hand crack above a juniper tree to the first belay of that route. Climb the next dihedral to the left of *The Slimy Spoon* to the same stratum that angles down to *Wave Rave*, but traverse left around a corner and up to the top of the Lower Ramp.

88. **The Slimy Spoon 8** ★ FA: Larry Dalke, Yves Gallet, Bill Harris, 1962. FFA: Erickson, Orr, Hurley, 1969. About 250 feet up the West Face Trail from the bottom of Pickpocket Buttress, there is a set of 7 railroad tie stairs. This route begins by a small tree 30 feet up and right from these stairs. Pass a small roof and ascend a dihedral to a ledge. Traverse left along a steep red band to a rotten gully, and continue to a belay beneath a rotten red roof. Climb a nice dihedral and belay on a ramp that angles down to the southeast to *Wave Rave*. Follow a zigzag, left-facing dihedral to the top of the Lower Ramp.

89. **Slime Monster 7** FA: Mike Brooks, Andrea Azoff, Jim Stuberg, 1986. Twenty feet right of *The Slimy Spoon*. Climb an inset, angle left to a roof, work left.

90. **The Greaser 7** FA: Pat Ament and Joe Fullop, 1962. Between *The Slimy Spoon* and *Earthquake*, climb a short, rotten red wall to a ledge. Zigzag up the wall, pass a roof on the right, and finish with a slab.

PICKPOCKET WALL

Pickpocket Wall is the southern extremity of the Lower West Face of Redgarden Wall. It is easily located at the junction of the Streamside Trail and the start of the West Face Trail. *Breakfast of Champions* looms over the initial steps of the West Face Trail.

91. **Earthquake 4** FA: Mike Brooks, 1982. Exact location unknown. About 40 feet left of *Breakfast of Champions*, go up a ramp until directly over a small "cave thing" and angle right about 20 feet to a ledge.

92. **Feel Free 6** FA: Jim Stuberg, Mike Brooks, Andrea Azoff, 1986. To the right of a large, right-facing edge, and left of *Protein Drink for Baby*.

93. **Protein Drink for Baby 8** FA: Mike Brooks, Andrea Azoff, Jim Stuberg, 1986. Ten feet left of *Lip Service*.

94. **Lip Service 9+** FA: Andrea Azoff et al., 1986. Just left of *Satyricon*, climb a left-angling crack and pull over the lip.

95. **Satyricon 11a** FA: Dan McQuade and Andrea Azoff, 1986. Derek Hersey free soloed it about 30 seconds later. Begin as for *Mr. Tomato* and climb a "small wall with a roof-crack thingie."

96. **Mr. Tomato A2** FA: Boddy and Brooks, 1986. Climb a zigzag, knifeblade crack about 20 feet left of *Unshown Sun*.

97. **Roof of the Unshown Sun A3/A4** FA: Ed Boddy, Mike Brooks, 1986. Rack: include hooks, sliders, knifeblades. Look for some fixed pro about 15 feet to the left of *Breakfast of Champions*.

98. **Breakfast of Champions 11a S ★** FA: Jim Erickson and John Ruger, 1975. A popular pitch. Where the trail makes a switchback near the wall, climb a small pillar, pull over a roof, and tackle a left-facing dihedral. Usually toproped.

99. **Captain Crunch 13b S** FA: Charlie Fowler et al., 1986. The very steep wall right of *Breakfast of Champions*. Up the face past a couple of bolts and pin to a lower-off spike.

PICKPOCKET WALL—SOUTHWEST FACE

100. **Perfect Lichenous 10b VS** FA: Jeff Achey and Matt Lavender, 1981. Climb the face about midway between *Pickpocket* and *Captain Crunch*.

101. **Spring Fever 9 VS** FA: Mike Brooks and Carl Harrison, 1981. Climb an overhang 10 feet left of *Pickpocket*, up and left via pockets, and pull over the lip at a yellow lichen streak.

102. **Pickpocket 8 VS ★** FA: Jim Erickson and David Breashears, solo, 1976. A pitch—best soloed. Up the pockets.

103. **Steak Dinner 9 VS** FA: Chip Ruckgaber, solo, 1986. Up the blunt southwest arête.

104. **South Face 7 VS** FA: Unknown. Climb the short, smooth wall. . . more of a boulder problem.

SOUTH FACE OF LOWER RAMP
The following routes can be reached by hiking beneath the Roof Routes to the base of the Lower Ramp and then scooting around to the south and west.

105. **Quo Vadis 8 ★** FA: Mike Brooks, 1981. Up and left from *Vertical Smile* is a similar crack system (or perhaps it is the same one). Climb it to the east-facing slab of the Lower Ramp.

106. **Vertical Smile 7 ★** FA: Carl Harrison and Jim Stuberg, 1981. From *Wave Rave*, scramble up a ramp to the west for about 70 feet to the base of a "Bastille-like crack." Move up and left into the crack, on up to a right-angling crack, and up to the easy slab of the Lower Ramp.

107. **Wave Rave 12b/c** FA: Brooks and Delaney, 1986. FFA: Fowler and Copeland, 1986. Climb a large roof past 2 bolts and a pin beneath the southeast corner of the Lower Ramp.

108. **Zombies on the Lookout 9+ S** FA: Griffith and Ament, 1980. From *Tiny Line*, scramble south and up a bit to a ledge. Traverse out onto the south face and climb steep, friable rock up to the easy slab of the Lower Ramp.

109. **Lime Line 8** FA: Stuberg, Brooks, Coy, Harrison, 1981. Climb the obvious groove to the left of *Tiny Line*.

110. **Tiny Line 8** FA: Griffith and Ament, 1980. Begin about 30 feet south of *Canary Pass*. Climb a thin crack in a southeast-facing wall to the easy slabs of the Lower Ramp.

111. **Lemon Line 7** FA: Brooks and Stuberg, 1981. Begin just left of *Candy-O*. Climb a crack and turn a small roof on the left.

112. **Candy-O 6** FA: Jim Stuberg, Solo, 1981. Begin about 20 feet south from *Canary Pass*. Climb a crack and turn a small roof on the right.

REDGARDEN WALL—TOWERS ONE AND TWO FROM THE SOUTHWEST

REDGARDEN WALL—SOUTHWEST FACE

Climbs on the southwest face of Redgarden Wall are described left to right, starting from the top of the Lower Ramp, then down and left to the Roof Routes Area. Some routes end on the Upper Ramp. From here, descend by rappel either down *Pigeon Crack*, *Rosy Crucifixion*, or the rappels at the base of *The Naked Edge*. However, *Grand Giraffe*, *Ruper*, *T2*, and *Jules Verne* continue past the Upper Ramp to the summit of Redgarden Wall, whence one may scramble down the *East Slabs Descent* or rappel back to the Upper Ramp via Chockstone Chimney.

ROUTES STARTING FROM THE LOWER RAMP

The following 10 routes all begin from the summit of the Lower Ramp, which is reached by scrambling up the Lower Ramp from the Roof Routes area. This is technically Class 4, but somewhat polished.

113. **Doub-Griffith 11c S ★** FA: Pitch one, Eric Doub and Eric Guokas, 1981; of *Doub-Griffith*, Eric Doub and Christian Griffith, 1981. Classic. *Doub-Griffith* starts by stepping left from the extreme end of the top of the Upper Ramp. In fact, it is just as easy to begin by stepping right from the extreme right end of the Vertigo Ledge. These two ledges are separated by about 20 feet of exposed 6 traversing. The route follows the sweeping arête left of *Super Slab* but makes traverses back and forth from the belays on that route, and in fact follows its second pitch. P1. Climb a steep wall with a thin but protectable 11c crack, then angle up and right around the corner to join *Super Slab* (a little runout). P2. Follow the second pitch of *Super Slab*. P3. Traverse left to the arête; up past 2 bolts and a fixed pin (11a/b), then continue straight up about 40 more feet to the belay on *Super Slab* below its final pitch. P4. Angle up and left past a bolt (10b) then run it out to a tiny ledge below the crux. Up the arête past 4 bolts (11b) to headwall where runout 9 climbing up and slightly right gains the final jugs.

114. **Dubious Graffiti 11c S ★** FA: Jeff Achey and Dan Stone, 1985. This variation to *Doub-Griffith* straightens out the line by connecting directly from the first pitch to the third. At the top of the crack on P1, climb straight up over a small roof past a bolt (11a) to a ledge and optional belay just under a bolt. A 10d move past this bolt gains easier (9) but runout climbing just right of the arête to join the third pitch of *Doub-Griffith* at a small ledge. Finish up this.

115. **To RP or Not to Be 12a S/VS** FA: Derek Hersey and Steve Andrews, 1987. Derek's mind-control classic, probably still unrepeated. Begin with *Super Slab* or *Doub-Griffith*, and climb to near the top of the second pitch. Step around to the left, make hard moves up and left past hidden

REDGARDEN WALL—SUPER SLAB AREA, SOUTHWEST FACE

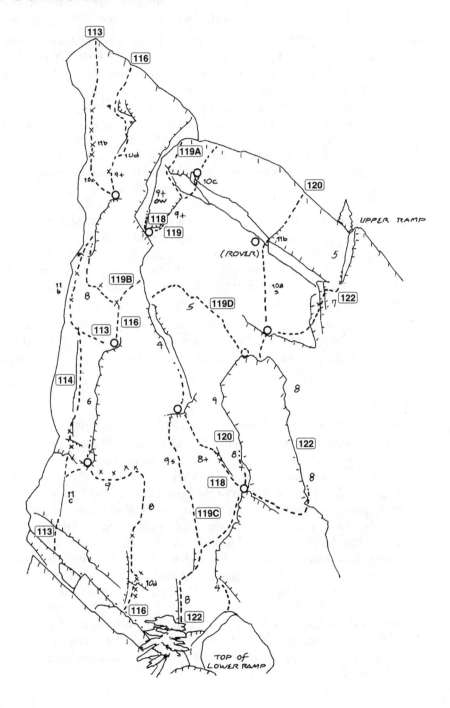

pockets, then straight left to a rest stance on a small ledge. Climb straight up for about 20 feet (4 or 5mm perlon around small flake), make a committing move left and mantel up onto a "thank God ledge." Climb up and right to the belay at the base of the last pitch of *Super Slab*. 120 feet.

116. **Super Slab 10d ★** FA: Layton Kor and Rick Horn, 1961. FFA: Pat Ament, Richard Smith, and Tom Ruwitch, 1967. FA P4 variation: Rob Candelaria, Misa Giesey. This is one of the all-time classics of Eldorado. From the top of the Lower Ramp, scramble up a ledge to the west about 35 feet and belay beneath some fixed pins. P1. Climb past an undercling (10c), move left into a corner and ascend about 50 feet, traverse left along some old pins, then up a short wall (9) to a belay stance. P2. Blast up a moderate, left-facing dihedral and belay after about 75 feet (6). P3. Move up about 20 feet to a fixed pin (this is where *Superspar* angles up to the right), work left around a blind corner (8), and straight up for 50 feet to a good belay stance in a dramatic setting. P4. Climb straight up the magnificent slab past a bolt (9) to a shallow, left-facing corner (old pin scar, good small/medium wire). Step right and master 15 feet of difficult, thin face (crux). Pull left back into the shallow corner, up to the roof, out to the left, and straight up to the top of the slab (9). **Variation:** To P4; head up to the bolt, then angle up and right (keep right of the shallow, left-facing corner) on small edges all the way to the top (10d, VS).

117. **Poached Eggs 10c S** FA: Rob Candelaria, Jim Royce, 1975. Start from the Lower Ramp, about halfway between the start of *Super Slab* and the start of *Ruper*. Climb thin cracks, and head straight up the face. Merge with *Grand Giraffe* about halfway up P3.

RUPER AREA

The next six routes all start in the same place, and share the same first pitch.

118. **Grand Giraffe 10a ★** FA: Layton Kor and George Hurley, 1960. FFA: Bob Culp, George Hurley, 1961. Classic. This famous route climbs the entire southwest face of Redgarden Wall. The crux is a spectacular off-width crack. P1. From the top of the Lower Ramp, climb the first pitch of *Ruper* to the belay niche at the base of the *Rover* dihedral (8). P2. Climb a flake and left-leaning diagonal crack (9) to a spacious belay ledge. The slot to the left of this pitch is 10 and seldom done. P3. Cruise a long, easy pitch up to a belay in a notch at the bottom of the ominous, off-sized fissure (4). P4. Struggle up the wide crack and chimney to the Upper Ramp. Traverse the ramp and descend to the upper end of a huge, arching roof (the *Exhibit A* cave) (Class 4). P5. Climb straight up the steep wall for about 75 feet, traverse right, then straight up to a belay in a short, left-facing dihedral (6 S). P6. Angle up and left along steep strata (7 S), then up and slightly right all the way to the saddle between Towers One and Two.

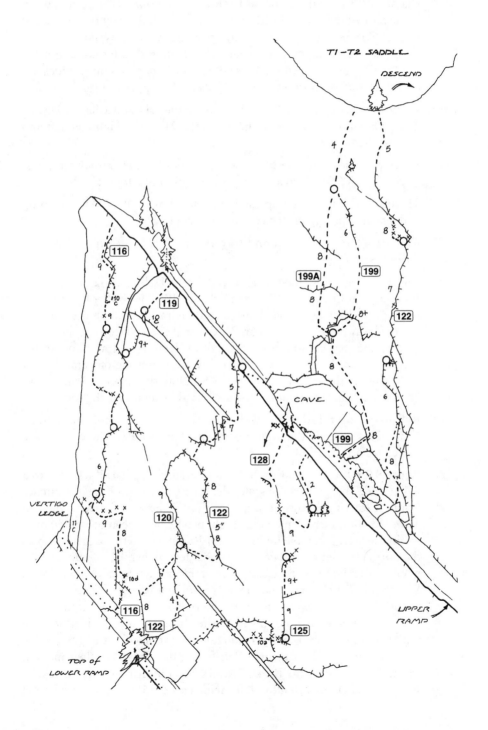

119. **Art's Spar 10d/11a ★** FA: Steve Wunsch, Jim Erickson, Art Higbee, 1973. Classic. P1. Climb the corner as for *Ruper* and *Grand Giraffe,* and belay at the base of the *Rover* dihedral (8). P2/3. Climb the next two pitches of *Grand Giraffe* (see topo). P4. Move right from the belay, go up a right-facing corner (9+), jam out through the exciting roof (crux), and belay atop the "spar." The roof has become a little harder since a block recently fell out. A short, easy pitch leads to the Upper Ramp.

119a. **Electric Aunt Jemima 10b/c** FA: Rob Candelaria and Charles Deane, 1975. On P4 of *Art's Spar,* at the top of the 9+ corner, climb out left and around the final roof.

119b. **Superspar 10d** Combine the first 2 pitches of *Superslab* with the last pitch of *Art's Spar* to create a superb variation (see topo).

119c. The original line started up the initial dihedral on P1, then headed up and left up a poorly protected crack system (9 S).

119d. Climb the *Rover* dihedral and traverse left across an exposed wall to *Grand Giraffe* (5).

120. **Rover 11c S ★** FA: Layton Kor and Larry Dalke, 1962. FFA: Steve Wunsch, Jim Erickson, 1973. Semi-classic. P1. Climb P1 of *Ruper* and belay at the base of a large, left-facing dihedral. P2. Climb the dihedral (9) to a belay on top of the pillar. P3. Go up the steep face via a thin crack (10a S) and step left to a belay beneath the roof. P4. Move down to the right and turn the roof at a small, awkward, left-facing dihedral (bolt at crux), and up the steep wall above (9+ S). Note that pitches 3 and 4 can be easily combined, avoiding the awkward belay under the roof.

121. **Roll over Rover 11d ★** FA: Rob Candelaria, Greg Finnof, Jim Royce, 1986. This ascends the arête just right of *Rover* P2. The clip-ins are difficult. 75 feet, 3 bolts.

122. **Ruper 8 S ★** FA: Layton Kor, Bob Culp, Ed Risley, 1961. Rack: RPs to a # 4 Friend. This great route scales the entire Southwest Face in 6 pitches from the top of the Lower Ramp to the saddle between Towers One and Two. Do not underestimate the climb; people have been benighted high up on the face. Scramble up the Lower Ramp, climb through a notch to the north, and set the belay on a ledge 8 feet higher. P1. Climb an easy pitch on the right (2) or a clean, protectable corner/crack on the left (8). Work up into a chimney and move around to a belay ledge on the arête to the right. P2. Traverse down to the right, then back up into the famous *Ruper* crack. Climb this for 75 feet to a good belay ledge on the right (8). Bring some 4-inch pro and don't get your knee stuck! P3. Move right on the ledge, up through left-facing dihedrals (6), then make a short, wild traverse (the Ruper Traverse) to the east with terrific exposure (7), and climb a shallow, left-facing corner (5) to a pine tree on the

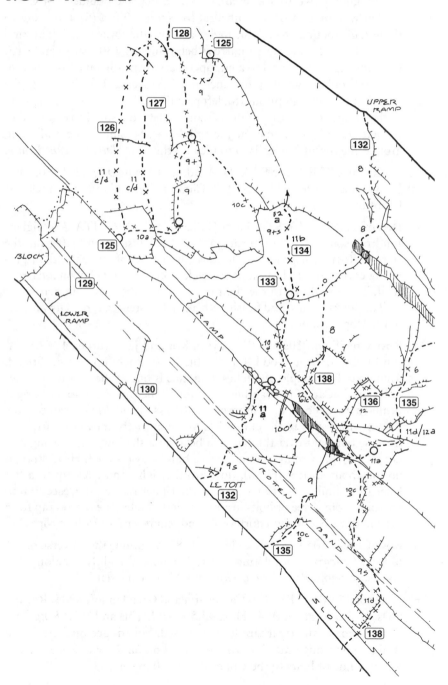

Upper Ramp. Traverse the ramp to the upper end of a huge arching overhang (cave), climb down into it (Class 4) and follow a rut in the brushy gully down to a level area above a massive boulder. P4. Climb the left wall of a left-facing dihedral for about 30 feet (6), move out to the left, up about 25 feet (7 S), angle back into the corner, out left around an overhang (5) and up to narrow belay stance: 130 feet overall. P5. Continue up the dihedral to a cramped belay beneath a massive roof (6, 90 feet). Look for an old piton anchor. P6. Move out left, then up to the roof past two ancient pitons (8), left past the end of the roof. Straight up to the juniper tree at the saddle (7), or out left to a small tree and up to the left side of the juniper at the saddle (4). Scramble east and south around the top of Tower Two to pick up the *East Slabs Descent Route*.

123. **Ducks on a Wall 11b/c S** FA: D. Arndt and Kevin Donald, 1970. FFA: Jim Collins and John Horn, 1979. Climb a thin and difficult crack just left of the *Ruper* crack.

124. **Deception Passed 10c S** FA: Larry Dalke, solo (?), 1967. FFA: Art Higbee, Jim Erickson, David Breashears, 1975. Begin just up and left from the start to *Rosy Crucifixion*. Surmount a narrow roof and ascend a right-facing corner, out right to a poor crack, then up to a belay on a narrow shelf. Traverse down to the right to the end of the shelf, out across the wall on funky flakes, and finish with a crack system that runs up and left to the Upper Ramp.

125. **Rosy Crucifixion 10a S** ★ FA: Layton Kor and Jack Turner, 1962. FFA: Jim Erickson, Steve Wood, Ed Wright, 1970. Rack: up to a #2 Friend. Though only a couple of pitches long, this is one of the all-time classics of Eldorado Canyon. Scramble to the top of the Upper Ramp, back right behind a huge block, up a short corner (Class 4) and down a ramp to the now-obvious start to the climb. P1. Make one hard move to start, then traverse out right over thin air to a belay in a shallow, right-facing corner (10a S). P2. Climb straight up to a bolt belay (9+). P3. Head straight up for about 45 feet (piton), down to the right, and back up to a flat ledge (9). Climb a short easy pitch to the Upper Ramp (4). Descent: Rap the route from a tree or bolts just up and left. (Note: The second rap from the end of P1 overhangs enormously and requires two 175-foot ropes.)

125a. **Rosy Cheeks 10a** FA: Derek Hersey, 1987. Continue the traverse on P1 of *Rosy Crucifixion* for 25 more feet, then up and slightly left along thin cracks, to rejoin *Rosy Crucifixion* on P3 below the flat ledge.

126. **Predator 11c/d S** ★ FA: Rob Candelaria and Greg Finnof, 1986. Rack: 9 QDs, #4 Rock (at roof), #7 Hex, #2.5 Friend. This and *Wild Kingdom*, its neighbor to the right, are long, exposed, bolted face pitches. Climb straight up through the roof from the first bolt on *Rosy Crucifixion* and follow a line of bolts to the Upper Ramp. 50 meters.

127. **Wild Kingdom 11c/d S ★** FA: Rob Candelaria, Greg Finnof, 1986. Rack: 8 QDs, #4 Rock, #7 Hex, #2.5 Friend. Begin with *Rosy Crucifixion* and traverse to a shallow, left-facing corner, then climb straight up along a line of bolts to the Upper Ramp. 50 meters.

128. **Plastic Jesus 11c/d ★** FA: Roger and Bill Briggs, 1985. Follow *Rosy Crucifixion*. Where P3 breaks off to the right, go up and left to a faint crack that is followed to the large pine tree with slings on the Upper Ramp.

129. **The Gem 11b S ★** FA: Bob Horan, 1984. A large flake-block is perched at the top of the Lower Ramp, just above a smooth, flat slab. Angle up and right past a fixed pin, then straight up a thin crack in the middle of the slab and exit left at the top.

130. **Last Rite 10b** FA: Michael Gilbert, Wendell Nuss, mid-1970s. A.k.a. *True Confessions*. Either way, mediocre. Scramble about 200 feet up the Lower Ramp to a point near the end of a deep slot on the right. Climb a small roof and ascend a prominent, right-facing, right-leaning corner, move right, then back left, and emerge on a long ramp just below *Rosy Crucifixion*.

131. **Revelation 12a VS** FA: Larry Dalke and Cliff Jennings, 1967. FFA: Skip Guerin and Chip Ruckgaber, 1983. Scramble up the Lower Ramp about 130 feet to a small, cavernous formation. Climb a right-leaning, overhanging chimney just left of *Le Toit* (11b), over a roof (10a/b), and up a corner to the broad ramp that is continuous with the *Wisdom* belay cave. Climb the left side of a rotten pillar up to a huge arching roof, out a poorly protected finger crack (12a VS), up and right through a second roof and right to join *Le Toit* at the top of the second pitch (10c S).

THE ROOF ROUTES

132. **Le Toit 11a (9 S) ★** FA: Layton Kor and Bob Culp, 1962. FFA: Duncan Ferguson, Bill Putnam, Jim Erickson, 1971. Variation: Roger Briggs, Larry Hamilton, 1972. Rack: up to a #3 Friend. Begin about 40 feet up along the Lower Ramp from *Wisdom*. P1. Angle out to the right beneath a small roof and zigzag up to a belay on a wide ramp that is continuous with the belay cave of *Wisdom*. The crux is near the top of the pitch (11a). P2. Angle right (awkward), then power across the roof, past a bolt, up to a ledge, with bolts (10d). P3. Traverse right for 50 feet along a ledge, and belay at a hole at the top of a ramp (0). P4. Move up and right and follow a series of short corners to the Upper Ramp (8 S). **Variation:** Begin P1 20 feet down and right at a thin crack. Head straight up to intersect with the regular P1. (10d)

ROOF ROUTES AREA

133. **The Rosy-Toit 10c S ★** FA: Steve Wunsch and Hunter Smith, 1973. This is a very dramatic pitch that connects *Le Toit* with *Rosy Crucifixion*. From the top of P2 of *Le Toit*, angle up and left into a large, right-facing corner (9+ S). At the top of the corner, move left past 2 pitons and follow the strata up to the bolt belay on *Rosy Crucifixion*.

134. **Le Toit Direct 12a S/VS** FA: Layton Kor and Larry Dalke, 1963. FFA: Rob Candelaria, Charles Deane, 1970s. Start at the bolted belay on top of P2 of *Le Toit*. Climb up to a thin, right-facing dihedral (modern bolt), up to an ancient bolt "protecting" the crux, step right, then up to a roof, then up and left over the roof, into a groove. Belay. Up left to the Upper Ramp.

135. **The Wisdom 11d/12a S ★** FA: Layton Kor and Pat Ament, 1962. FFA: of first pitch, Ed Webster et al., 1975; main roof, Art Higbee, 1975; of entire route, John Bachar, 1978. Classic. The famous roof on P2 is well protected, but P1 is somewhat runout and P3, a classic Eldorado "11d" has lost one or two holds over the years. Begin about 50 feet up the Lower Ramp, just above the end of a long slot. P1. Angle up and right beneath a diagonal roof (10c S), up through a rotten band, and up to the right to a belay in a deep recess. P2. Climb up and right to clip pro, down along the lip of the roof, then crank up onto the face and up to a bolt belay beneath another roof (11b). P3. Traverse right to a break in the overhang, go straight up a bulging wall to a higher roof (11d/12a S), then angle right to the *Psycho* slab and a 2-bolt anchor.

136. **Saint Eve 12b/c** FA: Layton Kor and Pat Ament, 1962. FFA: Christian Griffith and Dale Goddard, 1985. This is the free version of the original aid finish to *The Wisdom*. From the belay above the main roof, move left, turn the roof, up a small right-facing, right-leaning dihedral, then traverse right to join the Bachar finish.

137. **Tube Sock Tan Line 11 b/c VS** FA: John Sherman and Alec Sharp, 1982. Scramble up the Lower Ramp about 50 feet and set a belay just below the end of a deep slot. Climb up beneath a right-leaning, right-facing corner, traverse right past a bolt or pin, then climb straight up to the low end of the belay cave of *The Wisdom*.

138. **Scary Canary 12b/c S ★** FA: of *Canary Pass*, Layton Kor and Pat Ament, 1963. FFA: of first pitch, Roger Briggs, 1979. FA: of *Scary Canary*, Roger and Bill Briggs, 1980. Classic. This has a great deal of difficult climbing. Get up onto a diagonal rib of rock just up from the bottom of the Lower Ramp. P1. Follow a right-facing corner up to the left end of a slot (11d), up and left to a shallow, right-facing flake (9 S), and straight up to a bolt anchor beneath the main roof. The original *Canary Pass* (IV 7 A4) turned the roof and aided up across the headwall from here. Continue up to the

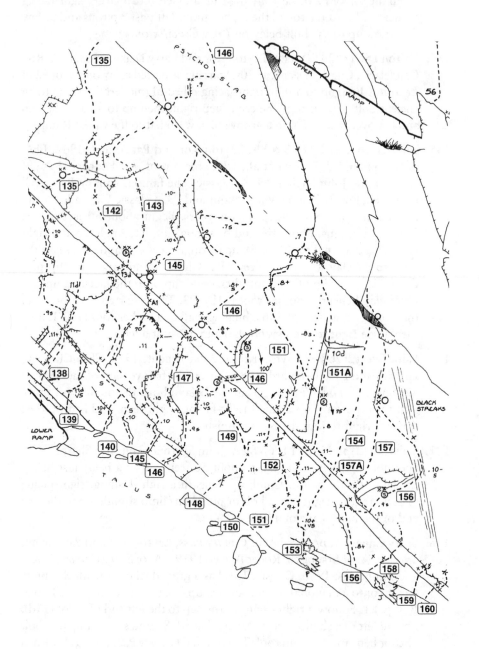

left (8) and belay in the recess beneath the Wisdom Roof. P2. Start up the Wisdom Roof, but where that route goes right, climb up and left into an awesome, overhanging dihedral. Continue up (12) for about 20 feet and, at a piton, turn the roof via flakes. Climb up and right past 2 bolts (11), then straight up the wall (9) to the easy traverse on *Le Toit*.

139. **Dangerous Acquaintances 11d VS** ★ FA: Alec Sharp, John Sherman, Matt Lavender, 1982. FA: variation, Derek Hersey. This was led on-sight. Sherman: "One of the most impressive leads I've ever seen; Alec must have been up there about two hours." Begin in a little alcove at the base of the Lower Ramp, about 20 feet left of *Temporary*. Climb up through the roof, move right and up a short, left-facing, right-leaning corner, angle up and left 10 feet along the strata (good cams), then up and right along a right-facing flake to hard moves at an undercling onto the face above. Tiptoe up to a fixed anchor. **Variation:** Head straight up the face above the right-leaning corner, straight up to the undercling (12a VS).

140. **Temporary Like Achilles 10c S A1** ★ FA: Pat Ament and Larry Dalke, 1967. FFA: of first pitch, John Bragg and Steve Wunsch, 1974. Begin at a flake about 12 feet left of *Evangeline*. Climb either side of the flake (10c), angle up and left along a rotten band, then fire straight up the face past 3 bolts to a 2-bolt anchor (9+). The original route aided the roof, belayed, followed a short, right-facing flake, then angled up and right toward *Evangeline*. **Variation:** Instead of angling up and left above the flake, head straight up (11a) then rejoin the line. This was the original free line.

141. **The Undertaker 13d** FA: Ben Moon, belayed by Gary Ryan, 1991. This is the free version of the *Temporary Like Achilles* roof. At the time, this was the hardest route in Eldorado Canyon. Amazingly, it still is. Since 1991, holds have broken, and it awaits a new ascent (at an even harder grade?).

142. **Huck Off 12b** ★ FA: Cameron Tague saw the line, got approval from the FHRC, and placed the bolts. After a few attempts and falls, he let his belayer try the moves. Willie Mein promptly redpointed it, 1999. Rack: QDs, TCUs. From the lip belay of *Temporary Like Achilles*, move left and angle up past 4 bolts to join *The Wisdom*. Good climbing, but last bolt almost clippable from *The Wisdom*.

143. **Hands in the Clouds 12a** ★ FA: Mark and Scott Tarrant, 1987. Rack: 5 QDs, Stoppers, and #3 Friend. This wild pitch begins from the bolt belay at the lip of the *Temporary Like Achilles* roof. Move up and right to a bolt, up and slightly left past two more bolts, left to a fourth bolt at a small roof, then up and right to the *Psycho* slab.

144. **Unnatural Desires 10d VS** FA: Alec Sharp and Dave Weber, 1982. Begin with *Temporary Like Achilles*, but climb up and slightly right through the initial roof to an obvious A-shaped hold, up and left to *Temporary*, then up and right along a left-facing corner to the top of *Evangeline*.

145. **Evangeline 11b/c A1** ★ FA: Pat Ament and Mike Van Loon, 1967. FFA: first pitch, Steve Wunsch and John Bragg, 1974; upper wall, Alec Sharp and Matt Lavender, 1981. Rack: up to a #1.5 Friend. Classic (including the headwall above the roof). Begin at a short, left-facing corner about 10 feet to the left of *Psycho*. P1. Climb up through the low roof (10b) to a conspicuous, short ledge, then power up via strenuous moves to a 2-bolt belay (11b/c). P2. Aid the roof and swing up to a 3-bolt anchor. P3. Zig out to the right past 3 bolts, up to the left, up a thin crack (10c), and onward to a belay at the base of *Psycho* slab. P4. Up and right past a couple of bolts, move right, then straight up the middle of the slab to the upper ramp (9).

145a. **Zealot 12a** FA: Candelaria, R. Wright, J. Garber, toprope, 1986. Start up P1 of *Evangeline*, then go up and slightly left from the short ledge at mid-face.

145b. It is also possible to traverse to *Temporary Like Achilles* from the second bolt, up and left along the strata above the low roof of P1 (10b S) via *Unnatural Desires*.

146. **Psycho 12d** ★ FA: Layton Kor and Huntley Ingalls, 1962. FFA: Steve Wunsch, 1975. The roof pitch was likely the first 12 in Colorado. Now harder, as some holds have deteriorated. Look for an arching, right-facing dihedral with a sling belay just above the roof. Begin at a short, right-angling ramp. Climb up through the brown band to a small, right-facing dihedral. Right at a bolt, up a shallow, left-facing corner to a bolt, and right to the belay (11a). Lower off, or climb the roof (crux) to a sling belay in an arching corner. Exit the corner to the left and zigzag up the headwall as shown in the topo. The last pitch across the slab is a beauty.

147. **Wasabe 12c** ★ FA: Dan Michael, Paul Piana, Mark Sonnenfeld, 1988. Begin with the first part of *Psycho*, then follow a line of bolts up and slightly left (11b). Lower off or climb the roof (12c). 7 bolts.

148. **Fire and Ice 12a** ★ FA: Pat Ament and Tom Ruwitch, 1967. FFA: of first pitch, Pat Adams, 1981; of second pitch (roof), Alec Sharp and Matt Lavender, 1981. A popular testpiece. Begin just up from *Guenese* at two shallow, left-facing corners and follow the chalk marks up and right past 3 bolts to an anchor beneath the roof. Lower off or climb the roof into a right-facing corner. **Variation:** At the roof, go up past 2 bolts to the left of the dihedral (12b/c).

149. **Slow Dancing 11c VS** FA: Alec Sharp and Dan Hare, 1981. From the second bolt on *Fire and Ice*, climb up and left to the top of the first pitch of *Psycho*.

150. **Determinator B2** FA: Rob Candelaria and friends, (toprope), 1987. Begins near *Fire and Ice* and angles up to the middle bolt on *Downpressor Man*.

151. **Guenese 11a** ★ FA: Layton Kor and Ron Foreman, 1962. FFA: Steve Wunsch, Jim Erickson, Scott Stewart, 1972. FA: Variation, David Breashears and Kevin Worral, 1977. Rack: RPs and 6 QDs for first pitch; up to a #3 Friend to continue. This is one of the most popular of the roof routes, largely because it is relatively easy and is well-protected. Begin about 60 feet left of a large juniper tree (20 feet left of a pine tree). The long, right-facing dihedral above the roof is easy to see. Angle up and right across the wall past a pin and a bolt, then straight up past a downward-pointing flake to a 2-bolt anchor beneath the roof (11a). Using a "fingertip bucket," crank out to the lip, pull up into a dihedral (11a), and cruise up to another 2-bolt anchor. Rappel 75 feet or pull around to the left by an old piton and continue as shown in the topo (9+). **Variation:** Climb straight up the dihedral (10d).

152. **Downpressor Man 12b** ★ FA: Mark Rolofson and party, 1986. Climb past the pin to the first bolt on *Guenese*, then straight up past 2 more bolts to the anchor at the top of *Fire and Ice*.

153. **Clear the Deck 11a VS** ★ FA: Eric Guokas, 1983. Begin down to the right from *Guenese*, climb up to an obvious, narrow pedestal, then move up and left to join that route. Can be toproped from *Guenese*.

154. **The Shining 12c/d (TR)** FA: Rob Candelaria, Matt Baruch. Start as for *Clear the Deck*, but head straight up. Over the roof between *Guenese* and *Kloeberdeath* and up the face above. Pass the right end of the roof at the top end of the *Guenese* dihedral and finish on easy ground above, merging into *Kloeberdanz*.

155. **Mean Lean 11d** FA: Rob Candelaria, 1978. Climb *Kloeberdanz* up to the roof, then traverse just beneath the roof all the way to *Psycho*.

156. **Kloeberdanz 11a S** ★ FA: Layton Kor and Larry Dalke, 1963. FFA: of third pitch, Dalke and Wayne Goss, 1965; of entire route, Steve Wunsch and Jim Erickson, 1974. Starts beneath a prominent, right-facing/right-arching, obtuse dihedral above the main roof, and 30 feet left of a notable juniper tree. Climb a jagged, right-facing corner to the roof, crank to the right, then pull over the roof (11, difficulty depends on body size). Retreat here, or climb the headwall to a sling belay. Move right past the end of the roof (10b S) and up a black streak to a narrow strance with a

bolt. Angle up to the left (unprotected) and climb a shallow, right-facing corner to a belay in a rotten band (9+ S). Climb a crack and deep groove to the Upper Ramp. **Variation:** From the narrow stance with the bolt, continue straight up the black streak (9+).

157. **Kloeberdeath 13b FA:** Rob Candelaria placed the bolts and tried it (with Mic Fairchild, and Jim Royce) first but was unable to clip the original first bolt (out on the lip). Candelaria returned, placed a new, lower bolt to protect the initial upside-down moves and redpointed the pitch. However, in the meantime, Jim Karn led the pitch using a six-foot-long quickdraw preplaced on the bolt at the lip, 1987. Rack: #3 Friend and 6 QDs. Follow *Kloeberdanz* to the roof, then climb straight out the upside-down arête and up the wall for 45 feet to join the belay on *Kloeberdanz*.

157a. **Lipsync 12b FA:** TR; Candelaria, 1987, led by David Light, 1988. Traverse left from the second bolt on *Kloeberdeath* to join *Guenese* "at the lip."

158. **Guokatron 12d S FA:** Darius Azin and Mark Tarrant, 1986. About 25 feet right of *Kloeberdanz* and 70 feet left of *T2*, and behind a large juniper, move right across the wall, straight up through the roof (1 bolt), then up the 8 S headwall to the sling belay on *Kloeberdanz*.

159. **Private Idaho 11d ★ FFA:** Mike Brooks and Todd Montgomery, 1986. About 50 feet up and left from *T2* and to the right of the large juniper tree are 2 bolt routes through the broad roof. *Private Idaho* is to the left. Power through the roof past 2 bolts. 40 feet. Lower off.

160. **Clever Lever 12a/b ★ FA:** Michael Tobias and Brian Robertson, 1970s. FFA: Greg Lowe, 1976. *Clever Lever* is just right of *Private Idaho*. Using an undercling and other bizarre moves, power up and to the right and turn the lip. 40 feet. Lower off.

T2 AREA

From *Jules Verne* to *Old Bad Aid Crack*, the roof is close enough to the ground to be more or less within arm's reach.

161. **Jules Verne 11b/c S ★ FA:** Pat Ament and Larry Dalke, 1967. FFA: of first pitch, Bill Putnam, 1971; of fourth and sixth pitches, Steve Wunsch and Jim Erickson, 1975; of entire route, Roger Briggs and Rob Candelaria, 1976. First on-sight free solo: John Arran, mid-1980s. This long route is one of the classics of Redgarden Wall. P1. Begin with *T2*, but pull up to the left at the lip of the roof, angle up and left following old pins and bolts up small, left-facing dihedrals, turn a shallow roof and head straight up to a belay on *The Ramp* (11 S). P2. Ascend a shallow, right-facing dihedral to a ledge. P3. Follow a long, left-facing corner/chimney, continue to the Upper Ramp (8+). P4. Ascend a long, left-leaning, right-facing dihedral (10c). (Optional belay here.) Place good pro, then run it

REDGARDEN WALL—TOWER TWO AND SOUTH BUTTRESS FROM THE WEST

REDGARDEN WALL—TOWER TWO AND SOUTH BUTTRESS FROM THE SOUTHWEST

out up the face above to the rotten band (11a), then angle left, still 10, to a belay stance. This infamous pitch has seen a number of 40-foot falls by some pretty competent climbers. P5. Climb straight up past a small roof/ corner, then angle left to a belay in the middle of the face (7). P6. Ascend straight up to a ledge just left of the fourth pitch of *The Naked Edge*, up and left through an unprotected roof (10d), and belay on a slab. Alternatively, climb the last two pitches of *The Naked Edge*. P7. The last pitch climbs straight up a moderate slab to the notch at the top of *The Naked Edge* (9).

162. **T2 11a S ★** FA: Layton Kor and Gerry Roach, 1959. FFA: Dave Rearick and Bob Culp, 1962. FA Variation A: David Light (?). FA Variation B: Layton Kor and Jack Turner, 1961. Rack: up to a #3.5 Friend. Though it has some poor sections, this is one of the classic routes of Eldorado. The climb begins directly under the imposing prow of *The Naked Edge* on Tower Two. Two pitches gain the right end of the Upper Ramp, from where the upper pitches snake up to join a prominent, right-facing dihedral to the left of the arête of *The Naked Edge*. Start right off the trail. Locate a chalked-up flake about 12 feet above the ground and a baby angle in a drilled hole up and to the right. P1. Crank up and right and head for the pin (crux). Climb right, then straight up (8) to a bolt belay on a ramp. P2. Step to the left of an obvious arête and ascend a decomposing chimney to the Upper Ramp, or better, climb the second pitch of *Jules Verne* a bit farther up to the left. Hike northwest along the ramp for about 70 feet and belay beneath a black-washed, vertical groove. P3. Climb the groove for about 60 feet, make a daring traverse left to reach a long finger crack that arches across the wall to the left, and belay along the crack after about 60 feet (9). P4. Continue up and left in the crack to the massive, right-facing dihedral and up to a belay on a narrow ledge (8). P5. Move up and left through a rotten red band with little or no pro (9 S) and belay in a groove. P6 and P7. Follow the groove/ledge up to the northwest and eventually finish at the tree at the top of *Ruper* (6). **Variation A:** Pull directly over the bulge above the rotten band on P5, and head for the top, (9). **Variation B:** From the long, final traverse, one may climb straight to the summit of Tower Two (7).

163. **The Stanford Roof 11c** FA: Jim Collins, 1979. Just right of *T2*, pull over the roof using an undercling and merge with that route.

164. **On Edge 11 VS** FA: Kevyn Heap and Lee Barbour, 1971. Two unrelated pitches. P1. Begin about 15 feet right of *T2* and pull over the roof. Pick a line up the wall between *Old Bad Aid Crack* and *T2* (unprotected), climb to the Lower Meadow and belay. P2. To the left of the third pitch of *Redguard* is a steep crack and corner. Climb this past a conspicuous flake that hangs out in space and merge with *Redguard* at the bi-level hole.

REDGARDEN WALL—SOUTH BUTTRESS
OVERVIEW FROM THE WEST

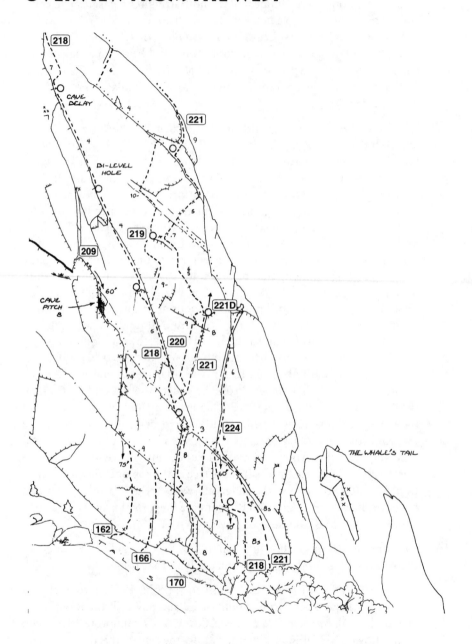

TOWER TWO—SOUTHWEST FACE

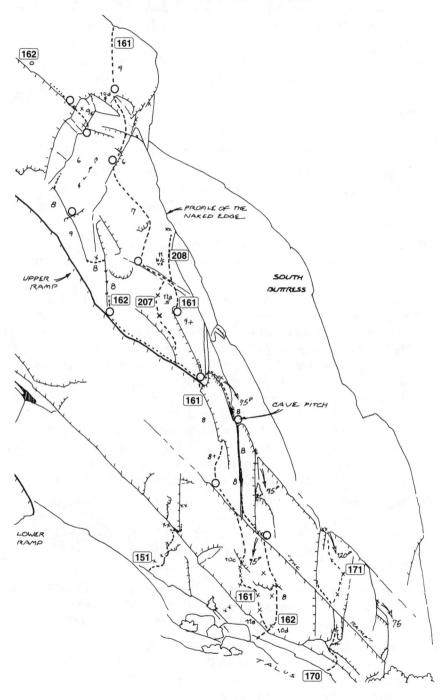

165. **Young Good Free Face 11c** FA: Henry Barber and Pat Ament, 1977. Barely an arm's length left of *Old Bad Aid Crack*, pull over the roof and go right or left. This must be awfully close to *On Edge*'s P1.

166. **Old Bad Aid Crack 11c S ★** FA: Stan Shepard and party, 1961. FFA: Duncan Ferguson and Chris Reveley, 1974. Begin about 20 feet right of *T2*, where the roof comes nearest the ground, and crank up onto the wall. Climb straight up to the left of a thin crack, then pull to the right of the crack and continue up to *The Ramp*.

167. **To the Moon 11** FA: Dan McQuade, toproped, 1986. Just left of *Neurasthenia*, climb up and left through the roof and join *Old Bad Aid Crack*.

168. **Neuraesthenia 11 S** FA: Dave Wilson and Alfredo Len, 1980. Begin about 15 feet left of *Touch and Go*, climb up through a roof past a bolt, move left into a dihedral and up to belay on *The Ramp*. Step left and climb the arête left of *Touch and Go*.

169. **Scratch 'n' Sniff 12a** FA Mark Rolofson, Stu Ritchie, 1989. Direct version of *Neurasthenia*. Climb over the same roof, then head straight up past 3 more bolts.

170. **Touch and Go 8+ ★** FA: Pat Ament and Gary Spitzer, 1966. Rack: up to a #2 Friend. A classic and coveted pitch. If one approaches via The Streamside Trail and up the switchbacks to the Roof Routes, this begins where the trail first reaches the rock. Fifteen feet to the right of the start, thick trees crowd the base. Move up to the roof, go left, then pull up (strenuous) to a good stance above the roof (8). Climb up through a slot and a short finger crack, move left on *The Ramp* (Route 174), and fire up a beautiful, obtuse, right-facing dihedral (crux near the top). 125 feet. **Variations:** One may also begin in a right-facing dihedral to the right of the first section (9 S), or via a left-leaning flake to the right of that (8), or via a shallow, right-facing dihedral to the right of that (9 S), all of which are good pitches, but currently pretty overgrown and neglected.

171. **Bolting for Glory 10a ★** FA: Andrea Azoff and Richard Rossiter, 1988. Originally toproped by Mike Brooks. A fine pitch. From *The Ramp* at the top of the first half of *Touch and Go*, climb straight up past 3 bolts (crux), then arc up and left past a fourth bolt to join *Touch and Go* near the top.

172. **Subliminal Seduction 10b** FA: Mark Wilford, free solo, 1976. Twenty feet right of *Touch and Go*, and behind a tree, climb a wall up through the apex of a roof (bolt) and up thin cracks above, to end on *The Ramp*.

173. **Nolo Contendere 10c** FA: Steve Dieckhoff, Mark Miller, 1992. 3 bolts added by Steve Dieckhoff in 1993. Rack: QDs, small wires. Follow *Subliminal Seduction* to *The Ramp*, then head up and right past 2 more bolts and compete in *The Contest*.

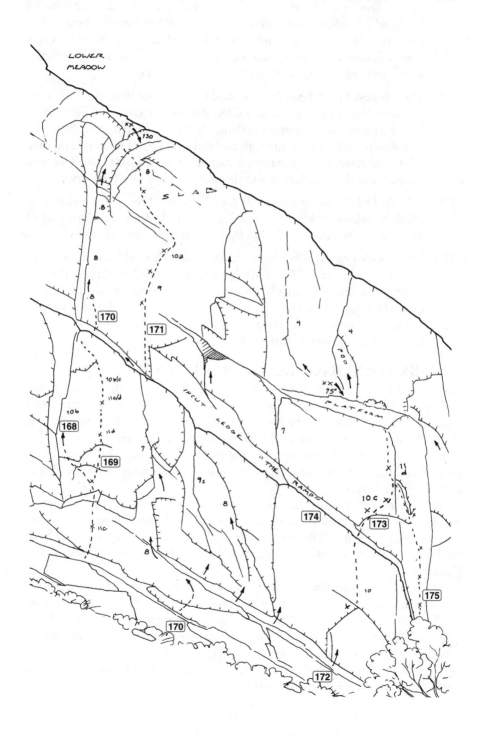

174. **The Ramp 5** A rapid means of ascent to the Lower Meadow, a means of descent from the first sections of *T2*, *Touch and Go*, etc., and a useful landmark. *The Ramp* follows the strata up and left from the base of *The Contest* and extends just past *Jules Verne* P2. To access the Lower Meadow, take *The Ramp*, then follow a 7 hand crack or a blocky corner a little to the left to gain the bolts atop *The Contest*.

175. **The Contest 11d** ★ FA: Chip Ruckgaber and Mike Brooks, 1988. First free solo: Derek Hersey. Rack: 5 QDs. Around the corner to the right of *Touch and Go* is a slightly overhanging, black, bolted wall. Begin up *The Ramp*. Pull up onto the wall and follow a line of bolts up and then left to the arête, then up past one more bolt on the west side. The crux lies between the fourth bolt and the arête and is a wee bit hairy.

176. **A Little Dab'll Do Ya 12b/c** FA: Derek Hersey 1987 (toprope), led by Mark Rolofson, 1989. Above and slightly right from the third bolt of *The Contest* is a thin crack that leads up to the Lower Meadow.

177. **Psyche-Gill-Logical 10b** FA: Pat Ament and Dale Goddard, 1984. Technically a variation on P1 of *Redguard*, but described here as the last short route on this part of the wall, under the Lower Meadow. This takes the finger crack right of *A Little Dab'll Do Ya*. Climb the first 20 feet of *Redguard*, step left to a finger crack, and climb directly up to the bolt belay at the top of that pitch.

CLIMBS STARTING FROM THE UPPER RAMP

There are just a few climbs that go from the ground to the summit of Redgarden Wall: *Psycho Pigeon*, *Ruper*, *Jules Verne*, *T2*, *Grand Giraffe*, *Redguard*, and *Anthill Direct*. All these except *Redguard* and *Anthill Direct* have to cross the Upper Ramp. This large ledge angles from the base of the majestic prow of *The Naked Edge* up and left to merge into the cliff at the far left edge of the South Face. In addition to the upper sections of *Ruper*, *T2* etc., many other fine climbs start from this ledge.

Approach: *Ruper* gives the easiest approach to the left end of the Upper Ramp, though this can be busy. Otherwise many of the roof routes (*Rosy Crucifixion*, etc.) will work. The extreme lower right end can be approached from the Lower Meadow via an exposed traverse left under the start of *The Naked Edge* (watch for loose rocks).

Descents: A. Downclimb to the lower end of the Upper Ramp (be VERY CAREFUL of loose rock). Climb up and around a little buttress at the bottom of The Naked Edge to find a bolt anchor on the sloping platform beneath the first pitch. Rappel 75 feet to the southeast and find another bolt anchor hidden behind a south-facing block. Rappel 150 feet southwest to the ground, or 75 feet to a bolt anchor on a sloping ramp on the route T2 (Route 162), then a final 75 feet southwest to the ground.

B. Locate a tree with slings near the top of *Rosy Crucifixion*, about halfway up the Upper Ramp. Rappel from here or at a pair of bolts 15 feet above (atop *Predator*). Rappel 100 feet (30 meters) to a ledge with 2 bolts, then rappel 180 feet (50 meters) to the Lower Ramp. Note that this requires TWO ropes. Note also that *Rosy Crucifixion* is a very popular climb. Do not use this descent when there are parties on the route. In addition, the upper rappel requires swinging to the right to gain the bolted ledge on *Rosy Crucifixion*. The lower rappel is mostly free, and lands partway up the Lower Ramp (this descent is not for beginners). Two 60-meter ropes are recommended, to get farther down the Lower Ramp.

C. Descend from the top of the Upper Ramp by rappelling 150 feet to the west, down *Pigeon Crack*. The beginning of this descent is identified by hard-to-find slings around a spike of rock at the NORTH side of the top of the ramp and a couple of yards down on the west side.

D. Just south of the upper rappel point of Descent C, downclimb to a large tree on a slab. Rappel 75 feet from here to a 2-bolt anchor atop *Song of the Dodo*. From here, rappel 80 feet/25 meters to Vertigo Ledge. This last rap route is preferable to *Pigeon Crack*.

178. **Mellow Yellow 11d S ★** FA: Larry and Roger Dalke, 1968. FFA: Steve Wunsch and John Bragg, 1975. FFA: of seam in roof; Dan Michael and Mark Sonnenfeld, 1986. Classic. This is an awe-inspiring route up the southwest face of Tower One. Begin near a pine tree at the northwest extreme of the Upper Ramp. P1. Climb a roof, then up and slightly left, then up and right (9) into a right-facing dihedral and a belay beneath a massive, A-shaped roof. P2. Turn the roof (crux) and climb 20 feet higher to belay. P3. Move up and through the next roof (11c) and belay at the top of a thin, left-facing dihedral. P4. Climb straight up (9) to a huge overhang with an A4 seam and angle left to the last pitch of *The Yellow Spur* (6 S). **Variation:** The A4 seam in the big roof has been freed (12a) with the addition of some bolts.

Note: Upper Psycho Pigeon (Route 54) takes off from just left of Mellow Yellow.

179. **South Face of Tower One 10c S ★** FA: Layton Kor and Bob Culp, 1962. FA: Duncan Ferguson, Chris Reveley, Dudley Chelton, 1974. Begin a short way to the west of *Exit Stage Left*, climb up past a piton (crux), through a small roof, and up to belay stance in a shallow corner. Angle up and left past old pitons, beneath a large diagonal roof (9+), and finish with an exquisite arête, the last pitch of *The Yellow Spur* (6 S).

180. **Mushy Peas 10a S** Derek Hersey, Barry Brolley, 1990. Rack: include extra #5 RPs. Just after the small roof on P1 of *South Face of Tower One*, head up and left to finally reach *Mellow Yellow* above the large roof.

REDGARDEN WALL—UPPER SOUTHWEST FACE OVERVIEW

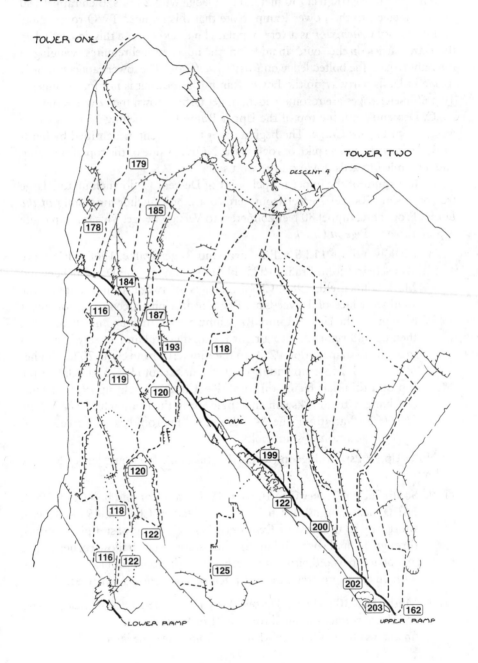

TOWER ONE

TOWER TWO

DESCENT 4

179

185

178

184

116

187

193

118

119

120

CAVE

199

120

122

118

122

116 122

125

200

122

202

203 162

LOWER RAMP

UPPER RAMP

REDGARDEN WALL—UPPER SOUTHWEST FACE, LEFT SIDE

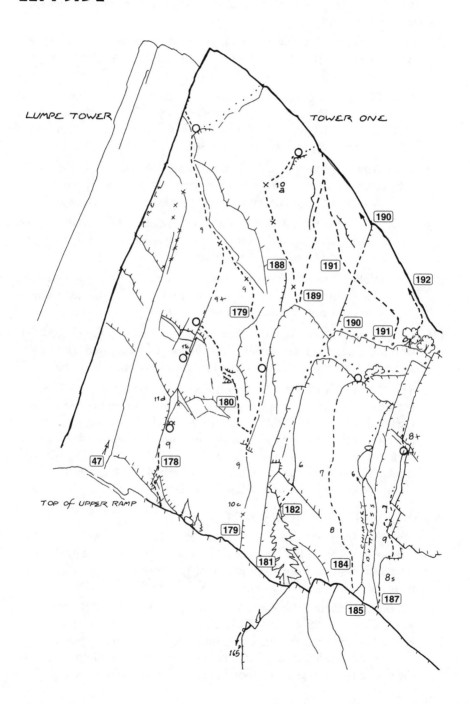

LUMPE TOWER

TOWER ONE

10 a

190

188   191

189

190   192

179   191

47   178

TOP OF UPPER RAMP

180

182

179

181   184

185

187

165

The next few routes all finish on Italian Arête Ledge. To descend from here, either hike east onto the slabby east face of Tower One to pick up the *East Slabs Descent Route,* or rappel *Chockstone Chimney* to the Upper Ramp. This is a double-rope rappel from bolts.

181. **Exit Stage Left 5** FA: Pat Ament and party, c. 1962. Begin about 15 feet left (west) of the tree of *E.L. 100* and climb a long, left-facing corner to Italian Arête Ledge.

182. **E.L. 100 7** FA: George Hurley and Gary Spitzer, 1966. This unusual route ascends a Douglas-fir for 40 feet. Perhaps 35 feet to the left (west) of *Chockstone Chimney,* climb the obvious large tree, pull up into a crack, over a roof, and straight up to Italian Arête Ledge.

183. **Short Arm Inspection 10c/d** FA: Jim Erickson, 1980. Climb the corner behind the tree of *E.L. 100* until it intersects *Exit Stage Left,* climb a thin crack through an overhang, and finish via pockets to the right of the arête.

184. **Body Tremors 8 S ★** FA: Bob Culp and Chuck DeWoodie, 1969. Steep and good quality. Begin just left of *Chockstone Chimney* and climb the steep, pocketed face as shown in the topo.

185. **Chockstone Chimney 6** FA: Ray Northcutt, Dallas Jackson, Cary Huston, 1956. This is the deep, left-facing chimney with a large chockstone near the top of the Upper Ramp, 150 feet up from the *Exhibit A* cave.

186. **Consummation Nite 11c/d** FA: Christian Griffith and Dale Goddard, 1984. Climb the narrow face between *Chockstone Chimney* and *The Italian Arête.* The first pitch is 9. The second (crux) takes a crack in the headwall.

187. **The Italian Arête 9 S ★** FA: Layton Kor and Larry Dalke, 1962. Steep, exciting. Start just right of *Chockstone Chimney.* Angle up around onto the south side to gain a thin crack, up the crack (8), through a roof (9), and up another 50 feet to a belay. Climb up to a roof in decomposed rock and pass it via an obvious crack (8+). Descent: one double-rope rappel down *Chockstone Chimney* (look for bolts) or hike off to the east along a ledge and pick up the *East Slabs Descent* at the saddle.

SMOKE AND MIRRORS AREA

Five routes start from Italian Arête Ledge to gain the summit of Tower One. Descent from here can either be by rappel back to Italian Arête Ledge (see *Smoke and Mirrors*); or from the summit of the Tower One by scrambling north, then east to join *East Slabs Descent*; or by rappelling *The Dirty Deed.*

188. **Smoke and Mirrors 10a ★** FA: Mic Fairchild, solo, 1998. Bolts placed by Mic Fairchild, 1999. Rack: QDs, small, medium cams. The best of the five routes here. Start at the left end of this ledge and head up past 3 bolts. Descend by locating a slung block on the slabs above the climb. Rappel to the east, then traverse back around to rejoin Italian Arête Ledge.

REDGARDEN WALL—UPPER SOUTHWEST FACE, RIGHT SIDE

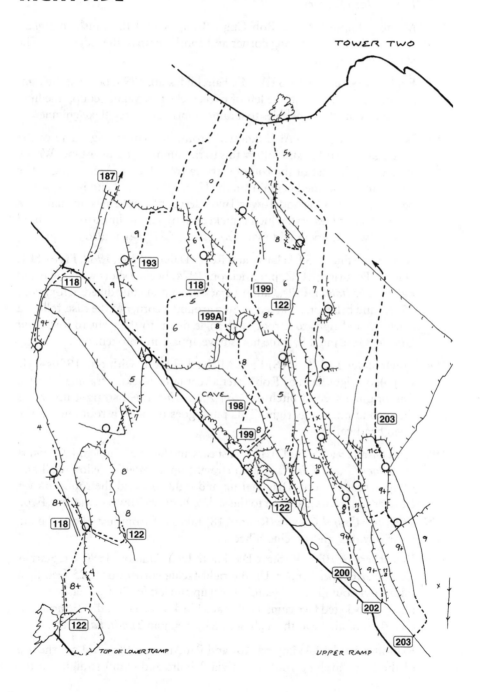

189. **There's a Cowboy Up There! 8** FA: Chris Archer, Roy Mclanahan, 1988. Start as for *Smoke and Mirrors*, then head up and slightly right to join *Exploratory Surgery*.

190. **Memory Lapse 8 S** FA: Bob Culp. Begin behind the finish to *Italian Arête*. Follow a left-facing corner and continue up to the ridgecrest. The rock is not so hot.

191. **Exploratory Surgery 8+ S** FA: Mic Fairchild, solo, 1998. Begin at the right end of the ledge. Climb the left of two cracks to a vague scoop, (medium nut) then out left on pebbles to a ramp. Finish at a large flake/chimney.

192. **Wrong Way Up 5 S** FA: Unknown. From the extreme right end of the ledge, gain the ridge and follow this to the summit of Tower One. *Wrong Way Up* is the last of the routes starting from Italian Arête Ledge. The next routes described begin from the Upper Ramp and end in the saddle between Tower One and Tower Two. Descent from here is normally via the *East Slabs Descent*, which is picked up by scrambling around behind Tower Two. Rappelling down *Chockstone Chimney* is also an option.

193. **Saint Augustine 11 S** FA: Larry and Roger Dalke, (8 A4), 1968. FFA: of P1, Duncan Ferguson; of P2, Jim Erickson, 1974. Begin a short way down and right of *The Italian Arête*. Climb a crack in a left-angling dihedral for about 45 feet and belay on a flat ledge. Step around a corner to the east, follow a crack up and right to a roof, and angle down to the right to join *Saint Giraffe*. Once rated 9, some holds have apparently broken.

194. **Much Slater 11d (9 S/VS)** FFA: Michael Gilbert (with one 1980s-style yo-yo); on-sight flash by Rob Slater a year later. Rack: extra small Aliens. The original second pitch of *Saint Augustine* aided straight up where the second pitch jogs right. This pitch goes through a roof and up the steep headwall.

195. **Saint Giraffe 9+ VS** FA: David Breashears and Steve Mammen, 1975. Start up *Upper Grand Giraffe*. Climb straight up a smooth, yellow wall and belay beneath a roof. Diagonal up and right to avoid the roof, up over another roof (crux), and on to the saddle between Towers One and Two.

Note: *Upper Grand Giraffe* (Route 118) takes off from just above the big cave, up the obvious, right-facing dihedral.

196. **Deutscherweg 10b/c VS** Steve Dieckhoff, Liese Ammon. 1990. P1. Start as for *Upper Grand Giraffe*. Up the right-facing corner about 25 feet, then follow a runout diagonal seam (10b/c) up and left for 20 feet. Easier climbing up a pocketed face gains a belay at a block with a thread. P2. Surmount the 10a roof above at the highest notch, then join *The Italian Arête*.

197. **Exhibit A 8+ A4** FA: Layton Kor and Pat Ament, 1963. Aid out the top of the huge, arching roof (cave) via 3 bolts and climb straight up the

vertical wall (8 S) to a sling belay at the left side of a smaller, arching roof. Finish as for *Alice in Bucketland.*

198. **A Minor 11 S** FA: Rob Candelaria, 1978. Start as for *Alice in Bucketland*, go straight up and cross the roof where it is about a body-length wide. Rejoin *Alice in Bucketland* shortly above.

199. **Alice in Bucketland 8+ S** ★ FA: Scott Woodruff and Dan Hare, 1976. Rack: up to a #3.5 Friend. Classic. Spectacular. A good alternative to *Upper Ruper* if this is crowded. Start at the low end of the big cave. P1. Climb up a short ramp, make a committing move right, across the roof, to monster jugs. Pull around, then angle up and left across the vertical wall to a sling belay beneath a smaller arching roof (8 S, 120 feet). P2. Venture up to the right and turn the upper roof (8+) to the right of its apex. Angle left, then straight up to a left-facing dihedral and belay at its top (7). P3. Climb directly up to the saddle between Towers One and Two (0).

199a. **Phallus In Suck-It-Land 8** ★ FA: Richard Rossiter and Ken Brink, 1986. Climb around the roof to the left of the sling belay, straight up the wall past two shallow roofs, and right to the belay at the top of the left-facing dihedral (8).

Note: The next route to the right is *Upper Ruper* (Route 122), starting just left of the obvious, left-facing dihedral, which it follows for two pitches.

200. **The Serpent 10b (9+ S)** ★ FA: Layton Kor and Larry Dalke, 1962. FFA: Jim Erickson and Art Higbee, 1974. FA: variation A, Chris Revely and Pat Adams, 1976; variation B, Chris Reveley and John Ruger, 1974. Rack: include a couple of 3- to 4-inch cams for heucos. This follows a left-leaning, left-facing dihedral system for 4 pitches. Begin about 30 feet up the ramp from the start to *Le Void*, to the left of a shallow, left-facing corner, which arches up and left. P1. Over a bulge (9+ S) and up the face to a thin crack and optional belay (just below the first bolt on *Rise Above*). Traverse left to the arête and up into a steep dihedral. Up this past 2 bolts (crux) to a surprising belay ledge (10b). P3. Climb the face left of the dihedral, lieback, and make a traverse right around a blind corner (10) to belay by a tree. P4. Step left and proceed as shown in the topo.

200a. Climb the initial dihedral of P1 on the left, up through a roof, then traverse straight right to the optional belay stance.

200b. Climb straight up the dihedral system of P3, past the blind traverse, to where it fades. Go left, then right, and back to the normal route.

201. **Rise Above 12a** FA: Mark Tarrant, Ray Atkinson, Scott Tarrant. A.k.a Mr. Malcontent. Follow P1 of *The Serpent*. Where *The Serpent* twists

left 40 feet up, continue straight up to gain a line of 8 bolts following progressively thinner climbing just left of a left-facing corner. At the top, arch left to the belay ledge of *The Serpent*.

202. **Le Void 11d/12a ★** FA: Larry Dalke and Pat Ament, 1963. FFA: Steve Wunsch, Jim Erickson, 1976. P2 was flashed on sight by the first ascentionists. FA: of the right dihedral on P1; Art Higbee, 1977. A superior route with good gear, except for just below the roof. Perhaps more than 100 feet up the ramp from its low point, and 30 feet down from *The Serpent*, locate a pair of left-leaning, left-facing dihedrals. P1. The right one is 11b, the left is 9+. Choose your corner, ascend to a horrific, overhanging crack along a downward pointing flake (11+) and belay at a precarious stance. P2. Climb the thin crack (11d/12a) and the large roof above and belay after about 40 feet. Continue up the slab to join the finish to *T2*. A 60-meter rope allows you to do P1and P2 in one pitch, for a top quality, fully 12 pitch.

202a. **Avoid 9+** FA: Roger and Bill Briggs, 1973. Escape to the right from the first belay of *Le Void*, to join P2 of *Love Minus Zero* (9+).

202b. **Chased Away 10b/c** FA: Jim Collins and Chip Chace, 1978. Traverse right from the top of the overhanging finger crack of *Le Void* and join *Love Minus Zero* at the far side of a 10 slab.

203. **Love Minus Zero 11c S ★** FA: Pat Ament and Tom Ruwitch, 1967. FFA: of first pitch, Erickson, Reveley, Higbee, 1973; of second pitch, R. and B. Briggs, 1973; of entire route, Breashears, Higbee, Ruger, 1975. Begin a short way up the ramp to the left from *T2*, below the low end of a thin crack. Angle up and right to gain the crack, follow it up and left for 100 feet and belay on a ledge. Traverse left, climb an unprotected, left-facing corner (9+), and belay on a stance beneath a large roof. Climb the roof (crux) and continue up the steep headwall to join the last part of *T2*.

204. **T Minus Zero 12a VS** FA: Rob Candelaria and Erik Fedor, 1986. This is a direct line on the *T2* finger crack. Begin between the black groove of *T2* and the start to *Love Minus Zero* and ascend a thin, incipient crack.

Note: Upper *T2* (Route 162) starts up the vertical, blackened groove 70 feet up the Upper Ramp.

205. **King Tut 9** FA: Charlie Fowler and Bill Feiges, 1977. Begin up Upper *T2*. At the level of the leftward traverse, go right along a flake and belay. Ascend an overhanging, left-facing dihedral, exit right, and climb up the slab to join *Jules Verne*.

206. **Fools Burn 10b/c S** FA: Rob Candelaria and Roger Briggs (?); or Jeff Lowe, Kevin Worral, and David Breashears, 1970s. Climb straight up the wall between the black groove of *T2* and the left end of the roof of

Green Willow Wall. Jam around the right side of a roof, and intersect the brown band on *Jules Verne.*

206a. **Ghouls Turn 11c VS** FA: Steve Levin and Roger Schimmel, 2000. Climb the thin seam right of *Fools Burn,* to the *Fools Burn* anchors. The face right again has been toproped, and another pitch has been led, by Cameron Tague and Steve Levin, to connect the arching overhang on *Green Willow Wall* into the upper section of *Ghouls Turn.*

207. **Green Willow Wall 11d ★** FA: Chip Chace and Dan Michael, 1987. Rack: up to a #4 Friend. Start near the bottom of the Upper Ramp, under the long, arching overhang that begins about 20 feet left of *Jules Verne.* Head straight up over the right end of the overhang, work up and very slightly left past 2 bolts, then up and slightly right to the rotten band on *Jules Verne.*

Note: P4 of *Jules Verne* (Route 161) follows the long, left-leaning, right-facing dihedral rising from the bottom of the Upper Ramp.

208. **Lene's Dream 11b/c S ★** FA: Roger Briggs and Scott Woodruff, 1976. Climb the dihedral and crux headwall of P4 of *Jules Verne* to the rotten band, then climb straight up to the top of the second pitch of *The Naked Edge.* This is a beautiful, exposed, continuously difficult pitch. Protection is poor on the lower section, but improves once *Jules Verne* is departed.

209. **The Naked Edge 11a/b ★** FA: Layton Kor and Bob Culp, 1962. FA: of P5; Kor and Rick Horn, 1964. FFA: Jim Erickson and Duncan Ferguson, 1971. FFA: of P5; Larry Dalke, 1966. FFA: of original P2; Rob Candelaria, Dave Breashears, 1974. FA: of variation D; Rob Candelaria, Mic Fairchild, 1988. Rack: RPs up to a #4 Friend. "The Edge" follows the great south arête of Tower Two. It starts from a sloping ledge located immediately right of the bottom of the Upper Ramp, and above a cave at the top of The Lower Meadow. It is usually reached via *Touch and Go,* though *The Ramp* gives the technically easiest approach. From the top of *Touch and Go,* a long pitch romps up and left into the Cave Pitch, whence steep 8 moves lead straight up to the ledge at the base of P1. Any other route leading to The Lower Meadow will suffice. The start can also be accessed from The Upper Ramp by a short, steep Class 4 scramble up and right from the extreme right end of The Upper Ramp. If using this approach, be very careful of loose rock. P1. From the sloping belay ledge above the Cave Pitch, climb a superb finger crack about 3 feet right of the arête to a 2-bolt belay on a slab (11a, 70 feet). P2. Climb along the left edge of the slab past a couple of bolts, go left around the arête (9), and up a fading crack to a spectacular stance (10b). P3. Up the arête for about 50 feet to a tiny alcove (#3 Friend), out right to a mantle (8), up and finally right to a large, sloping ramp beneath a bomb bay chim-

REDGARDEN WALL SOUTH FACE FROM THE BASTILLE TRAIL

ney (120 feet). P4. Work up a shallow corner with fixed pins and into the bomb bay chimney. Climb out the right side of the chimney to a tiny perch on the arête (11a S, 60 feet). Beware of rope drag. P5. Move up and right in a shallow corner (11a/b), swing around to the right side of the arête, and power up a hand-to-fist crack (10d) in an overhanging, right-facing dihedral to a belay on a sloping shelf on the right (60 feet). P6. Traverse around to the west side of the arête and follow the strata of the rock up and left to a break along the crest (5, 75 feet). Escape to the northeast past some trees and along a ledge to reach the *East Slabs Descent*. **Variation A:** The original aid version of P2 moved right from the belay and then skirted around the slab with A4 nailing. This goes free at 10c S. **Variation B:** Instead of struggling into the chimney on P4, continue up and right (11d S) from the flake with the fixed pin. **Variation C:** Instead of even starting up P4, traverse the strata up and left to join *T2*. **Variation D:** From belay under P5, traverse left until it is possible to head up into the large and obvious dihedral, just left of *Sickness Unto Death*. Climb this to the top. Double ropes are recommended. (12a [?] VS), Mic sez: "butthard."

The next three routes all start from the 2-bolt belay at the start of *The Naked Edge*.

210. **Genius Loci 11c** FA: Alan Nelson, Karl Mueller, Alan Bartlett, 1989. Rack: 9 QDs. This steep, thin, bolted pitch ascends immediately left of the first pitch of *The Naked Edge*. After the first 70 feet, traverse right to belay as for end of P1 of *The Naked Edge*. The pitch originally extended farther, past 2 more bolts, but they have been removed.

211. **Slow Train Comin' 11a** FA: Jimmy Ratzlaff, Steve Hadik. Rack: QDs. Beautiful slab. Follow 8 bolts just to the right of the first pitch of *The Naked Edge*. Belay as for top of P1 of *The Naked Edge*.

212. **Fool's Journ 9+ S** FA: Peter Hunt, Steve Ilg, 1985. Begin just down and right from the rappel anchor at the base of *The Naked Edge*. Climb a poorly protected slab to the right, then follow *Edgewise* back left to the anchor at the top of P1 of *The Naked Edge*.

212a. **Edgewise 8** FA: Dan Hare and Scott Woodruff, 1977. Start from the last pitch of *On Edge*. Follow the strata of the rock up and left to the top of the first pitch of *The Naked Edge*.

213. **Overhanging Headwall A4** FA: Jim Logan and Dick Erb, 1967. Climb *Fool's Journ* to the headwall, then climb a lichenous, left-facing corner to the broad slab below *The Diving Board*. A free lead of all the hard climbing on this pitch has been claimed, but this claim is refuted by the belayer involved.

REDGARDEN WALL—TOWER TWO FROM THE SOUTHEAST

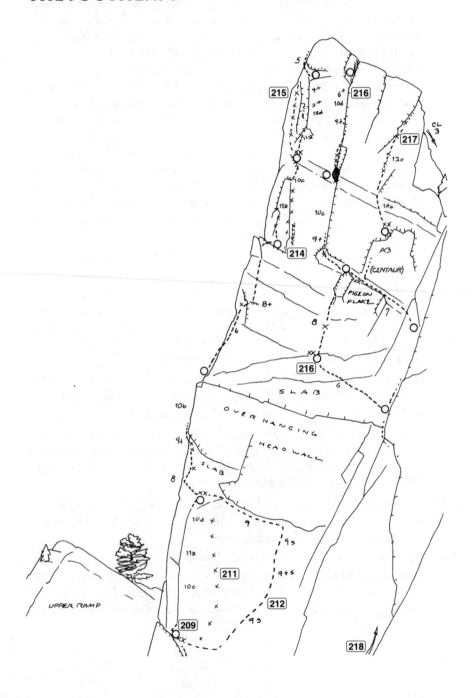

REDGARDEN WALL—TOWER TWO, NAKED EDGE CAVE AREA

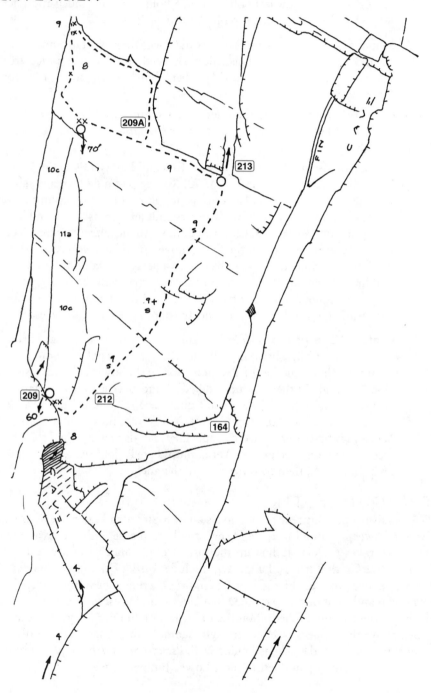

214. **Wingless Victory 13b** ★ FA: Christian Griffith and Mark Sonnenfeld, 1986. Classic. Climb the overhanging arête just right of P4 of *The Naked Edge*. Crux at the last bolt. 60 feet, 5 bolts. Recommended approach: Rappel 150 feet from the top of *The Naked Edge*.

215. **Sickness Unto Death 12b** ★ FA: Christian Griffith, Rusty Holcomb, 1989. Rack: 7 QDs, #3 Friend. This wildly exposed pitch breaks out left from the start of P5 of *The Naked Edge*, then climbs past 4 bolts to the top. Crux low down.

The next two routes tackle the huge, overhanging headwall right of *The Naked Edge*, and left of the upper pitches of *Redguard*. They both break out left from high up on *Redguard*.

216. **The Diving Board 11a** ★ FA: Layton Kor and Larry Dalke, 1962. FFA: Roger Briggs and Jim Erickson, 1972. Rack: up to a #4 Camalot, shop-vac. Classic. Spectacular. The crux is popular with birds. From the top of the black ramp on *Redguard*, traverse out left across a slab and belay at the base of a steep wall. Climb straight up to the left side of the Pigeon Flake (8). From the top of the flake, move up and left into an out-leaning, left-facing dihedral and power up to a belay in a cave (10b/c). Climb out through the top of the cave, up a short corner, right, then left, and up an overhanging hand-fist-offwidth crack (11a). Belay in an inclined groove, then scramble off to the north to join the East Slabs Descent.

217. **Centaur 12c** ★ **or 10d A4** FA: Pat Ament, Tom Ruwitch, Roger Briggs, 1967. FFA: of P2, Christian Griffith, 1986. FA: Variation, Brad Bond. Climb the first 5 pitches of *Redguard* to the shallow cave. Traverse left along a ramp (7) then aid up a dihedral and over a roof to a hanging belay at 2 bolts (A3). The second pitch originally aided up to a left-facing dihedral near the top (8, A4). This pitch, however, goes free at 12c, and is best approached by rappel. P1 has also been bolted for a free ascent, and is an open project. **Variation:** Where P1 jogs right, nail straight up a thin crack, then traverse right to the anchor.

THE SOUTH BUTTRESS

The massive South Buttress encompasses all of Redgarden Wall right of Tower Two and sweeps around to the east, eventually to merge with the East Slabs. *Redguard* takes the classic line up the huge trough/dihedral between Tower Two and the South Buttress. Landmarks include *Anthill Direct*, which ascends the prominent prow to the right of *Redguard*. There is a beautiful, steep face low down and right of this, ascended by *Genesis*, and *C'est la Vie*, which takes the huge, right-leaning dihedral on the right. Lower Juniper Ledge is the large bench above the *Genesis* face. To the right again, behind The Whale's Tail, lies the water-streaked and blackened Bulge Wall. *Pseudo-Sidetrack* follows a prominent diagonal ramp up and left to meet Lower Juniper Ledge.

REDGARDEN WALL FROM THE SOUTHEAST

Tower One
Lumpe Tower
Shirttail Peak
Hawk-Eagle Ridge
East Slabs Descent Route
South Buttress
209
226
232
252 260
Wind Tower
Whale's Tail

REDGARDEN WALL—TOWER TWO FROM THE SOUTH

Approach by heading up the talus from the cement slab. *Genesis* and the prominent dihedral of *C'est la Vie* will be right in front of you. Descend via the *East Slabs Descent*, or various rappels listed in the text.

218. **Redguard 8+ S ★** FA: Dick Bird, Cary Huston, Dallas Jackson, Dale Johnson, and Chuck Merley, 1956. FA of variation: Paul Mayrose and party, 1965. Rack: up to a #3 Friend. This was the first route to scale the entire height of Redgarden Wall and has become a coveted classic. This is also a very hazardous route, often poorly protected, loose in places, polished, and committing, and has claimed its share of victims. From the cement slab, scramble up the talus to the base of Redgarden Wall and follow a footpath west to a small clearing about 75 feet west of *Genesis* and about 30 feet east of the obvious bolted line of *The Contest* (Route 175). P1. Climb up a blackened, improbable looking, shallow corner for about 70 feet (8 S) and traverse 20 feet left to a 2-bolt belay on a shelf. This pitch is called The Birdwalk after its originator, Dick Bird. P2. Climb the right crack of two (4), work up into a prominent groove with a 2-bolt anchor, and climb all the way to its end below a huge, black-washed dihedral. P3. Do a short lieback (4) up into the dihedral and climb up the left wall for about 100 feet (4) to a belay stance on the left. P4. Up the narrowing ramp (left wall) for 140 feet (4) to a "bi-level hole." P5. One more long pitch up this system to a shallow cave (4). P6. Move out onto the steep right wall and climb to a narrow ledge (7). Traverse left (north) into the deep cleft between the top of the South Buttress and Tower Two, out around the left side of a huge chockstone and belay at the top of the route. Climb up and east over the shoulder of the South Buttress to catch the *East Slabs Descent Route*. **Variation:** Climb about 20 feet above the bi-level hole, move out onto the right wall and belay. Climb a crack and ledge system up and right for about 75 feet to a bulge. From beneath the bulge, move left some 20 feet and take a shallow, right-facing inside corner to the top (8). There are many other easier variations awaiting rediscovery.

CLIMBS STARTING FROM THE LOWER MEADOW

Immediately right of upper *Redguard*, a narrow face towers above The Lower Meadow, bounded on the right by *Anthill Direct*. The Lower Meadow is approached most easily via *Touch and Go*, *Redguard*, or *The Ramp*. Two routes begin from The Lower Meadow. There is no known Upper Meadow, though it is rumored to exist.

219. **Red Ant 10b/c** FA: Jim Erickson and John Behrens, 1980. Head up P3 of *Redguard* to a good belay ledge. Climb the wall on the right past a small, right-facing corner, go about 40 feet left, and up to a belay ledge on *Anthill Direct*. Work up to a diagonal band, traverse left, master a roof via a hand crack (crux), and continue up and right to the direct finish on *Anthill Direct*.

REDGARDEN WALL—SOUTH BUTTRESS FROM THE SOUTH

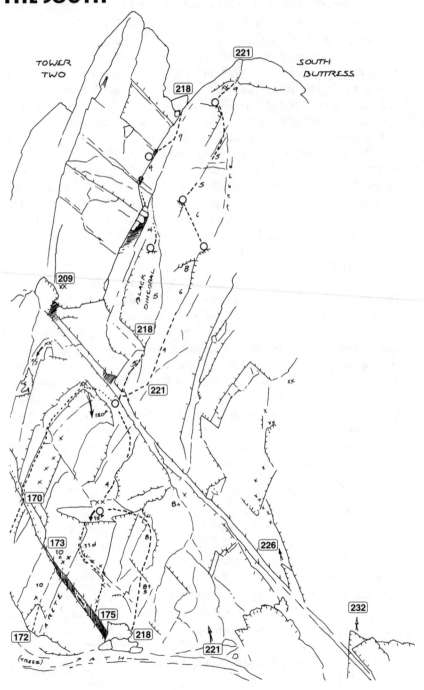

220. **Semi-Wild 9+** ★ FA: Charlie Fowler, Dan Stone, Glen Randall, 1978. This follows the obvious dihedral/crack line left of P2 of *Anthill Direct*. Start from The Lower Meadow and follow the crack over a small overhang. Finish up *Anthill Direct*. Topo on page 298.

221. **Anthill Direct 9 S** ★ FA: of P1; Harvey Carter and Sheldon Schargart, 1958. FA: of entire route; Layton Kor and Rick Tidrick, 1961. FA: of direct finish; Royal Robbins and Pat Ament, 1964. Rack: SR. Combined with *Touch and Go*, this is one of the best 8 outings in Eldorado (9 with the direct finish). Start just left of the pedestal at the bottom of *Genesis* and well to the right of *Redguard*. P1. Climb an awkward, blackish ramp for about 70 feet, move left around a bulge (8 S), back up into a groove, and belay at a 2-bolt anchor on a huge ledge (The Lower Meadow). P2. Climb a clean face up to a crack and left-facing corner, then power over a black bulge (8) to a belay ledge. P3. Angle up and left along a dark lichen streak (6 S), traverse left to a ledge, and belay. P4. Climb up into a shallow, right-facing corner, up an exposed crack with some old pins (5), and back to the left to a belay in a groove beneath a bulging roof. P5. Traverse right beneath the bulge, past a couple of old pitons, lieback up the crack /corner (9) to where the angle eases off, and belay. P6. Climb 150 feet of moderate terrain and traverse off to the north to catch the *East Slabs Descent*. **Variation A:** Start P1 via *Redguard*, (more direct) up to The Lower Meadow. **Variation B:** Climb *Touch and Go* to The Lower Meadow. (Recommended.) **Variation C:** The original P5 shuffled off to the north via the groove/ledge (see *Anthill*). **Variation D:** On P3, climb directly up to the arête. Follow this (6) to rejoin the route partway up P4. Topo on page 298.

222. **Dancing from Within 9+** FA: Kyle Copeland, roped solo, 1985. Parts of this obscure route may follow *Chromium Shore* or *Sidetrack*. P1. As for *Redguard* P1. P2. From the belay, move right, over a small roof, and up a thin crack (Crack 'n' Ups) to a belay (9+). P3. Climb a line right of *Anthill Direct* to belay as for *Pseudo-Sidetrack* on Lower Juniper Ledge. Topo on page 298.

223. **Chromium Shore 9+** FA: Mike Brooks and Chris Snyder, 1980. Climb a crack system to the right of P2 of *Anthill Direct*. Topo on page 298.

224. **The Sidetrack 8** FA: Rick Horn and Dave Dornan, 1961. FA: of variation, Bob Culp and John Link, 1968. A forgotten route in the middle of nowhere. P1. Climb the first 80 feet of *Anthill Direct* to a point beneath a rotten red overhang and belay (8). P2. Turn the roof near some old bolts, enter a groove, and diagonal left to a belay ledge. Climb up the obvious crack and chimney system to Lower Juniper Ledge. **Variation:** One may also turn the roof a few feet to the right (8). Topo on page 298.

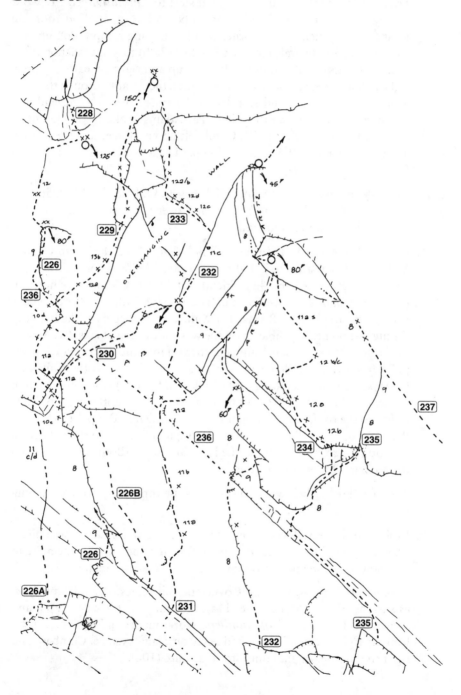

225. **The Book of Numbers 12c** ★ FA: Larry Dalke and Cliff Jennings (8 A4), 1967. FFA: Darius Azin and Mark Tarrant, 1986. Rack: up to a #3.5 Friend. Begin with the funky, original start to *Anthill Direct*. P1. Work up to a rotten diagonal band (groove) beneath a squared-off roof and right-facing corner, up the corner to a left-leaning ramp (10c), up past some pins, then up and right past 3 bolts (12a/b) to a bolt anchor at the base of the upper dihedral/roof. P2. Arc up and right beneath the large, right-facing dihedral/roof to the apex (12c), then crank through the apex at a wide crack (11) and step left to belay (#2.5 and #3 Friend and Stoppers). Be careful on this pitch; Pat Adams broke his ankle falling awkwardly from the crux. P3. Climb left about 30 feet to a steep crack and go straight up (10a) to Lower Juniper Ledge (see *Anthill* and *Pseudo-Sidetrack*).

225a. **Left Side of Roark 10b/c S** FA: Jeff Achey and Bill Feiges, 1977. Start as for *Book of Numbers*, climb up to and over the first overhang on P1, and exit left to join *Sidetrack*.

226. **Genesis 12c** ★ FA: Jack Turner and Bob Culp, 1962. FFA: Jim Collins, 1979. The hardest route in Eldo until 1984. FA: Variation A, Chris Archer 1995. Rack: #2 and #2.5 Friend and 8 QDs. Classic. Due north of the cement slab (southwest side of The Whale's Tail) some large blocks rest against the base of Redgarden Wall. *Genesis* begins at the left atop the highest point. Scramble up on the west side of the blocks. P1. Ascend the large, left-facing, left-leaning corner up into the A-shaped roof and pull left onto a foothold near two pitons (10d). Climb mostly straight up (11a) past 2 bolts and along the left side of a flake (9) to a 2-bolt anchor. Lower off, 80 feet, or P2. Continue upward past another pair of bolts (crux) to the roof, and then right to a 2-bolt anchor. Rappel 125 feet, or P3. move up and right (9+) and do the original finish up a steep dihedral (9) and face to Lower Juniper Ledge. **Variations:** (Both toproped from the anchor 125 feet up *Genesis*.)

226a. The face directly below the anchors can be toproped at 11c/d, joining *Genesis* just over the roof.

226b. **Moi et Toi 12c** FA: Bob Horan, 1990. Using a bolt on *Lakme* as a directional, toprope the face left of *Pansee Sauvage*, then up the 12c arête to the right of *Lakme* before veering left to the *Genesis* anchor.

227. **Exodus 11b/c** ★ FA: Leonard Coyne and Bill Feiges, 1977. Climb *Genesis* to the bottom of the flake (11a), then move out left past a pin and some bolts to *The Book of Numbers*. Work out around the large, right-leaning, right-facing dihedral and belay on a small stance. Climb up and right to join the original finish to that route (10a).

228. **Leviticus 12c** Mark Sonnenfeld, 1986. Rack: RPs, QDs. Start atop P1 of *Genesis*. Climb straight out the overhang past 3 bolts.

229. **Lakme 13c ★** FA: Christian Griffith, 1987. Rack: 8 or 9 QDs and a #4 Rock (above the last bolt). A Griffith testpiece with good pro. Begin by climbing *Genesis* up through the apex and past the second bolt. Where *Genesis* angles up and left to the flake, follow a line of bolts out to the overhanging arête on the right (12b), then straight up (crux) to the anchor above *Desdichado*. 5 bolts. Rappel 165 feet.

230. **Le Boomerang 11d ★** FA: Chip Ruckgaber, Ken Goto, and others, 1987. First free solo: Derek Hersey, 1992. This is a connecting pitch between the first 50 feet of *Genesis* and the 2-bolt belay on *C'est la Vie*. The airy diagonal traverse feels longer than it really is. Power up into the A-shaped roof on *Genesis* (10c), but instead of pulling around to the left, continue straight up to a bolt (11a/b). It gets harder. Continue, all the way to *C'est la Vie*. 4 bolts.

231. **Pansee Sauvage 11b S ★** FA: Bolted on the lead by C. Griffith with Pat Ament and Gray Ringsby, 1984. The lowest bolt was added in 1987, not by Griffith. Rack: 3 QDs and a skyhook (optional). The mind of the savage is fresh and resourceful. Begin this superb face pitch about midway between *C'est la Vie* and *Genesis*. There are 3 bolts, one at each crux. At the third bolt, go straight right, up and left, then directly up to the 2-bolt belay on *C'est la Vie*. 80 feet.

232. **C'est la Vie 11b or 9 ★** FA: of first pitch, Rick Horn and Pat Ament; of complete line, Ament and Jeff Wheeler, 1962. FFA: Bob Williams and Dave Ohlson, 1974. FA: of variation A, Layton Kor and Cub Shaefer, 1963. FA: of variation C; Henry Barber and John Bragg, 1973. Rack: up to a #2 Friend. Another Ament masterpiece . . .this route takes the giant, right-leaning dihedral due north of the cement slab. Begin atop some large flakes that lean against the base of the wall. P1. Step up to gain an incipient crack in a shallow, left-facing corner and climb straight up to a blunt flake. Move right (9) and undercling/lieback around a prominent, left-facing flake to a toprope anchor at 60 feet. Climb up through an apex (8), exit right, up to a stance, traverse left across a slab (9), and belay at 2 bolts in the dihedral. P2. Climb straight up the baffling, right-leaning dihedral (crux) to a belay on a pedestal with 2 bolts. Rappel 150 feet to the ground, or P3. climb the roof to the east (8) and belay at a rock horn. From here one may climb off to the east via *Pseudo-Sidetrack* (4). The Arête Variations follow the arête right of P2. **Variations: A.** From the "apex" on P1, go up and right and around a blind corner (8+) to the belay above *Whistle Stop* (optional), then move back around to

the left and up the exciting arête (8+) to a piton belay. **B.** From the stance above the apex, move out left onto the slab (9) and climb a thin crack up to the arête (9+). (This crack can also be reached from the bolted belay in the corner, by traversing right.) **C.** From the rock horn belay above the main dihedral, pull up over the lip of the roof (10a VS) and work straight up to Lower Juniper Ledge (or downclimb *Pseudo-Sidetrack*.) **D. Deceptive Bends 11b S** FA: Pat Ament and Rick Horn. FFA: Jim Collins and Brian Harder, 1979. Climb up and left through the roof from the top of the main dihedral of *C'est la Vie*.

233. **Desdischado 13c** ★ FA: Christian Griffith, 1986. This is perhaps Christian Griffith's finest and most difficult route. P1. Follow *C'est la Vie* into the dihedral. Climb up through the crux (11b) (maybe belay here), and arc out left along a line of bolts to the arête. This is extremely strenuous, with the crux near the third bolt. From the fourth bolt, climb up over the lip of the roof (12a/b) to a 3-bolt anchor on the original upper part of *Genesis*. Rappel 165 feet. There is an open project on the obvious break below *Desdischado*, and parallel to it, intended to finish up *Lakme*. This has 2 bolts and an empty 9mm sleeve, plus a fixed pin.

234. **Je T'Aime 12c (10d S)** ★ FA: Christian Griffith and Chris Hill, 1986. Rack: A #2 Friend at the undercling (or just solo up to the first bolt) and 4 QDs. This very sustained route ascends the beautiful, dark green face between *C'est la Morte* and *C'est la Vie*. Bolted on the lead, from hooks. Climb the first 60 feet of *C'est la Morte*, clip the first bolt, and make difficult moves to get established at the bottom of the face. Clip the next bolt and make some hard moves along the overhanging arête (12). The third bolt often has a cheater sling. From the third bolt, move up along a flake, then when the obvious line appears to go straight up, make crux moves out into the middle of the slab to reach the fourth and last bolt (a very difficult clip-in). Work up and slightly left via very difficult and sustained face moves to the top of the slab. 100 feet.

235. **C'est la Morte 9** ★ FA: Duncan Ferguson and John Bragg, 1974. This is a fine, varied pitch. Begin atop some large blocks that lean against the base of the wall about 25 feet left of *The Flakes*. Climb an unprotected ramp up and left to an undercling (6 S), lieback up and right, make a tricky step around (8), and climb straight up an RP crack (crux) to join *Whistle Stop*.

236. **The Inderekt 11c S** FA: Steve Dieckhoff, Gary Ryan, 1993. Rack: TCUs, #2 Camalot, QDs. Named for Derek Hersey. Start as for *C'est la Morte*. Follow the stratum up and left on the obvious break past *C'est la Vie*, (crux, be careful with obvious delicate flake just before *Pansee Sauvage*) to finish on *Exodus*. 60-meter pitch.

237. **The Flakes 9-** ★ FA: Larry Dalke and Pat Ament, 1961. FFA: Duncan Ferguson, Jim Erickson, Bill Conklin, and Dave Clark, 1970. FA: of variation B, Jeff Achey, 1980. Begin in a prominent, left-facing dihedral and flake system to the left from *Whistle Stop*. Climb up the tricky corner (8), undercling left (8+), climb up around a flake out of the left-facing system, and up to the belay above the ramp on *Whistle Stop*. Finish with that route. **Variation A:** Continue up under the left-facing flakes all the way to the belay (more sustained). **Variation B:** The first crux can be avoided while adding a new one by climbing in from the start of *C'est la Morte* (8+).

238. **Whistle Stop 9-** ★ FA: Tom Quinn and David Jones, 1958. This is an exciting pitch up a steep and beautiful face. Begin by hiking around to the west side of The Whale's Tail and back to the east into the gully between it and Redgarden Wall. Just below and left of a large chockstone, climb straight up for 15 feet, up a diagonal ramp to the left, and belay just past its top (this belay can be skipped, making a 150-foot pitch). Climb up a finger crack (7) until it fades into the face, straight up past a bolt (crux), place a #3 or #4 Friend under the roof to protect the second, and traverse straight left about 25 feet to an old piton belay. Note that the original line avoided the upper face and diagonalled right to join *Anthill*.

THE BULGE WALL

The vertical black face immediately behind The Whale's Tail is known as The Bulge Wall. Approach: Head up the gully behind either side of The Whale's Tail and gain a broad platform (the east gully is easier). To escape from the top of *The Bulge*, *Blackwalk*, and the like, traverse round to the north and intersect the *East Slabs Descent Route*. One may also rappel or lower off from bolt anchors atop some of the routes.

239. **Cleopatra Says. . .10a S/VS** FA: Christian Griffith and James Epp, 1980. Begin down to the left from *The Anthill*, go up a slab, and over a 4-foot roof to join that route.

240. **Horizontal Beginnings 7** FA: Chip Ruckgaber, David Hague, Marc Hirt, 1981. Begin down and left from *The Anthill*, and presumably right of *Cleo Says*, at the right end of a roof, climb up a slab, and up over a roof to join that route.

241. **The Anthill 5** FA: Dale Johnson and Dick Bird, 1956. This may have been the first route completed on Redgarden Wall and like *Redguard*, spans the height of the South Buttress. Climb *Pseudo-Sidetrack* to Lower Juniper Ledge (routes are the same to here). Follow the stratum (a red ramp) up to the west to the exposed arête of the South Buttress and belay. Traverse around to the left onto the southwest face and join *Anthill Direct*. Climb

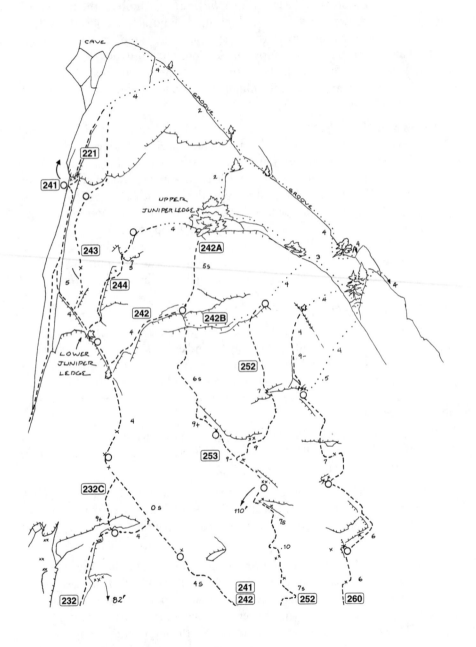

BULGE WALL

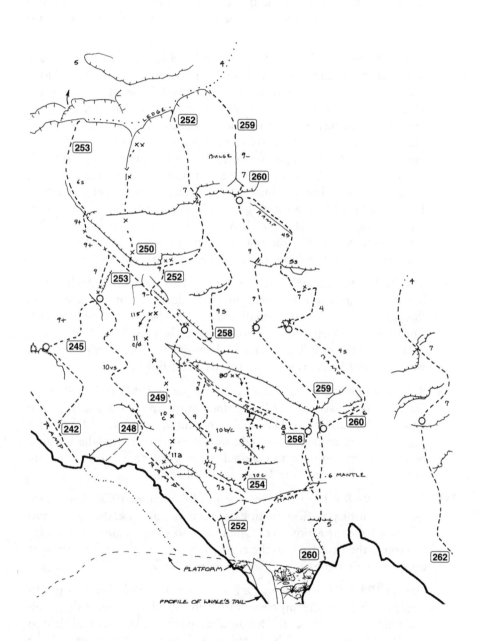

steep cracks up and left (crux) to a belay in a groove beneath a bulging roof. Follow the stratum of the rock up and left (northwest) until it is possible to ascend moderate slabs up onto the shoulder of the South Buttress. Climb an easy pitch up the shoulder of the buttress (about 100 feet) and traverse north across the east face to catch the *East Slabs Descent Route.*

242. **Pseudo-Sidetrack 4 S ★** FA: Stan Shepard and Don Davis, 1958. This is a popular "beginner route," but beware of occasional runouts and long diagonal traverses. Begin near the west end of the grassy platform behind The Whale's Tail. P1. Follow a ramp up and left and around a bulge (3) to a belay with a poor anchor. P2. Continue up and left along the sloping strata for about 90 feet and belay beneath a crack with many pin scars (maybe an old pin or two). P3. Climb straight up the crack (4) for about 50 feet, then diagonal to the left along another ramp to a small tree about 30 feet short of a huge ledge with an ancient juniper tree (Lower Juniper Ledge). Move up and right in a blocky, left-facing dihedral (4) to another large ledge and belay.P4. An easy finish drops down to another ledge and traverses off to the east (see topo). **Variation:** An exciting, direct finish goes straight up from the belay (5 S) to Upper Juniper Ledge.

243. **The Archer-McLanahan 10a** FA: Roy McLanahan, Chris Archer. Follow *Pseudo-Sidetrack* to Lower Juniper Ledge. Start up the next pitch, then head up the face to a small, left-facing dihedral (old bolt to left). Continue up and left past a horizontal crack, then up a face above (crux). Belay under the roof. Up and right, then over the roof to easier terrain, where *Anthill Direct* is joined above its direct finish.

244. **PA's Variation 8 S ★** FA: Pat Ament and party, 1964. Follow *Pseudo-Sidetrack* to Lower Juniper Ledge, then move up the left-angling ramp about 20 feet and belay. Diagonal right and up through a bulge into a big, left-facing corner, move right out of the corner near the top (old bolt), then up and over an exposed bulge (crux) to a belay on a slab. Traverse off to the right to Upper Juniper Ledge.

245. **To Night 9+ S ★** FA: Chris Reveley and John Ruger, 1974. A nice face pitch with little pro. Begin with P1 of *Pseudo-Sidetrack*, then go up and left to a belay at a tiny tree. One may also climb higher on *Pseudo-Sidetrack*, then cut back to the right to reach the belay. Climb straight up, then angle right to the 2-bolt anchor of *Night*.

246. **Pilgrim 10d ★** FA: Montgomery, Brooks, Hruby, 1987. Begin as for *To Night* and belay at the tiny tree. "Move up and left to a purple sling," up and right past 2 bolts (crux), follow a ramp left to a bolt, up and right to a bolt, and on up to a 2-bolt anchor. A third pitch climbs straight up through a bulge to a bolt and pin belay.

247. **High Noon 11a** ★ FA: Todd Montgomery, Dan Hruby, Mike Brooks, 1987. Climb P1 of *To Night* to the belay tree. Work up and right past 2 bolts, up and left to a horizontal break (#2.5 Friend), traverse right, and up past two more bolts to a 2-bolt belay.

248. **Night 11b/c VS** ★ FA: Layton Kor and Larry Dalke, 1967. FFA: Jeff Achey and Paul Meyers, 1980. This ascends the exquisite black face to the right of *Pseudo-Sidetrack*. Good line, bad protection. Begin as for *Blackwalk*, but after the first 10 feet, angle up to the left past *A Breed Apart*, up through a narrow roof, and zigzag up to a 2-bolt belay as shown in the topo. Climb a short headwall (9) and finish with *Walking the Talk*.

249. **Back in Black 11c/d** FA: Mike Brooks, Andrea Azoff, 1989. Takes the face between *Night* and *Blackwalk*. Follow 6 bolts to double-bolt anchor. Crux near the top. 115 feet.

250. **Blacktop 11b S** FA: Malcolm Daly, Sari Nicoll. 1998. Rack: QDs, TCUs/ Aliens after second bolt. A 90-foot-long bolted pitch past 4 bolts, up a black streak on the face above *Back in Black*. Double-bolt anchor.

251. **A Breed Apart 11b/c S** FA: John Allen and Alec Sharp, 1981. Poorly-protected, lichenous. Climb through a roof up and left from the start to *Blackwalk*, then straight up to join the last few feet of the first pitch of that climb.

252. **Blackwalk 10b/c S** ★ FA: Layton Kor and T.J. Boggs, 1962. FFA: Jim and Dave Erickson, 1969. Rack: up to a #2 Friend, but only a #2 Friend and a few QDs are of any use on the first pitch. A classic face climb. Begin near the middle of the grassy platform behind The Whale's Tail. P1. Climb a slabby, left-facing corner up and right to an overlap. Angle up and left (8 S) to a bolt beneath an undercling, work up and slightly left to 2 bolts about 18 inches apart (crux), climb up to a ramp (8 S), then left and up to a 2-bolt belay. Rappel 100 feet or continue with the original P2 (9) as shown in the topo.

253. **Walk the Talk 9+ S** ★ FA: Duncan Ferguson, Bill Putnam, Jim Erickson, 1971. This long, exposed pitch begins with the P2 of *Blackwalk*, then follows a left-angling roof up to the west for about 50 feet, breaks through the roof, and goes straight up to easier ground. Traverse off to the north.

254. **Backtalk 10c S** ★ FA: Todd Montgomery and Mike Brooks, 1986. Begin as for *Blackwalk* at a short, left-facing corner, move up right to an overlap, left a move or two, then more or less straight up past a bolt, a #1.5 or #2 Friend placement, another bolt, and a half-driven LA to a 2-bolt anchor. 75 feet. A second pitch over the roof above the 2 bolts (9+ S) was soloed by several people, including Derek Hersey, Charlie Fowler, and John Arran, 1986, before anyone actually led it.

255. **Backstroke 11c/d S** FA: Jimmy Ratzliff and Austin Weis, 1987. Rack: a few wires, TCUs, and QDs. Climb the face between *The Bulge* and *Backtalk*, then move left to the bolt anchor on the latter. 75 feet.

256. **Fade to Black 11d** FA: Steve Dieckhoff, Mark Miller. 1992. Traverse left from the *Backstroke* crux thru the crux of *Blackwalk* to join *Back in Black* below its crux.

257. **Fade to Night 11** FA: Rolando Garabotti, Michael Gilbert. 1996. Follow *Fade to Black*, then continue left to join *Night*. 60-meter pitch.

258. **Dessert 9 S ★** FA: Layton Kor and Larry Dalke, 1962. Rack: up to a #3 Friend. Steep and exciting, good rock. Begin with P1 of *The Bulge*. From the belay, move left, up a short wall (8 S), then make a long traverse up and left to the bolt belay on *Blackwalk*. Move down to the right, up a steep, unprotected wall (9 S), right beneath a roof, up a slab to another roof (7), and up easier slabs to belay on a big ledge. Traverse off to the north to intersect the main descent.

259. **Shades of Gray 9 S ★** FA: Pat Ament, Cam John, Gray Ringsby, 1979. Begin a short way left of *The Bulge*. P1. Climb the left-facing dihedral (9), and belay at a fixed pin about 6 feet left of the first belay on *The Bulge*. P2. Climb up through the overhang just right of its low point and follow a left-angling crack to a belay in a small, red, right-facing corner. P3. Climb straight up from the alcove (9), pass a roof at a short, angling crack (9), and up a slab to the bolted belay beneath the final pitch of *The Bulge*. P4. Up the nice 9- crack above.

260. **The Bulge 7 S ★** FA: Layton Kor and Ben Chidlaw, 1957. An Eldorado classic. Cruxes are protected, but easier sections are runout and not so easy to find. There have been a few accidents, mainly to seconds, on this climb. The pitches traverse to and fro, making a competent second a must. Begin at the far east end of the once-grassy bench above The Whale's Tail. P1. Climb up a few feet to a short crack that angles up to the left (25 feet below a shallow, left-facing corner), move up and right over a bulge, do an exciting mantel just right of the left-facing dihedral (6) and work straight up to a belay beneath an overhang. P2. Move right about 15 feet via underclings, then up and left about 60 feet to a belay at a bolt and piton. P3. Move up and right 10 feet, straight up for 20 feet, and left a few feet to a bolt. Step left and down slightly, up and left a few feet to a narrow stance (7 S), then up and left for 50 feet to a belay on a sloping stance with bolts. P4. Scuttle off to the right, across the face to join the east slabs (6 S). Traverse north (right) to reach the main descent route. **Variation:** On P4, climb straight up the excellent 9- crack.

Chip Chase on Centaur *(5.12c), Redgarden Wall.* RICHARD ROSSITER PHOTO

LOWER EAST FACE

This is the short wall right of The Bulge Wall, and below The East Slabs. Approach from The Wind Tower Trail. Look for a large pine tree near *Balance of Terror*.

261. **Sticky Feet 9 S** FA: Carl Harrison and Paul Meyers, 1981. Begin about 20 feet left of *The Whittle Wall*, climb straight up to a semi-sling belay from a chickenhead at a horizontal crack. Continue straight up just left of the green concavity on *The Whittle Wall* (crux) and onward to easier ground.

262. **The Whittle Wall 7 S ★** FA: Pat Ament and Jean Juhan, 1964. Begin about 40 feet down and left from the big pine tree across from Wind Ridge. Climb a ramp that angles up to the left and work straight up to a belay in a greenish hollow. Traverse right for 30 feet, then up and left along a steep ramp and through some bulges (crux). Continue on easier terrain until it is possible to traverse north to join the *East Slabs Descent*.

263. **Genuine Risk 11a S** FA: Erickson and Jim Garber, 1980. Start as for *The Whittle Wall*, but climb straight up. Stay between *The Whittle Wall* and *Balance of Terror*.

264. **Balance of Terror 9** FA: Jim Erickson, solo, 1973. Start behind the big tree. Climb a groove about 15 feet left of *East Overhang*. This skirts the steep face taken by *East Overhang*.

265. **Pompidou Centre 12d** FA: Christian Griffith. Toprope the face left of *East Overhang*. Up the face, traverse left along an undercling flake, and continue up the left side of the flake.

266. **East Overhang 10d** FA: Pat Ament and Jim Erickson, toprope, 1971. First lead (?): Derek Hersey, free solo. FA: variation, Eric Doub, 1982. A short, overhanging wall to the right from the big pine tree. **Variation:** Ascend the wall just left (11).

267. **Mental Cruelty 11a** FA: Jim Erickson, 1981. Overhanging, pocketed wall 7 feet right of *East Overhang*.

268. **East Side 6** There is a huge pine tree against the wall just across the gully from Wind Ridge. Begin about 30 feet to the right of this tree and climb up the east face until it is possible to angle right to the main descent route.

269. **Noggin 7** FA: Jim Stuberg and Mike Brooks, 1981. Find a tongue of rock with three cracks in it and climb the vertical crack on the right.

270. **Bank of America 12a** FA: John Allen, 1981. Climb a short, left-leaning, thin crack up a short, overhanging wall 50 yards across the gully and uphill from *Cinch Crack*.

REDGARDEN WALL FROM THE SOUTH

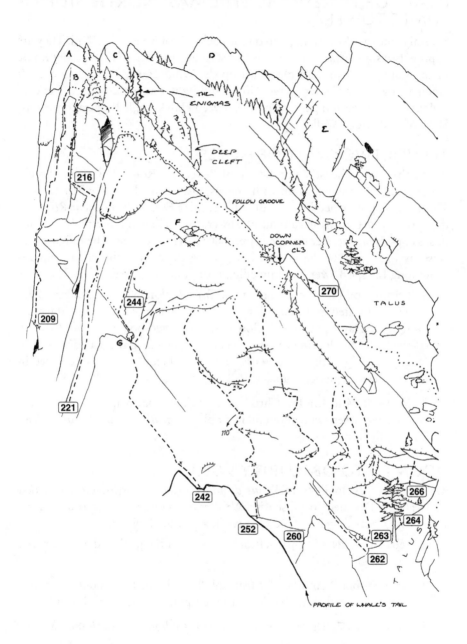

THE SUMMIT AREA
(WALL OF HOLES, THE ENIGMAS, NORTH SIDE OF LUMPE TOWER)

Several routes are located high up on the back side of Redgarden Wall. They are approached somewhat conveniently by ascending the *East Slabs Descent Route* or the slabby area to the right. Start up the Wind Tower Trail, then cut left along a ledge toward a large tree. Go up and right, passing around or beneath a giant chockstone and gain the gully between Hawk-Eagle Ridge and the East Slabs of Redgarden Wall.

TOWER TWO/WALL OF HOLES

Above the large chockstone at the top of *Redguard* (Route 218) is an obscure but attractive east-facing wall, with heucos, just below the top of Tower Two. This area is approached by ascending the regular *East Slabs Descent Route* all the way to just below the summit of Tower Two. Though admittedly tedious, this is considerably easier than the approach for The Enigmas. The Enigmas are close by (one gully to the north), but gaining them from this point requires summiting Lumpe Tower and rappelling north into the correct gully.

1. **Scrutiny on the Bounty 11b ★** FA: Bret Ruckman, Bruce Miller, 1997. This is located in the corridor just above the top of *Redguard*. Start just right of a large pine tree. Follow 6 bolts to a two-bolt lower-off. Crux by the fifth bolt, leaving the steep heucos and gaining the slab above. The relationship of this route with *Dizzy Miss Lizzy*, a toprope reported in the previous guide, is unclear.

2. **Venus de Milo 13a** FA: Christian Griffith and partner, 1986. Find bolts on a very steep wall, about 30 feet right of *Scrutiny on the Bounty*. Crux near the top.

DOOMED TO OBSCURITY WALL

About 100 yards uphill from *Venus de Milo*, locate a north-facing, heucoed wall. This is Doomed to Obscurity Wall, and it contains three routes. First ascents are claimed by a Boscoe McTavish, a.k.a. Joe Huggins.

3. **Seize of Holds 8** Slightly left of the center of the pocketed area, climb a vertical gray band.

4. **Orifophobia 9** Another 50 feet uphill, find two large boulders and a steep, pocketed arête that leans to the right. "Swing up and over."

5. **Slots of Fun 7** "Under *Fear of Holes* (*Orifophobia*) is roof/dihedral with a hand crack. . . pump it."

LUMPE TOWER/THE ENIGMAS

The Enigmas are located in a deep gully between Lumpe Tower and the Middle Buttress, which can be seen from the parking lot. A wide, irregular trough descends from here to the brushy gully between Redgarden Wall and Hawk-Eagle Ridge. This is a complex area of cliffs, caves, ravines, and poison ivy. Above and right of a wide cave (which looks like a mouth) high in the trough, is a buttress with deep gullies on either side. From near *Bank of America*, scramble northwest up steep slabs, then work south into the left gully and locate three bolted climbs on a steep north-facing wall below a giant chockstone. These climbs are called The Enigmas and ascend the overhanging north side of Lumpe Tower.

1. **The Recreant 12b/c** FA: Matt Lavender, 1988. Rack: 5 QD and a #3 and #4 Friend for the belayer. This route is 30 feet downhill from *Viva la Figa*. 4 bolts to a double-bolt anchor.

2. **Viva la Figa 12c** FA: Dale Goddard and Matt Lavender, 1988. Climb the face to an obvious, overhanging arête between *The Recreant* and *Lex Loci*. 6 bolts to chains.

3. **Lex Loci 12d** FA: Matt Lavender, 1988. Climb an overhanging wall, with 6 bolts leading to chains, to the right of *Viva la Figa*. Avoid the loose flake left of the fifth bolt.

REDGARDEN WALL—THE ENIGMAS

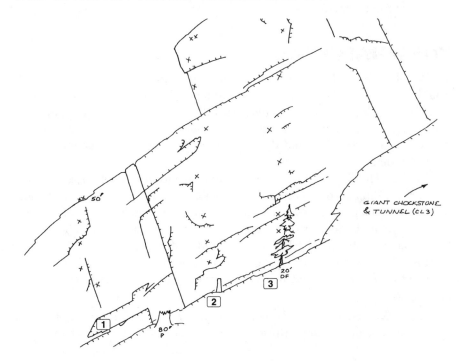

LUMPE TOWER/NORTH SIDE

A scramble under or around the giant chockstone brings one to the col between Lumpe Tower and The Middle Buttress. Several climbs have been done here on the north-facing continuation of the Enigmas wall. This wall becomes the summit block of Lumpe Tower. Rather than bushwhack up the east slabs, a nicer approach might be a quick romp up one of the West Face of Redgarden Wall routes, like *Swanson's Arête*.

4. **Escape Artist 7** FA: R. Rossiter, solo, 1980. This is the line of least resistance from the north col to the summit. Lieback or jam a short, steep, left-facing corner at the northeast side of the summit block, above the giant chockstone.

5. **Burning Desire 10d** FA: John Warren and Dan Hare, 1981. Climb the obvious wide crack to the left of *Dream Weaver*.

6. **Dream Weaver 10a** FA: Jim Erickson, solo, 1978. From *One Night Stand*, scramble east and north down a gully for 80 feet. Climb a hand crack in an east-facing, overhanging, pocketed wall.

7. **Soap Dodger 10** FA: Joe Hladick and Carl Harrison, 1981. Climb the crack right of *Dream Weaver*.

8. **One Night Stand 11d** FA: Jim Erickson, 1979. From the col on the north side of the summit of Lumpe Tower, climb a pair of obvious, overhanging finger cracks.

THE WHALE'S TAIL

The Whale's Tail is the 200-foot-high, curvilinear tower directly across South Boulder Creek from The Bastille. There is a large cave at the bottom of its south face. This lower south face has numerous difficult boulder problems and short routes that see a great deal of traffic. The low-angle east face provides an introduction to slab climbing, and the west face provides an introduction to easy crack climbing.

To reach The Whale's Tail, just walk across the footbridge. To descend from the summit, rappel from slings down the west face to the big ledge at the bottom of the crack pitches. Note that this may be more than half a rope. Alternatively, downclimb the northeast ridge to a point where it is easy to hop off to the flat bench between The Whale's Tail and Redgarden Wall (Class 4). This ridge is narrow and exposed, and the inexperienced will require a belay.

Routes are described left to right, starting from the left edge of the west face.

1. **No Problem 6** FA: (?) Stuberg and Tom Wilmering, 1980. Begin at the west end of the flat platform between the northeast arête of The Whale's

THE WHALE'S TAIL FROM THE WEST

Tail and the start to *The Anthill* on Redgarden Wall. From the huge chockstone in the gully, angle up and right for 30 feet to a small ledge, then up and left via a crack.

2. **Ahab 8** FA: Carl Harrison and Randy Kath, 1981. Up and left from *The Yorkshire Ripper*, below an undercling and roof, climb out to the right on flakes to the edge of the roof, undercling left to the break at the left side of the roof, turn the roof and head for the top.

3. **The Yorkshire Ripper 10c** ★ FA: Derek Hersey, Barry Brolley, Keith Ainsworth, 1987. Begin about 25 feet up and left from the start to *Jack the Ripper*. Climb a left-leaning groove for about 15 feet (crux), step right, back left to the groove, and belay on a good ledge. Traverse right (9) all the way to the arête, which is climbed to the top on the north side.

4. **Jack the Ripper 9+ (8 S)** ★ FA: Larry Dalke, 1966. FFA: Jim Erickson and Mike Hartrich, 1973. FA Variation B: Pat Ament, 1979. An Eldorado mini-classic. Begin on a ledge at the base of a huge, right-facing dihedral at the left (north) side of the west face. This is where the gully between The Whale's Tail and Redgarden Wall narrows down. Climb the slab (that forms the left side of the dihedral) up to the big roof (8 S), hand-traverse right across the right wall to the arête (9+), and shoot for the top. **Variation A:** The right wall of the dihedral may also be crossed lower down at a diagonal groove (9 S). **Variation B:** The 8 S slab may be avoided altogether by climbing in from a point higher up in the talus gully.

5. **C'est What? 11c** ★ FA: Fred Knapp, Erik Fedor, 1989; free solo, Derek Hersey. Rack: QDs, RPs for start, medium Friend to protect moves to first bolt. This was the last route bolted before the Eldorado Canyon bolting ban. Start up *Jack the Ripper*. Step right onto the steep face and follow bolts to an anchor. Lower off.

6. **Schwa 9+** FA: Brooks and Dennis Smith, 1981. The exact line of this route is not known. Right of *Jack the Ripper*, climb a roof via a crack, and work up to the alternate lower traverse on that route.

7. **New Cambria 6** FA: Lynn Smith, Mike Brooks, Dennis Smith, 1982. Begin at the bottom of the *Ripper* dihedral, then angle out right across the wall to the arête left of *West Crack*.

8. **Left Arête 8 S** ★ FA: Pat Ament and Cathy Pfeffer, 1980. A super clean route with exposure. Begin as for *West Crack,* but angle out to the left arête as soon as possible and blast for the summit.

THE WHALE'S TAIL FROM THE WEST

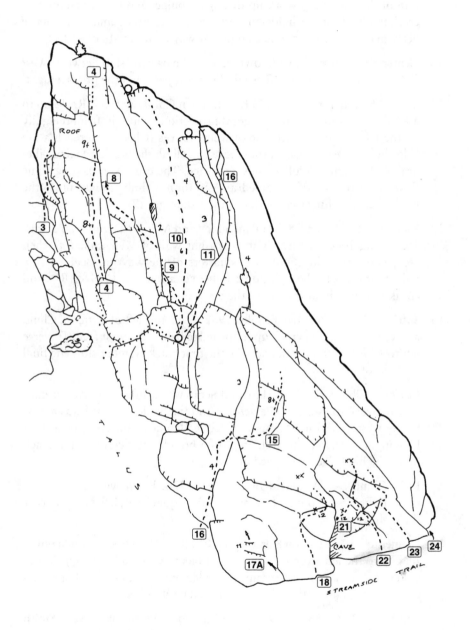

9. **West Crack 2 ★** FA: Unknown. Rack: up to a #2.5 Friend. A great climb for novice leaders—or anyone else. Begin from the big ledge at the bottom of the west face, work up through a bulge, and jam a magnificent crack (with lots of face holds) to a belay alcove near the summit. A practice belay may also be set in a hole about halfway up (after about 45 feet).

10. **Center Face 6 S ★** FA: Unknown. Climb the narrow slab between *West Dihedral* and *West Crack*. The climbing is superb, but the pro is naught.

11. **West Dihedral 4 ★** FA: Layton Kor and Ben Chidlaw, 1959. Rack: up to a #4 Friend. A fine pitch with good protection. Climb in from the gully on the left and make a couple of weird moves (Class 4) to reach a big ledge below the west face. From the ledge, climb the big, left-facing dihedral at the right side of the flat west face. The crux is in passing some flakes near the top of the dihedral. **Variation:** Climb straight up to the big ledge, via a finger crack that arcs to the right (7).

12. **Video Feedback 12a S ★** FA: Paul Sibley and Mike O'Donnel (on-sight), 1986. This bold venture climbs the right wall of *West Dihedral*, then escapes to the right about three-quarters of the way up. Begin with a flake that leads to the right, up a bulge via a thin crack, place RPs and crank to the right at the top of the crack.

13. **Soft Parade 11a** FA: Mike Brooks, 1982. Begin just left of *Buffoon*. Climb an overhanging, thin crack up to the ledge below the west face. Traverse left to *Jack the Ripper* (!), and take the first crack system below the final traverse of that route.

14. **Buffoon 10b/c S** FA: Dan Hare and Scott Woodruff, 1976. About midway between the start to *Clementine* and the big ledge that leads across to the west face routes, a short ledge leads out to the right beneath a hanging, left-facing dihedral. Step off a boulder and climb a thin crack up to the big ledge mentioned above.

15. **Kid's Climb 8+** FA: David Breashears, 1976. Begin with *Clementine*, move right after about 20 feet, and climb a square-cut, left-facing corner through a roof.

16. **Clementine 5** FA: Layton Kor and Ben Chidlaw, 1959 (second pitch only). Just up to the left from the boulder problems, climb a left-facing corner system (5) for about 60 feet up to a ledge on the west arête. Follow an easy crack (0) up to the false summit of The Whale's Tail.

17. **Smith Overhang A3** FA: Dennis Smith and Mike Brooks, 1981. Smith later died on Mount Robson. Aid over the roof just left of *N.E.D.* via a hook on a loose flake. **Variations:** Just left of *Smith Overhang* are two fine, moderate boulder problems. **A.** *Lunge Break* begins at the bottom

THE WHALE'S TAIL—SOUTH FACE

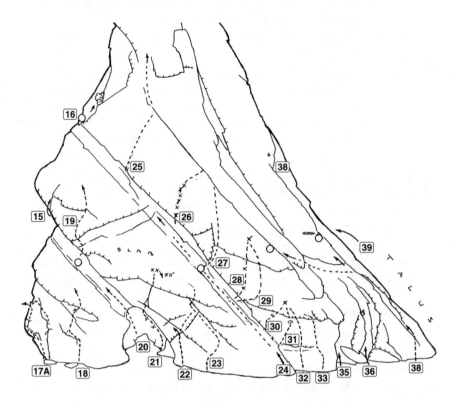

of the crack, angles left on obvious holds, then makes a long reach (a dyno for the altitudinally challenged) to a big lip (11). **B.** The right one goes up a weird crack to a heelhook (9), then traverses off to the left.

18. **N.E.D. 12b/c ★** FFA: Alan Carrier and Adam Grasowsky, toprope. Led by Charlie Fowler, 1979; Free-soloed by Bob Horan. This is a popular toprope problem, rarely led. This is the first obvious line to the west of the cave. Make some unusual moves up to a wide roof, stretch out past a fixed pin and up over the lip.

19. **Swelling Itching Brain 9** FA: Jim Stuberg and Carl Harrison, 1981. Begin with *Pigeon Exit* and continue to a point just above *N.E.D.* Climb up and right at a small V-groove, gain the west edge of the *Spoof* slab, pull over a roof, and up a slab to *Clementine.*

20. **Pigeon Exit 7** FA: Unclaimed. Here is an unparalleled opportunity to wallow in mounds of pigeon droppings and to clip into historic, rotting slings from the 1960s. Begin inside the cave on the west side and follow a rotten stratum of rock up and out.

21. **Monument 12c** FFA: Scott Woodruff, mid-1980s. FFA direct finish: Dale Goddard, 1989. Popular. Begin on the east side of the cave and follow chalked-up holds past 3 bolts. Finish up the crack at the top of *Horangutan*. **Variation:** There is a direct finish past a fourth bolt at 13a, up to bolts and chains.

22. **Horangutan 12b** ★ FA: Paul Sibley, Kevin Donald, Ron Cox, 1970. FFA: Dick Cilley, toprope, late 1970s. Led free by Bob Horan and Chip Ruckgaber, early 1980s. Horan later free-soloed the route. Begin at a series of chalked up, overhanging jugs, just right of the cave, up to an apex, left along a crack with two pins, then straight up a short crack to a 2-bolt anchor.

23. **Urban Gorilla 12a** ★ FA: Chip Ruckgaber, toprope, 1982. Led by Bob Horan, 1985. Begin a short way to the right of *Horangutan*, up and left along a diagonal roof, and up over the main roof.

24. **Spoof 8+** FA: Layton Kor and Bob Culp, 1962. This ancient tour takes a diagonal ramp formed by the strata of the rock and follows it all the way around to the west face. Begin about 35 feet to the right of the cave. The crux is in the first 25 feet of the route. Finish with any west face route or climb off to the north. There are also several difficult variations that climb the overhang above the ramp

25. **Smoof 8** FA: Pat Ament and Cam John, 1978. Near the end of the *Spoof* traverse, climb a roof (6) and veer right to join *Dirty Sam*.

26. **Men of Steel 7 A3** FA: Greg Miller and Mike Brooks, 1986. About 12 feet left of *Spoof Roof*, tackle a severe overhang via a bolt and two tied-off pins. Move right from the lip of the roof to a small belay.

27. **Spoof Roof 9+** FA: Bill Roos and Diana Hunter, 1974. Climb the first 70 feet of *Spoof* to a break in the overhang, and up you go. Beware of rope drag.

28. **M 10a/b** FA: led by Mike Brooks, 1986. From the third pin on *Spoof*, pull up to the right past a couple of bolts, over the roof, and up to a bolt belay.

29. **Second Coming 11a** FA: Mike Brooks and Todd Montgomery, toproped, 1986. Climb up to the third pin on *Spoof*, move right and straight up to the bolt anchor on *M*.

30. **Free Speech 12a** FA: Brooks, toproped, 1986. Climb up and left 10 feet past *Amputee Love*, then up and right past 2 huecos and over the roof to 2 bolts.

30a. **Continuous Free Speech 9+** FA: Ken Trout, Martha Trout, 1999. Rack: Bring Aliens and RPs. From the anchor bolts atop *Free Speech*, head left a few feet, then up on steep jugs but poor gear, past a lip (9+ S/VS), to finish on the easy slab at the bolts of *M*. This may intersect with the upper section of *Second Coming*.

31. **Amputee Love 12d** FA: Harrison Dekker, toproped, 1984. Climb up the first few moves of *Spoof*, then angle up and right to a solution hole and pull over the roof.

32. **Bowling for Tourists 11a** FA: Brooks, toproped, 1986. Begin just right of the base of the ramp of *Spoof* and climb straight up the bulging wall to a bolt.

33. **Amazon 10c** FA: Mike Brooks, toproped, then soloed, 1986. Climb the bulging wall about 12 feet right of the start to *Spoof*. "Go up jugs (sorta) staying left of the small roof that's 20 feet off the ground, then straight up to a single bolt belay."

34. **Gut Feeling 10b/c** FA: Jim Stuberg and Carl Harrison, 1981. About 6 feet left of *Dihedral Two*, take a left-angling line through the roof.

35. **Dihedral Two 8+** FA: Unknown. This is the left option of two, polished, right-facing dihedrals.

36. **Dihedral One 10d** FA: Unknown. Not to be confused with the preceding route, this is the next smooth dihedral to the right (east).

37. **Dirty Sam 8** FA: Pat Ament and Phil Dean, 1963. FA variation: David Breashears, 1976. Climb in from the east slabs or begin with *Dogma*. Belay at a crack above the beginning to *Spoof* and proceed as shown in the topo. **Variation:** Climb the upper face farther to the right.

38. **My Dogma Got Run Over by My Karma 6** FA: Mike Brooks, 1986. Begin at the far east side of the south face, go up a shallow, left-facing dihedral, and up the slab to a belay at a horn. Continue straight up to a finger crack (crux) and on to the summit.

39. **East Slabs 0 to 4** The easiest and safest line begins about halfway up the talus along the east side, climbs up to a belay at a large juniper tree, and follows a groove up to the summit.

40. **The Northeast Arête Class 4** This is the easiest downclimb from the summit. To do it as a route, hike up around either side of The Whale's Tail to the grassy platform beneath the short north face. Step up onto the arête where it is about 3 feet high and follow it to the summit. It is obvious to stay on the left side of the arête. There is very little protection.

NORTH ROCK

This is a small, mediocre, north-facing crag about 100 feet northwest of the top of Hawk-Eagle Ridge. Jim Erickson did the first routes during one of his solo binges of the late 1970s; in 1981, Carl Harrison climbed all the routes that Erickson missed. Approach as for Hawk-Eagle Ridge or by hiking up the gully below the east ridge of Shirttail Peak from East Draw.

1. **Off the Wall 9** FA: Jim Erickson, c.1979. Begin at the left side of the wall. Go up to a roof, angle 20 feet right, turn the roof, and finish with either of two easy cracks.

2. **Flake 6** FA: Carl Harrison, 1981. Begin about 35 feet to the right of the above and climb straight up past the left side of a flake.

3. **First Crack 2** FA: Erickson, c. 1979. Climb the 4-inch-wide crack that goes past the left side of the flake.

4. **Joyous 7** FA: Harrison, 1981. Climb a shallow, arching, right-facing dihedral about 20 feet right of *First Crack*, change cracks partway up and continue to the top.

5. **Second Crack 3** FA: Erickson, c. 1979. After a *Joyous* start, continue to the right into the right-hand crack and go straight for the top.

6. **You Jane 5** FA: Harrison, 1981. Begin with *Joyous*, then hand-traverse right, crossing *Second Crack*, to the top of the wall.

7. **Ledge to Ledge 6** FA: Harrison, 1981. About 50 feet right of *Second Crack*, climb a shallow, right-facing dihedral to a ledge, move left into another dihedral and finish with the last few feet of *You Jane*.

8. **EZ Chimney Class 4** A few feet right of the preceding route is a chimney with a tree in it that can be used to get back to the ground.

9. **Botanical Crack 6** FA: Harrison, 1981. Sounds wonderful. Six feet right of the chimney.

10. **Green Finger 8** FA: Harrison, 1981. Climb a finger crack to the right of the preceding route.

HAWK-EAGLE RIDGE

This ridge runs parallel between Redgarden Wall on the west and The Rotwand on the east. It arises just north of Wind Tower and climbs to the northwest for about a thousand feet. It is home to dozens of obscure routes, but has a few that have become popular. The area can provide shelter on very windy winter days. All routes are on the southwest side of the ridge and are approached via The Wind Tower Trail and the lower part of the *East Slabs Descent Route* for Redgarden Wall.

1. **Peters Out 5** FA: Pat Ament and Paula Munger, 1975. FA Variation A: Erickson, Wunch, Bob Godfrey, 1978. FA Variation B: Mike and Pete Werner, 1978. Climb the far northwest arête of Hawk-Eagle Ridge, bypassing a roof band on the left. **Variation A:** Climb a hand crack through the roof. **Variation B:** Climb through the overhang a bit farther to the right.

HAWK-EAGLE RIDGE

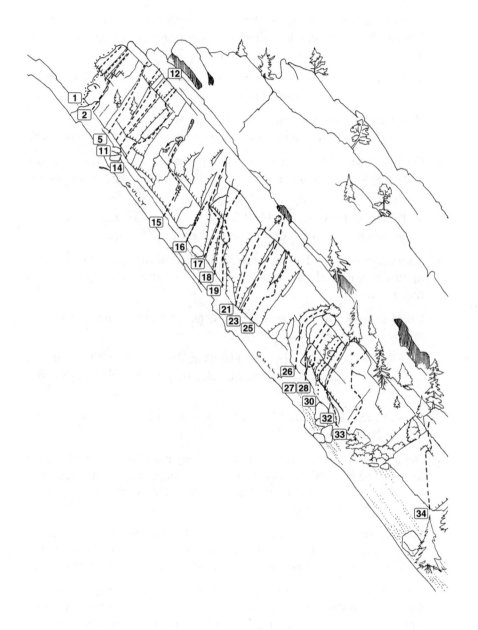

2. **Siberian Khatru 8** FA: David Hague and Marc Hirt, 1981. Begin at a shallow inset about 20 feet left of *Central Park*, scoot up a slab to a finger crack and climb it through a roof.

3. **Central Park 7** FA: Huggins, Brooks, Stuberg, 1981. A few feet left of *The Larch*, climb a crack to a big, square inset capped by a narrow roof, and through the roof at its extreme left.

4. **The Larch 6** FA: Brooks, 1981. Six feet left of *Howard Placebo*, climb a crack and the right end of a narrow roof above an inset.

5. **Howard Placebo 6** FA: Stuberg and Placebo, 1981. Begin a few feet left of *I've Been Sick* and follow a crack up past the left side of a large roof.

6. **I've Been Sick 7** FA: Harrison, 1981. Ten feet left of *Walk About*, follow a crack system up to a big roof, climb the roof at its right and continue to the top.

7. **Walk About 4** FA: Harrison, 1981. Begin at a wide slot 6 feet left of *Times Square*, up to a roof, and on to the top via a crack.

8. **Times Square 7** FA: Harrison, 1981. Just left of the *Uncle Ernie*, climb up to a hanging, left-facing dihedral, over a small roof, and onward via finger cracks.

9. **Uncle Ernie 6** FA: Harrison, 1981. Begin at a slot behind a tree and follow a crack to the top.

10. **Pepe Le Peu 6** FA: Stuberg and Harrison, 1981. About 20 feet left of *Devo*, climb a right-angling finger crack past a tree to a broken roof that is climbed via large holds.

11. **Crystal Graze 8** FA: Harrison, 1981. Begin a few feet left of *Devo*, climb to a crack, and at the roof move left to *Pepe Le Peu*.

12. **Devo 8** FA: Stuberg, Brooks, and Joe Huggins, 1981. Begin about 10 feet left of *Roof's Way*, climb a long, left-facing corner up to a red roof, turn the roof on the right, move back to the left above the lip of the roof, and straight up to a tree.

13. **Wet Dream 9 S** FA: Stuberg and Harrison, 1981. Climb the first 6 feet of *Roof's Way*, hand-traverse right and up to a break in the roof, turn the roof, move right, follow a ramp to its end, then up the arête to the top.

14. **Roof's Way 10a S** FA: Layton Kor and John Link, 1968. FA Variation A: Jeff Lowe and Charlie Fowler, 1978. FA: variation B, Jim Erickson, 1980. This route ascends the west side of a prominent buttress about 30 feet after the approach gully changes from brush to rock slabs. Climb up through a hollow, traverse right, and up through two roofs to a belay at

a tree. Climb straight up to a hand crack through a third roof. **Variation A:** Begin with a dihedral past a short bulge (9). **Variation B:** Climb the right of 3 cracks above the ledge at the top of *Roof's Way*.

15. **Stay Hungry 10d** FA; Dan Hare and Scott Woodruff, 1980. About 75 feet down the gully from the prominent buttress of *Roof's Way*, climb a thin crack in a flake to the right side of a roof, undercling left around the roof, and up to a block. Rappel 75 feet.

On the face betwen *Stay Hungry* and *Yellow Brick Road*, there is an incomplete project. There are 2 bolts on top, and a couple of bolts low down (placed prior to the bolt ban). The first 30 feet are about 11d, and have been toproped by Leslie Coon. The face directly above, up to the bolts on top, is steep, blank, and likely around 13–14 in difficulty.

16. **Yellow Brick Road 6** FA: Unknown. Begin a short way left of *Self Abuse*, climb up into a right-facing system, and angle right to join that route above the roof.

17. **Self Abuse 10b/c** FA: Jim Erickson and Dan Stone, 1976. Climb a right-facing inside corner, just left of *January Playmate*, and jam out the left side of large roof.

18. **January Playmate 8** FA: John Behrens and Jim Erickson, 1969. Climb the left crack in the inset mentioned above, angle left beneath an overhang, move right and follow a crack to a rotten ledge, 20 feet to another ledge, and on to the top.

19. **January Rush 9** FA: Duncan Ferguson, 1976. FA variation, Duncan Ferguson and Kevin Donald, 1980. Climb the right of two cracks in an inset that is left of the arête of *Heart of Gold*. **Variation:** Once above the crack that is in a left-facing dihedral, one may continue up the face (10 S).

HEART OF GOLD/RUSH BUICK AREA

These are good climbs, located above a narrow section of the gully. Below here the gully is wide and vegetated, with bushes and scree; above, the gully floor is rock slabs, blending in with the upper East Slabs of Redgarden Wall.

20. **Heart of Gold 12a ★** FA: Dan Hare and Kris Hanson, 1988. Rack: QDs. Excellent. Climb the first 12 feet of *Rush Buick*, move left, and follow a line of 11 bolts up the wall to the right of the arête. Thirty-one meters long; a 60-meter rope will only just allow lowering.

21. **Rush Buick 7 ★** FA: Jim Erickson and John Behrens, 1969. Just right of the bolted arête of *Heart of Gold*, climb a classic, right-facing dihedral. Rappel 100 feet.

22. **Emergency Brake 9+** FA: Dan Hare and John Warren, 1984. Begin 10 feet right of *Rush Buick*, up over a deceptive bulge, move left and up

past 2 bolts to a thin crack, then right around an overhang to belay in a cave. Rappel *Rush Buick*.

23. **Nobody's Home 9** ★ FA: Stuberg and Harrison, 1981. To the right of *Rush Buick* and below a conspicuous cave, climb 2 right-facing dihedrals, one after the other, straight up to the cave. . . and see if anybody's home.

24. **Mountains out of Molehills 8** FA: Dan Hare and Alan Bradley, 1981. To the right of *Rush Buick*, find a pinnacle that is separated from the wall. Climb a short, right-facing dihedral to a horizontal crack, right to the arête, and past a tricky bulge.

25. **The Squeamish 10b/c S** FA: Dan Hare and Todd Bibler, 1983. Rack: should include a clip stick, tape, and extra RPs. Climb a right-facing flake that stops after about 25 feet, right, then left into a big, right-facing dihedral, up to a roof, right and over a rotten black roof, and belay in a cave. Climb off left to *Rush Buick* and rappel.

26. **Prime Time Climb 10b/c** FA: Harrison and Stuberg 1981. About 6 feet left of *Die Heeda Rule*, climb an off-width to an overhanging hand crack.

DIE HEEDA RULE/TOMBSTONE AREA
Here are two of the better routes on the ridge. There are the remains of a large felled tree at the base. and they are about level with a prominent cave (which looks like a mouth) on the East Slabs of Redgarden Wall.

27. **Die Heeda Rule 11b** ★ FA: Duncan Ferguson, solo, 1975. Climb the overhanging, straight-in corner via a thin crack.

28. **Brother Jug 10a** FA: Carl Harrison, 1981. Begin with *Die Heeda Rule*, up to a horn, lean out right to a jug, crank over the roof, finger crack to another roof, and up the face.

29. **Resisting Arête 10b/c** FA: Dan Hare and Katy Cassidy, 1983. Begin in the *Bowling Alley* and climb partway up, move out left at a bolt and up the arête.

30. **Bowling Alley 6** FA: Harrison and Stuberg, 1981. This is the chimney left of the *Tombstone* roof, inhabited by an oversized bowling ball.

31. **Bold Finger 10a** FA: Ken Duncan and Scott Blunk, 1977. Climb a finger crack through the roof about 10 feet left of *Tombstone*.

32. **Tombstone 11a** ★ FA: Jim Erickson and Paul Sibley, 1970. Rack: up to a #4 Friend. This is one of the few routes to become popular on the ridge. Climb a weird crack through the large overhang just left of *Plinth*.

33. **Plinth 10b/c S** FA: Scott Woodruff and Dan Hare, 1976. FA: variation, Dan Michael, Casey Newman, Jeff Butterfield, Bill Feiges, 1980. About

HAWK-EAGLE RIDGE—LOWER SOUTHWEST FACE

80 feet up from *Crack-Tree-Face* and left of a break in the ridge, is a diamond-shaped, south-facing wall. Climb up and right, left into mid-face, up and left to a left-angling ramp, and right from a bolt into an inside corner. **Variation A:** Toprope straight up from the bolt via a black streak. (This may have been bolted and led.)

34. **Crack-Tree-Face 8** FA: Harrison, solo, 1981. Begin near the left side of an inset, just left of a right-facing dihedral, climb a plumbline up past a flake by a dead tree, over a tiny roof, and voilà.

35. **The Bean 4** FA: Stuberg, solo, 1980. Climb a left-facing dihedral to a large tree.

36. **Tekneek 9** FA: Harrison and Stuberg, 1981. The exact location of some of these routes is uncertain, this one being a case in point. See topo.

37. **Skip and Go Naked 8** FA: Dave Kozak, solo, 1980. Climb the short wall 45 feet left of *Uninspiring Wall.*

38. **Short One 6** FA: Jim Stuberg, 1981. Climb the wall at its lowest point.

39. **Uninspiring Wall 5** FA: Steve Wunch, 1970. Climb the wall up through a square roof.

40. **Rupee Dog 8 S** FA: Carl Harrison, 1981. Climb the middle of the smooth wall.

41. **Heva 9 S** Eric Doub and Dan Montgomery, 1977. Just left of *Low Profile,* climb the smooth face via a right-angling crack.

42. **Low Profile 7** FA: Carl Harrison, 1981. Begin in some bushes below a roof and follow a plumbline up the face.

43. **Jupiter 9 S ★** FA: Jim Erickson and Jim Hofman, 1970. About 80 feet up the gully from *Cinch Crack*, climb a 15-foot, straight-in corner and continue up a smooth face.

44. **Leapfrog 8** FA: Pat Ament, 1970s. Pull over the roof at a shallow inset 20 feet left of *The Crab*, and follow a crack that diagonals to the right.

45. **The Crab 7** FA: Stuberg, 1981. Climb the large inside corner up and left from *Cinch Crack.*

46. **Stranglehold 7** FA: Dan Hare and Alan Bradley, 1980. Just up and around the corner from *Cinch Crack*, up a short inside corner, move right under a roof, then up and left at some buckets.

47. **Cinch Crack 12b ★** FA: Unknown. FFA: John Bragg, 1978. Flashed on-sight, by Patrick Edlinger. About 75 feet above the big chockstone of the *East Slabs Descent*, a large roof hangs out over the gully. The route is obvious and impressive. . . a hand and finger crack through the middle of the roof (usually has a couple of fixed nuts). Lower from a bolt anchor.

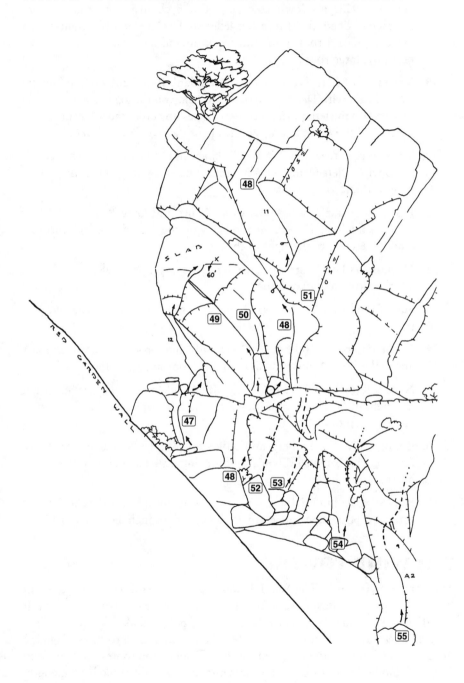

48. **Dead on Arrival 11c S ★** FA: Unknown. FFA: Jim Erickson and Scott Stewart, 1973. Just down from *Cinch Crack*, climb a 12-foot-long, clean, left-facing dihedral (7) to a big ledge and belay. Go up a right-facing dihedral, pass a roof (pin), and work up and left past another pin beneath the large roof (crux).

49. **Road to Nowhere 11c S** FA: Steve Sangdahl, John Baldwin, the Lumex. 1985. Begin with *Dead on Arrival* and belay on the big ledge. Climb the dihedral on the left and a crack that angles up across the left wall (crux), go around the arête, and up to the anchor above *Cinch Crack*.

50. **Those Fertile Years 7 A2** FA: Jan Delaney and Mike Brooks, 1986. Climb the obvious, left-facing dihedral that goes straight up from the beginning of *Road to Nowhere*.

51. **Lips Like Sugar 12a/b ★** FA: Colin Lantz and Greg Robinson, 1987. Begin as for *Dead on Arrival* and belay on the big ledge. Climb through a line of 6 bolts to the right of that route.

52. **Mr. Loyko's Diet Plan 9+** FA: Mike Brooks, toproped, 1986. Up through a little corner and over a roof.

53. **Stay Tuned 9+** FA: Brooks, 1986. Start right of *Mr. Loyko*, and join that route.

54. **Smear Campaign 10d** FA: Ed Body and Mike Brooks, 1985. Begin just above the chockstone and climb up past a protruding block.

55. **Nails to Nowhere 9 A2** FA: Greg Miller and Jan Delaney, 1986. Begin just right of the chockstone, angle up and left from a block, over a roof, and back up to the right.

56. **Bikini 7** FA: Jim Stuberg and Mike Brooks, 1981. Begin just above *Hooker*, climb a dihedral on a south-facing wall, and halfway up turn an overhang on the right.

57. **Hooker 9** FA: Jim Erickson, solo, 1979. Begin well below the chockstone, at the low point of the ridge. Angle up left and through the center of a roof.

THE WIND TOWER

The narrow pyramid of The Wind Tower rises 300 feet directly above South Boulder Creek and is host to several of the most popular routes in Colorado. It is difficult to estimate how many thousands of people make ascents of *Wind Ridge*, *Tagger*, and *Calypso* each year, but the fact that these routes seldom are unoccupied stimulates the imagination. Nearly all of the routes on The Wind Tower lie along the south and west faces and are up to three pitches in length. The routes on the south face are, with some exception, more difficult and poorly

THE WIND TOWER FROM THE SOUTHWEST

protected. On the west face, the routes are lower-angle and better protected, but there is loose rock, especially near the summit, and one should be reluctant to climb directly beneath another party.

To reach The Wind Tower from the parking lot, cross the footbridge, then hike up The Wind Tower Trail (for the west face) or hike east a short way along The Streamside Trail to the south face. To descend from the summit, scramble north along the ridge for about 100 feet to a U-shaped notch with a bolted rappel anchor. Make a short rappel or downclimb (4) to the steep and loose slope below, where the upper end of The Wind Tower Trail can be picked up. There is a long, rotten ledge system two pitches up that traverses the entire west face. This is exposed and dangerous in places but allows for a third-class, walk-off from all routes, including those on the south face. A better escape from the top of the routes, however, is to rappel from two bolts at the top of *Recon*, near the dying tree. Rappel 80 feet, then rappel 100 feet down the first pitch of *Calypso*. **Rockfall from human carelessness has caused several serious accidents on The Wind Tower. PLEASE BE CAREFUL.**

1. **Bent Dog 8** FA: Jim Stuberg and Mike Brooks, 1981. Climb a short face about 50 feet up and left from *Wind Ridge*.

2. **Day 444 (rating unknown)** FA: Jim Stuberg and Mike Downing, 1981. About 40 feet left of *Wind Ridge*, at a small buttress, climb a crack, hand traverse right, up the left of two dihedrals, and up a crack at a dead tree.

3. **Variety 8** FA: Carl Harrrison, 1981. About 20 feet up and left from *Wind Ridge*, climb a dihedral, an arête, and a finger crack to join *Breezy*.

4. **Breezy 4 ★** FA: Unknown. Rack: up to 3 inches. This route follows the obvious, left-facing dihedral system just left of *Wind Ridge*. Start about 40 feet up and left from *Wind Ridge*. Traverse right into the large dihedral system. Continue straight up via a zigzag crack system to the walk-off ledge. Take the obvious exit or continue to the summit via a clean, V-shaped corner, up around a large tree, and right to finish with the last 40 feet of *Wind Ridge*. **Variation A:** Start as for *Wind Ridge*, head up the slabby dihedral on the left (6), and continue up to join the regular route. **Variation B: Erickson's Wide Crack 8+** FA: Jim Erickson. An overhanging slot on the right looms after about 100 feet. Finish with *Wind Ridge*.

5. **Wind Ridge 6 ★ or 8 ★** FA: Layton Kor and Jane Bendixon, 1959. FA: of variation, Phil Olinick, 1981. Rack: up to a #2.5 Friend. This takes the skyline ridge as seen from the footbridge. From the huge block that leans against the face, hike up around the lower buttress of *Wind Ridge* and cut back south onto a ledge with a Douglas-fir. P1. Climb straight up to a large flake, then step right onto the exposed ridge (8). Otherwise, jam and stem up and slightly left 20 feet, and hand-traverse the top of the aforementioned flake to join the arête above the 8 crux. This variation

THE WIND TOWER—WEST FACE LEFT

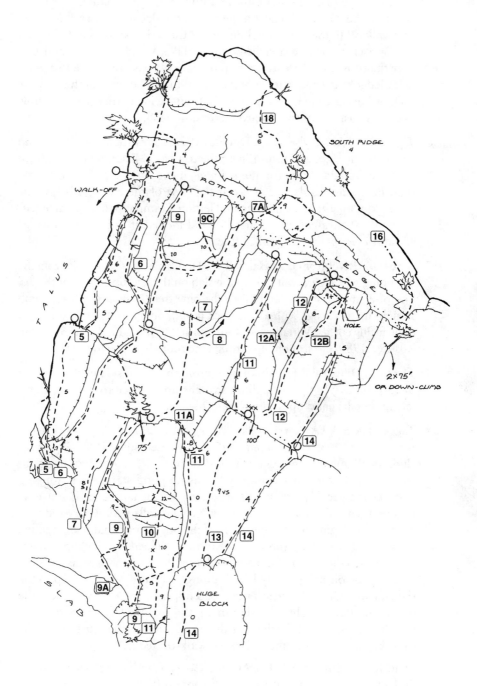

goes at a tricky 6. Continue straight up the ridge to a belay on a big in-sloping ledge (5). P2. Step right and power up into a crack that keeps going all the way to a belay on the walk off ledge (6). Either bag it here and walk off to the north, or climb one of the weirdest roofs in Eldorado. P3. Weasel up behind a right-pointing flake, stand up on it, and pull over the roof (6). Work straight up the face (4) past a big tree to a good belay ledge a few paces north of the true summit. Be very careful of loose rock on this last pitch. **Variation:** P3. A left-facing corner with a double overhang just left of the "weird flake roof" (10).

6. **Tigger 5 ★** FA: Maybe Kevin Donald, 1970s. This route parallels *Wind Ridge* on the right and joins it near the top of P2. Begin on the platform with the Douglas-fir as for *Wind Ridge*, move up and right and follow right-facing dihedrals to a belay at the base of the dihedral below the upper roof on *Tagger*. Climb up and left on a ramp, up through an exciting roof (5), straight up a crack (5), and move left to join *Wind Ridge* about 40 feet below the walk-off ledge.

7. **Across the River from Butt Hair 9 S** FA: Duncan Ferguson, 1974. From the beginning of *Tagger*, continue up the slab on the left, up a seam at the left side of a small buttress, and up to the pine tree ledge. From here, climb straight up to a bulge with a thin crack (crux), up the face above, and up a right-facing corner. **Variation A: Roof Finish 9-** FA: Jim Erickson and Raoul Rossiter, 1980. Go straight up through the roof above the top of the route.

8. **The G.Y. Dihedral 8** FA: Unknown. From the south side of the ledge at the top of *Calypso Direct*, climb straight up the face to a steep, right-facing dihedral and up to the walk-off ledge.

9. **Tagger 10c S ★** FA: Larry Dalke, Pat Ament, 1962. FFA: Jim Erickson, Jim Walsh, 1968. FA: *Roofed Out*, R. Rossiter, solo, 1980. Rack: include small, medium wires and TCUs/Aliens for P1. Note that the popular first pitch, though technically 9, has no good stances for stopping and placing gear. There are some good placements, but it is not easy finding them. There have been a few ground falls here where the gear has ripped. Begin about 30 feet left of the huge block that leans against the wall. P1. Climb up through a shallow A-shaped roof, (9) up and left around the edge of the big roof, and straight up to the ledge with the pine and 2-bolt belay. Belay here if doing just P1, or continue up to the right-facing dihedral beneath the broad upper roof and belay below the mid-point. P2. Straight up and stem out through the left side of the final roof (crux). #2 or #2.5 Friend at the lip. Optional belay just above the roof. Finish up a nice dihedral to the walk-off ledge.

9a. **I Did It My Way 9 S** FA: Pat Ament, 1970s. Climb a right-facing dihedral straight up to the left side of the roof on P1.

9b. **Roofed Out** 7 FA: R. Rossiter, solo, 1980. Avoid the crux roof by underclinging off to the right

9c. **Fear and Loathing** 10b/c FA: Jeff Butterfield and Doug Madara, 1980. From this traverse one may climb up through the right side of the overhang.

10. **Salvation** 12a/b S ★ FA: Mike Van Loon and Pat Ament, 1960s. FFA: Jeff Achey, 1980. FA: variation, Rob Candelaria, 1986. From the start of *Calypso* (left option), climb up a steep, poorly protected slab and out through a roof with a bolt. **Variation:** Climb in under the roof from the left (12).

11. **Calypso** 6 S ★ FA: Layton Kor, Larry Dalke, Pat Ament, 1961. The park rangers reckon P1 to have more accidents than anywhere else in the Canyon. The traverse at the end of P1, once protected by some old pins, is now difficult to protect and pretty polished. A fall by the leader from the end of the traverse can result in a nasty swing back into the dihedral. Competence required. Begin just left of the huge boulder that leans against the wall. P1. Climb the slot between the boulder and the wall (6), or the smooth face 5 feet to the left (8), or traverse in from a tiny, left-facing flake 10 feet farther left (5). Work up into the large, right-facing dihedral above the block. Jam and stem up to a roof, undercling and lieback around to the right (6) and up 25 feet, place a nut to protect your second, and traverse 10 feet down to the right to a 2-bolt anchor. P2. Move up and left into a vertical crack (6) and continue up to a belay stance just below the walk-off ledge. (This is also P2 of *Recon*.) P3. Choice of finishes from here; see topo.

11a. **Calypso Direct** 8 ★ FA: Pat Ament and Larry Dalke, 1965. Climb out the left side of the *Calypso* roof to the ledge with the pine on *Tagger*.

12. **Reggae** 8 ★ FA: Unknown. Rack: up to a #2 Friend. This is one of the best moderate pitches on The Wind Tower. From the 2-bolt anchor on *Calypso*, move down and right about 10 feet, then up a large, right-facing dihedral with little roofs. The crux is a superb finger crack and slot at the top (wired Stoppers). Belay *à cheval* on a natural bridge.

12a. **Jimmy Cliff** 7 S FA: Kevin Donald, 1980. Traverses left out of the dihedral on a brown band of rock, (7 S), and join P2 of *Recon*.

12b. **Rastaman Roof** 9 FA: R. Rossiter, Solo, 1981. Branch right below the crux and climb a crack out the center of a natural bridge.

13. **Wind Tower Slab** 9 VS ★ FA: Russ Kirkpatrick and George Meyers, 1970. First led by Jim Erickson, 1972. Climb the middle of the slab between *Calypso* and the groove of *Boulder Direct*. The pitch is usually toproped.

THE WIND TOWER—WEST FACE RIGHT

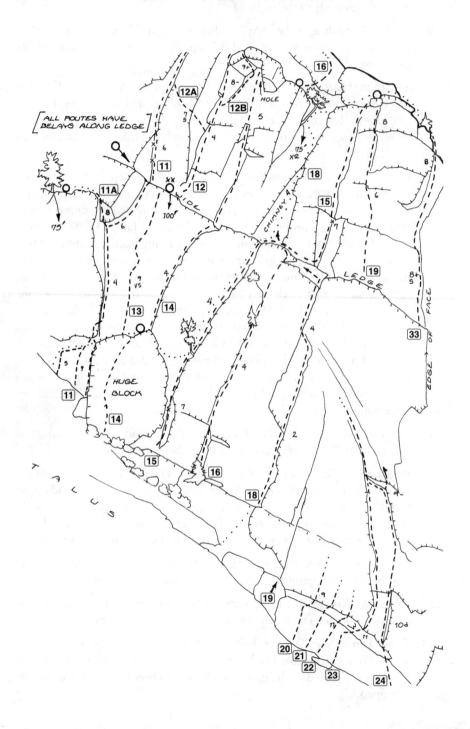

14. **Boulder Direct 5** ★ FA: Unknown. P2, R. Rossiter, solo, 1978. This is a pretty good route and deserves more attention. P1. Climb the outside of the big block that leans against the wall and belay in a cozy niche at its top (0). Go up an easy groove (Class 4) or the more interesting face to its right (4) and belay on the wide ledge at mid-face. P2. Climb straight up the face, through a slot (5), and on up beneath a natural bridge. Walk-off, downclimb, or head for the summit.

15. **West Overhang 7** ★ FA: Unknown. Climb the slot behind the right side of the huge block (6+) and up the easy chimney above. Move right on the mid-face ledge, up a short dihedral to a roof (crux), and on up to the south end of the walk-off ledge.

16. **The Bomb 4** ★ FA: Dick Bird and Dallas Jackson, 1956. This was probably the first route done on The Wind Tower. It is the easiest way to the summit. The first pitch may have been the same as for *Recon*. P1. Begin on the ledge about 20 feet to the right of the big block, up a short, right-facing corner into a prominent groove, past a tree, and on up to the big ledge at mid-face. P2. Move left, climb a chimney, and belay on a good ledge above a juniper tree. Work up onto the scenic south ridge (4) and continue to the summit. Beware of loose rock.

17. **The Governor's Climb 5** FA: D. Lamm. This ascends the slab between routes *Recon* and *The Bomb*. There is (or was) an old rusty bolt and hanger at the top of this pitch.

18. **Recon 6** ★ FA: Cleve McCarty and Ted Rouillard, 1957. Begin at the far right end of a ledge that leads south from the block. P1. Climb a left-facing dihedral, over a roof (0), and up a crack to the big ledge at mid-face. Traverse left about 50 feet and belay at 2 bolts. P2. Climb the steep crack (6) that is usually done as the second pitch to *Calypso*. Belay with a poor anchor in a large recess along the rotten walk-off ledge or rappel from the new bolts. From here, traverse out right around an exposed roof (4), back north to belay at a tree, and on up the south ridge to the summit. Otherwise scramble up the ledge (CAREFULLY) for about 60 feet to a break in the overhang, up this (4), and left to join the last 50 feet of *Wind Ridge*.

19. **Lemmings 8** FA: Dan Hare and Scott Woodruff, 1979. Begin in the next system right of, and down from, Recon. Climb straight up to the big ledge at mid-face. About 30 feet left of *Left Out*, climb the face to a crack through a roof.

20. **Hard Up 9+** ★ FA: Mark Norden and Bruce Adams, 1974. This is a nice little pitch. Master the left side of the roof (RPs) and romp up the face above. Finish with *Left Out* or the last pitch of *Lemmings*.

Joyce Rossiter on the Rainbow Wall *(5.13a), Wind Tower.*

21. **Raisin Bran 9** FA: Mike Brooks and Todd Montgomery, 1983. Squeezed between *Smooth Z* and *Hard Up* is another line through the roof.

22. **Smooth Z 11b/c** FA: Darius Azin, 1986. Rack: #2 and #2.5 Friends. Just right of *Raisin Bran*, turn the roof via 2 underclings.

23. **Endless Summer 11b/c S** FA: Kevin Donald, Duncan Ferguson, David Breashears, Rob Candelaria, 1980. Climb the overhang a few yards left of *The Uplift*, and down a little from *Smooth Z*. Climb a right-facing dihedral, through a roof, and up to the broad ledge that truncates the west face. A second pitch allegedly goes up between *Left Out* and *Lemmings* (8).

SOUTH FACE

The following routes ascend the very steep south face of The Wind Tower. Cross the footbridge and follow The Streamside Trail east beneath the south face.

24. **The Uplift 10d VS** FA: Pat Ament, Jan Sacherer, Roger Raubach, 1964. FFA: Duncan Ferguson and John Searls, 1974. Begin a short way to the left of *The Muscle Up*, go over a roof, up a clean, right-leaning, left-facing ramp, over a second roof, and finish with *Futile Laments*.

25. **The Muscle Up 12c VS** FA: Bob Horan, 1986, toproped by Christian Griffith, 1985. Begin to the left of *King's X*. Climb straight up through the arched roof.

26. **King's X 10d ★** FA: Layton Kor and Larry Dalke, 1967. FFA: Ron Cox and Paul Sibley, 1971. FA Variation A: Chris Archer, Keith Gotschall 1993, variation B; Chris Archer, Pete Athans, Eric Reynolds, 1998. Begin about 25 feet to the left of The Lower Triangle (a flat buttress formed by two converging ramps), and to the right of the arched roof of *Muscle Up*, find lots of chalk and a fixed pin at a bulge. Climb up through the perplexing bulge (10c), then up and left to the low point of a roof (often festooned with slings), optional belay. Step right, (wires, #2 Friend) and straight up (crux) past a couple of fixed pins through the A-shaped roof (watch for the rope catching in the apex) to a good belay stance a few feet above it. Twelve feet higher is another stance, usually equipped as a rappel anchor. Rap or continue (9) up the awkward, right-facing dihedral to a large ramp, which connects to the west face. **Variations:** Both variations start from the belay at the lip of the *King's X* roof. **Variation A:** Traverse left to the arête (8). **Variation B:** From the same belay head up and a little left (10 to 15 feet), then traverse left (9).

27. **Futile Laments 9** FA: Pat Ament and Tom Higgins, 1979. From the old belay 40 feet up *King's X*, climb straight up, past a roof, and join the arête between the south and west faces. Up to a broad ledge. Downclimb *Boulder Direct*, or continue up any route that ascends from this ledge (see topo).

THE WIND TOWER—SOUTH FACE LEFT

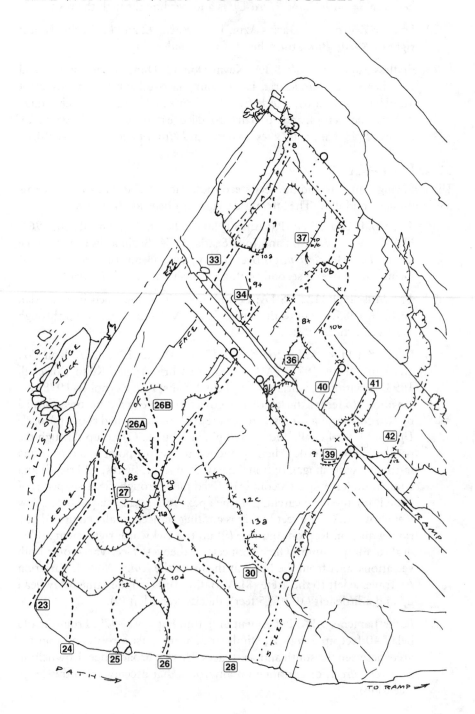

28. **Black Wind 11b/c S** FA: Led by Jeff Lowe, 1981. This route apparently begins to the left of the dihedral below *Rainbow Wall* and right of the start of *King's X*, either crosses or joins *Awesome Robots*, and merges with *King's X* at the A-shaped roof of P2.

The following three routes begin from, or to the left of, a large left-facing, right-leaning dihedral that forms the left side of The Lower Triangle, and leads up (4) to the pedestal at the beginning of *The Yellow Traverse*.

29. **Awesome Robots 10** FA: Kyle Copeland, 1983. FFA: Mike Brooks and Trip Halbkat, 1984. Begin this obscure line as for *Rainbow Wall*, reach left for an undercling, and traverse left to the roof on *King's X*.

30. **Rainbow Wall 13a** ★ FA: Kyle Copeland and Mark Hill, 1983. FFA: Bob Horan 1984. First on-sight flash, Ben Moon, 1991. Rack: a #2 Friend and 6 QDs. The first 5.13 in Eldorado Canyon. Scramble about a third of the way up the left-facing dihedral of The Lower Triangle, undercling out to the left (9, #2 Friend), stretch up to clip the first bolt, and follow a line of bolts up and left to easier ground. The crux is by the second bolt, but the rest of the pitch is sustained and difficult to decipher.

31. **Diffraction 10a** FA: Kyle Copeland (9 A3), 1983. FFA: Charlie Fowler and Copeland, 1986. Climb about halfway up the dihedral described above, move out around a flake, and straight up to the finish of *The Yellow Traverse*.

32. **Lower Triagonal 9+** FA: led by Jim Erickson, 1978. Follow a crack along the right side of the south face of The Lower Triangle, then straight up (crux) to the belay pedestal.

UPPER SOUTH FACE

The following four routes begin from a diagonal ramp, halfway up the south face, which may be reached by traversing in from the west face or by climbing up to it via *The Yellow Traverse*, *King's X*, et cetera. This ramp is detached from, but in line with, the ramp forming the east side of The Lower Triangle.

33. **Left Out 8** FA: Steve Wunch with a "backrope," 1971. Farthest left of the routes on the upper south face. Pretty much follows the arête between the south face and the west face. Begin at the upper left (west) end of the ramp mentioned above, just left of *Disguise*. Climb up into a small dihedral, pass an awkward bulge (crux), up a narrowing ramp, and up a short, weird corner to the pine tree at the top of the south face.

34. **Disguise 10b S/VS** ★ FA: Bill Briggs and Pat Ament, 1977. Rack: up to 1 inch. Begin in a slot just down and right from *Left Out* or from the ramp near the finish to *King's X*. Power up over an unprotected roof (8), then up and slightly left (9+) to a bulge with an old fixed pin. Move right (crux) and on up to the pine tree at the top of the face.

THE WIND TOWER—UPPER SOUTH FACE

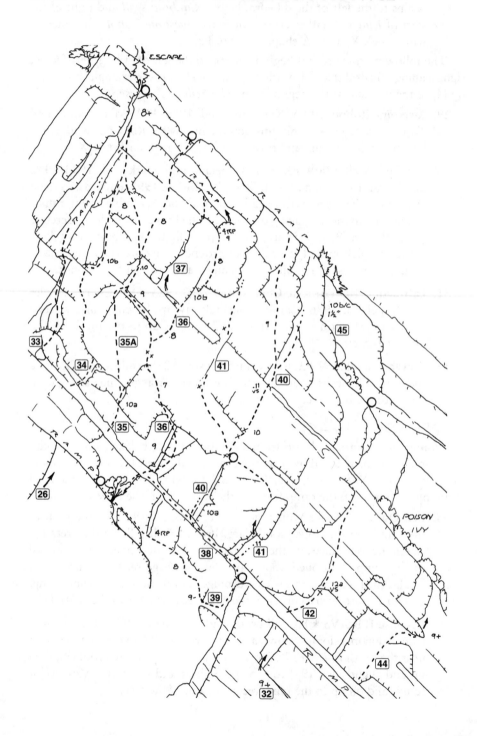

35. **Balls of Fire 10c VS ★** FA: Charlie Fowler and Mike Munger, 1978; variation: Chip Ruckgaber, Mike Schlauch. This is a good line but it's pretty runout. Begin about 25 feet up and left of *The Metamorphosis*, just down from the finish of *King's X*. Make hard, unprotected moves up into a right-leaning, left-facing dihedral, and stem up to the 2-bolt anchor on that route. Angle up and left into a shallow corner (pro possible), up over a bulge (crux), and on up to the pine tree at the top of the wall.

35a. **Variation** From the starting moves, head straight up the face to a small roof. Head right to rejoin *Balls of Fire* just below the crux bulge.

36. **The Metamorphosis 10b S ★** FA: Pat Ament and Gordy Ryan, 1967. FFA: Jim Erickson and Art Higbee, 1973. Rack: up to a #3 Friend. One of the classic face routes of Eldorado. It is dead-vertical, sustained, moderately runout, and has a fine, exposed position. Begin from a belay just above a small vine maple tree at the low (east) end of the ramp described above. Move up and right into a tricky, left-facing corner (9+), then up and left to a 2-bolt anchor (optional sling belay). Step right and up to another bolt, up and right past a down-pointing flake (10b), up a pocketed section, over a bizarre bulge (9, #4 RP), then up and left on a narrow ramp to a belay down and right from a pine tree.

36a. **Xanthomorphosis 10b S ★** Combine *Lower Triagonal* and *The Yellow Traverse* with this pitch for a nice outing.

37. **Ur-ine Trouble 10b/c S** FA: Steve Wunch and Jim Erickson, 1973. This is a variation to the upper part of *The Metamorphosis*. From the second bolt, move up and left and climb a right-leaning, right-facing dihedral. Good climbing, not much protection.

The following routes begin from a ramp that angles up to the west from a point along the east side of the south face, directly beneath *Southeast Chimney*. This Class-3 ramp tapers to a rounded pedestal after 100 feet and forms the right side of a broad buttress known as The Lower Triangle.

38. **Blackjack 10a S/VS** FA: Layton Kor and Pete Robinson, 1963. An impressive lead for its time. Climbs the ramp that forms the right side of The Lower Triangle, then continues up and left to the southwest arête. Starts below *Southeast Chimney*. Climb to the apex of The Lower Triangle (The Pedestal), climb up into a nasty diagonal chimney and follow it up to a belay at a vine maple tree at the beginning of *The Metamorphosis*. From here, do one of the routes on the upper south face or follow the continuation of the ramp around to the west face.

39. **The Yellow Traverse 9- VS ★** FA: Layton Kor and Stan Shepard, 1960. Rack: a #4 RP. This pitch, which parallels the crux of *Blackjack* from below, is basically unprotected but for the easier moves near its end.

Begin from The Pedestal, drop down a bit to the west, move out onto a tiny ledge, then work up and left (west) to the belay for *The Metamorphosis* at the vine maple. Be wary of a large, detached block near the end of the pitch.

40. **Deutsch Sturheit 11b VS** FA: Thomas Nolting and Chip Ruckgaber, 1986. Begin from The Pedestal atop The Lower Triangle. Follow *Blackjack* a ways, then ascend a funky, diagonal chimney for 20 feet and climb a right-leaning, left-facing dihedral (10a) to a 2-bolt belay. Angle up and right past 2 pins, over a bulge (crux), and straight up.

41. **Scotch and Soda 11b/c S ★** FA: Layton Kor, Charles Roskosz, 1962. FFA: Jim Erickson, Art Higbee, 1973. This made a bit of a splash back in the 1970s and may still cause people to wonder if they should be on the rocks or not. Begin from The Pedestal. Move up and left to get under the roof, then up and right into the apex. The climbing is sustained, and the crux is clearing the roof. Go up and left to a bolt belay. Follow the strata up and left, then up and right, pass a bulge (10d), and climb a right-leaning corner to the ramp at the top of the south face.

42. **Sheer Terror 12 VS** FA: Skip Guerin and Chip Ruckgaber, 1983. A bold lead, climbed without any toprope/rappel inspection or practice. Between The Shark's Head and *Scotch and Soda* is a horizontal roof with a rounded apex. Climb through the apex (crux), protected by an ancient upside-down pin, belay on the upper end of the poison ivy ledge of Shark's Head, and continue as for that route.

43. **11b/c ?** An alleged route climbs through the low point of the overhang between The Shark's Head and *Sheer Terror*.

44. **Calamine Roof 10a** FA: Kevin Donald and partner, 1980. The Shark's Head is a large finger of rock that points downward to the east above the lower part of the ramp. Route named for Kevin Donald's visit to a hospital after the first ascent. From the ramp, climb up to and around the right side of The Shark's Head, then up to a belay on a ramp. This is covered with poison ivy, and perhaps the route deserves a "VS" rating because of this. P2 goes up and left and finishes with *Hand Crack*.

45. **Hand Crack 10b/c** FA: Jim Erickson and Raoul Rossiter, 1980. From the cave at the top of the first pitch of *Southeast Chimney*, traverse 30 feet left and climb a short, overhanging hand crack to some trees on the ramp that leads to the top of the south face. This crack serves as a logical finish to the next three routes west from *Southeast Chimney*.

46. **Southeast Chimney 4** FA: Cleve McMarty, Bill Becker, Ward and Ted Koeberle, 1957. The actual chimney is about 60 feet up in the back of a right-facing, right-leaning corner. Begin in a vegetated trough to the east

of the left-leaning ramp, climb the chimney, move up and left to a belay by a small cave. Continue up and left along the strata to the top of the south face, thence up the south ridge to the summit. The original line goes right from the top of chimney, then up the south edge of the east face to the south ridge. **Variation A: Hot Toes 7 S** FA: Gray Ringsby and Pat Ament, 1979. This is the best of several variations. Begin on the ramp mentioned above, climb up a short way, and make an unprotected traverse to the east to the base of the chimney.

47. **Wind Tower Wire Route 7** FA: Mike Downing and Gary Cudd, 1980. Climb the steep, pocketed wall about 15 feet to the right of *Southeast Chimney* to a slab.

48. **V2J 10 S** FA: Jim Morrison, Vicki Coulter, Jim Stuberg, 1986. Begin with "a tiny dihedral between *Tidal Wave* and *Southeast Chimney*" and continue up the southeast arête to the summit. Four pitches.

49. **Tidal Wave 8** FA: Jim Stuberg and Carl Harrison, 1981. Begin about 30 feet to the right of *Southeast Chimney* and climb another right-facing corner for 130 feet to a small cave. Move out right to a crack system and climb large holds up to a tree.

HURRAH RIDGE

This is the small rock island in the gully between The Rotwand and The Wind Tower.

1. **Hurrah Ridge 7** FA: Pat Ament and Roger Dalke, 1964. Climb the north-west arête. 90 feet.

THE ROTWAND (THE RED WALL)

This is the steep red wall that rises along the east boundary of the park. It is a couple of hundred feet high and climbs some 1,500 feet to the northwest before it fizzles out in the forested gully below the east ridge of Shirttail Peak. The rock is shattered and loose, the protection poor, and the climbs unpopular.

To approach, cross the footbridge to the north side of South Boulder Creek and follow The Streamside Trail east, past The Wind Tower, to the bottom of the crag. To descend from the lower routes, it is easy enough to hike down and around the east side of the ridge. One may also rappel from an iron railing just west of an old lookout structure that is a vestige of early resort days, or rappel the southwest face from trees in many places. To descend from the upper routes, one may scramble around the east side to the top of the ridge, thence down the gully and back to the bottom. Note that the lower part of the gully on the west side of The Rotwand is about 0 in difficulty. Note also that the boundary of the park is just east of the ridgetop. To descend to the east requires crossing land belonging to the Eldorado Artesian Water Company. This is part of their water catchment area, **please do not pollute or disturb it.** Rappel the west face if possible. On the south side of The Rotwand, the park boundary lines up with the new dam, and then cuts right under the ruins of the old lookout house. Please do not trespass on private land.

1. **Hi-Fi 7** FA: Mike Brooks and Dennis Smith, 1981. Find a V-shaped dead tree at the upper extreme of the wall. Begin just south of the tree, climb straight up to a V-shaped roof 30 feet off the deck, skirt a large overhang on the right, then up and right across a smooth slab to the top.

2. **Time Bomb 9 S** FA: Dan Hare and George Russel, 1980. Start below a flake/crack at the right edge of a clean slab. Turn a roof to reach the flake, and climb the crack to its top. Diagonal left to a horizontal band and up the center of a smooth wall about 20 feet to the right of a right-facing dihedral.

3. **Poison Dwarf 8 S** FA: Jim Stuberg and Carl Harrison, 1981. Somewhere between *Looney Tunes* and *Time Bomb*, locate a "vegetated line" left of a small tree. Ascend a short, right-facing dihedral and finish on face holds.

4. **Skimpy 8 VS** FA: Jim Stuberg and associates, 1981. Begin a couple of hundred feet down from the top of the ridge and just left of a ramp the angles up to the right. Climb up and left, pass a roof (crux), and climb the headwall to 2 trees at the top of the long ledge that runs along the upper wall.

5. **Sic Mix 8 VS** FA: Mic Fairchild, solo, 1994. Start near a tree three-quarters of the way along the bottom of the west face. Zigzag first up left to a tree, then right to the big ledge. Poor rock.

6. **Baron von Barnhart's Eiger Dreams 7** FA: of all pitches described, Rob Cassady, Steve Conrad, 1993. Begin close to, or just right of, the start of *Sic Mix*, at the break in the overhang. P1. Climb past a tree and angle right, over an overhang (loose) to the top of the lower tier. P2. Up a short finger crack, then past a tree on a clean face to the top. There are two variations of P2: **Variation A:** Scramble 50 feet right down the ledge, climb up a slab, then an overhang to the top (8/9). **Variation B:** Scramble left, up the same ledge, then climb an overhang to the top (6).

7. **Looney Tunes 9 S** FA: Jim Stuberg, Mike Brooks, Carl Harrison, 1981. Follow an obvious line 20 feet left of *Beatnik*. 145 feet.

8. **Beatnik 7 VS** FA: Jim Stuberg and Mike Brooks, 1981. Begin across from the top of Hurrah Ridge, perhaps 70 feet up to the left from *Dumb Wadie Bird*. Angle up and right to 3 trees and continue up to the big ledge that runs along the upper ridge. Walk left about 120 feet and climb a chimney to the left of the last pitch of *Dumb Wadie*.

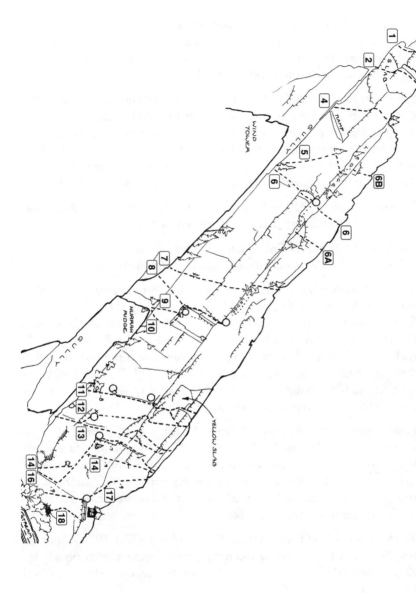

DIE ROTWAND (THE RED WALL)—SOUTHWEST FACE

9. **Yes Fragile 8 S** FA: Dave Kozak and Mark Lane, 1980. Begin near the top of Hurrah Ridge (the buttress in the gully between The Rotwand and The Wind Tower) and ascend to a belay at a large tree. Climb straight up to the long ledge and choose a finish.

10. **Dumb Wadie Bird Warble 8 VS** FA: Larry Dalke and Pat Ament, 1963. Continue up the gully below the southwest face for another 160 feet past *Kinder Rooten* and find this weird route left of an "ugly groove." P1. Climb a short pitch up to a tree on the left and belay. P2. Climb a slab up into a chimney and belay on a ledge system that runs the rest of the way up the wall. Hike left for 100 feet. P3. Finish with a groove.

10a. **Raygun (Rating?)** FA: Jim Stuberg and Ray Riechert, 1981. Ascend an overhanging, left-facing dihedral to the left of P2.

10b. **Let It Be 9** FA: Direct finish, Dudley Chelton, Bob Hritz, Bob Wade, 1973. This direct finish climbs straight up from the second belay.

11. **Kinder Rooten 9 VS ★** FA: Layton Kor and Pat Ament, 1963. FA: of variation, led by Jim Erickson, 1972. Scramble up the gully about 50 feet past the buttress of *Lady Godiva* and belay in a hollowed-out area. Climb straight up to a tiny tree and belay (8). Climb 70 feet of easier rock and step left to a belay ledge. Step right, turn the roof to a slab, then go straight up and over a smaller roof (9-) and on to the top. **Variation:** At the final roof go right, then left. One may also bypass this last roof by scooting around its right end.

12. **Lady Godiva 9 VS** FA: Larry Dalke and Cliff Jennings, 1966. FFA: Jim Erickson and Art Higbee, 1973. As the wall curves around to face southwest, a rotten buttress rises up, just left of a roof. Climb the rotten buttress and angle left above a roof to a belay with a bolt. Climb 70 feet straight up to a ledge and belay. Move right and master three dangerous roofs enroute to the top of the face.

13. **The Sampson Effect 9 VS** FA: Bob Wade and Bob Culp, 1975. Climb the first 30 feet of *Lady Godiva* and head straight up to a belay on a ledge. Zigzag around the right end of some roofs and up a steep headwall (crux) to the top.

14. **Hit the Deck 8 VS** FA: Carl Harrison, Mike Brooks, and Jim Stuberg, 1981. Climb the face just left of *Elitist Picnic* to the belay tree on *Rotwand Route*. A second pitch takes the face about 20 feet to the right of *Rotwand Route*.

15. **Elitist Picnic 9 VS** FA: Larry and Roger Dalke, 1965 (A4). FFA: Carl Harrison and Tom Jasbutis, 1980. From the start of *Rotwand Route*, climb up and slightly left past a small tree to the belay tree on that route.

16. **Rotwand Route 7 VS** FA: Layton Kor and John Auld, 1960. Not far to the left (west) of *Endangered Species*, climb a steep, right-angling ramp to a stance, then make a long, ascending traverse left to a tree and belay. Ascend a broken, left-facing system past another tree to the top of the face.

17. **Endangered Species 9 VS** FA: Carl Harrison and Sandy East, 1981. Begin a short way west of the "cavern of the weeping wall." P1. Climb straight up to a belay at the left end of the iron lookout railing. P2. Angle up and left, then goes straight up. Both pitches are 9 and are very poorly protected.

18. **Simple Harmonic Motion 10b/c S** FA: Led by Dudley Chelton, 1973. This neat little route climbs the wall just left of a shallow cavern with a "weeping wall" and follows a narrow ramp up and right to finish at the right end of the iron railing of the lookout house. Be warned that there are some healthy patches of poison ivy in this area.

19. **Syphillis Waffle 9+ S** FA: Leonard Coyne, 1978. Work up through some roofs to the left of *Dalke's Folly*.

20. **The Rotwand Girdle 9 VS** FA: Bob Hritz and Hunter Smith, 1973. For the gourmand. Begin just left of the "weeping cavern" as for *Simple Harmonic Motion*, climb up about 40 feet and begin a thousand-foot, diagonal traverse, staying near the middle of the wall, all the way to the top of the ridge.

The final two routes are currently on Eldorado Water Company property. Their property line begins at the dam, runs up the cliff, then skirts just below the old gazebo. The landowners are currently friendly toward climbers, but please avoid trespassing on their land, and respect their rights as landowners.

21. **Dalke's Folly 9** FA: Larry Dalke, c. 1963. This was originally done as a boulder problem. It ascends a short steep wall a bit east of the dam. Find the line of least resistance.

22. **Paul's Wall 11a** FA: M. Brooks. This route follows a couple of bolts to a point where you can lower off. Loose, mediocre, and the bolts appear to be gone.

ELDORADO EAST

EAST DRAW

Directly above Eldorado Springs, a rocky hogback ridge rises northward to a wooded summit above Shadow Canyon. Between the hogback and the rugged east slope of Shirttail Peak, The Old South Mesa Trail winds its way up a broad,

U-shaped draw, passes over a scenic divide, and descends into Shadow Canyon. This ancient path begins on private property in Eldorado Springs and is about three-quarters of a mile long. It is the most direct approach to Shadow Canyon, and provides access to the main Mesa Trail, and the following crags. One walks through town on private roads and right up someone's driveway to access this trail. It is imperative that hikers and climbers proceed respectfully so that public access to this unique area is not lost. Remember, there is no public parking in Eldorado Springs.

ISLAND ROCK

This is the large, dark block with an obvious chimney, across the gully from a big, orange wall, and on the north side of the east ridge of Shirttail Peak. Hike directly up to the feature from The Old South Mesa Trail.

1. **Eldorado Pool Girls 5** FA: Mic Fairchild, solo, 1996. Start at the left corner of the north face (northwest corner of the crag), and head up the north ridge to the summit.

2. **Cher's Liposuction Workout 8 S** FA: Mic Fairchild, solo, 1996. Start in a recess left and down from *Cro-Magnon Man*. Power over a bulge, then climb the face above to the summit.

3. **Cro-Magnon Man 7** FA: Carl Harrison, Jim Stuberg, Scott Kimball, 1981. Climb the chimney that splits the east side of the rock.

4. **Overhanging Crack 10** FA: Chip Ruckgaber, c. 1982. Climb a crack to the right of *Cro-Magnon Man*.

5. **Enlightening Arête 9 S** FA: John Warren and Dan Hare, 1982. This is the northeast-facing arête to the right of the chimney.

WALL OF FLAME

The west side of East Draw is formed by the rugged east slope of Shirttail Peak, at the south end of the South Ridge of South Boulder Peak. In the midst of this maze of buttresses and steep gullies, a conspicuous orange wall overhangs to the southeast. Perhaps equidistant between this wall on the north and a massive block split by a chimney on the south, is a smaller, southeast-facing wall: the Wall of Flame. Approach via The Old South Mesa Trail and hike west up the side draw to the base of the rock.

1. **The Blue Flame 11b/c** FA: Mark Tarrant and Dan Hare, 1989. This short route goes up and left on the left of the face, past several bolts.

2. **Fire Storm 11d ★** FA: Dan Hare and Mike Engle, 1989. Rack: #2.5, #3 and #3.5 Friends, QDs. Climb the first 15 feet of *You'll Go Blind*, go out left, up past 5 bolts, and belay at a tree.

3. **You'll Go Blind 11b/c S** ★ FA: Dan Hare and John Warren, 1982. Rack: up to a #3 Friend with 2 #2s. Climb a right-leaning crack in the center of the wall. 50 feet.

4. **Carnal Knowledge 12a VS** FA: Eric Guokas, 1980s. Rack: up to a #3 Friend. A thin crack to the right of center. 1 bolt (?). This route is easily toproped.

5. **Hwang Ho A3** FA: Scott Rourke, Kathy Miller, 1988. Rack: include KBs, Bugaboos, small tri-cams, RPs, TCUs, wires, Big Bros. This climbs the prominent, steep, red, south-facing wall just above Wall of Flame. Climb a shallow, left-facing dihedral up into a crack and left-leaning dike, past a bolt, to a ledge.

SOFA PATROL

About halfway up the hogback ridge, on the west side of the crest, locate a 30-foot, orange, overhanging, west-facing wall. Approach via The Old South Mesa Trail and hike east, cross-country directly up to the objective. Beware of rattlesnakes.

1. **Sofa Patrol 12b** ★ FA: Unknown. Climb up the center of the short but high quality face via toprope.

2. **Couch Potato 12b/c** FA: Unknown. A toproped line with dynamic moves to the right of *Sofa Patrol*.

RATED ROUTE INDEX

Dandi-Line 214
Doctor Michael Solar ★ 211
E-Z Corner, Ridge Four 55
E.L. 100 306
Escape Artist 338
Escergot 153
Flakey Floont 274
Ghetto Cruiser 165
Gimli 237
The Greaser 276
The Green Dihedral ★ 87
Hi-Fi 370
Horizontal Beginnings 327
Hurrah Ridge 369
I've Been Sick 348
Jawa 139
Jimmy Cliff S 359
Joyous 346
Kaisho 169
Knight's Move ★ 203
Lady Fingers 209
Lemon Line 278
Let It Vee 161
Little Face, Ridge Two 39
Low Profile 352
Men of Steel (A3) 344
Mesca-Line ★ 214
Noggin 334
Northeast Arête, Supremacy Rock S ★ 146
Nova S 138
Pigeon Exit 344
Premonition 275
Rewritten ★ 256
River of Darkness 209
Roofed Out 359
Rotwand Route VS 373
Rush Buick ★ 349
S&M ★ 206
Shadow 272
Slime Monster 276
Slots of Fun 336
South Face, Pickpocket Wall VS 278
Speakeasy S 200
Srinagar 207
Stranglehold 352
Tales of Ulysses 198
Tampon 209
Those Fertile Years (A2) 354
Times Square 348
Twilight 142
Verschneidung ★ 229
Vertical Smile ★ 278
Waiting Room 247
West Chimney, The Bastille ★ 127
West Overhang, Wind Tower ★ 361
The Whittle Wall S ★ 334
Wide Crack, Ridge Two 39
Wind Tower Wire Route 369
Wind Tunnel ★ 217

5.8

Ahab 340
Bent Dog 356
Birthday Blow 39
Blind Mouse 235
Bob's Arête ★ 61
Body Tremors S ★ 306
Book of Dreams ★ 65
Breakfast in Bed ★ 127
Bridge-it Bardot 129
Bridget the Midget 217
Bushwhack Crack S 200
Calypso Direct ★ 359
Catnip 96
Cher's Liposuction Workout S 374
Coffee Break with Joe 207
Crack-Tree-Face 352
Crystal Graze 348
Culp's Fault ★ 82
Dead Letter Department 215
Deep Water 65
Devo 348
The Direct Finish 227
Dirty Sam 345
Doris Gets Her Oats 247
Dumb Wadie Bird Warble VS 372
Edgewise 313
Fickle Finger of Eight 139
First Unknown 236
Five Fang Overhang 210
Flakes, The Prow 89
The G.Y. Dihedral 358
Gambit ★ 189
Gonzo ★ 161
The Good Ship Venus 218
Green Finger 346
The Green Slab 252
Hang Ten 207
Hit the Deck VS 372
Horse d'Oeuvre 214
The Hot Spur 247
Initial Route 232
Inverted Vee 210
Jag 247
January Playmate 349
Leapfrog 352
Left Arête, Whale's Tail S ★ 340
Left Out, The Wind Tower 365
Lemmings 361
Lime Line 278
Linga Line (A2) 88
Long John Wall ★ 221
Loose Cannon 53
Lost in Space 248
Lower Mellow Yellow 268
Lunar Avenue S 211
Memory Lapse S 308
Mountains out of Molehills 350
Neato 182

5.9+

ROUTE NAME INDEX

IN MEMORIUM

The Late Great Derek Hersey

Clockwise from top: On Vertigo, *roof routes on Red Garden Wall,* and Rosy Crucifixion.
PHOTOS DEREK HERSEY COLLECTION

Free solo on pitch 5 of The Naked Edge. DEBBIE GREGG PHOTO

ACCESS: It's every climber's concern

The Access Fund, a national, non-profit climbers' organization, works to keep climbing areas open and to conserve the climbing environment. Need help with closures? land acquisition? legal or land management issues? funding for trails and other projects? starting a local climbers' group? CALL US!

Climbers can help preserve access by being committed to leaving the environment in its natural state. Here are some simple guidelines:

• **STRIVE FOR ZERO IMPACT** especially in environmentally sensitive areas like caves. Chalk can be a significant impact on dark and porous rock—don't use it around historic rock art. Pick up litter, and leave trees and plants intact.

• **DISPOSE OF HUMAN WASTE PROPERLY** Use toilets whenever possible. If toilets are not available, dig a "cat hole" at least six inches deep and 200 feet from any water, trails, campsites, or the base of climbs. *Always pack out toilet paper.* On big wall routes, use a "poop tube" and carry waste up and off with you (the old "bag toss" is now illegal in many areas).

• **USE EXISTING TRAILS** Cutting switchbacks causes erosion. When walking off-trail, tread lightly, especially in the desert where cryptogamic soils (usually a dark crust) take thousands of years to form and are easily damaged. Be aware that "rim ecologies" (the clifftop) are often highly sensitive to disturbance.

• **BE DISCREET WITH FIXED ANCHORS** *Bolts are controversial and are not a convenience*—don't place 'em unless they are *really* necessary. Camouflage all anchors. Remove unsightly slings from rappel stations (better to use steel chain or welded cold shuts). Bolts sometimes can be used pro-actively to protect fragile resources—consult with your local land manager.

• **RESPECT THE RULES** and speak up when other climbers don't. Expect restrictions in designated wilderness areas, rock art sites, caves, and to protect wildlife, especially nesting birds of prey. *Power drills are illegal in wilderness and all national parks.*

• **PARK AND CAMP IN DESIGNATED AREAS** Some climbing areas require a permit for overnight camping.

• **MAINTAIN A LOW PROFILE** Leave the boom box and day-glo clothing at home—the less climbers are heard and seen, the better.

• **RESPECT PRIVATE PROPERTY** Be courteous to land owners. Don't climb where you're not wanted.

• **JOIN THE ACCESS FUND!** To become a member, make a tax-deductible donation of $25 or more.

The Access Fund

Preserving America's Diverse Climbing Resources
PO Box 17010 Boulder, CO 80308
303.545.6772 • www.accessfund.org